INSIGHT ⊙ GUIDES

SWITZERLAND

⊙ Walking Eye App

YOUR FREE DESTINATION CONTENT AND EBOOK AVAILABLE THROUGH THE WALKING EYE APP

Your guide now includes a free eBook and destination content for your chosen destination, all for the same great price as before. Simply download the Walking Eye App from the App Store or Google Play to access your free eBook and destination content.

HOW THE WALKING EYE APP WORKS

Through the Walking Eye App, you can purchase a range of eBooks and destination content. However, when you buy this book, you can download the corresponding eBook and destination content for free. Just see below in the grey panels where to find your free content and then scan the QR code at the bottom of this page.

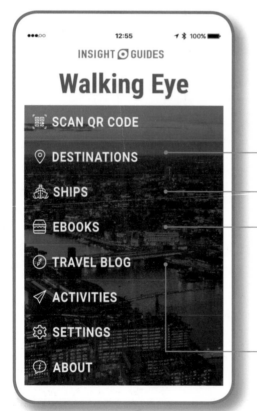

Destinations: Download your corresponding essential destination content from here, featuring recommended sights and attractions, restaurants, hotels and an A–Z of practical information, all for free. Other destinations are available for purchase.

Ships: Interested in ship reviews? Find independent reviews of river and ocean ships in this section, all available for purchase.

eBooks: You can download your free accompanying digital version of this guide here. You will also find a whole range of other eBooks, all available for purchase.

Free access to travel-related blog articles about different destinations, updated on a daily basis.

HOW THE DESTINATION CONTENT WORKS

Each destination includes a short introduction, an A–Z of practical information and recommended points of interest, split into 4 different categories:

• Highlights
• Accommodation
• Eating out
• What to do

You can view the location of every point of interest and save it by adding it to your Favourites. In the 'Around Me' section you can view all the points of interest within 5km.

HOW THE EBOOKS WORK

The eBooks are provided in EPUB file format. Please note that you will need an eBook reader installed on your device to open the file. Many devices come with this as standard, but you may still need to install one manually from Google Play.

The eBook content is identical to the content in the printed guide.

HOW TO DOWNLOAD THE WALKING EYE APP

1. Download the Walking Eye App from the App Store or Google Play.
2. Open the app and select the scanning function from the main menu.
3. Scan the QR code on this page – you will then be asked a security question to verify ownership of the book.
4. Once this has been verified, you will see your eBook and destination content in the purchased ebook and destination sections, where you will be able to download them.

Other destination apps and eBooks are available for purchase separately or are free with the purchase of the Insight Guide book.

CONTENTS

Travel Tips

TRANSPORT

A – Z

LANGUAGE

FURTHER READING

Maps

LEGEND
𝒫 Insight on
📷 Photo Story

THE BEST OF SWITZERLAND: TOP ATTRACTIONS

△ **The Matterhorn**. Switzerland's iconic pyramidal peak towers above the resorts of Zermatt and Saas Fee. The 478-metre (14,692ft) mountain was first scaled in 1865; the climbing season runs from mid-July to mid-September. See page 178.

▽ **Bern**. Encircled by the mighty Bernese Alps, the bear-loving Swiss capital has a Unesco-protected Old Town and a 16th-century astronomical clock. See page 119.

△ **The Ticino**. Italy and Switzerland come together in the southern Ticino region, from the gardened shores of Lago Maggiore to glittering Lago di Lugano. Expect palm trees, pizzas, piazzas and gelato. See page 183.

△ **San Bernardino Pass**. Driving the San Bernardino Pass, which dates to Roman times, is a breathtaking experience. The high mountain pass takes in lakes, meadows, valleys and peaks as it swerves round 18 hairpin bends in the Graubünden region near the Italian border. See page 208.

△ **Basel**. Straddling the Rhine near the border with France and Germany, historic Basel has a beautiful Old Town and 13th-century Münster cathedral. Try to time your visit to coincide with Fasnacht, Basel's spectacular three-day Lenten festival. See page 265.

△ **St Moritz**. This glitzy Swiss ski resort in the Upper Engadine was the birthplace of Alpine tourism in 1864. See page 216.

▽ **Zürich**. With a heavenly lake, an Old Town huddled around the banks of the Limmat River and plenty of culture, Zürich is more than just the banking capital. See page 227.

△ **The *Bernina Express***. The historic railway between Chur and Tirano (Italy) is a scenic and engineering marvel. A Unesco World Heritage site, the panoramic route goes through 55 tunnels and across nearly 200 viaducts and bridges. See page 219.

▽ **Lake Geneva**. Western Europe's largest lake – 72km (45 miles) long – known to the French as Lac Léman, is punctuated by its soaring monumental fountain, the Jet d'Eau. Geneva itself, home to the Palais des Nations, has a proud history and an international outlook. See page 149.

△ **Luzern**. Switzerland's quintessential lake town. Set against an Alpine backdrop, historic Luzern is car free, with ancient covered bridges and sparkling new concert halls. See page 293.

THE BEST OF SWITZERLAND: EDITOR'S CHOICE

Zürich Kunsthaus.

BEST MUSEUMS AND GALLERIES

Zentrum Paul Klee. Bern's showcase to the great Swiss artist contains 4,000 works in a building designed by Renzo Piano. See page 123.

Landesmuseum Zürich. The country's most visited cultural museum offers a fascinating insight into Swiss history, politics and culture. See page 233.

Kunstmuseum Basel. The oldest art collection in the world. Its outstanding selection of 19th- and 20th-century art contains pieces by Paul Gauguin and Wassily Kandinsky. See page 270.

Fondation Beyler. This private collection in Riehen, near Basel, boasts 300 Cubist and Impressionist works and dazzling, regularly changing one-off shows. See page 79.

Museé Olympique Lausanne. A must for those travelling with kids and sports fanatics. Head here to learn about the Games' golden moments through lots of photography and fun activities. See page 163.

Zürich Kunsthaus. Immerse yourself in the fine art museum's 4,000-strong collection of paintings, sculptures and installations, spanning Swiss to French art. See page 233.

BEST FESTIVALS

Fasnacht. Many Swiss cities enjoy this Lenten festival, but Basel's Fasnacht is the biggest and the best. See page 270.

Locarno Film Festival. Held over 10 days in August, this popular event includes new films shown on a giant screen in the beautiful Piazza Grande. See page 193.

Zürich Street Parade. This wild techno parade around the lake is attended by tens of thousands of euro fans every summer. See page 236.

Montreux Jazz Festival. Major international names in jazz, blues and pop converge at this lakeside town every July. See page 166.

The Lucerne Festival. A series of classical music concerts in summer animate the lake city. See page 297.

Theater Spektakel. All the city's a stage in Zürich for 18 days over July and August. Theater Spektakel, one of Europe's leading contemporary performing arts events, puts on 40 productions at 13 stages. See page 236.

Beth Ditto performing at Montreux Jazz Festival.

BEST LANDSCAPES

Jungfrau. The railway to reach this Alpine wonderland stops at Europe's highest-altitude station. See page 133.

Emmental Region. Drive or bike the undulating valley roads of the Emmental Cheese Route past dairies and chateaux. See page 124.

Swiss National Park. Founded in 1914, this pristine national park has more than 80km (50 miles) of well-defined paths from which to explore the landscape. See page 215.

Bodensee. The area around Lake Constance is a scenic oasis of vine-covered slopes, orchards, forests and medieval towns. See page 254.

Bürgenstock. Take the rocket-like lift to the summit of this Central Switzerland peak for incomparable views over Lake Luzern. See page 309.

Lago di Lugano. The lake of the Ticino's southern-most city dazzles at night. Its shimmering lights and mountain and lake silhouettes stretch towards Italy. See page 195.

Appenzellerland. Rolling green hills, flowery meadows and rugged mountains meet quirky rural traditions here. See page 258.

Rhine Falls. The grand spectacle of crashing water can be enjoyed from observation points at the foot of the falls in Neuhausen am Rhein-fall. See page 251.

Val Morteratsch. Encounter fearless ibex, chamois or deer on the mountain slopes around the Morteratsch Glacier. See page 219.

The Jungfraubahn in front of Eiger's North Face.

BEST ARCHITECTURE

Chiesa di San Giovanni Battista. The futuristic 1986 church in the Valle Maggia is the work of Ticino Tendenza architect Mario Botta. See page 194.

Bellinzona Castles. Up on a rocky peak, the crenulated 15th-century Castelgrande and its fortifications are Unesco World Heritage listed. Castello Montebello and Castello Sasso Corbaro are also among the best-preserved medieval castles in the country. See page 190.

Altstadt Bern. The Rosengarten is a great place to enjoy views over the capital's medieval Old Town. See page 121.

The Gotthard Base Tunnel. The world's longest Alpine rail tunnel is the latest of the region's extraordinary engineering feats. See page 184.

Kloster St Johann Müstair. In a remote Grisons valley, this 8th-century convent is a treasure trove of ancient murals and frescos. The fresco in the south apse dates from the Carolingian period. See page 215.

Vaud Castles. There are about a dozen Vaudois castles open to the public. Located near Lac de Neuchâtel, visit the mighty bastion of the Château de Grandson. See page 284.

Schaffhausen to Stein am Rhein. Take in the medieval half-timbered houses and hilltop fortresses of the Upper Rhine villages. See page 251.

BEST LAKE ACTIVITIES

Cruise the Vierwald-stättersee. Steamers depart regularly from the quays in Luzern and take in various sites on the "Lake of the Four Forest Cantons". See page 296.

Bike about the Zürich-see. Grab a free Züri rollt bike and explore the lakeside on two wheels. See page 240.

Stroll Geneva's Lakeside Gardens. Lap up Lake Geneva/Lac Léman from the prestigious Ariana Park of the Palais des Nations. See page 158.

Skate Lac de Joux. In late winter, this Jura lake freezes to form a huge free ice-skating rink. Skates can be hired at the lake. See page 147.

Thun Lake Festival. The open-air summer Thunerseespiele puts international and local musicals on centre stage; www.thunersee spiele.ch.

Make sure to sample Switzerland's delicious raclette.

Hiking trail around Lake Luzern.

BEST ALPINE DRIVES

San Bernardino Pass. Tackle 18 bends to reach the formidable mountain ridge of San Bernardino. See page 208.
St Gotthard Pass. Make a dramatic entry to the Ticino via the northwestern St Gotthard Pass. See page 186.
Furka Pass. View the great tongue of the Rhône Glacier tumbling through the valley of the Valais. The Furka Pass featured in a car chase in James Bond's *Goldfinger*. See page 181.
Bernina Pass. Flanked on all sides by the highest Swiss peaks, swerve your way from St Moritz to Tirano. See page 222.

The spectacular Furka Pass.

BEST FOOD & WINE

Cheese. Emmental is just one of some 450 regional cheeses, along with Gruyère, Appenzeller, pungent Schabziger and Vacherin Fribourgeois. Many varieties are best enjoyed as fondue, combined with kirsch and shared among friends.
Chocolate. Mounds of Toblerone and Lindt await. Other artisan producers, such as Zürich's Sprüngli, Teuscher and Läderach, are all there to be tried.
Raclette. Cheese melted before the fire, scraped onto boiled potatoes and eaten with gherkins is more than a meal – it's a ritual.
Lebkuchen. The five-centuries-old Basel Autumn Fair is an excuse to pig out on this delicious gingerbread.
Bread. Ogle up the heavenly displays of baked goods at a *Bäckerei-Konditorei*, such as plaited brioche, *Taillaule Neuchâteloise*.
Spätzli. Dive into a plate of squiggly egg noodles.
Cured meats. The most famous is *Bündnerfleisch* from Graubünden, cured with salt and Alpine herbs.
Bratwurst. Enjoy a veal *Kalbsbratwurst* sausage, pork *Bratwurst* or spicy *Bauernbratwurst*, washed down with a beer.
Wine. Sip some crisp white Chasselas wine produced at the Unesco-classified terraced vineyards of La Côte, on the northern side of Lake Geneva.
For more insight into Switzerland's food and wine, see page 85.

BEST HIKES

The Aare Valley. From the trails at the heart of the Bernese Oberland, eye up the almost-Caribbean colours of lakes Thun and Brienz. See page 126.
Staubbach Falls. Hike to these spectacular falls in the Lütschine Valley, outside the picturesque village of Lauterbrunnen. See page 134.
Heidi's Village. Follow the red markers in Maienfeld to the Alpine Heidi-Hüsli hut, supposedly home to the heroine of the Swiss novel. See page 206.
The Swiss Trail. Looping round one end of the Urisee, this Central Switzerland walk has views over Lake Luzern and the historic Rütli meadow of William Tell fame. See page 310.
Gemmi Pass. The walk from Leukerbad into the Bernese Oberland demands reasonable fitness and takes about four hours. See page 177.
Eiger Trail. On no other trail will you get such a thrilling close-up look at the Eiger's famous North Face without climbing it. See page 133.
Doubs Regional Natural Park. Hiking trails crisscross this Jura reserve. One of the best is the Trans Swiss Trail, stretching from St-Ursanne to Mendrisio, Italy. See page 282.

Off-piste skiing in Engelberg.

BEST ALPINE ADVENTURES

Bike the Nufenenpass. Spiral down the country's highest road passage, from the Valais to the northern Ticino's Val Bedretto. See page 181.
Interlaken. An adventure hub for base jumping, canyon swinging, zip lining, hang gliding and river rafting. See page 127.
Off-Piste Thrills. The Laub Wall of Engelberg's Mount Titlis is a death-defying run (for experts only). See page 308.
Golden Eye **Bungee Jumping**. Follow in Bond's footsteps and leap from the Verzasca dam in the Ticino. See page 105.
Grindelwald. Set out on strenuous (but rewarding) treks in the Eiger, Mönch and Jungfrau massif, or rock climb the Eiger's North Wall. Don't take this challenge lightly – at least 64 climbers have died attempting this feat since 1935. See page 132.
Summer & Glacier Skiing. Don your bikini and hit the pistes of the glaciers at Zermatt, Saas Fee and Verbier on skis or snowboard. See page 101.
Sledging in St Moritz. From the 360° panoramas of the Muottas Muragl, the run winds through 20 corners to the valley floor. See page 216.

BEST LITTLE TRAIN JOURNEYS

Gurtenbahn. Since 1899 day trippers have flocked to the funicular railway that climbs the resident mountain south of Bern. See page 123.
Mount Rigi. Take the Alpine railway to the "Queen of the Mountains" east of Luzern and gaze over the snow-capped giants of the Jungfrau region. See page 139.
Niesenbahn. A quaint funicular runs to the top of Niesen for unparalleled views of the Eiger, Mönch and Jungfrau. See page 127.
Mount Pilatus. The country's steepest rack railway runs from Alpnachstad through Alpine meadows to the summit, Pilatus Kulm. See page 307.
Uetlibergbahn. Zip away from Zürich's downtown to the top of its local mountain for dream panoramas over the lake and city. See page 243.
St Moritz to Zermatt. The *Glacier Express* and regular trains cross the Bernese Alps with terrific vistas at every turn. See page 138.
Monte San Salvatore and Monte Brè. Both the Ticino peaks can be scaled by funicular. On a clear day you can see all the way to Milan. See page 198.

Mount Pilatus accommodates a steep rack railway.

Sunset at Kronberg, near Appenzell.

The Unterwalden steamboat is proud to be Swiss.

Historic bridge in Ticino.

Lake Luzern obscured by a sea of fog.

A MAGNET FOR MYTHS

A country of cliché-defying contradictions, Switzerland has long been romanticised and misrepresented.

Flower-laden cattle.

The popular image of Switzerland is so riddled with myth that books which try to set the record straight hardly know where to begin. Faithful representations are constantly vying with the image of bankers and milkmaids, chocolate and watches, ski resorts and yodelling. Most famously the country has had to live with the words of Orson Welles in *The Third Man*, who deemed that the only upshot of five centuries of Swiss peace and democracy was the cuckoo clock. One Swissophile academic, after studying the nation's civilisation, confessed doubts as to whether Switzerland should even exist, for the home of William Tell has no natural frontiers, no common language, no unifying culture and no dominant religion.

Nonetheless, it has been a sought-after holiday destination since 1863, when Thomas Cook first organised package tours from Britain. Lord Byron's *The Prisoner of Chillon* and Conan Doyle's climactic struggle between Sherlock Holmes and Professor Moriarty at the Reichenbach Falls helped romanticise the mountainous country, as did Johanna Spyri with her popular Heidi stories. Visitors have not always been kind. Ernest Hemingway found the streets so clean he expressed a desire to foul them.

The Titlis Rotair rotating gondola.

The "peace-loving" Swiss were, up to about 150 years ago, almost constantly at war with themselves or others. Many of these conflicts were orchestrated by powerful neighbours in order to keep the Swiss state intact and neutral, but domestic squabbles threatening this haven included civil war, peasant uprisings and religious disputes. Somehow, the Swiss always managed to pull themselves back from the brink.

Significant developments taking place in other European countries were often dismissed by the Swiss. In deciding to "opt out" in this way, Switzerland subconsciously set the early parameters for making the country what it is today. Nineteenth-century nationalists advocated language ties as a prime criterion for setting the frontiers of modern Europe. The Swiss ignored this, as they did the idea that centralised government was desirable or that a monarch was necessary. "The Swiss believe," says one of them, "that they are rational and realistic. They are not. They will take pains to define a principle, immediately think of a dozen exceptions to the rule, then say it's better to use common sense. In other words, they believe in the principle of no principles."

The iconic Matterhorn.

LAKES AND MOUNTAINS

Switzerland's steep valleys and soaring peaks were formed by powerful
geological upheavals and the erosive effects of the great Ice Ages.

Famous for its superb mountain backdrop, the
Alps constitute 60 percent of Swiss territory.
This great rocky barrier divides northern Europe
from the Mediterranean world and extends in a
1,200-km (750-mile) long arc from the French
Riviera to the gates of Vienna. Another, lesser
range of mountains, the Jura, defines the country's northwestern frontier with France, while
between the Alps and the Jura extend the varied
landscapes of the Plateau or Mittelland. In this
latter, relatively low-lying area, the majority of
the country's population live and work, many of
them clustered around the glorious lakes which
make up for Switzerland's lack of a sea coast.

THE SHAPING OF THE MOUNTAINS

Infinitely complex in detail, with every valley and
every peak quite distinct from every other, the
geology of the Alps is relatively simple, though
the extensive timescale involved and the tec-
tonic forces exerted are almost beyond human
comprehension.

The Great Aletsch glacier.

The country's first foundation consisted of an
enormously thick layer of crystalline rock. Around
300 million years ago, this bedrock was subjected
to great pressure and folded into what are sometimes referred to as the First Alps. These predecessors of today's mountains eventually sank
beneath the surface of an ocean, which gradually filled up with sediments, many of them rich
in fossils. This process extended over tens of
millions of years, until it was interrupted by the
northward drift of the ancient continent of Africa.

Beginning roughly 100 million years ago,
rock material which had once extended over a
distance of about 500km (300 miles) from north
to south was compressed into an area no more
than 200km (120 miles) across. The more or

less orderly layering of rocks in chronological
sequence was disturbed almost beyond recog-
nition, as the remorseless pressure folded one
layer over another, forming a wave-like surface. In places, the Earth's crust fractured, and
magma from the interior spewed from volca-
noes. About 3 million years ago, a final thrust
heaved the rocks skyward to form a high mountain range, the basis of today's Alps.

THE ACTION OF THE ICE

The present outline of the mountains is mainly the
result of successive Ice Ages, the last only ending some 10,000 years ago. At one point, virtually
the whole of Switzerland lay buried beneath a vast
sheet of ice, from which only the occasional peak

protruded. This was the era of the glaciers, the slow but relentless movement of which sculpted much of the landscape into its present form. The characteristic U-shape of many an Alpine valley is a sure sign of its former occupation by a glacier, while many of the country's lakes fill basins originally scooped out by ice, then dammed by material deposited when a glacier had come to a temporary halt. Mighty ancestors of today's Rhine, Rhône and lesser rivers flowed out from the glaciers, sweeping rocky debris with them which, when dropped, gave the lowlands their present shape. As the ice sheets underwent their final (to date) retreat, the climate improved, and the land they had bared was colonised again by plants and animals, first by a tundra-like vegetation of mosses, lichens, dwarf shrubs and trees, then by the conifers (pines, firs, spruces) which rise to today's tree line, then by the deciduous trees (alder, willow, oak, beech, ash and sycamore) which form the woodlands of the Plateau and the Alpine valleys.

SWISS CLIMATES

Switzerland is affected by Atlantic, continental and Mediterranean weather systems, while the intricate combinations of altitude, slope and exposure to the sun mean that many parts of the country have a whole range of local climates within a very limited area. This is very obvious in many an east–west Alpine valley, where the shaded, north-facing (ie, southern) slopes of the valley will be clad in dense coniferous forest, while the sunny, south-facing (ie, northern) side of the valley is a cheerful patchwork of villages, farm buildings, fields and meadows. The severity of the climate increases rapidly with height, but this can be offset by a southerly location, exposure to the sun, or the presence of a great body of water helping to maintain more stable conditions; thus the steep north shore of Lake Geneva is one great vineyard, while the highest vines in Europe are to be found in the canton of Valais above the valley of the Rhône, where fine wines are made from grapes harvested at an altitude of 1,100 metres (3,600ft). Together with the other southern cantons of Ticino and Graubünden, the Valais is known in German as the "Sonnenland", where the bare rock and contorted arolla pines of the heights contrast with a luxuriant Mediterranean vegetation of figs and chestnut trees on the lower slopes and in the valleys. Surprisingly warm conditions prevail too in the low-lying parts of the cantons of Vaud and Neuchâtel, protected from Atlantic winds and rain by the great wall of the Jura Mountains.

The vineyards of St Saphorin, Lake Geneva.

⊘ WINDS OF CHANGE

Landlocked Switzerland is subject to seasonal winds that blow through its valleys from the farthest corners of the continental landmass.

One such wind is the cold, dry **Bise**, which sweeps in across the Vaud and Neuchâtel plateau from eastern Europe. The northern side of the Alps is much affected by another wind: the **Föhn**. Blowing from the south, the warm Föhn unloads its moisture as it rises, crosses the ridge line and, warm and dry, sweeps down the northern valleys, melting snow, scorching plants and giving people headaches, or even depression. When villages were built of wood, devastating Föhn fires were common.

ENVIRONMENTAL THREATS

Nowadays, the Föhn (see box) is of less concern than global warming, acid rain and pollution generally. The country's 1,828 glaciers are good indicators of climatic change. Most have been retreating for some time, and in 2016 Switzerland was reported to have 40 fewer snow days a season compared to the 1970s. The Morteratsche glacier, a national treasure and popular tourist

In the course of the 20th century, more than a quarter of the area of Switzerland's permanent ice – covering about 100 sq km (38 sq miles) – disappeared, as a result of climate change and pollution.

vital function as avalanche inhibitors and soil stabilisers. The death of trees, particularly conifers, because of acid rain, is not therefore simply an aesthetic issue, but one of the survival of Alpine communities and the safeguarding of communication routes.

THE JURA

Rising to a high point of 1,723 metres (5,650ft), the 200-km (120-mile) -long Jura range consists of a regular succession of rounded ridges and trough-like valleys running southwest–northeast.

attraction, is shrinking fast. And while the tongue of the Rhône glacier once reached the valley floor at Gletsch, visitors wanting to admire this mighty natural phenomenon at close quarters now have

Autumnal colours, Poschiavo.

to make their way much further up the valley. The sudden melting is also creating instability in mountainous regions, where massive rockfalls have occurred where retreating glaciers no longer support some areas of the mountain.

Environmental pollution has been an issue for some time in this small, landlocked country. Chemical spills in the Rhine have made the headlines, as has the sudden mass death of fish in the country's lakes, but the most taxing environmental problem has been the erosion of Alpine forests, aggravated by atmospheric pollution from motor vehicles, in particular from the thousands of trucks driving daily through the Alps.

In Switzerland, mountain forests are not simply admired for their beauty, they frequently have a

The mountains are made of limestone, formed in the Jurassic era, which bears their name, and squeezed into these shapes by the same forces which shaped the Alps. On the French side of the border they descend in a series of stepped plateaux, while on the Swiss side they form a formidable cliff up to 1,000 metres (3,000ft) high.

Cattle graze on the upland pastures and most slopes carry forests of beech or spruce, while most human activity is concentrated in the parallel valleys where roads and railways run. Communication between the valleys is via *cluses*, transversal ravines cut perhaps by the rivers. As so often in Switzerland, lakes form a transition between mountains and lowland regions; the Jura dips its toe into two beautiful bodies of water, the Bielersee and the Lac de Neuchâtel. From the crest of the range, there is a magnificent prospect of the Savoy Alps on the French shore of Lake Geneva, Europe's largest Alpine lake, 310-metres (1,000ft) deep and covering an area of 580 sq km (220 sq miles).

THE MITTELLAND

Plateau it may be, but the Swiss Mittelland is far from flat; lying at a height of 350–1,200 metres (1,100–3,600ft), most of it consists of undulating hillsides interspersed with level areas along the

Varied scenery, Appenzell.

bigger rivers or on dried-out lake beds. Farmland alternates with woodland, villages with cities, all linked by a dense network of roads and railways.

Though the Plateau only occupies 30 percent of the area of Switzerland, it is the home of two-thirds of the country's inhabitants. At its junction with the mountains, lakes have formed, providing favourable sites for great cities like Geneva, Zürich and Luzern. In the western part of the Plateau, from the rim of Lake Geneva northeastwards towards Zürich, the favourable climate and the fertility of the soil encourage arable farming, even the cultivation of crops such as tobacco.

Further east, beyond Zürich, in the cantons of Thurgau, St Gallen and Appenzell, rainfall is heavier and grazing is dominant, with rich grasslands enhanced by the presence of fruit trees and orchards whose blossom makes a splendid spectacle in springtime.

The southern edge of the Plateau is overlooked at a number of points by great ramparts of rock seeming to guard the approach to the Alps. Lake Luzern is dominated by Rigi, Bürgenstock and Pilatus, the Appenzell country by the Säntis.

THE FAMOUS PEAKS

The Alpine heartlands are further south, reaching their greatest elevation in the Valais Alps, which extend eastward from Mont Blanc. Here stands the awesome pyramid of the Matterhorn (4,477 metres/14,700ft), close to the country's highest peak, the Dufourspitze (4,634 metres/15,200ft). To the north, beyond the valley of the Rhône, are the summits of the Bernese Oberland, culminating in the Finsteraarhorn (4,274 metres/14,000ft) and the famous Jungfrau (4,158 metres/13,600ft) – accessible even to day-trippers by rack railway.

For all their grandeur of bare rock, snow and ice, few parts of the Alps are nowadays really remote. The mountain valleys have long been areas of human settlement as well as important corridors of communication. The Oberland and the Valais Alps are separated by the deep cleft occupied by the Rhône, prolonged eastwards by the valley of the Vorderrhein. This is one of the most prominent features in any map of Switzerland, an east–west trench running from Martigny in the Valais right across the southern part of the country to Chur in the canton of Graubünden. At Andermatt, this valley meets the ancient trade route coming up the valley of the Reuss towards the St Gotthard Pass and the cities of northern Italy, thereby forming one of the great crossroads of Europe.

The traffic-filled roads and busy rail networks of these major corridors contrast with lesser valleys, where a traditional way of life has only relatively recently begun to be transformed. Hanging high above the Rhône is the valley of the little River Lonza, the Lötschental, its string of villages still made up of severe, dark timber houses. Until the beginning of the 20th century, when a rail tunnel was bored beneath the Lötschberg and a station was built at the bottom of the valley, the only connection with the outside world was on foot over the high Lötschenpass, or by steep mule track to the valley of the Rhône. A road only climbed up to the Lötschental to end its isolation in the 1970s.

View over Lake Geneva to Mont Blanc.

Monti di S. B

Aelen

S. Mouritio

hocret

Bucato di zables

Vila noua

Buglia de bonda...

Zhilium

S. Gingo

Tonon

Latove

Furiau

Ripaglia

DE BERNESSI

Viue

SEPTENTR

Clerola

Gule

Loter

Losanna

Morges

Moden

Torente

O bonua

Orba

Laserra

VERO DISSEGNO DEL LAGO DI GENEV

Scala di miglia x Italiani.

Fosegni

Alonzo

Baleis

Celi

Figli

Budli

Doueino

Veizi

Bela grada

VILA

Nemaie

S. Gioere

Bona

Moton

Badia di Contuorna

Badia de deua mont

Cofegli

Virr

Lanri

Giusi

Anbesi

Vesona

Galegiarda

GENE
VUA

Vetri

Terni

S. Gioulin

irate d'reinigi

Meridies

Qui son
Qui son ...

Tanhiere
xeni da
... Ma

Vetri

STRADA DI LION

Vepli de Core Panu
da EA ...

Palificata

Versois

Copet

Neon

Feligni

Diuona

Gess

S. Clgudio di
borgogna

Borgo S. Geruasio

Penei

Sacone

Fornei

Logra

Chiana

Colonge

Paso della
Clussa

Lani

Berra

Perera

RODANO F.

Monte di
Hardrossa

Bona Villa

Narni

Beorgi
Fomali

Bella riua

DECISIVE DATES

Habsburg Emperor Rudolf's entrance into Basel, 1273.

PREHISTORY

c. 10,000 BC
After the great Ice Age, hunter-fisher folk settle in the Mittelland.

c. 400 BC
Rhaetians enter the south-eastern parts of the country; Celtic tribes settle in the south-west. By 58 BC Germanic tribes force the powerful Celtic Helvetii tribe to migrate to Gaul.

ROMAN AND HOLY ROMAN EMPIRES

58 BC
Julius Caesar pursues the Helvetii, defeating them at Bibracte in Burgundy.

58 BC – AD 400
The Romans occupy a defensive area along the Rhine and Danube, settling with the Celts in relative harmony.

c. 500
The Alemanni tribes invade from Germany, driving out the Romans and taking possession of northern Switzerland, while the Burgundians take the south. The Rhaetians hold out in Grisons.

c. 600
Irish monks St Colomba and St Gallus bring Christianity to Switzerland.

614
Founding of the St Gallen monastery, later to become one of Europe's major seats of learning.

771
King Charles, the future Charlemagne, unites Switzerland as the kingdom of the Franks. The country is divided up into shires, which form the basis of the present canton demarcation.

834
The Treaty of Verdun divides the country up into the old kingdoms of the French Burgundians and the Germanic Alemanni.

RISE OF THE SWISS CONFEDERATION

12th and 13th centuries
Noble dynasties including the Habsburgs, Savoys and Zahringens found many of today's main cities, developing power bases and autonomous regional authorities.

1291
Death of Habsburg Emperor Rudolf triggers instability leading to the legendary Oath at Rutli Meadow, the proclamation of the Swiss Confederation and the heroic story of William Tell.

1315
Decisive defeat by Schwyz peasants over Austrian Habsburgs at the Battle of Morgarten. Consequent Schwyz importance leads to the denomination Schweiz, Switzerland.

1351–53
Zürich, Bern, Glarus and Zug join the Confederation, which now numbers eight cantons.

1386–88
With further victories against the Austrians at the Battles of Sempach and Nafels, the confederacy is de-facto autonomous.

1389
A truce ratified by Albert III, Duke of Austria, guarantees peace for seven years and legitimises the Swiss Confederation.

1415
Twenty-year peace treaty signed between Austria and the Confederation.

The Battle of Grandson, 1476.

1476
Major victory for the Swiss Confederation army in the Burgundian Wars against Charles the Bold.

1499
The Basel Treaty ends the Swabian War, the last great conflict between Swiss communities and the Habsburgs, and the Empire concedes Swiss independence.

1501–13
Enlargement of the Confederation to 13 cantons, adding Basel, Schaffhausen and Appenzell. The *Dreizehn Orte* of the Old Swiss Confederacy lasts until 1798.

1515
The Confederation is defeated by the French at the Battle of Marignano; by way of an ensuing peace settlement, the Confederation agrees never again to take up arms against the French.

THE AGE OF RELIGIOUS CONFLICT

1518–23
Swiss Reformation leader Ulrich Zwingli becomes priest at Zürich's protestant Grossmünster church and gives rousing sermons against Catholicism.

1524
Zwingli marries a rich widow, scandalising the church for his breach of celibacy.

1524–28
Reformation spreads, splitting the Confederation. Schaffhausen, Bern, Basel, Grisons and St Gallen join the reformists, while Zug, Fribourg, Lucerne, Uri, Unterwalden, Schwyz and Solothurn remain Catholic. 1529: Zürich attacks the five Catholic members of the Christian Union, sparking the Kappel Wars.

1531
The religious civil warring continues. The Christian Union, allied with Austria, bites back and Zwingli is killed.

1536
Reformation in Geneva under the guidance of John Calvin. Vaud canton conquered by Bernese troops.

1555–1563
Growth of Catholic Counter Reformation further divides the Confederation and forces Protestants to seek refuge in Zürich.

1616–48
Switzerland remains neutral during the Thirty Years' War, culminating in the Peace of Westphalia treaties which endorse the Confederation's independence.

THE ENLIGHTENMENT

1712
The Treaty of Aargau establishes Protestant dominance in the country but protects the rights of Catholics. The economy flourishes, with the pastoral countryside offset by booming

John Calvin and four syndics at the College of Geneva.

Fighting for women's suffrage, 1971.

urban industries, particularly watch and clock making.

1755
Voltaire's arrival in Geneva rocks the Calvinist establishment; after several attempts, he establishes a theatre in the city in 1766.

1798
The Helvetic Republic, a centralist parliamentary system based on the new French model, is formed after Napoleon invades.

1815
Switzerland's neutrality is established at the Congress of Vienna, recognised by European powers in The Treaty of Paris, which ended the Napoleonic Wars.

1848
Centralised power bolstered with the creation of a Federal Constitution, but cantons maintain extensive self-determination.

1864
Signing of the first Geneva Convention and founding of the Red Cross Organisation.

STAYING NEUTRAL

1901
Red Cross founder, Henri Dunant, is jointly awarded the first ever Nobel Peace Prize.

1914–18
The Swiss preserve their neutrality during World War I, despite regional tensions over affinities.

1920
First meeting of League of Nations, Geneva.

1939–45
Switzerland is again neutral in World War II, but contributes generously to post-war economic reparations.

1942
Switzerland condones assisted suicide, which can be performed by non-physicians, for non-selfish motives. Euthanasia remains illegal; its decriminalisation is subject to ongoing debate.

1945
Founding of United Nations, with Geneva as European headquarters.

1955
Opening in Geneva of European Centre of Nuclear Energy (CERN).

1963
Switzerland joins the Council of Europe in Strasbourg after heated discussions about the subject of neutrality.

1971
Women's suffrage finally granted in national referendum (a previous bid failed in 1959).

1979
The region of Jura is made into a canton.

1980
The Gotthard Tunnel, linking Switzerland to Italy, opens to road traffic.

1994
Referendum outlaws racial discrimination and denial of Nazi Holocaust; laws tightened against illegal immigrants.

1995
After pressure from Jewish groups, Swiss Banking Association reveals about US$57 million is held in

dormant bank accounts, opened by German Jews before World War II.

1998
Swiss banks agree to a US$1.25 billion settlement of claims linked to Nazi Holocaust victim assets.

2001
The Swiss vote to stay outside the EU.

2002
The country votes to join the United Nations; negotiations and bilateral agreements with the EU begin.

2004
Agreement with EU on taxing accounts in Swiss banks held by EU taxpayers.

2005
Referendum vote goes in favour of opening job market to workers from the 10 newest European Union countries.

Opposing posters regarding the UN referendum, 2002.

2006
Referendum vote supports plans to amend Swiss asylum laws, making them some of the strictest in the West.

2008
Switzerland joins Europe's passport-free Schengen zone.

2009
The country slips into official recession but soon recovers.

2010
Women ministers get historic cabinet majority in Federal Council.

2011
Following Japan's Fukushima nuclear plant disaster, Switzerland is the first European country to announce phasing out of nuclear power by 2050. The Swiss franc pegged to euro.

2013
Switzerland's parliament sets a 62-year deadline for recovery

Train in the Gotthard Base Tunnel.

of unclaimed assets from Holocaust survivors and families, which will then be turned over to the State.

2014
Referendum vote approves controversial quotas on immigration, proposed by the right-wing Swiss People's Party.

2015
The franc is unpegged from euro exchange rate by the Swiss National Bank; EU-Switzerland agreement on automatic exchange of financial information on bank accounts of each other's residents from 2018.

2016
Parliament refuses to introduce quotas on immigration as per 2014 referendum, instead voting in a compromise immigration law prioritising Swiss citizens in new job vacancies. The 57km (35-mile) Alpine Gotthard Base Tunnel, the world's longest rail tunnel, is opened.

2017
Referendum votes support making it easier for third-generation immigrants to gain citizenship and the banning of new nuclear power stations from 2018.

Roman Corinthian column, Vaud.

BEGINNINGS

The earliest settlers in Switzerland were Celts who built their wooden homes on stilts by the shores of its now-famous lakes.

During the unusually severe winter of 1853 the level of Lake Zürich fell to an unprecedented low level, exposing a swathe of sticky mud around the shoreline. Enterprising residents realised that shoring up the perimeter would provide a windfall of free land, and they got busy with spade and shovel.

The eager opportunists of Obermeilen, a village about 39km (24 miles) from Zürich, found their digging impeded by what appeared to be a forest of wooden props just beneath the surface. Someone had the sense to summon the distinguished Dr Ferdinand Keller from Zürich and he, probably with the ancient Greek historian Herodotus in mind, was able to proclaim the discovery of one of the vital missing links in Switzerland's prehistory. The props, he concluded, were evidence of an ancient Celtic tribe who built their houses on stilts over the water.

Aquatic settlement at Lac de Morat.

CRO-MAGNON ANCESTORS

Tools found among the props were made of stone and bone rather than metal, indicating a date earlier than the Bronze Age, which is generally put at about 1500 BC onwards. Traces of human presence in Switzerland of course go back much further. A fragment of jaw found in the Jura has been identified as belonging to a woman who lived about 50,000 years ago; a more complete skull from Neuchâtel is that of a young Cro-Magnon adult of about 12,000 BC. Caves which housed prehistoric troglodytes have been found near Geneva, Villeneuve and Thayngen. The significance of the submerged props near Obermeilen was as evidence of people who constructed their homes, and quite elaborate ones at that.

Hundreds of similar aquatic villages, some with as many as 40,000 piles driven into the mud,

have subsequently been discovered in lakes, rivers and swamps. The Swiss lake-dwellers, like the troglodytes before them and the so-called Beaker people of western Europe afterwards, remain shrouded in prehistory. The transition to recorded history begins with Roman literature of the 1st century BC. The lake-dwellers had by then been replaced by other Celts and a branch of the Etruscans, the Rhaeti (Raeti), a people probably Celtic in origin who inhabited what is now southern and eastern Switzerland and were defeated by the Romans in 16 AD.

The Romans annexed present-day Switzerland to the Roman Empire in 15 BC. Because the Swiss "province" lay between Italy and the Roman defensive lines along the Rhine and the

Danube, it was crucial to the security of the Roman world; Romans fortified key mountain passes and applied all their renowned road-building skills to the territory.

Switzerland is much richer in Roman remains than is popularly supposed. Baden, a well-known spa near Zürich, was described by Tacitus as "a place which during long years of peace had grown to be a city, much frequented on account of the attraction of its salubrious waters". The greatest Roman city, though, was Aventicum, the modern Avenches, where a complex of palaces, temples and triumphal arches was enclosed by a wall some 7km (4 miles) in circumference.

THE ALEMANNI

Roman ruins bear testimony to the empire buckling under the pressure of the Germanic tribes at the turn of the 5th century AD. The Alemanni took possession of northern Switzerland; the Burgundians seized the south. Secure in the mountain fastnesses of Graubünden, the Rhaeti alone escaped almost untouched, whereas what is now Ticino was driven closer

Julius Caesar and his army subdue the Helvetii.

⊘ RESISTING THE ROMANS

The Helvetii were the most powerful of the Celtic tribes and lived between lakes Constance and Geneva, in the Alps and on the Jura. By 58 BC, pressure from German tribes had forced the Helvetii to migrate en masse to Gaul. With their bridges burnt behind them, 368,000 men, women and children assembled in Geneva on 28 March 58 BC for the exodus, only to find their exit across the Rhone barred.

The barrier was Julius Caesar and his army, then embarking on his conquest of Gaul. The emigrants slipped past the Roman cordon but they were pursued and caught at Bibracte, near the modern town of Autun in Burgundy. In his *Commentaries on the Gallic Wars*, Caesar pays tribute to the fighting spirit of the Helvetii, whose last stand was behind a makeshift barricade of oxcarts. Their resistance held out from 1pm until sunset, but the outcome against the drilled legions was inevitable and they were obliged to return whence they had come, albeit with the promise of Roman protection in the future and a large measure of self-governance in what became known as Helvetia.

The Etruscan Rhaeti refused to succumb to Rome for another 40 years, and one of the more colourful accounts of their resistance has Rhaeti women, frustrated by their lack of weapons, hurling their suckling children at the conquerors "through sheer exasperation".

to Italy, sharing that country's fate under the Ostrogoths and Lombards well into the Middle Ages. The foundations were laid for the German-French-Romansh-Italian components of modern Switzerland.

The mutual hostility of the Alemanni and Burgundians was tempered by the common threat of the Franks under Clovis, but to no avail. The Franks were routed in 469 and the Burgundians in 534 at Autun, where the Romans had turned back their Celtic predecessors. The whole of modern Switzerland, Ticino excepted, was again

> The legacy of the Romans in Switzerland is apparent in the Romansh language, still spoken in Graubünden, which is a combination of Roman Latin and the Tuscan dialect of the Rhaeti.

united in subjugation to a single power, its future bound up with the varying vicissitudes of the Merovingian, Carolingian and Frankish rulers for centuries to come.

Clovis had sworn that if he defeated the Alemanni he would convert to Christianity, and he was duly baptised on Christmas Day, 496. As the champion of orthodox Christianity, he was as opposed to the heretical Arian Christians as he was to heathens. The Burgundians were numbered among the former, the Alemanni among the latter; so, the history of Switzerland from the Merovingian kings to Charlemagne's coronation as Holy Roman Emperor in 800 was closely allied to the religious upheavals of the age.

BAND OF IRISH MONKS

The task of reasserting orthodoxy in Switzerland fell, curiously, to a caravan of tattooed, long-haired Irish monks who set out in 610 under the leadership of St Columba, armed with stout sticks and with a spare pair of boots slung round their necks. They followed the course of the River Limmat past Zürich to the lakeside village of Tuggen. "This place pleased them," says a chronicle of 771, "but not the evil ways of the dwellers. Cruelty and mischief ruled in their midst, and they were given over unto heathen superstitions." These included toasting their gods with beer. Gall, Columba's

zealous assistant, threw the images of the local gods and the drinking vessels into the lake, where-upon the enraged Alemanni drove them away.

The monks transferred their attention to Pregentia (Bregenz), which they were advised was a hotbed of heathen practices. Gall found this to be true and again destroyed the local icons.

Ordered out of the country for his actions, Columba led his band of monks across the Alps into Italy, but Gall was too unwell to travel and stayed behind in the forest east of Arbon. In 614

The Baptism of Clovis, c. 850.

he founded the famous monastery which bears his name (see page 257).

Alemannia, which had so doggedly resisted Christianity, became the seat of other great monasteries: Rheinau, founded in 724 by the Visigoth Pirminius, Pfäfers and Einsiedeln. Each of these monasteries established a network of parish churches which accelerated the complete conversion of Switzerland, effected a revolution in agriculture and cleared huge expanses of forest.

CONFLICT WITH THE POPE

As the Merovingian kingdom collapsed under the weight of its crimes and incapacity, it split into what were known as Austrasia and Neustria, in effect the same Burgundian-Alemannic dichotomy which existed in microcosm in Switzerland. Eventually the two halves were reunited as the Kingdom of the Franks under Charles, later Charlemagne, in 771. Crowned Holy Roman Emperor by Pope Hadrian in 800, Charlemagne suddenly found himself almost on a level with the Pope, who, however, exceeded the secular power of kings by virtue of vast papal estates and wealth. The papacy and the imperial throne were then closely matched rivals for the leadership of the Western world.

Statue of Charlemagne, Zürich's Grossmünster.

As long as Charlemagne and Pope Hadrian remained on fairly friendly terms, conflict did not materialise, but the danger signs were evident in Switzerland. Clerical land barons were not inclined to take their orders from the secular counts. They insisted on a legal immunity which made them answerable only to the imperial crown. An ambiguous chain of command spelt potential trouble.

The threat was realised soon after Charlemagne's death in 814. His heir, Ludwig the Pious, was barely able to contain four rebellious sons, and on his death the empire was carved up among the three survivors: Lothar, Ludwig the German and Charles the Bald. The division, ratified by the Treaty of Verdun in 834, split Switzerland along the old lines. The Teutonic Alemanni joined the other subjects of Ludwig the German, and the Romanised Burgundians those of Lothar.

The Kingdom of Burgundy, of which the Swiss "Kingdom of Transjurane" was but a small portion, eventually succumbed to the sheer incompetence of its successive kings and in 1032 it was swallowed up by Conrad II of Germany after the battle of Morat. Swiss Alemannia fared little better. Two attempts to revive an independent Duchy of Alemannia failed, so that the two principal parts of Switzerland fell under the sway of the German empire. Ticino, in the south, was wrapped up in Italian affairs, while the three so-called Forest Cantons of Switzerland were considered too remote to be of interest.

FAMILY FEUDS

During the 12th and 13th centuries, most of Switzerland was ruled by the German kings and emperors, but beneath that was a feudal patchwork which produced four great families, each of whom attempted to wrest Switzerland for itself. All failed utterly, although two of them, the Savoys and Habsburgs, ended up elsewhere with a kingdom (Italy) and a dynastic empire (Austria-Hungary) apiece.

The other two families, the Zähringers and the Hohenstaufens, continued the 11th-century struggle between Henry IV – both King of Germany and Holy Roman Emperor – and Pope Gregory VII. When the dust settled the Hohenstaufen family emerged as the shaky holders of the Duchy of Alemannia while the Zähringers had created a power base in the town and

☉ THE FIRST CHRISTIANS

According to tradition, Christianity first put in an appearance in Roman Helvetia in the person of Mauritius, the commander of a Christian legion posted there from Egypt. He fell victim to a purge of Christians by the Emperor Maximilian and was executed at a place in the present-day Valais, whose name was later changed to St Maurice to honour his martyrdom. In any case, it seems that Switzerland had a bishop, either Theodor or Theodul, as early as 381. In general, however, this was a false dawn for the new religion and over the course of a couple of centuries the remnants seem to have been infused with a good deal of heresy.

estates of Zürich, one which they used as a springboard to become the masters of almost all of modern Switzerland by 1127.

The system of defence with which the Zähringers attempted to consolidate their hold had a profound effect on the future shape of the country. They fortified a number of strategic villages and converted them into cities with chartered privileges. A small settlement on the banks of the Sarine became Fribourg; others grew into Burgdorf, Morat and Thun. The centre of the defensive line between Fribourg and Burgdorf formed a stronghold at Bern.

A further 100 or more fledgling towns were founded in the following century, and it was reckoned that a traveller in the lowlands passed a town gate every 20km (13 miles) or so. Not all the towns survived, but the successful ones steadily attained a measure of independence which they were ready to defend against any aggressor. As they were seldom strong enough to do so alone, they sought alliances with kindred communities or powerful princes, and Switzerland began to resemble a scaled-down version of the Greek city-states. The urban population remained relatively modest: by the end of the Middle Ages, Basel had between 9,000 and 12,000 inhabitants; Geneva, Zürich, Bern, Lausanne and Fribourg had about 5,000 each.

HOLY DEADLOCK

Berchtold V's death in 1218 without an heir unleashed a violent struggle for possession of his estates between two formidable rivals, Thomas of Savoy and Count Rudolf of Habsburg. In a decisive battle at Chillon, on the shore of Lake Geneva, Thomas defeated Rudolf's forces, but he did not have long to relish his victory. He died a few months later (in 1268) on his way home from a trip to Italy. His achievements were squandered by the gross incompetence of his brother, Philip.

The future of Switzerland hung in the balance and the territory might easily have disintegrated. Added to all the independently minded new towns were scores of princelings not knowing which way to turn during the deadlock over the succession to the Kingdom of Germany and the Holy Roman Empire. The powerful church estates, recognising no temporal authority within the country, were torn between loyalty to the semi-divine imperial crown and their duty to the papacy.

> *Flattered by Charlemagne's many visits to the city, Zürich still refers to the Holy Roman Emperor as the "fountain of its intellectual life".*

PUSH TO GREATNESS

Pope Gregory's ultimatum to the German princes was that if they could not agree among themselves on a new emperor he would impose one. Their response was to submit the name of a sup-

Fortified cave dwelling, St Gallen.

posed nonentity whom they could keep under their thumb. The nominee was Count Rudolf of Habsburg, then 55 years of age. He could number among his accomplishments the "great slaughter" of forces loyal to troublesome bishops, a stirring battle (at Zürich's behest) against the unsavoury Count of Regensburg, and the capture of a few castles. In the Terrible Times, however, that made him a rather ordinary German princeling and not necessarily imperial material.

Newly crowned nevertheless, Rudolf set about laying the foundations of the great Habsburg dynasty. His aims in Switzerland were first to cut Philip of Savoy down to size and then to acquire as much land as he could, especially from the abbeys.

The abbots of St Gallen were forced to cede land and farms; the monastery of Murbach, then in financial difficulties, was made to surrender Luzern. Any estate whose ownership was

> *The authenticity of William Tell's heroics has long been disputed, even by Voltaire, who observed that "this whole business about the apple is highly suspect."*

Count Rudolf of Habsburg winning a tournament.

in doubt went straight into the Habsburg bag. Rudolf's gobbling up of Switzerland is considered to be the catalyst of Swiss political history. All that had gone before served merely as a prologue to the Swiss Confederation.

REBELLION OF THE FOREST CANTONS

The setting for these contentious events was the three so-called forest cantons – Unterwalden, Schwyz and Uri – on Lake Luzern, north of the Alps. What distinguished the Alemanni inhabitants of this region from the rest of the nation was that in their remote station they had escaped rigorous feudalism. Since time immemorial the valleys of Uri and Schwyz had enjoyed virtual self-government under popular

assemblies – *Markgenossenschaft* – which ran contrary to the structured tiers of feudalism.

Subsequent events in Uri are rather confusing and as such are typical of the general mêlée surrounding the birth of the Swiss Confederation. While the nuns of the Abbey of Our Lady in Zürich collected the tax revenue, political overlordship was given first to the Zähringers and then, when that family petered out, to the Habsburgs when they acquired the governorship of Zürichgau, an extensive district which included all three forest cantons.

The fact that most of the population were free peasants, and thus had the right to bear arms and to serve abroad, gave them delusions of grandeur and importance. They believed they were free of all feudal obligations except to the emperor himself. The coronation of Rudolf as emperor brought matters to a head: the emperor whom they were prepared to love and the titular overlord whom they instinctively hated were at a stroke one and the same person. Which would it be: love or hate?

The traditional version of events provides one answer. It says that Rudolf could have been loved if he had been willing to adjudicate personally over the theft of goats and other items of parochial business, but as emperor he was far too busy. He appointed agents to deal with such things, and they were not good enough for the proud free peasants. The conventional view is that the agents were "covetous and cruel tyrants who taxed, fined, imprisoned, and reviled the unfortunate inhabitants".

The tyranny of Rudolf's agents, most notably Landenberg and Gessler, of William Tell fame, drove the forest canton people to unite in rebellion, asserting their allegiance in the historic pact of 1291 (see page 41). The resultant birth of Swiss liberty was not a spontaneous explosion against Habsburg tyranny, however, but a refinement of earlier alliances among communities who probably derived the idea of such leagues from Italy. In fact, some say, there was no Habsburg tyranny.

Nevertheless, the inhabitants of the forest cantons would have had enough to alarm them in the remorseless expansion of the Habsburg estates which created a de-facto cordon around them. The Swiss whom William Tell symbolised were undoubtedly exceptionally sensitive to the threat of outside interference.

WILLIAM TELL

Whether William Tell ever really existed is uncertain, but Switzerland's most famous folk hero is memorialised throughout the country in the form of statues and monuments.

The origins of the William Tell legend are rooted in the country's early history, when the German King, Albrecht of Habsburg (son of Rudolf), held sway over his subjects through the tyrannical activities of tax-collecting bailiffs. One of the most unpopular was Hermann Gessler, Albrecht's imperial governor in Altdorf, the Alpine capital of the canton of Uri. The haughty and spiteful Gessler placed his hat on a pole in the town marketplace, and gave orders that all passing should show due reverence by kneeling before it.

A local countryman named William Tell blatantly ignored the hat and was arrested. The biting sarcasm in the exchange between a furious Gessler and the unrepentant Tell gets lost in translation, but the well-known outcome was Tell being ordered to shoot an apple off his son's head. The arrow was right on target. "Had I injured my child," Tell told Gessler, referencing a second arrow, "this second shaft should not have missed thy heart."

Tell was taken in chains to Gessler's dungeon in Axenstein, which meant crossing the lake by boat. When a violent storm erupted, the oarsmen, who were unfamiliar with these waters, untied Tell and told him to steer them to safety. Instead, on reaching the shore, Tell jumped out and pushed the boat adrift. Gessler and his crew managed to save themselves, but by then Tell had vanished. He had not gone far. Tell knew the route Gessler would take back to his castle, and was lying in ambush when the governor appeared. The arrow held in reserve now found its mark through Gessler's heart. "This is Tell's shaft," Gessler gasped with his dying breath.

The basic story and various embellishments, culminating in the dissidents in the meadow at Rütli launching a full-scale rebellion, paint a picture of freedom-loving Alpine republicans who were willing to submit themselves to a decent German king like Frederick II but were capable of delivering a devastating riposte to tyrants like the ghastly Habsburgs.

"All this seems to have been invented," observed the sceptical Swiss historian François Guilliman in a private letter in 1607, "to nourish hatred against Austria."

Ironically, Guilliman was one of those responsible for nurturing the figure of William Tell, but the story owes its universal currency to a 1804 play by Schiller and

William Tell shooting the apple from his son's head.

Rossini's well-known opera, first performed in 1829. Schiller, a German, never set foot in Switzerland and his knowledge of Swiss history was largely gleaned from Johannes von Müller's *History of Switzerland*. The William Tell story, which von Müller believed totally, was offered as Switzerland's contribution to the rampant spirit of Liberty, Equality and Fraternity.

Waspish historian Christopher Herold argues that the first to challenge the truth of the Tell legend, "was saved from national disgrace and possible lynching only by the fact that his books were so dull and unreadable that few people were aware of their existence."

Von Müller's research was taken up by other historians, however, and was boosted by the discovery of the original document of the Pact of 1291 (see page 41). It transpired that very similar legends (the archer, the object on his son's head, the second arrow held in reserve) crop up in mythology over northern and central Europe and even in Asia Minor."

The Three Confederates During the Rütli Oath, 1780, by Johann Heinrich Fussli.

SWISS CONFEDERATION

An independent Switzerland emerged at the end of the Middle Ages, during which it established its prowess at cunning and ruthless warfare.

The three forest cantons signed their "Perpetual League" pact on 1 August 1291, barely two weeks after Rudolf's death. "The people of the valley of Uri," it proclaimed in Latin, "the democracy of the valley of Schwyz, and the community of the mountaineers of the Lower Valley, seeing the malice of the age... have promised in good faith to assist each other with aid, with every counsel and every favour, with person and goods, within the valleys and without, with might and main, against one and all, who may inflict upon any one of them any violence, molestation or injury, or may plot any evil against their persons or goods..."

The declaration laid down the basis of a legal code with the proviso that "we will accept or receive no judge in the aforesaid valleys, who shall have obtained his office for any price, or for money in any way whatever, or one who shall not be a native or a resident with us."

Rudolf died bitterly disappointed that he had not been able to secure the non-hereditary succession to the imperial throne for his son Albrecht, and the family reverted to being mere dukes when the crown went instead to Adolf of Nassau. The loss of imperial status made the Habsburgs a less imposing force in the eyes of the Swiss Confederation, which almost immediately entered into an alliance with Zürich and an anti-Habsburg coalition which sprang up in eastern Switzerland.

Zürich attacked Winterthur, a Habsburg town, in 1292, but was severely defeated. The Habsburg Duke Albrecht retaliated by besieging Zürich and eventually regaining the crown for the Habsburgs. Albrecht was subsequently assassinated in an ambush, however, and on his death the German crown slipped away from the family again, this time to Count Henry of Luxembourg.

Coat of arms of the confederated cantons.

NIGHT OF VIOLENCE

The violence was not one-sided. In 1314 a band of Schwyz men attacked the Habsburgs' abbey at Einsiedeln and made off with the monks as prisoners, even taking the monastery's cattle. The following year, in 1315, the infuriated Habsburgs resumed hostilities.

Duke Leopold assembled at Zug an army which included contingents from Luzern, Winterthur and, remarkably, Zürich. On reaching the hamlet of Haselmatt, near Aegeri, his ill-prepared force began the steep ascent of Morgarten.

Above a particularly tricky part of the ascent the defenders were waiting for them. Weighed down by heavy armour, the Austrians and their Swiss allies barely had time to look up when an avalanche of rocks and tree trunks descended on them from the Figlerfluh, a spur on the ridge of Morgarten. The Confederates rushed into the confusion brandishing their fearsome halberds

> The monastery of Konigsfelden, near Baden, was built in 1308 by Elisabeth, the widow of King Albrecht, on the spot where her husband was slain in ambush by a gang of Swiss nobles.

The Battle of Morgarten.

(long spears with an axe blade on one side and a pick on the other). The Austrians could retreat only by the way they had come. The retreat turned into flight, the flight into slaughter; many who escaped as far as a lake were drowned by the weight of their armour.

PEASANTS TRIUMPH

The Battle of Morgarten, a victory celebrated in Switzerland to this day, was possibly the first triumph in medieval Europe of peasants on foot over mounted knights. "When the fight was over," the chronicle records, "the men of Schwyz pulled off the weapons of the killed and drowned, robbed them also of their other possessions, and enriched themselves with arms and money." The occasion was commemorated by the construction of a chapel to St Jacob, but perhaps the best epitaph is a quotation attributed to the Austrian duke's fool before the action: "You have taken counsel how best to get into the country, but have given no explanation of how you are going to get out again."

The surprise victory over the Austrians boosted the forest cantons' prestige among their peers and more regions were drawn into the Confederation. In 1332 Luzern was the first town to join up, followed by Zürich (1351), Glarus and Zug (1352), and Bern (1353), making a total of eight members. After Bern, however, the rural cantons were wary of the balance tilting towards the cities, and no more cities were admitted until 1481. Zürich seceded from the Confederation but rejoined when not even the military assistance of Charles VII of France could stave off defeat.

A similar league was formed in Rhaetia, where the city of Chur joined surrounding villages and valleys in the "League of the House of God". The spread of such leagues was propelled by the bankruptcy of the smaller feudal lords in an economic climate devastated by the Black Death, bad harvests and starvation. Forced to pawn their feudal rights, they saw them being snapped up by prosperous cities. Bern bought the Hasli Valley from the impoverished lords of Weissenburg and with it the feudal rights over its inhabitants. Ironically, the new "lords" in such circumstances were in no hurry to extend to their acquired subjects the freedom which they valued so highly for themselves.

THE VIENNA PEACE TREATY

Successive Habsburg dukes never gave up the idea of reclaiming the Swiss lands lost to the Confederation and for a while succeeded in regaining Zug. Zürich was the main target, however, and it was only saved in 1351 by the intervention of the forest cantons. In time, the Swiss took the offensive. Luzern launched attacks on surrounding Austrian strongholds, Zug on the castle of St Andreas near Cham, Zürich on Rapperswil and Schwyz on Einsiedeln. In June 1386, Duke Leopold III, nephew of the loser at Morgarten, proposed to deal with the Swiss once and for all, at the Battle of Sempach (see box).

In 1389, after another Austrian defeat, this time at Näfels, a seven-year peace treaty was signed at Vienna which gave the Confederation undisputed possession of conquered lands, which is not to say that the Habsburgs did not attempt to seduce Zürich back into the fold by various diplomatic subterfuges. A 20-year peace treaty signed in 1415 was an altogether more reliable indication of Austria's willingness to accept what had happened. Although the Confederation was still technically within the German Empire, the bond was growing meaningless. Germans began to refer to the inhabitants of the confederate states collectively as Die Schweiz, after Schwyz, the state which to them seemed most representative of their increasingly distant neighbours.

In spite of apparent progress towards a constitution, the Confederation still fell some way short of a comprehensive government. It was a union of the loosest kind, in which the members were neither fully equal nor all bound to one another. Zürich kept a rather frigid distance from Luzern, for example, and Luzern

The death of Arnold von Winkelried at the Battle of Sempach.

⊘ ARNOLD VON WINKELRIED

The victory of the Confederates at the 1386 **Battle of Sempach** was due at least partly to the bravery of one Arnold von Winkelried, a national hero with similar hazy historical origins to those of William Tell.

The Austrians took to the field in full armour; the Swiss infantry faced them in a wedge-shaped formation. Unusually, the Austrian knights dismounted and advanced on the wedge with their halberds levelled. The tactics worked as, even with halberds 2.5 metres (8ft) long, the Swiss could not get close enough to strike.

The Swiss were dropping like flies and defeat seemed certain when things took a miraculous turn. "A good and pious man," says the chronicler, "stepped forward from the Swiss ranks". The Swiss are reluctant to believe that it was anyone other than Arnold von Winkelried. "I will cut a road for you; take care of my wife and children!" he cried.

The enterprising von Winkelried spread his arms wide and threw himself forward, forcing a number of levelled lances to the ground. His comrades charged over his fallen body and through the gap to engage the enemy at close quarters, the style of fighting at which they excelled.

Duke Leopold himself was killed but when his body was laid out, the Swiss having won a resounding victory, it was noticed that mysteriously his head bore no visible wounds.

from Glarus. The charters of each of the various states were very different. The rural cantons tended to be quite genuinely democratic, with magistrates appointed by popular assemblies, while in the cities the supreme power was lodged with the magistrate, who dispensed liberality downwards more or less as he pleased.

Nevertheless, during the 15th century Switzerland began to assume the proportions of a major European power. Its military prowess had already been amply demonstrated, and

Death of Charles the Bold in the Battle of Nancy.

⊘ THE COVENANT OF SEMPACH

The Covenant of Sempach, drawn up after the battle in 1386, has been described as "the first attempt, made by any people, to restrain somewhat the fury of war, to regulate military disciples and leadership by intelligent, humane law." Five centuries before the Geneva Convention, it provided for the humane treatment of the wounded and included such clauses as: "Women should not be attacked unless they warned the enemy by an outcry or fought themselves, in which case they could be punished as they deserved." The enlightened covenant also reflected the growing identity of the "Schweiz" as a separate nation.

now the economic foundations also looked solid. After the pan-European depression of the 14th century, the Confederation grew rich on cloth, wool and linen or, in the case of Zürich, silk. The attraction of money, as opposed to the barter goods which had generally been the currency previously, took precedence over political power.

This development was not quite as high-minded as it may appear, however, because much of the capital which created the new wealth was plainly and simply war booty, the fruits of victory over the richest ruler in Europe, Charles the Bold of Burgundy.

THE BURGUNDIAN WAR

The Swiss were so confident of their military superiority that they looked on foreign wars as unremarkable business opportunities. They did not realise that in this instance they were being manipulated by the notoriously wily Louis of France, who would benefit by assuming large swathes of Burgundian territory. The war was undertaken, says one historian, "at the instigation of France, for the interest of France, and in the pay of France".

Hostilities commenced in 1476, with Bern declaring war on Charles the Bold in the name of the Confederation. While Charles was away in Germany, Bernese troops invaded Burgundy and took Héricourt. On his return, Charles marched on Bern by way of Lake Neuchâtel, pausing to take the town of Grandson and either hanging or drowning 412 prisoners.

The first engagement proper at Neuchâtel took place on 2 March 1476 when, after an initial skirmish, the Burgundians were surprised by a sudden Swiss offensive. Their retreat was so hasty and disorderly that the booty left behind was unbelievable. Among 420 pieces of artillery and a huge quantity of general stores there were also diamonds and a golden casket containing holy relics including nothing less than pieces of the true cross and the crown of thorns. It was said that the booty included enough silk to enable the Confederate peasants to scorn clothing made from anything less for years. In contrast, the loss of life was minor.

Charles returned within a few weeks with a force of 25,000 men and laid siege to Morat, pounding the city with artillery fire which tore down part of the town wall and destroyed houses. Knowing that Bern would be next if Morat fell, the Confederate forces marched to the city with a force as large as the Burgundian besiegers, who included a number of English archers. The result was one-sided: between 8,000 and 10,000 of Charles's men were killed, against a few hundred Swiss losses.

Two days after the battle, a decisive victory for Charles's opponent, the Duke of Lorraine, a body was recovered from a frozen lake. It had been half-eaten by wolves but the exceptionally long

> "It is a horrible, fearful sight, that of so many dangling corpses," reported the Duke of Milan's ambassador with the Burgundian forces at Grandson, taken by Charles the Bold in 1476.

fingernails – an affectation of Charles the Bold – left little doubt as to its identity.

DIVIDING THE BOOTY

The spoils of the Burgundian war were colossal but their division, as far as the rural cantons were concerned, was so loaded in favour of the cities that the question of admitting yet more cities to the Confederation, in this instance Fribourg and Solothurn, brought the country to the brink of civil war.

Providentially, however, peace was maintained by the future saint, Niklaus von Flue. He worked out a compromise which admitted the towns to the Confederation in return for abandoning their other alliances. He proposed a new covenant, the *Stanser-verkommnis* (Agreement of Stans), which would in future regulate the division of spoils. Niklaus's canonisation followed some five centuries later.

MARY AND MAXIMILIAN

The death of Charles the Bold and the disintegration of the Duchy of Burgundy in the 15th century was as momentous and unexpected as the collapse of the Soviet Union would be in the 20th. The duchy was in reality an empire which included the Netherlands and Belgium and went all the way south to the Mediterranean. Now, the Low Countries were able to reassert their own

identities, and what had so recently been Louis XI's relatively insignificant kingdom assumed the dominant role in what became modern France. The role of the Swiss in bringing about Charles's demise was not as significant as his own bad judgement, but Swiss soldiers won great admiration and were perceived throughout Europe as the most useful to have on one's side.

Charles the Bold's terminal difficulties began with a hitch in the proposed marriage between his daughter Mary and Maximilian, son of the Habsburg Emperor Frederick.

Danse Macabre illustration by N. Manuel.

The marriage eventually took place and rescued Habsburg finances in what was undoubtedly their darkest hour. The Swiss soldier who had to a large extent paved Maximilian's way to a handsome inheritance was, with perfect impartiality, reaching for Maximilian's throat.

Maximilian's mistake was to offer the Swiss the hand of friendship. He suggested they forget about their Confederation and join instead the Swabian Bund, a new league headed by himself. War was soon raging along the whole line of the Rhine, from Basel to the borders of Vorarlberg and Graubünden, at the very idea. The so-called Swabian War lasted six months and was punctuated by the acts of valour now expected of Swiss troops.

SEVERING GERMAN LINKS

The peace treaty signed at Basel on 22 September 1499 secured the liberation of Rhaetia from the German Empire, incorporating it into

> "Here you might observe men's disposition – caution and cunning" wrote the reformist Zwingli, about the Swiss military tactical skills. "They pretend one thing, but hope to get another."

Statue of Hans Waldmann.

the Swiss Confederation and effectively reducing the links between the Confederation and the empire to a mere formality. This step was tantamount to acknowledging its independence. Formal independence, however, was not declared until the Peace of Westphalia, 150 years later.

The Confederation's burgeoning prestige attracted applications for membership from Basel and Schaffhausen in 1501. When Appenzell joined the Confederation in 1513 the number of members stood at 13, and there it remained for the following three centuries.

The activities of Swiss mercenaries from the 15th to 19th centuries really belong to the history of other nations' problems rather than

Switzerland's, but in the interest of symmetry it may be worth noting that having helped France and the Habsburgs in their difficulties with Burgundy, and having then turned on the Habsburgs, the Swiss again demonstrated perfect impartiality by taking up cudgels against France.

ITALIAN ALLIANCE

The Swiss actually began on France's side, the occasion being the invasion of Italy in 1494. The switch in their loyalties was the work of Matthäus Schiner, a man who began life as a street urchin but went on to become a cardinal and a confidant of Pope Julius II. The Pope was of course alarmed by French ambitions in Italy. Schiner suggested to him that the Swiss might be open to an offer of money, indulgences and other incentives. They were: a five-year alliance between the Papal See and Switzerland was duly signed. The Swiss drove their recent allies out of Lombardy and reinstated the Sforzas in Milan, which became a Swiss protectorate. The French bounced back but the issue was settled, so it seemed, at the Battle of Novara, which decided the matter in 1513.

The rural cantons were uncomfortably aware that the balance of power previously shared with the cities was slipping away. Zürich, Bern and Luzern could between them field twice as many men as all the other cantons put together. Zürich, in particular, was behaving like a sovereign state under its "ambitious and readily bribed" burgomaster, Hans Waldmann, "whose manifest opulence gave the lie to his affectation of republican simplicity".

Of humble origins himself and "Squire of Dubelstein" only by a fortuitous marriage, Waldmann personified the contempt of the urban nouveaux riches for the agrarian peasants by ordering them to put down all their large dogs because they were spoiling the hunting.

TORTURE AND EXECUTION

Five hundred peasants of Knonau marched on Zürich in protest and, taking Waldmann prisoner, gave him a taste of the rack in the Wellenberg state prison. Waldmann had spent some time in Wellenberg for youthful excesses, and there were not a few jilted mistresses who probably wished he had never been let out, but on this occasion the rack failed to extract a confession which would have invoked the death penalty. Undeterred, the city council voted to let him die anyway. Thousands turned out to watch him being led to the block in a meadow outside the city walls. He is said to have looked back at the city longingly before lowering his head. "May God protect thee, my beloved Zürich, and keep thee from all evil," were his parting words. His death was followed by rioting and many more executions as the plutocrats tightened their grip on the city to the exclusion of the country districts. After centuries of debate Zürich finally elected a monument to Waldmann in 1937.

While enterprising merchants could amass fortunes in the towns, the economy as far as rural people were concerned was still all about mercenary soldiering. Unfortunately for them, warfare was becoming too expensive for prospective employers. Developments like artillery, now essential, put the cost of even small wars beyond the means of minor, bad-tempered princes, traditionally the most regular source of employment. Moreover, the Germans had woken up to what they were missing and their mercenaries were competing for what business there was.

THE BATTLE OF MARIGNANO

Novara had been a great triumph for Swiss arms, but, when Francis I acceded to the French throne soon afterwards and immediately marched on Italy to restore French honour, three cantons – Bern, Fribourg and Solothurn – refused to fight. Cardinal Schiner, his sacred mission yielding to the profane, took command of the depleted Swiss forces. The two armies met on the road to Marignano on 13 September 1515. Battle raged inconclusively until midnight, was broken off, and resumed at dawn. In the afternoon, the French destroyed the dykes holding back the Lambro, and the plain on which the majority of the Swiss troops stood was suddenly flooded. The orderly retreat from this impossible predicament so impressed Francis that he ordered his men not to pursue.

There was also some solace in the "Eternal Peace" concluded with France afterwards. The Swiss possession of Ticino was acknowledged, although the future "Italian" canton was not granted that status until 1805.

The trauma of defeat weighed heavily on the Swiss. They tried immediately to raise another army, but the response was lukewarm. That afternoon on the road to Marignano saw France and Switzerland change places on the ladder of European power. A loose Confederation without a strong central authority was suddenly and dramatically exposed as an inadequate anachronism. Switzerland was reduced from a great power to a small neutral state, and it was in no condition to face the schismatic wrench of the Reformation.

The Battle of Marignano.

⊘ SOLDIERS FOR HIRE

Historian J. Christopher Herold aptly summed up the Swiss skill at balancing war and peace: "Beginning in the Middle Ages, [the Swiss] sold military service to foreign powers in the form of mercenaries. In order to exercise their military profession undisturbed and to enjoy its fruits in peace, they soon adopted a policy of neutrality – that is, the territory of Switzerland became neutral, while its citizens took part, on an impartial basis, in every European war for several centuries. The Swiss, who now consider themselves the first free and peaceful nation of the Continent, gave their name to an occupation usually involving both servitude and belligerency."

THE REFORMATION

Switzerland stood at the heart of Europe's religious upheaval, its cities erupting in flames as redoubtable reform leaders challenged the authorities.

The impact of the Reformation was doubly hard on Switzerland because, while Martin Luther in Germany concentrated on theology and was content to leave politics to the princes, Huldrych Zwingli drew no such distinction between religion and politics. He wanted a total overhaul of Swiss society, top to bottom.

ZWINGLI ROUSES THE MASSES

Born in Wildhaus in 1484, Zwingli was educated in Basel and Bern with a view to entering the church. He was a gifted student and entered into serious correspondence with scholars like Erasmus in Holland.

Never a natural bookworm, however, Zwingli went campaigning in Italy, although he became increasingly sceptical about the Swiss mercenary tradition and expressed his objections so forcefully that a public uproar made it prudent to retreat for two years to the abbey at Einsiedeln. The abuses within so appalled him that he redirected his critical energies, and this brought him to the attention of the Zürich council, which had decided that the city's reputation for wickedness required a vigorous remedy.

Zwingli's first sermon as the newly appointed "plebanus" was a rousing address which had people talking about "a new Moses who had arisen to save his people from spiritual bondage". The scholar Platter, sitting in the congregation, "felt himself lifted off the ground by his hair". Unlike Luther, Zwingli did not challenge papal authority over the sale of indulgences and the like. He was at first more inclined to outline a new state modelled on the Greek ideal, but he came round to the view that in order to build a new society it was necessary first to destroy the old. His targets were the mass and the worship of images.

Huldrych Zwingli.

THE FOREST CANTONS REBEL

In 1524 Zwingli showed what he thought of clerical celibacy by marrying a rich widow, and in the same year he was supported by the government in ordering the removal of all pictures and images from churches. By cutting ties with the diocese of Constance, Zwingli created in Zürich what was virtually its own state religion. The reforms were adopted readily in the northern and eastern cantons, but the forest cantons were steadfastly conservative and Roman Catholic. The Reformation was to them a product of the cities and for that reason alone suspicious if not downright evil. The forest cantons issued a warrant for Zwingli's arrest in case he entered their territory.

The Swiss factions looked beyond their borders for support, the Reformers to Germany and the Catholics to Austria. The split deepened and in 1529 Zürich declared war on the forest cantons. The confrontation of the two armies at Kappel was cooled at the last moment by diplomacy. Zwingli was disgusted by this pact and predicted that the Catholics would one day hold sway and then there would be no mercy.

In a way, Zwingli was right, because when the armies squared up again in the same place two

> The 16th-century Genevese were the most decadent citizens of Switzerland. Their moral plateau was a city statute that levied a modest charge on men who kept more than one mistress at a time.

years later the forest cantons had four times as many men as the Zürich force. On this occasion battle was not averted, and Zwingli was killed, along with many of his relatives and most of the Zürich city council. His body was quartered, burnt and "scattered to the wind". Leadership of the Zürich movement passed to his son-in-law Heinrich Bullinger, who found it expedient to concentrate on ecclesiastical matters and leave politics alone.

CALVIN'S CAUSE

In one sense, John Calvin, the second giant of the Swiss Reformation, picked up where Zwingli left off, but Zwingli's work was mainly about Zürich and the conversion of German-speaking Switzerland while Calvin's was about Geneva and French-speaking Switzerland. Calvin and Geneva were improbable bedfellows. He was born in Picardy, northern France, in 1509, "a northern Frenchman of superior intelligence and learning, but of a gloomy, austere disposition." The Genevese were the least austere people in Switzerland. They were gamblers and wine-lovers, and kept a red-light district busy.

After the collapse of the Roman Empire, the city was passed around various masters, but at an early date it became an episcopal see, the

bishops reaching some kind of accommodation with the House of Savoy which controlled the territory all about. In 1421, however, Duke Amadeus VIII of Savoy usurped the see and it was entrusted to a motley collection of Savoyard hangers-on and royal offspring.

GENEVA HOT-BLOODS

Rebellion against the Savoyards produced the three musketeers of Geneva's history: Bezanson Hugues, Philibert Berthelier and François Bonivard, the last immortalised – with poetic licence

John Calvin.

– in Byron's romantic poem, *The Prisoner of Chillon*. They were a slightly anarchistic band of hot-bloods known as the "Children of Geneva". The first was decapitated by the bishops in 1519, the second fled, and Bonivard, about whose life Byron actually knew very little, was imprisoned in Chillon.

Wishing to rid themselves of the autocratic Savoyards, the Genevese turned to the Swiss Confederation, then at the pinnacle of its military prestige, and to Bern in particular. Bern was by then under Zwingli's influence and the price of its support was that the Genevese had to reform. Guillaume Farel, a fanatical preacher from Neuchâtel, was chosen as the man for the job.

Farel's arrival in 1532, two years after Bonivard had been locked up for the second time, precipitated a storm, the city dividing into supporters of the Confederation, known as the Eydguenots, and those who realised they preferred Savoy, the so-called Mamelukes. Egged on by Farel, the former invaded the cathedral in 1535, ripped apart everything except its walls, and led their dogs and mules inside the hallowed walls to add the proverbial insult to injury. Defrocked priests trampled on their robes while the beleaguered Catholics could only pray for a miracle.

Calvin (right) and Farel in Geneva.

It was Geneva's misfortune at the height of this religious tension suddenly to become the coveted target of three avaricious neighbours: Francis I, the victor at Marignano, the Emperor Charles V and Geneva's supposed ally, Bern itself. Bern got there first with a force of 6,000 men but fear of French intervention inhibited them and saved the city from annexation. The Bernese forces captured the castle of Chillon, however, and freed Bonivard.

Bonivard discovered that Geneva had changed in his enforced absence. His abbey

> The Spanish scholar Servetus unwisely passed through Calvin's Geneva on his way to Italy. He was not only a Unitarian but unsound on infant baptism. Servetus was publicly burnt to death.

had been seized and secularised, and the whole city looked gloomy. The difference was John Calvin, whom the fiery Farel had taken on to help him clean things up. For the moment, Calvin's proposed remedy was altogether too rigorous for the Genevese and in 1538 both he and Farel were banished. Farel returned to Neuchâtel and stayed there for the rest of his life, but within three years violent infighting on the Geneva council and the renewed threat of a Bernese occupation led to an invitation to Calvin to return.

CALVIN'S MORAL CRUSADE

Accepting Geneva's offer – on his own terms – Calvin now set about his mission with a vengeance. The Genevese were less aware of the intricacies of his doctrine of pre-destination than of the impact of the Consistory, his tribunal of 12 civic worthies who passed judgement on all spiritual and moral matters, public and private. They had the power to enter houses on suspicion of depravity, and laid down the law on the clothes, including the colour, and on what and how much people ate. Drunkenness, blasphemy and agnosticism were put into the same criminal category as murder.

In 1556 John Knox, the Scottish Calvinist, visited Geneva and described it as "the maist perfyt schoole of Chryst that ever was in the erth since the dayis of the Apostillis." By then, most of Calvin's opponents had bolted from the city, but his writings, which could be construed as a charter for capitalism in that they sanctioned the charging of interest on loans, went down well in Scotland and New England. No fewer than 24 printing presses ran day and night churning out his works in a number of languages. More than 2,000 of his sermons and 4,721 letters survive. "His religious enthusiasm was able to triumph over bodily ailments" says one of the more sympathetic biographers.

attack on their religion in 1602 by Charles Emmanuel I of Savoy, who was re-living the old Savoyard dream of making Geneva his own. The Savoyards crept up on the city on the night of 11 December and several were halfway up the walls when the alarm was given. Citizens in nightshirts rushed out and the invaders were beaten off at the cost of several lives. To guard against any repetition, Geneva signed a treaty with Henry IV of France, but the treaty did not come cheap. The city had to surrender to him its main agricultural hinterland, the

Zwingli's death at Kappel.

LAST LECTURE

Calvin died in 1564, his parting words being a stern lecture to those who came to pay their respects. The institutions he left behind in Geneva were soon severely tested by the gentler form of persuasion employed by St Francis of Sales, the champion of the Counter Reformation. By eliminating the more scandalous abuses of the Catholic Church, he managed to win back the entire countryside south of Lake Geneva. The city itself remained loyal to Calvinism and it was at the risk of his life that St Francis, while officially the Bishop of Geneva, paid one or two clandestine visits.

The Genevese took – and take – considerable pride in the way they saw off a perfidious

Pays de Gex, and it was hard to imagine how Geneva would be able to feed itself.

CONTINUAL CONFLICT

Unpleasant as the Reformation and Counter Reformation had been in Switzerland, the discomfort paled in comparison with the Thirty Years' War, which began at the start of the 17th century as a war about Bohemia and religion, developed into a trial of strength between France and the Habsburgs, and tore central Europe to shreds. The Swiss cantons were neutral, but atavistic instincts were aroused by war swirling around them and the Swiss population was divided, rooting for one side or the other.

VOLTAIRE'S THEATRE

Geneva was roused from its Calvinistic state of self-denial when Voltaire arrived in the city in 1755 and introduced its citizens to the theatre, with all its perceived vices.

Voltaire, less commonly known as François-Marie Arouet.

Voltaire spent most of the last 20 years of his life in Switzerland, although he returned to Paris just before he died in 1778. The French author's writing to date would not have been at all to the taste of the previously libertine but now thoroughly chastened burghers. He found his métier in writing a wicked satire on the pompous Duke d'Orléans, which earned him a six-month banishment from Paris. He continued to comment on the unfortunate duke's character and was therefore brought back to be thrown into the Bastille. A spell in England opened his eyes to the intellectual traditional of Isaac Newton, John Locke and other empiricist philosophers of the 18th century.

By now, Voltaire was producing an impressive flow of literature, and on returning to France showed an unsuspected talent for making money, buying shares in the government lottery and selling corn to the army.

Voltaire's romantic attachments kept pace with his rising fame and fortune and earned him the patronage of Madame de Pompadour. Nevertheless, he carried

on pricking personalities, including the Prussian Frederick the Great, for whom he happened to be working at the time, living in one of Frederick's palaces and drawing a pension of 20,000 francs. When Voltaire then showed up in Geneva, an unlikely place for someone with his kind of background, it was a matter of waiting to see what he would get up to next in spite of his protestations about being on the brink of death and wishing only to lead a quiet life.

In the event, Voltaire bought an estate, Les Délices, on the outskirts of Geneva, pottered about his garden, and was charming to everyone he met in Genevese society. He invited a select gathering to meet his house guest Lekain, the greatest French actor of the day. Lekain, Voltaire and his niece, Mme Denis, gave a reading from one of his works, Zaïre. "Never saw I so many tears shed," Voltaire wrote later, "never were the Calvinists so tender..." His mind was made up – Geneva must have a theatre.

At his announcement of this, Geneva caught its breath. The Consistory fulfilled expectations with such an explosion of moral outrage that even Voltaire, to whom controversy was meat and drink, thought it prudent to decamp to Lausanne until things cooled down.

Voltaire returned quietly the following year but soon revived the issue by writing in the Encyclopaedia that Geneva needed a theatre that would "unite the wisdom of Sparta with the polish of Athens". This apparently inoffensive claim nevertheless raised the hackles of the other great man of contemporary Switzerland, and former friend, Jean-Jacques Rousseau, who fumed that while he had nothing against theatre, per se, it would corrupt the innocent Genevese, leading them to the road to levity, ruin and perdition.

Undaunted, Voltaire opened his theatre at Les Délices; the city closed it down. He tried again at several other locations, always with the same result. Geneva at last got a purpose-built wooden theatre in 1766 and the Puritans promptly put a torch to it. Voltaire swore that Rousseau was responsible. The flames attracted a crowd of citizens armed with buckets, but on realising that it was the theatre they are reputed to have emptied the buckets with a cry of "Let those who wanted a theatre put it out!" The ironic outcome to this feud is that when Rousseau died he was buried in the Pantheon in Paris – alongside Voltaire.

HUGUENOT WEALTH

Geneva had difficulty feeding itself with the loss of the Pays de Gex to Henry IV of France, but the French Huguenots provided the solution. They were artisans, watchmakers and jewellers, merchants and, above all, financiers. In little more than a century, Geneva became one of the wealthiest cities in Europe. On the political front, the Peace of Westphalia, which concluded the Thirty Years' War, ratified Swiss independence. The Swiss states were no longer, even in the loose sense which had long been the case, part of the German Empire.

The Swiss, quiet and prosperous while the rest of Europe was at war, used the Peace of Westphalia as a cue to fight among themselves and let the economic advances slip away. It was almost as if the Confederation needed an external threat to remain in one piece. Without it, the states went off on their own. Neuchâtel and St Gallen were paragons of unbending absolutism; Bern, Fribourg, Solothurn and Luzern aped the oligarchies based on birth and inheritance. Only the forest cantons were even remotely democratic. Society split along class lines too: a minor peasant protest against new taxation struck such a popular chord that a proletarian uprising exploded over much of central Switzerland.

The peasants themselves were "hards" pitted against "softs", the former chopping off the beards, ears or both of those who were thought not to be pulling their weight. The poorly equipped peasants were no match for their common enemy, however, and both their principal leaders, Christian Schibi and Nicholas Leuenberger, were captured, tortured and executed.

SECOND WAVE

The religious wars were fought all over again on slight pretexts. The First Villmergen War (1656) was sparked by the imperiously Catholic Schwyz sending three of the handful of Protestants living in the canton to be dealt with by the Inquisition in Milan, and eventually had Bern and Zürich at war with all five Catholic states. War threatened in St Gallen in 1697 because Catholics wished to carry the cross upright in a procession through the streets. The Second Villmergen War, which again saw St Gallen in the thick of the action, was over who should provide the labour for the construction of a new road. The Pope was drawn into the dispute and it was only settled after a bloody victory by the combined Zürich and Bern armies.

The manipulative hand of Louis XIV of France was behind much of the religious ill-feeling of the 17th century. To begin with, he needed Swiss mercenaries – between 6,000 and 16,000 a year – for his wars and was prepared to offer commercial privileges in return. Switzerland ended

John Calvin preaching from his deathbed.

up, though, as a dependency of the French Crown in all but name, and things might not have stopped there had France not been kept in rein by Britain and the Netherlands. Swiss envoys were treated to lavish entertainment at the French court and it was said that they were beguiled into playing the king's poodles. When Louis XIV remarked that all the money he had paid for Swiss troops would have paved the road from Paris to Basel with gold pieces, the Swiss replied – in one celebrated exception to their sycophancy: "You forget Sir, that with the Swiss blood spilt in the French service you might fill a canal from Basel to Paris."

In the 17th and 18th centuries the leading cities of the Confederation took on different characters. Zürich was the seat of liberal and intellectual progress, Bern of politics and finance, and Geneva of science. Zürich, like all fully fledged members of the Confederation, had its subject lands, and the liberal tenden-

> "Man is born free; and everywhere he is in chains" – the resounding opening to Rousseau's Social Contract.

Jean-Jacques Rousseau.

cies stopped there to be replaced by the sort of patriarchal governor much admired by Goethe. Landolt von Greifensee, a case in point, advocated compulsory church attendance and believed that flogging was an effective means of discipline.

FRENCH ELITE

Bern was resolutely French in language and manners. Its constitution was elitist, with all power vested in 360 families. The middle class had no political rights but were given the run of trade, education and religion. The lower class, which included foreigners, were not permitted to own houses or have their children baptised in the city. They were not allowed to enter the market

before 11am, by which time their betters (or their betters' servants) were supposed to have done their shopping. In 1744 a group of citizens led by a certain Henzi presented a petition asking for some of these regulations to be relaxed. Henzi paid for the presumption with his life.

Geneva, which had previously been under the heel of Calvin's Consistory, was rocked to its foundations in 1755 by the arrival of Voltaire. He was there, he said blandly, to see out his twilight years (he was then 61), but those who assumed this meant a mellow, uncontroversial retirement were in for a rude awakening (see page 52).

REVOLUTIONARY SHOCK

As France had long been Switzerland's most powerful ally, the Revolution sent shockwaves through the Confederation. It was opposed, naturally enough, by those with a vested interest in the divinely appointed social and political order: the cantonal governments, the privileged urban classes, the church and, of course, the French aristocratic refugees, most of whom congregated in Solothurn, Fribourg and Neuchâtel. It was supported by the subject territories, the French-speaking parts and by Swiss émigrés in Paris. The opponents could have found an ally in imperial Austria, but there was always the fear of Austrian territorial ambition in Switzerland. France, whatever its government, was seen as the best available guarantee against Austrian aggrandisement. All in all, it suited Switzerland to be neutral.

Franco-Swiss relations, on tenterhooks because of the Revolution, were tested to the limit on 10 August 1792 when the Paris mob stormed the Palace of the Tuileries, where the job of protecting the French royals was in the hands of the Swiss Guard. It seems that once his personal safety had been secured, Louis XIV ordered a ceasefire, whereupon the mob turned on the guard and massacred nearly 800 of them. Ten days after the incident, the French Assembly dismissed the Swiss mercenaries serving elsewhere and sent them all home without pay. Many of them, particularly the officers, promptly switched sides, fighting for the anti-revolutionary coalition under Austrian command and British pay.

The Swiss revolutionaries in Paris shook off the general Swiss outrage at the massacre of the Guard to press for the French "liberation" of Switzerland. The French Government was cautious. Almost the whole of Europe had imposed a blockade on France, and only the Swiss frontier was open to admit a long list of materials provided by indiscriminating suppliers in Austria, Italy and Hungary.

In 1798 French attitudes hardened under the growing influence of Napoleon Bonaparte. A pretext was found to occupy the southern shore of Lake Geneva, the first such foreign invasion in the Confederation's his-

three forest cantons were defiant. They would be "burnt beneath their blazing roofs", they said, "rather than submit to the dictates of the foreigner". They were hopelessly outnumbered, however, and after the fall of Glarus and Schwyz the resistance focused on the town of Stans, in Nidwalden.

The French commander called 9 September 1798 the hottest day of his life: "Like furies, the black legion of the French galley-slaves slew and raged the district through." The defiance ended in smoke and blood that night.

The Elephant Carousel by Antoine Caron: the elephant represents Geneva, under attack from Catholic forces.

tory. Laharpe, who had long borne a grudge against Bern, reminded Napoleon that the city possessed a treasure trove of gold. Bern was the military mainstay of the Confederation but, abandoned by the other members and paralysed by internal dissent, it could not withstand a French assault.

THE SACK OF BERN

On 5 March the French Army entered the city and went to work. The contents of the treasury were carted off in 11 wagons together with the city's three mascots, bears named Erlach, Steiger and Weiss.

The 10 city cantons acquiesced in the Helvetic Republic proclaimed by France, but the

⊘ ROUSSEAU'S FAMILY VALUES

Jean-Jacques Rousseau was born to French parents in Geneva in 1712. Although he spent most of his life wandering about, he claimed never to have lost his love for the city. Once, on leaving after a return visit, he was so overcome by emotion that he fainted.

At the time of his row with Voltaire over the theatre, Rousseau was extolling the nobility of savagery, the innocence of childhood, the wickedness of civilisation. Critics have pointed out that Rousseau's damp-eyed adoration of childhood hardly squares with the fate of the five children he fathered by an illiterate servant, Thérèse le Vasseur. He despatched the lot to foundling hospitals.

📷 TRADITIONAL COUNTRY LIFE

Life continues in much the same way as it always has in the rural communities of the Alps, with their distinctive music, crafts and style of dress.

One of the most remarkable features of Switzerland is the coexistence of two contrasting economies: the dynamic, ultramodern one of industry and business, and the rural, farming economy that is, at least in mountain areas, highly traditional. Farms in the Alpine valleys and highlands are small scale and family run. High government subsidies have helped to stem the generational drift away from the land; now, if anything, younger generations are returning, driven by a craving for traditional, authentic ways of life. Consequently, Switzerland has been less affected by the pervading western European phenomenon whereby rural communities rapidly transmute into commuter villages. The Swiss in general take tremendous pride in their traditional countryside heritage, which embodies much more than the caricature of bearded, yodelling, alphorn-playing, flag-tossing farmers in traditional dress – and plaited milk can-carrying Heidi's – seen at touristy folklore shows.

THE SOUND OF MUSIC

Yodelling, with its ululating high falsetto and low chest notes, was developed from the calls of Swiss herdsmen and, like the national instrument, the melancholy alphorn, was used as a way of communicating across mountain valleys. The alphorn, made of a hollowed pine trunk up to 4 metres (13ft) in length, was first described in 1555 and originated in the traditional rural village of Appenzell and the Bernese Oberland. By the early 19th century, the alphorn had come perilously close to disappearing from use but, from the 1820s, a cultural revival rescued it from this ignominious fate. Apparently, herdsmen used to play it to soothe the cows while they were being milked.

Children and Alpine herdsmen dress in traditional costume for the time-honored cattle procession to summer pastures in Alpstein. Yodelling can be heard to the accompaniment of cow bells.

Alphorn players perform on the last day of the international Alphorn Festival in Nendaz.

Traditional wood-carved houses are common in the area around Lake Brienz.

The art of woodcarving

Around Lake Brienz is a community of craftsmen who use local wood such as linden to create works of art – from music boxes and trinkets to sculptures. Even the architecture and the buildings with heavy, ornate wooden balconies reveal the craftsmanship that has made the town of Brienz the unofficial woodcarving centre of Switzerland.

Woodworkers have passed on ancient skills from generation to generation, creating the ornamental objects and practical items which are sold in the region's studios and craft shops. You can learn more about the craft at Brienz's Woodcarving Museum (Hauptstrasse 111; tel: 033 952 13 17; www.museum-holzbildhauerei.ch), Switzerland's first museum dedicated to the art, boasting an extensive collection of antique carvings and wooden music boxes. Nearby is a violin-making school, Geigenbauschule Brienz (Oberdorfstrasse 94; tel: 033 951 18 61; www.geigenbauschule.ch; office Mon–Fri 8–11.45am, 1.30–5pm), which has occasional concerts and other cultural activities throughout the year.

Traditional cheesemaking survives in the Swiss valleys and mountains.

A flock of sheep graze in the afternoon sunshine in the Italian-speaking Ticino canton.

There is an astonishing variety of regional dress in Switzerland: some 400 different types have been recorded. Here, Alpine residents of all ages don traditional Appenzell costumes to take part in the local cattle drive, accompanied by cows and white Appenzell goats.

THE MAKING OF MODERN SWITZERLAND

The country preserved its neutrality through two world wars, and ended up even richer and more stable than before.

The Helvetic Republic was largely a French invention, formed physically and politically to suit the purposes of France. The French restructured the area, backed a new constitution with a centralised republic (enacted in 1798) and re-divided the cantons. Bits of the south were chopped off and given to French-controlled Italy, Neuchâtel was completely cut off and Mulhausen was attached to France. The remainder was divided into 23 cantons under a rigidly centralised French-style executive. The constitution imitated the individual liberties introduced by the French Revolution (particularly those of the French Constitution of the year III, 1795) but the loss of local autonomy was resented, as were the new taxes and hostility to religion. The ultimate humiliation was the choice between signing a perpetual military alliance with France, thus ending Swiss neutrality, and outright annexation.

The constitution, which lasted from 1798 to 1803, was made unworkable by constant brawling among the Swiss. By 1803 Napoleon had had enough: they could have their cantons, their neutrality and even their judicial torture. Under the Mediation Act, the 13 cantons were restored as quasi-sovereign states, and six new fully autonomous ones were created: Aargau, St Gallen, Graubünden, Ticino, Thurgau and Vaud. But for the rest of the Napoleonic Wars, Switzerland continued to be a vassal state to France, serving them for industry and as a battleground. As mediator of the Swiss Confederation, the Emperor reserved the right to recruit 16,000 men in Switzerland through a defensive alliance, and thousands of Swiss soldiers died during Napoleon's Russian Campaign.

A 19th-century open-air assembly in Uri canton.

THE ROAD TO NEUTRALITY

The Congress of Vienna, convened to unstitch the Napoleonic Empire after its collapse in 1814, saw Swiss patricians lobbying furiously to regain their former rights, and it was only through much banging of Swiss heads that the Big Four – Austria, England, Russia and Prussia – got them to agree to a loose federation. The cantons, now numbering 23, would be almost autonomous with just a few federal functions exercised by rota among Bern, Zürich and Luzern.

With Napoleon finally disposed of, the Treaty of Paris, signed on 20 November 1815, guaranteed Switzerland's perpetual neutrality.

Switzerland's borders were established by the treaty as they are today. The Confederation lost

Mulhouse but regained an enlarged Geneva, the Valais and Neuchâtel. The former territory of Basel was shared with Bern.

While the international status and map of Switzerland were now secure, the domestic scene during the next 15 years of so-called Restoration was chaotic. Cantons insisted on minting their own currency, and customs barriers between them were so cumbersome that international traders used other routes. The rift between conservatives and progressives widened, culminating down the line in the Sonderbund War.

In 1830, inspired by the July Revolution in France which saw King Charles X dethroned, the mood switched to Regeneration, a curious misnomer, for what ensued was a period of utter chaos. Disgruntled peasants in the various cantons pursued their highly disparate dreams, unified only by a general desire to cut the aristocracy down to size.

The Federal Tagsatzung, (Federal Diet), the executive body, was so impotent that in 1832 seven cantons including Luzern and Zürich formed a breakaway federation of sorts, and other factions followed. These groupings then re-arranged themselves so that the Confederation was effectively divided into two bitterly antagonistic camps: "an ominous state of affairs, calculated to make every patriot tremble for the result..."

As tension mounted between opposing religious groups, the canton of Aargau "set the whole country ablaze" by abolishing all monasteries and nunneries, thereby antagonising the Pope and the Emperor of Austria whose ancestors had founded the monastery of Muri. The compromise was to save the nunneries but get rid of monasteries.

COUNCIL OF WAR

In 1844, Luzern, one of the Catholic cantons, decided that its religious interests would best be served by handing over its education to the Jesuits. Extremist Protestants launched guerrilla raids on the city, with 100 para-military volunteers killed and 1,900 captured in one attack. The seven predominantly Catholic cantons linked up as the Sonderbund, declared an Act of Succession and appointed a Council of War. Prince Metternich, the Austrian Chancellor and one of the architects of the new Switzerland at the Congress of Vienna, watched these developments aghast. Switzerland, he wrote, "presents the most perfect image of a state in the process of social disintegration..."

The civil war pitted the 415,000 conservative, Catholic inhabitants of the Sonderbund alliance against nearly 2 million in the largely Protestant federated cantons. The Sonderbund was difficult to defend. The forest cantons held a strong central position, but Fribourg was completely isolated and Valais was connected to the others

1844–5 raids in Switzerland.

only by high Alpine passes. The federal forces picked off Fribourg first and then closed in on Luzern from all sides. The city surrendered without a fight, and the others soon followed. The campaign was over within 20 days, leaving 78 dead and 260 wounded.

The victors were lenient, the principal victims being the Jesuits, who were expelled. A new constitution was put to the vote, and although seven cantons opposed it they agreed to go along with the majority. The Federal Constitution of 1848 put foreign affairs and other institutions like the post office and customs under central control, restricted mercenary activities abroad and ensured that for the first time all cantons had democratic institutions. The Swiss had a plausible national government at last and were in a position to catch up with the rest of Europe.

In the years that followed, Zürich played a prominent role in federal affairs, and under the dynamic leadership of its liberal mayor, Jonas Furrer, enjoyed an unprecedented period of cosmopolitan cultural renaissance.

NEUCHÂTEL CRISIS

Revitalised by their growing democracy, the Swiss felt cocky enough to contemplate going to war with Prussia over the curious business

Zürich in 1869.

of Neuchâtel, the first crisis of foreign policy the young state had to face. Neuchâtel had been something of an oddity since 1707 when, in order to spurn the advances of Louis XIV of France, it had put itself under the ducal sway of Frederick II of Prussia. It remained a Prussian possession even after admission as a canton in 1814; it was thus a monarchical enclave within a republican confederation. These royalists refused to join the federal forces against the Sonderbund in 1847 and were overthrown by republican sympathisers.

TWO-DAY COUP

The following year, however, the Great Powers reinstated the Prussian king as the Prince of Neuchâtel. The Swiss would have none of it and went on recognising the republican usurpers. On 2 September Count Frédéric Pourtalès usurped the usurpers in a royalist coup and Neuchâtel was Prussian again – but only for two days. A hundred or so royalists were taken prisoner in the counter coup, but Frederick William IV of Prussia mobilised, and the Swiss responded by raising a force of 30,000.

Napoleon III, who did not wish to see the Prussian Army rolling up on his southeastern flank, offered to mediate, and Britain's Lord Palmerston reminded Frederick William of the guarantees of Swiss neutrality.

The agreement reached was that Switzerland would release the royalist prisoners, who would then return to Prussia, Neuchâtel would be given full cantonal rights within the Swiss Confederation, and Frederick William would give up his sovereign rights for all time although he could, if he liked, go on calling himself Prince of Neuchâtel. It was the last of the old struggles between Swiss and foreign authorities.

MERCENARIES AND REFUGEES

The twin problems caused by Swiss mercenaries abroad and political refugees remained unsolved. The 1848 Federal Constitution had forbidden any more military capitulations (ie, contracts to supply mercenaries) but it did not abolish those already in existence, two of which were with King Bomba of Naples and the Pope. These meant that, whether they liked it or not, Swiss troops were mixed up in the wars of the Italian Risorgimento, a situation which continued in defiance of the issuing of a new federal law in 1859 which tightened the ban on mercenary service.

In the same year a papal Swiss regiment was accused of atrocities after capturing Perugia; another unit was badly beaten the following year at Castelfidardo by an Italian army marching to join Garibaldi. About 4,000 Swiss "volunteers" fought in the American Civil War, mostly for the South, and 7,000 were killed fighting for France in World War I. Volunteering – even for the French Foreign Legion – was banned in 1927, the only exception being the Vatican Guard, founded in 1505 by Pope Julius II, whose contracts stipulate no combat duties.

The political convulsions of the mid-19th century created a flood of fugitives who chose

Instead of persecuted Protestants, 19th-century refugees in Switzerland included leading political figures such as Mazzini and Lenin, and, later, Mussolini.

to interpret Switzerland's internationally guaranteed neutrality as a safe haven for them. The country showed both profit and loss on its popular reputation as an asylum.

course did not agree and, at least to begin with, the majority of the population welcomed the refugees as martyrs, trying to find them work. The welcome cooled when the volume swelled to thousands and, unable to find work, they became public nuisances. The refugee question became a grave embarrassment to Switzerland, and its shadow today is the feeling, perhaps, that the vaunted secrecy of the country's banking system may shield rather too many unworthy causes.

In spite of difficulties with Neuchâtel, mercenaries and refugees, federal Swiss enjoyed

Satirical cartoon showing France, Prussia and Austria sweeping revolutionaries into Switzerland, 1848.

SWISS NAPOLEON

Louis-Philippe, the future "citizen-king" of the French, spent some years in Graubünden as a mathematics teacher, but on assuming the throne he objected violently when Louis Napoleon, who later succeeded him as Napoleon III, claimed asylum in Switzerland. Napoleon was in fact a naturalised Swiss and had become a captain in the Swiss Army. When the Diet refused to expel him, Louis-Philippe sent an army of 25,000 men to fetch him. Napoleon defused the danger by leaving Swiss territory and moving to London.

Louis-Philippe's actions reflected the not uncommon attitude that the price of Swiss neutrality was *not* harbouring fugitives. The Swiss of

internal peace, economic prosperity and respectability in foreign relations.

WAR AGAIN

As long as the European balance of power remained stable, the independence and neutrality of Switzerland were safe. When the balance was upset, cracks showed in the fabric. The 1870 Franco-Prussian War was a particular case in point because of the country's racial and religious composition. The political minority of Catholic Conservatives and the linguistic minority of the Radical-Democratic French cantons were united by the dread of Protestant Germanisation, as exemplified by the growth of Prussia. The threat existed in the possible Germanisation

⌕ THE RED CROSS

The distinguished Red Cross employs some 16,000 people in more than 80 countries worldwide, helping victims of armed violence and conflict. And it all started here.

Dunant helping the wounded at the Battle of Solferino.

International Geneva, familiar as the backdrop to so many peace conferences and summit meetings, is practically a state within a city. It is the address for scores of international organisations and even has its own postmark for their outgoing mail. It is no coincidence that the famous Red Cross, which has fluttered above ambulances in countless wars, is actually the Swiss flag with its colours reversed, nor that the Red Cross headquarters should be in Geneva.

Henri Dunant, the Red Cross founder, was born in Geneva in 1828 and made his fortune in Algeria as a grain speculator. He returned to Geneva to try to raise more capital but, faced with bureaucratic obstacles, decided to go to Napoleon III personally.

Dunant's efforts to secure an audience with Napoleon set something of a benchmark in sycophancy. He wrote a book, which proved beyond a doubt that Napoleon was heir to the Emperor Augustus – *The Empire of Charlemagne Re-established* or *The Holy Roman Empire Reconstituted by His Majesty the Emperor Napoleon III*, by J. Henri Dunant, director and

president of the Financial and Industrial Society of Mons-Djemila (Algeria), member of the Asiatic Society of Paris, of the Oriental Society of France, of the Geographic Societies of Paris and Geneva, of the Historical Society of Algiers, etc. Dunant had one copy printed, and then had to deliver it.

He tracked down Napoleon in Italy on the eve of the Battle of Solferino (1859). Understandably, the emperor had other things on his mind and, in the morning, so did Dunant. He found himself in the middle of one of the bloodiest battles in history – 33,000 casualties on the first day alone. Dunant threw himself into washing wounds and generally helping as casualties poured in at the rate of 55 a minute. After two days and nights without sleep, the man was a legend. It was almost irrelevant that Napoleon glanced at the book and said that for political reasons he could not accept it.

Dunant returned to Geneva and wrote a moving account of the horrors he had seen. *A Souvenir of Solferino* was a powerful plea for the creation of a neutral organisation that would care for the casualties of war. M. Gustave Moynier, president of the Society for Public Usefulness of Geneva, read it and thought the idea good. Dunant toured Europe drumming up support; the result was the signing of the first Geneva Convention in 1864.

Yet three years after the foundation of the Red Cross, Dunant left Geneva bankrupt. Wandering penniless, he thought of other ambitious schemes. But these came to nothing and pursuit by his creditors meant he could not stay in one place for long.

In 1887 Dunant returned to a semi-incognito existence in Switzerland, living like a hermit in the village of Heiden in Appenzell. A journalist discovered the fate of the founder of the Red Cross, and his scoop was quickly followed up by other newspapers. In 1901 the white-bearded hermit of Heiden jointly won the first Nobel Peace Prize – seized on by his creditors as an opportunity to renew their claims. Embarrassed by the financial failure of one of its own, Geneva questioned his claim to have founded the Red Cross.

Dunant had the last word. When he died in 1910, he left the Nobel Prize money he had saved to charitable institutions in Norway and Switzerland. His remaining creditors got nothing.

> *Switzerland's size meant that it would only ever be a pawn in Europe's power game, but the opening of the Gotthard Tunnel in 1882 made it a key player, with the best route from north to south.*

of the federal government, so logically they dug in their heels in favour of cantonal autonomy. The division between Centralists and Federalists was therefore a racial and cultural one, championed respectively by the Vaudois Louis Ruchonnet and the Federal Councillor Emil Welti, the latter campaigning on the slogan "One law, one army."

The obvious outsider in the fundamental Swiss split was Italian-speaking Ticino, where Conservatives and Radicals were practically of equal strength. Complaints of dishonest electoral practices led to demonstrations, riots and bloodshed, and for a while civil war within the canton looked likely. Elections in 1889 to test some democratic innovations brought Ticinese living abroad streaming home to vote. The parties even chartered ships to bring hundreds of voters back from Europe and all the way from America. The result was a draw but, under the majority system, the Conservatives gained two-thirds of the seats.

The Radicals took the law into their own hands, seizing public buildings, imprisoning the municipal council and declaring a provisional government. The arrival of two battalions of federal troops and a promise of proportional representation calmed things down. In 1892, the Radicals were returned to power.

THE NEW ECONOMY

A neutral Switzerland provided one carefree flank for all its neighbours; the critical question was whether Switzerland had the will and the power to prevent its neutrality from being invaded by someone else. It was probably as much as Switzerland could do in this respect to announce large increases in the mobility and striking force of its army and, all the while, lend its neutral territory profitably as the seat for international organisations.

The new tunnels, roads and railways were bad news for farmers, or so it seemed. The military efficacy of embryonic Switzerland depended to a

very large extent on a pastoral economy, that is to say non-labour-intensive stock-raising. Over the course of centuries, the forest cantons were joined and progressively dominated by others whose land was more conducive to mixed farming. Agriculture evolved so that by the middle of the 19th century the main activity overall was cereal production.

In the circumstances, cereal production increased so that the country generally had enough grain to cover domestic consumption for 300 days. Modern means of transport, however,

The first train to pass through the Gotthard Tunnel, 1880.

exposed the Swiss farmer to competition from as far afield as Russia. Swiss production costs and prices were too high compared to foreign cereals which, thanks to better transport, could now be imported with ease.

Swiss farmers turned to other things, and the cereal mountain shrank. By the end of the 19th century, the country was producing only what was needed to cover domestic consumption for six months.

Swiss farmers realised that they had turned full circle. Conditions were still excellent for stock-raising and dairy farming, so they once again invested their energies in these. Some things had changed. The demand from abroad was no longer for horse meat but for beef.

Cheese sold so well that it eventually accounted for more than a third of agriculture exports. The dairy industry also produced two novelties which have since become synonymous with Switzerland – chocolate and condensed milk.

SWISS WATCHES

The watch- and clock-making industry was forced (especially after World War I) to adopt factory methods for export sales. The industry as a whole went for volume, rising to control

French-speaking Switzerland, as ever, was suspicious of Germany, exceptionally so after its invasion of Belgium, and of the German outlook which had been gaining ground within the country. More than 220,000 "pure" Germans were living in Switzerland, half of them in Basel and Zürich alone. French-speaking Switzerland's sympathies were entirely with France and Britain. The Italian-speaking Ticinesi were for Italy. On the whole, German-speaking Switzerland felt a kinship with Germany and admired its rise in technology, industry and commerce.

Swiss patrol at an observation point on the southern frontier during World War I.

nearly 90 percent of total world production. By the 1970s it had slipped to about 40 percent and was still falling as the Swiss franc gained against the currencies in the watch industry's main export markets. A falling dollar meant that competitive American watches were cheaper, and of course the entry of the super-efficient Japanese manufacturers re-wrote the rules from top to bottom.

LOOMING WORLD WAR

In time, political conversation in Switzerland, as in the rest of Europe, hinged on the domino effect that began with the Habsburg Archduke Ferdinand's assassination in Sarajevo and resulted in World War I.

Many deplored the invasion of Belgium but still believed in Germany.

"On general cultural grounds as well as political I believe that a German victory is desirable," wrote Karl Scheurer, head of the Military Department of Bern canton in August 1914. A month later the German minister in Bern reported to his superiors: "From the very first day since the outbreak of war Switzerland has discreetly placed at our disposal her entire secret military intelligence service..."

The arrest and trial of two of Commander-in-Chief General Wille's staff officers for passing secrets to the Germans and Austrians led to calls for his resignation, damaging the morale of an army already on uneventful frontier duties.

Following two visits to the Alps by Queen Victoria, Switzerland suddenly became the fashionable holiday destination for the European middle classes. Anticipating the boom in winter sports, the first form of entertainment was joy-riding downhill on Schlitten, or toboggans, borrowed from villagers.

A few bombs were dropped but there were no serious breaches of neutrality. The real war for Switzerland was economic. Depleted agriculture was insufficient to feed the people and there was a constant danger of being cut off from imported food supplies and the raw materials necessary to keep industry running. An agreement with the central powers in 1915 allowed for the import of German and Austrian goods, but the Allies were less cooperative. The United States, however, guaranteed the supply of bread.

Some Swiss were ruined by the war; others did well. In the absence of foreign competition, it was like old times for farmers. The worst hardship fell on the working class, their bitterness exacerbated by the large number of foreigners who flooded in during the war – profiteers, deserters and conscientious objectors. There were also the Russian revolutionaries, Lenin, Trotsky, Zinoviev, Axelrod and Martov. Their presence made Switzerland look like the revolutionary capital of the world, and the idea of a general strike took shape among Swiss socialists as class divisions and economic pressures exploded in around 1916.

Though the Social Democrats – the political arm of the organised labour movement – had to cede to a federal order to call off the General Strike of November 1918, many of their demands were quickly met. Their victories included a 48-hour week, and most importantly proportional representation, which helped them gradually become the strongest party in parliament by 1943.

WORLD WAR II

With the prospect of a second war ever more likely, Switzerland took precautions against being caught out as before by filling its granaries. Neutrality in the event of hostilities was taken for granted, but an official German training manual gave a shock: its maps putting Switzerland firmly within the boundaries of the Third Reich. The Swiss German cantons were no less alarmed; it made them realise how different they were from the citizens of Germany, especially from the Fascists. When war broke out, the choice of Henri Guisan from French-speaking Vaud as Switzerland's new Commander in Chief marked a significant change from the previous German bias among the military. Mobilisation led to the call-up of 400,000 men, later increased to 850,000 with the inclusion of auxiliary services and the home

General Henri Guisan.

guard, out of a total population of only 4 million. In the early stages of the war, Swiss troops took up their usual positions along the borders, but with the fall of France, which left the country completely surrounded by the Axis, Guisan adopted a strategy that an enemy would be allowed to roll across the frontiers, where defence was difficult, in order to be met where conditions better suited the Swiss, in and along the Alps.

There is no doubt that the German High Command had plans for a Swiss invasion. They even had a codename, *Tannenbaum* (Fir Tree). Why the operation was not carried out remains a puzzle.

One theory is that Hitler believed the number of troops required was hardly worth what Switzerland represented in the way of raw materials. He already had use of the Gotthard Tunnel to get coal to his Italian allies, and the Swiss, he knew, had mined the tunnel and would blow it up at the first sign of an invasion. Hitler had a ready-made motive to invade if he needed one: his troops had uncovered in French headquarters at La Charité-sur-Loire a secret agreement on the exchange of information between Swiss and French intelligence, an ironic postscript to World War I. In any case, after the Allied landings in North Africa and France, he had other things on his mind.

Support for Switzerland joining the League of Nations.

⊘ THE LEAGUE OF NATIONS

Switzerland was enthusiastic about the proposed League of Nations after World War I, and, although it took no significant part in its creation, Geneva was selected as the seat of the League. Nevertheless, there was doubt whether Switzerland's neutrality would allow it to join; in 1920 the Declaration of London allowed Switzerland in "by reason of an ancient tradition". The Confederation would not be called on to take part in military operations, but it would be bound to observe economic sanctions as imposed by the League. When the chance to join was put to the Swiss electorate, the population voted in favour of joining by 414,830 votes to 322,937.

POST-WAR HELP

When peace was concluded, Switzerland devoted a generous proportion of its intact economy to post-war reconstruction. The full implications of Fascism in Germany and Italy ran deep, and the once bitterly divided Swiss cantons appeared as not such bad bedfellows after all.

However, the unified spirit of the wartime years was quickly upset by the effects of the Cold War. From 1948 the Communist Party had a strong influence, and tensions between Communists and opposing factions caused a

> *The right of Swiss women to vote and stand for federal elections only came in 1971, and women's right to vote in Appenzell-Rhoden cantonal elections was only passed in April 1991.*

deep rupture in Swiss society. Nevertheless, the economy purred from one boom to the next, propelled by huge reserves of capital and relatively cheap foreign labour. The question of giving the vote to women, refused in 1959, suggested to more-progressive onlookers that the Swiss were not merely quaint but antediluvian (a second referendum finally introduced universal suffrage in 1971). Conservatives and the lower-middle classes broke a taboo by asking aloud whether the country really wanted so many foreign workers, while students no longer blindly upheld the hallowed Swiss virtues, suggesting, for example, that they reject national service.

Even debate over the canton system, thought to have been settled in 1848, arose with the proposal to detach the Jura from Bern and make it a canton in its own right. To make matters worse, it emerged that political interests in Bern had bought votes to stifle such a move.

In 1995, the Swiss banking industry was found to have about $57 million in dormant accounts, many opened by German Jews before World War II, of which $8.6 million was in accounts under Swiss names. The Nazi Gold Scandal, as it became known, had a deep impact on the collective psyche, and in 1998 Swiss banks approved a US$1.25 billion settlement fund for claims relating to Nazi Holocaust victim assets. In 2013, Switzerland's parliament approved a

62-year timeframe for the recovery of unclaimed effects, after which time they will be turned over to the State.

CONTEMPORARY ISSUES

The Swiss, with their comfortable lifestyles, have traditionally regarded themselves as being immune from the rest of the world, and the average citizen is not interested in big changes that might disturb the peaceful equilibrium of life. However, in a landmark referendum in 2002, the country voted by a small margin to join the

immigration quotas and a cap on residence permits for foreigners proposed by the controversial Swiss People's Party (SVP). However, late in 2016, Switzerland's parliament rejected the bid, opting instead to pass a law prioritising its own citizens in new job vacancies (with no mention of quotas). The outcome signalled the country's desire to maintain ties with the EU, responding to EU pressure for Switzerland to observe bilateral agreements protecting free movement if they wanted to remain within the single market. Then, in early 2017, in a sign that conservatism

Referendums are a common feature of Swiss political life.

United Nations, thus overturning the result of a similar referendum held in 1986.

Gradually, Switzerland is increasing its political integration with the rest of Europe. Despite voting against joining the European Union in 2001, a bilateral agreement, which makes it easier for EU nationals to live in Switzerland, came into force in 2002. In 2005 a referendum went in favour of opening the job market to workers from the 10 newest EU countries, and in 2008 Switzerland joined Europe's passport-free Schengen zone.

The question of immigration has gained momentum since a 2006 vote backed plans to make Switzerland's asylum laws among the toughest in the West. In an important referendum in 2014, the public demanded stringent

is somewhat on the wane, a referendum paved the way for a fast-tracked citizenship process for third-generation immigrants, despite bitter opposition from populists and their political voice the Swiss People's Party.

The environment is of paramount importance to the nature-loving Swiss. In a May 2017 referendum, Swiss voters backed government plans to provide billions of dollars in subsidies for renewable energy and to ban new nuclear plants from 2018.

While immigration and employment are likely to remain the thorniest issues of the early 21st century, the majority of visitors will encounter a diverse, hospitable and polite people, eager to show you their beautiful country.

Cattle farmer in the Swiss countryside.

Masked reveller making music at Basel's famous carnival, Fasnacht.

THE SWISS

Stereotypically portrayed as being efficient and provincial, the diverse people of this wealthy nation are also nature loving and cultured, with a history of tolerance and freedom.

Although Switzerland is today one of the world's richest nations, for much of its history this tiny, landlocked country was relatively poor. Bereft of natural resources, its young men went abroad to earn a living, often serving as mercenaries. At home the philosophy of "waste not, want not" was drilled into the national character.

Characterised as being careful with money, tidy-minded and extremely environmentally conscious, the Swiss are masters of paying attention to detail. No wonder they are good at running banks, hotels and railways, as well as making watches and executing complex engineering projects. They are also – thanks to a long tradition of direct democracy and frequent referendums – an incredibly self-determined people.

Wealth is never discussed, nor flaunted. In general the Swiss are polite, always shaking hands when they meet or bid farewell, and raising glasses to one another with great ceremony before drinking. *Proscht*, *santé*, *salute*, even *Zum Wohl* and *Gsundheit*, are common toasts depending on what region you are in. Resolutely Swiss and regional at the same time, they fly national and cantonal flags as often as possible.

CURSE OF THE STEREOTYPE

The Swiss still suffer from international perceptions that they are either bland bankers in grey business suits or bearded farmers in quaint leather shorts. While examples of these do exist, in reality the population is surprisingly varied, in the innumerable dialects alone.

Some clichés generated from within are also open to question. Despite its long history of neutrality, sharp divisions have racked Swiss history, and though the civil warring of the 19th century is over, internal disputes are common. There

Watchmaker's shop in Bern.

are also deep contradictions. While women only gained the right to vote in 1971, its eight million inhabitants have a fairly unrivalled level of independence.

There is considerable, though understated, regional pride. Locals are rarely complimentary about the folks who live over the hill, or, more often, mountain. Each region loves to mock its neighbours. Stereotyped as being slow and dull, the Bernese are seen as conservative and rarely voting for new ideas, except for stronger environmental controls. They are divided from their Francophone neighbours to the west by the River Sarine, and an imaginary line called the *Röstigraben*, the Rösti ditch. This witty label conjured up by the Swiss press is a reminder that *rösti*, the crispy potato cake, is a Swiss-German delicacy. The Swiss French population meantime talk about the Bernese region east of the river as Outre-Sarine,

> F. Scott Fitzgerald maintained that Switzerland was a place where few things begin but many things end. Yet the psychiatrist Karl Jung and painter Paul Klee are high among Switzerland's influential innovators.

Taking a break from the slopes.

as if it were overseas, or even outer space.

The citizens of Zürich consider their eastern neighbours in Appenzell as the most workaholic and obstinate of the Swiss. German speakers, proud of their work ethic, tend to scorn what they see as the languid French speakers in the west. As recently as 1978, the French speakers in Bern Canton broke away to form the new canton of Jura.

The rest of Switzerland regards the Italian-speaking community in Ticino with suspicion because locals look as if they enjoy life too much. As for the folk in the Valais, they are regarded merely as odd: most speak French, the rest a German dialect that is incomprehensible to outsiders. There are even mixed emotions about the Romansh-speaking inhabitants

of Graubünden who wear traditional dress on a daily basis, and with admirable pride.

Zürich's increasingly laid-back, clubbing city slickers reckon they are far superior to those in the capital, Bern, while both view Basel and Geneva as borderline cases, barely in Switzerland at all.

DIRECT DEMOCRACY

Every Swiss canton has its own tax-raising powers, schools, police and courts. In the power-sharing arrangement between the national, cantonal and municipal governments, each individual community has the authority to decide on everything from utilities to public holidays and road maintenance. Major decisions are decided by national referendum, of which there are several every year.

High levels of Swiss independence and self-determination help to explain the country's decision to remain outside the European Union. The idea of joining the EU has been snubbed overwhelmingly in the past; in a national referendum in 2001, 22 out of the 26 cantons voted to remain outside the union. Meanwhile, following a 2014 referendum on immigration quotas, the EU stepped up pressure for Switzerland to abide by bilateral agreements for free movement in order to stay in the single market. The result was a compromise: in 2016, the Swiss parliament voted to pass an immigration law giving its residents priority in new job vacancies without imposing any specific quotas.

IMMIGRATION AND DIVERSITY

Switzerland is a country at the intersection of several European cultures. With no less than four national languages and amazing regional variation, diversity is deep rooted here. Whereas the majority of the 19th century was characterised by emigration, immigration levels have been significant since the 1980s, and immigration has become one of the most contentious issues in Switzerland in recent years (see page 67).

As of 2016, migrants accounted for nearly a quarter of the Swiss population. Most of the two million migrants are European; 10 percent are Asian. Arabic speakers now outnumber Romansh speakers, and a significant Muslim community resides in Basel, where they have long enriched the local population with their culture – and their food.

While communities generally live comfortably together, issues surrounding immigration have frequently caused division. In 2014, a referendum approved controversial immigration quotas proposed by the Swiss People's Party (SVP), whose antagonistic referendum campaign posters have included one showing three white sheep kicking a black sheep across the border. Although parliament responded by passing a compromise immigration law with no mention of quotas in 2016, the issue is far from resolved. In the same year, divisions were stirred up again when citizenship was refused to two Muslim girls who refused to swim with boys at school.

The traditional gap between progressive city dwellers and rural traditionalists is far more blurred in today's society, where many of the former have moved to the countryside and even many apparently conservative senior citizens see the clear benefits of migration.

GREEN, SPORTY AND TRADITIONAL

The Swiss are among Europe's most disciplined nature lovers. Environmental protection here is seen as a legal obligation, and many referendums tie in with environment and conservation issues. And with spectacular natural landscapes providing the perfect outdoor playground, the Swiss are keen skiiers, walkers, cyclists and climbers.

This is a sports-loving nation, where men and women excel internationally at snow and ice sports such as skiing, tobogganing, bobsleighing and curling. A few decades after the advent of British holidaymakers in the Alps in the 1850s, the Swiss took to downhill skiing and have never looked back. The first world Alpine championships were staged at Mürren in 1931. The mountainous terrain is also ideal for producing champions in air sports such as hang-gliding; while on flatter land Swiss equestrian competitors have an excellent record in showjumping, dressage and carriage driving. World-class rowers and sailors thrive on the numerous lakes.

Thanks largely to one outstanding star, Roger Federer, tennis has become almost synonymous with Switzerland over the past couple of decades. With 18 Grand Slam singles titles to his name in 2017, the 35-year-old Basel-born player and former world number one is viewed by some commentators as the greatest male tennis player of all time.

Advertising campaigns which once favoured traditional sports such as *Schwingen* (wrestling), today project a far more adventurous image, with pictures of young people engaging in extreme sports – bungee jumping, snowboarding, ice climbing or sky surfing. The scarier the better. And being landlocked has not stopped its surf team competing on the international circuit.

Across all the rifts between old and new, tradition and change, the Swiss across the board retain a passion for their roots. On Christmas Eve they flock back to their native villages, ready

St Moritz's Schlitteda festival.

to meet and greet childhood friends, sing carols and celebrate. At the same time, there has been a noticeable brain drain, mainly to North America, as highly qualified young Swiss move to jobs with better prospects.

TECHNICAL SKILLS

Another assumed facet of the Swiss character is ingenuity. Over the centuries, innovation has helped to overcome a lack of natural resources. Back in 1513, Urs Graf developed etching, the art of making prints from an engraved metal plate. In the 18th and 19th centuries, skilled watchmakers in the Jura made names like Rolex, Ebel and Rado world famous. The world's first electric oven was switched on at a hotel in St Moritz in 1889.

Switzerland has long been at the leading edge of technology. In 1981, at IBM's Zürich laboratory, Gerd Binning and Heinrich Rohrer won the Nobel Prize for their work on the scanning tunnelling microscope. At the European Centre for Nuclear Research, on the Swiss-French border near Geneva, scientists and engineers are probing the fundamental structure of the universe through powerful particle accelerators. CERN was also where the Internet was born in 1990, when physicist Tim Berners-Lee created the first browser-editor.

A traditional saddler, or Sennensattler.

⊘ WANING SWISS TAX APPEAL

Celebrities from Elle Macpherson to Elizabeth Taylor and Sean Connery have all chosen Switzerland as a home and fiscal paradise, shrinking their tax liabilities by as much as 90 percent and building lavish multimillion dollar homes. But Switzerland's days as a tax haven may be over. Keen to put an end to the country's reputation as a safe haven for illegal money, new laws came into effect in 2017 to address the country's bank secrecy, which fuels much of the tax evasion. Authorities in Bern signed an agreement with the US allowing the automatic, two-way exchange of information about bank accounts between the two countries, and a similar deal has been struck with the EU.

Other inventions include the Swatch watch, the Smart car and even the *trotinette*, the trendy micro-scooter that crowds the world's pavements.

FAMOUS RESIDENTS

Switzerland's combination of neutrality and tolerance has attracted a curious collection of celebrities over the centuries. Many have been French or German exiles with easy access to their homelands, such as John Calvin (1509–64). The French Protestant reformer moved to Basel, then Geneva, where he put into practice his theories that the church should control the state. He ruled Geneva like a dictator for 20 years.

In the 20th century, famous residents ranged from political radicals to reactionaries. Lenin the archetypal communist (1870–1924) left Russia to live in Zürich in 1914, where he wrote *Imperialism, the Highest State of Capitalism* (1917). Italian Fascist leader Benito Mussolini (1883–1945) fled to Switzerland as a young man, in 1902, where he began preaching revolution. He was thrown out for causing unrest. Among many exiled rulers have been the Shah of Iran, Mohammed Reza Pahlavi (1918–1980), and dictators such as Mobutu Sese Seko, president of former Zaire (1930–1997).

Then there was Einstein. Long before his fame, German physicist Albert Einstein (1879–1955) took Swiss nationality in 1901 and worked in the Patent Office in Bern. Four years later he published four highly advanced papers, one of which dealt with the theory of relativity.

HAVEN OF THE WELL-HEELED

Switzerland has long been seen as a peaceful hideaway for the fabulously rich. Untrammelled by paparazzi and sensational newspapers, residents have ranged from rock idols and film stars to Greek shipping billionaires and wealthy playboys. In 1952, comedian Charlie Chaplin (1889–1977) escaped the McCarthy political witch-hunts in the USA to settle in Corsier, near Vevey, and started a trend among the entertainment industry. As well as film stars such as Audrey Hepburn, Switzerland has been home to writer and wit Noel Coward, rock star Phil Collins and actor and writer Peter Ustinov. Stars living there today include Tina Turner and Shania Twain, while famous alumnae of its posh finishing schools included the late Diana, Princess of Wales, a former pupil at Rougemont.

LANGUAGE

Switzerland has no less than four official languages – German, French, Italian and Romansh – and that's before you come to the regional dialects.

Surely the Swiss are a nation of polyglots who switch between flawless German, French and Italian and have a better than average grip on English too? Not quite. The German-speaking majority for a start may read and write German, but their spoken language, Schwyzerdütsch, is neither official nor national and is incomprehensible across the border in Germany. Secondly, official French, as written by bureaucrats, makes purists cringe. Vernacular French is not at all bad, but each area has its own idiosyncrasies. Those in the Ticino can speak standard Italian, the third official language, but generally use dialects that would draw blank stares in Italy.

Romansh, national but not official, sounds something like a mixture of Italian and Swiss-German, though its roots are in Vulgar Latin, as for all Romance languages. Some believe the language owes also to the Rhaeti, who resisted the Romans, yet became predominantly Latin-speakers. Today it is spoken by about 50,000 inhabitants throughout Graubünden, though even then it is split into five different dialects in various regions. Romansh was declared a national language in 1938 to thwart Mussolini, who argued Graubünden was Italian and thus suitable for annexation.

On a national level, government documents are always delivered in the three official languages, while regional figures are addressed in their language. To try and make a bit of sense of the complicated situation, it is worth looking at the chronology of the language map.

German arrived in Switzerland with the Alemanni, who ousted the Romans. Schwyzerdütsch encompasses all of the Alemannic dialects spoken in Switzerland, designated as Low, High and Highest-Alemannic forms. The grammar is very different from standard German, Hochdeutsch, a relatively recent convention created by Luther's translation of the Bible. When a Swiss-German speaker is interviewed on German television, subtitles are used.

The Swiss read their newspapers and official documents in standard German, but speak one form or another of Alemannic. Highest Alemannic is, appropriately, the dialect of the people of the Alps, and while they can understand Low-Alemannic tongues,

Romansh on a traditional house near Klosters.

they are not always mutually understood. Radio and television use both German and Schwyzerdütsch. Swiss writers by their own admission generally come across as stilted when they write in German.

The history of French in Switzerland is a little less complex. In about AD 500, Helvetic territory split between the Alemanni and the Burgundians, who were also Germanic but gradually adopted the Romance language, which became French. In so doing they earned the derision of those who remained loyal to Alemannic. As for Romansh, it was "Kauderwelsch", gibberish.

Those of Burgundian stock held their ground and today about one-fifth of the population is French speaking. French is the sole official language in the cantons of Geneva, Vaud, Jura and Neuchâtel, and the majority language in Fribourg and Valais, spoken by two thirds of their citizens. The Swiss-French feel very much part of the cultural world of France.

Italian is the common language in the Ticino and in parts of Graubünden. Local Italian dialects amount to private languages, so someone from northern Ticino would be baffled by what is said in the south.

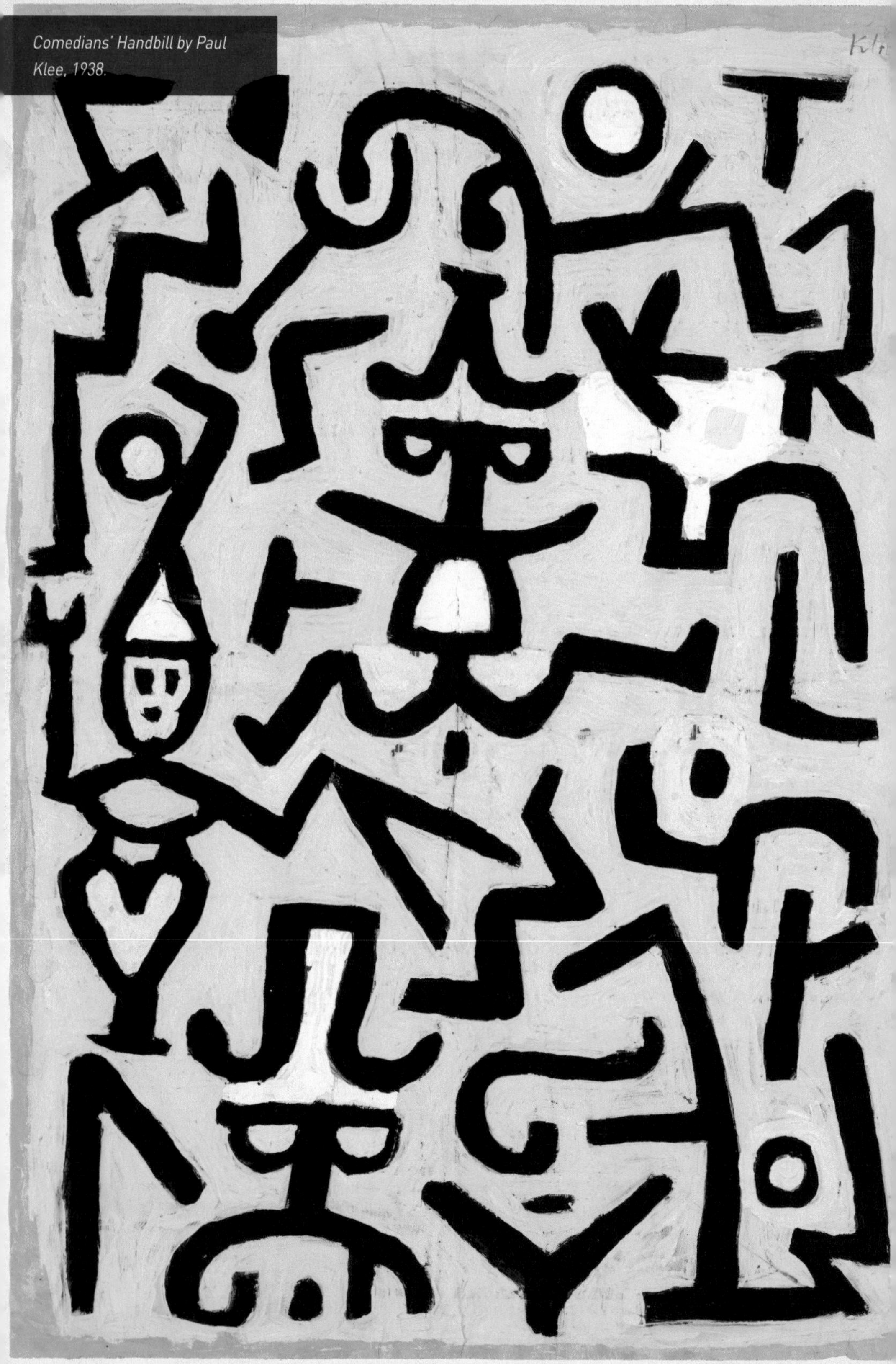

Comedians' Handbill by Paul Klee, 1938.

THE ARTS

For a supposedly conservative nation, Switzerland has produced some exceptional avant-garde artists and daring art forms over the past two centuries.

Switzerland's arts scene has exploded over the past couple of decades, reflecting the importance the Swiss place on art and culture in general. Private art, public art, classical and contemporary art, the thirst for art – viewing it, appreciating it and understanding it – has seen culture take a pivotal place in daily life. Since the beginning of the 20th century, museums and galleries have opened even in the smallest towns. A great variety of concerts take place across Switzerland throughout the year, with summer jazz and classical music festivals being particularly popular with visitors and locals.

PAINTING

This seemingly conservative nation inspired ground-breaking art forms in the 19th and 20th centuries. Imagine the astonishment of an audience at Cabaret Voltaire in Zürich on 8 February 1916. Confronted by artists banging

Mountain landscape by Ferdinand Hodler, 1914.

> The creations of leading 20th-century architect Le Corbusier can be seen all around the world: from Chandigarh in the Punjab and the Museum of Modern Art in Tokyo to the famous Notre Dame du Haut chapel in eastern France.

on bottles and shouting poems through hats, the nightclub-goers were witnessing the birth of a new art movement raging against orthodox ideas and calling for chaos: Dadaism. One of its pioneers was abstract painter and sculptor Jean (or Hans) Arp (1887–1966), born in Strasbourg but resident in Switzerland from about 1909. It was around that night in Zürich

that he met Paul Klee (1879–1940), a German citizen born near Bern, and one of the most imaginative masters of modern art. Despite his association with the German Expressionist group Der Blaue Reiter, the Bauhaus and the Surrealists, Klee belonged to no specific art movement, and retained an individuality using strong Africa-inspired colour and elaborate line drawings to convey his personal fantasies and semi-abstract dream images.

He is eclipsed as possibly the most influential Swiss artist of the epoch only by Ferdinand Hodler (1853–1918), who made his reputation as a realist but later turned to Symbolism. Despite seeing himself primarily as a figure painter, expressing ideas over images, it is his landscapes that speak most loudly. Many of those canvases – of untouched Swiss mountain and lake scenery – are on display at the major museums in Bern and Zürich.

SCULPTURE

Some of the 20th century's greatest sculptors were Swiss. The most innovative was Alberto Giacometti (1901–1966), son of Impressionist painter Giovanni. Able to draw and paint fluently as a child, he was 14 when he first sculpted his brother, Diego. Creating the first of his iconic

scrap metal, all highly polished and finished to eliminate the "junk" look. Bill's all-round talent included architecture, painting, writing and graphic design. Inspired by mathematics, his sculptures were often based on a helix or a spiral. Continuing Switzerland's innovative sculpting is Pipilotti Rist (1962–), whose installations, video and audio-visual works are displayed worldwide.

ARCHITECTURE

One of the most influential – and controversial – architects of the 20th century was Swiss: Le

Alberto Giacometti.

Giacometti's Buste de Diego.

spindly figures in 1935, he worked on them with a passion for the rest of his life.

Few sculptors intrigue the general public as much as Jean Tinguely (1925–1991) from Fribourg. He invented mechanical sculptures, including some that even painted pictures. In 1959, his *"metamatic-automobile-odorante-et-sonore"* created 40,000 abstract paintings while it was exhibited at the first Paris Biennial. Although his sculptures look eccentric, they carry an artistic message: "The machine allows me, above anything, to reach poetry," he said, and "The only stable thing is movement." Other prominent Swiss sculptors include Robert Müller (1920–2003) and Max Bill (1908–94). Müller worked with black-painted sheet metal, as well as chunks of

Corbusier (1887–1965), a master of modern architecture. Ironically, he struggled to find acceptance for his far-out ideas in Switzerland and most of his projects were achieved elsewhere. A modest painter (under his real name, Charles Edouard Jeanneret), he was heavily influenced by the Cubists' organic forms and clean lines. For him, simplification of design was a priority. Today's buildings still rely on his five-point guidelines for construction, ranging from the free-standing pillar to the roof garden. For him, a house was "a machine for living", and you can still see the villas that he designed in his home town of La Chaux-de-Fonds. Le Corbusier was multi-talented: his 1929 Barcelona chair is a design classic, displayed in museums.

Other influential Swiss architects include Ticino's Mario Botta (1943–), who designed the SFMOMA gallery in San Francisco, and Jacques Herzog and Pierre de Meuron, who – at the turn of the new millennium – won international acclaim for their conversion of a former power station into the Tate Modern gallery in London. One of their latest hits is the VitraHaus, added to the Vitra Design Museum in Weil am Rhein, Germany, in 2010.

At home they are best known for their signal box outside Basel railway station, and their

scene, has prompted gallery openings and expansions in Switzerland's major cities over the past decade, and have seen Basel and Zürich in particular become major international arts and cultural hubs.

Every major city has an impressive *Kunsthaus* (art gallery): Zürich, Geneva, Luzern, Lausanne and Bern, which also has an excellent Klee museum and arts centre, the Zentrum Paul Klee. Always check to see what is on at the Migros Museum in Zürich, where special exhibitions often juxtapose young Swiss talent with works by well-

Pavillon Le Corbusier in Zürich, previously Heidi Weber House, was Le Corbusier's last building.

green doctor's surgery, now a tourist attraction in Basel.

A couple of modern wonders studding the skyline of post-industrial Zürich West include the 2011 Mobimo Tower by Basel architects Diener & Diener, and Switzerland's tallest building, the 126-metre (413ft), 36-storey Maag-Tower by Annette Gigon and Mike Guyer. The pair carved out a name for themselves in museum design, with (among others) the Kirchner Museum in Davos, 1992, and Museum Liner in Appenzell, 1998.

GALLERIES

Interest in the country's exceptional 19th and 20th-century painters and designers, coupled with a thriving contemporary and public-arts

known artists. In Basel, there are two unmissable sites. One is in Solitude Park: the Mario Botta-designed Jean Tinguely museum, dedicated to his ingenious kinetic sculptures. The other is nearby, at Riehen, in a striking building designed by Renzo Piano. This houses the outstanding private collection of art dealer Ernst Beyeler, whose artist friends included Pablo Picasso.

In addition to these major galleries, Switzerland has some unexpected gems, such as the Fondation Pierre Gianadda. Set among vineyards in Martigny and opened in 1978, the gallery has staged crowd-pulling exhibitions of works by Gauguin, Modigliani and Matisse. The permanent collection includes Picasso, Toulouse-Lautrec and Cézanne, as well as outdoor sculptures by Arp, Brancusi, Rodin and Moore. These are regularly complemented by concerts featuring major international stars, such as Cecilia Bartoli and Itzhak Perlman.

MUSIC, BALLET AND FILM

Love of music starts at grass-roots level in Switzerland. Every village has a *Musikverein*, a music club, often with a *Hudigääggeler*, a combo of double bass, clarinet and the ubiquitous accordion. Traditional instruments still played include the *Hackbrett*, a stringed instrument, laid flat

Six, Arthur Honegger (1892–1955) is Switzerland's most famous musical son. He wrote for chamber orchestra and piano, for ballet and symphony orchestras. His *Symphony No. 4* was dedicated to Basel, while his 1923 tone poem, *Pacific 231*, is all about a railway engine.

Other noteworthy composers include Frank Martin (1890–1974) and Othmar Schöck (1866–1957). Thanks to contemporary composers such as the oboeist and conductor Heinz Holliger (1939–), modern music has a high profile in Zürich and Bern. Under the baton of Ernest Ansermet (1883–

Classical music played by the Engadine Symphony Orchestra.

and played with wooden spoons. The haunting echoes of the alphorn, the long, long horn, still fill the valleys on 1 August, Swiss National Day. Yodelling, the vocal way to send messages from one isolated community to another, is now used for entertainment.

Close to Germany, France and Italy, Switzerland has long been a retreat for world-famous musicians. In 1848, Richard Wagner (1813–83) fled Germany after the May Uprising. He settled in Zürich where he worked on his towering opera, *Der Ring des Nibelungen*. Some 60 years later, Russian composer Igor Stravinsky (1882–1971) wrote *The Rite of Spring* (1913) at Clarens, near Montreux. Although he was a member of a French group of composers nicknamed *Les*

1969), Geneva's Orchestre de la Suisse Romande built an international reputation, since matched by the Basel Sinfonietta, the Festival Strings Luzern and the Züricher Kammerorchester.

Switzerland's largest professional ballet company, resident at Zurich Opera House, has been directed by German Christian Spuck since the 2012/13 season. Since 1987, Lausanne has been home to Béjart Ballet Lausanne, founded by French-born choreographer Maurice Béjart, who renamed his ballet company after the city he so loved.

The Swiss are avid jazz fans. The feted Montreux Jazz Festival in July, which celebrated its 50th year in 2016, attracts up to 200,000 fans to listen to the world's leading musicians at the

> *Switzerland has long been a popular home for musicians, artists and writers. When English poet Lord Byron left Britain for good in 1816, he lived in Geneva with fellow poet Shelley.*

Stravinski Auditorium, the Montreux Jazz Club and Montreux Jazz Lab. Meanwhile, the generous mass of Festival-Off free events includes concerts in the surrounding communities, jazz in the park, jazz competitions and workshops for young musicians, late-night jam sessions at the Montreux Jazz Club, a pool party and strobe club.

In Verbier, the classical music festival is held in a giant tent, with spectacular views of the surrounding mountains, while Luzern's *Musikfestwochen* (Music Festival Weeks) are staged in Jean Nouvel's striking lakeside concert hall. Nyon's Paléo summer festival is more youth oriented. Recent concerts have featured the Red Hot Chili Peppers and Manu Chao. The country's biggest open-air concert pulls a crowd of nearly a quarter of a million to some 200 concerts in six days and nights. Each August, Locarno's international film festival is rated among the top half-dozen in the world.

The Swiss also have an affinity with country music, with festivals held during summer. The biggest, Country Night In Gstaad, has drawn some major names since it was first held in 1989, including Emmylou Harris, Travis Tritt and Dwight Yoakam.

LITERATURE

Two of the 20th century's leading German language writers were Swiss. One was dramatist Friedrich Dürrenmatt (1921–90). His plays, such as *The Visit*, performed both on Broadway and in London, and *The Physicists*, a surreal look at scientists, demonstrate his excellent plots and sense of theatre, as well as his acute perception of moral dilemmas and black humour. Max Frisch (1911–91) typified the extraordinary, all-round talent of so many Swiss artists. In his time both a philosopher and a journalist, Frisch designed and built his first house in 1943, the year his first novel was published. His play, *The Fire Raisers*, is regarded as a key text in the Theatre of the Absurd.

Until the 19th century, Switzerland inspired foreign writers rather than home-grown talent. Geneva was a hugely influential city in the early 18th century. The birthplace of the philospher and writer Jean-Jacques Rousseau (1712–78), Geneva attracted writers and philosophers such as Voltaire and Germaine de Staël.

German-speaking authors who lived and worked in Switzerland included the Austrian poet Rainer Maria Rilke (1875–1926) and German Nobel Prize author Thomas Mann (1875–1955). In *The Magic Mountain* (1924), Mann used a Swiss sanatorium to represent a microcosm of European

Dramatist Friedrich Dürrenmatt in 1960.

society. Another Nobel Prize-winning German novelist, Hermann Hesse (1877–1962), moved to Ticino in 1911, where he wrote *Steppenwolf* (1927).

Ireland's James Joyce (1882–1941) spent five years in Zürich, where he wrote *A Portrait of the Artist as a Young Man* (1916). Other residents included prolific Belgian novelist Georges Simenon (1903–89), creator of Maigret the detective, and Graham Greene (1904–91). In *The Third Man*, the film of Greene's novel, Harry Lime comments that "In Switzerland they had brotherly love, 500 years of democracy and peace, and what did they produce…? The cuckoo clock." Added to the script by Orson Welles, those lines epitomise the cynicism of Harry Lime; but Welles was wrong about the cuckoo clock. It was invented in Germany.

FROM ROMAN RUINS TO GLASS TOWERS

Although famous for its natural architecture, Switzerland's towns and cities contain an array of fascinating buildings dating back to Roman times.

Gothic architecture is symbolised by Europe's magnificent cathedrals. Switzerland has wonderful examples in Lausanne and Bern. More art than architecture, Lausanne's stained-glass rose window and the magnificent gilded triptych in Chur cathedral represent the heights of perfection reached by Gothic style. The cool, classical lines of Renaissance style can be seen in some of the mansions of the wealthy and in a few churches, for example San Lorenzo in Lugano. There are also beautiful baroque buildings; most notable are the cathedral and abbey at St Gallen dating from the 18th century. The Abbey Library, with its fabulous wooden inlaid floor, is a masterpiece of rococo style. Neoclassical styles and industrial architecture represent the preoccupations of the 19th century. In the 20th century Switzerland embraced the key architectural styles fashionable in the rest of Europe, from the *belle-époque* hotels of Montreux to Modernist buildings such as Le Corbusier's La Clarté glass and steel apartment block in Geneva. Postmodernism also has Swiss exponents including Bernhard Tschumi.

FROM ANTIQUITY

Avenches, Martigny and Nyon contain fine Roman amphitheatres. Romanesque style can be seen in Zürich's Grossmünster and the cathedral in Chur. Although much altered in later centuries, the St Gallen Portal of Basel's sandstone cathedral is a fine example of late-Romanesque style and decoration.

Eighteenth-century architecture at Brienz.

The setting and architecture of Fribourg are both spectacular.

The twin towers of the Romanesque Grossmünster in Zürich dominate the cityscape. They were rebuilt in the original and Gothic style after a fire in 1763.

Roche Tower in Basel, designed by Herzog & de Meuron.

Modernist medley

Swiss architects have made the most of the 20th-century development of reinforced concrete. Some of the country's most ingenious architecture has been employed in the building of impressive bridges and tunnels in the Alps. The opening of the world's longest road tunnel, the Gotthard, in 1980, was an engineering achievement which architects Rino Tami and Christian Menn designed to work well with the natural landscape. Then came the opening of the world's longest rail tunnel, the 57km (35-mile) twin-bore Gotthard Base Tunnel in 2016, providing a high-speed rail link under the Swiss Alps between northern and southern Europe.

Known as the "father of Swiss architecture", Karl Moser designed numerous buildings, including St Antonius Kirche in Basel (1931), which imaginatively used the then new medium of concrete. Le Corbusier's last building (1967), the predominantly glass Maison de l'Homme, is in Zürich. Ticino architect Mario Botta designed the Banca Gottardo, and the Museum Tinguely in Basel in 1996, capitalising on its riverside setting. Modern marvels include Basel's new Museum der Kulturen by Herzog & de Meuron and the extension of the Kunstmuseum Basel by Christ&Gantenbein; Jean Nouvel's Kultur und Kongresszentrum, KKL Luzern; and the much-awaited new wing of the fine arts Kunsthaus Zürich by architect Sir David Chipperfield, due to open by 2018.

St Gallen's beautiful Abbey Library, designed by architect Peter Thumb.

The Roman amphitheatre at Augusta Raurica.

The Kunsthaus Zürich will gain a striking and modern new wing.

Making cheese the traditional way.

FOOD AND WINE

There is a lot more to Swiss cuisine than chocolate, fondue and *rösti*, but they make a fine introduction to further delights.

When it comes to food, Switzerland has specialities that are known worldwide. What could be more indulgent than a bar of Swiss chocolate? More sensible than a bowl of muesli for breakfast? Or more convivial than sharing a fondue? Yet these are only a taste of the culinary story. This tiny nation crams in a host of local and regional dishes, often based on French, German and Italian traditions. However, in the Switzerland of today, you will also find modern, light and creative dishes, plenty of Asian eats and a thriving organic food scene.

The Swiss love of good, wholesome food starts young. Cookery lessons for boys and girls are on the curriculum of many primary and secondary schools. At regional markets, fresh fruit and vegetables delight the eye. A spiralling amount of these locally grown staples, along with farm-fresh meats and dairy products, are organic. The same can be said for city markets, as the Swiss – both rich and poor – opt to pay more for sustainably grown, seasonal produce sourced from individuals or co-ops in order to invest in their future. More than 12 percent of all agricultural land is farmed organically, but that rises to 20 percent in mountainous areas. And in Graubünden, more than half the farms are organic. Almost 80 percent of this produce is distributed by the main supermarkets, primarily Coop and Migros, where you will find extensive organic choices.

Common to all regions is careful preparation, with an emphasis on bold, unfussy flavours. Dishes still tend to complement the seasons, with portions appropriate to the weather. In winter, high in the mountains, they are hearty; in summer, down by the lakes, they are lighter. They are always satisfying, however; seldom

Rösti, a typical Engadine speciality.

has anyone stood up from a Swiss meal still feeling hungry.

FAMOUS CHEFS

Switzerland has produced many talented chefs, including several international stars. Freddie Girardet (now retired) and the late Philippe Rochat and Benoit Violier all came from here. A rising star is Andreas Caminada, whose Schauenstein Schloss restaurant in Graubünden is one of only a trio to hold three Michelin stars.

Many Swiss chefs have made their reputations abroad. Anton Mosimann, proud holder of a royal warrant, has lived and worked in London for over 40 years. A much younger Swiss chef to launch on to the international scene is

Zürich-born Daniel Humm, who is taking New York by storm at his contemporary American restaurant, Eleven Madison Park, where 11-course menus are standard fare.

DAILY BREAD

Bread is on the table at every meal in Switzerland, and the *Bäckerei* or *Bäckerei-Konditorei* (bakery-cake shop) is an institution of daily life no less so than in Germany or France. Only the breads in Switzerland tend to be a whole lot more stodgy and wholesome than in the latter,

offer daily in many bakeries countrywide. *Taillaule Neuchâteloise* is another braided bread from Neuchâtel, made with raisins, butter, milk, eggs and lemon rind. Its name comes from the French

> Thousands of Swiss regularly comb the forests for a multicoloured array of fungi (ilze, ceps or funghi), which are eaten fresh, or preserved and pickled for the months ahead.

Cuchaule, plaited bread seasoned with saffron, is eaten during the Bénichon harvest festival.

other than in the French-influenced regions, where it tends to be white and crusty.

Bakeries sell an astounding variety of breads and other *Backwaren* – many of these bakery products were once regional or festive specialities. In the French-speaking cantons for example, bread is often inscribed with a motif: diamonds in Geneva, a bishop's crosier in the Jura. Walnuts are incorporated into the dense, rye-based Valais loaves, while rye is also the main ingredient in the hearty Graubünden bread. For rustic farmers' bread *Bauernbrot* or *Burebrot*, white, rye and whole-wheat flours are mixed together. Breads once reserved for holy days and religious festivities, such as the brioche-like plaited *Züpfe*, are a Sunday brunch or party favourite, though on

tailler, meaning "to cut" – the dough is cut up with scissors and laid in the cake tin in a zigzag shape.

Also popular all over Switzerland is the Ticino's *torta di pane*, a dense, spicy cake made from stale bread, raisins, cinnamon, nutmeg, lemon and cocoa, covered with almonds and pine nuts.

FILLING FAVOURITES

Some of Switzerland's best-known dishes are among the simplest. Popular with hikers is the cheesy *Älplermakkaronen*. This belly-bursting version of macaroni cheese, with chunks of bacon and lots of cream, is often served in a wooden bowl at mountain huts during the summer. If there is one national dish, it has to be *Zürigschnätzlets*. Originally from Zürich, this diced-veal specialty gently cooked with cream and mushrooms is now found on menus across the country. Like many dishes, it is often accompanied by potatoes or the egg-noodle *Spätzli* – meaning "little sparrows". The longer squiggly *Spätzli* and the rounder *Knöpfli* – "little buttons" – are so widespread you can find ready-made versions in all supermarkets. But the best are *hausgemacht* (homemade), created in the chef's kitchen with the help of special sieves.

Charcuterie is another forte. Regional homemade sausages and dried meats reflect

however, can rise to the challenge of a *Berner Platte*, a casserole of sauerkraut and beans, garnished with meats such as *Zungenwurst* (tongue sausage), *Rippli* (smoked ribs) and *Siedfleisch* (boiled beef).

POTATOES AND FISH

Having long been a staple food, potatoes are transformed into a variety of dishes. Among the tastiest is *rösti*, a flat, round and crusty potato cake. Much crisper than hash browns, the potatoes are boiled, grated and then fried.

Pizokel, a type of Spätzli pasta.

Valais canton specialties.

harder times, when mountain communities relied on well-stocked larders to survive the winter. Nowadays air-dried beef is a delicacy, served in paper-thin slices. Best known is the tender and flavoursome *Bündnerfleisch* from Graubünden, cured with salt and alpine herbs, but the herb-flavoured *Walliser Trockenfleisch* from the Valais and smoked and dried *Mostbröckli* from Appenzell are equally popular in the eastern cantons. Every butcher takes pride in his own secret recipes for sausages. Accompanied by a beer and lashings of onion, nothing slides down easier than the hotdog-like *Kalbsbratwurst* (veal sausage), a *Bratwurst* (pork sausage) or spicier *Bauernbratwurst* (farmer's sausage). Only very hungry skiers and hikers,

Freshwater fish is also highly prized. As well as trout, lakeside restaurants serve delicate, salmon-like *Felchen*, and *Egli* or *Perchette* (perch), all in a variety of creative dishes.

MUESLI

One dish ensures that Swiss food has a healthy image. Around the world, muesli is enjoyed as a breakfast dish. As ever, the packet version bears little resemblance to the original. Invented in 1897 by dietary expert Dr Bircher-Benner in Zürich, muesli is often eaten in Switzerland as a light snack, rather than a breakfast dish. The Swiss call it *Birchermuesli*, in honour of its inventor, and today's muesli can be quite a creamy concoction. The ingredients of oat flakes, nuts and grated apple with a splash of water and lemon juice are often enriched with dried fruits and soaked overnight in creamy milk. Next day, it is served with a blob of yoghurt.

SEASONAL SPECIALITIES

Some dishes are prepared only for special festivals or religious celebrations. In early December, entire households bake huge batches of *Weihnachtsguetzli* Christmas cookies, which are presented to all visitors. At New Year, families

On Easter Sunday, goat and lamb are the traditional main course in many parts of the country. In German-speaking areas, *Osterfladen* is a must for dessert. With dried fruits, eggs and almonds, this is a pie or a rice tart, with a melt-in-the-mouth crust. In the autumn, every region has festivals, often marking the end of the harvest. The five-centuries-old Basel Autumn Fair is an excuse to eat *Lebkuchen* (gingerbread), *Magenbrot* (chocolate loaf) and *Rosenkiechli* (waffles).

As Christmas approaches, you can nibble on *Lebkuchen*, *Änisbrötli* (aniseed-flavoured

Cheese fondue – a dish for sharing.

in Basel give *Läckerli* (spiced honey biscuits) to their friends. Zürich has its own versions called *Züri-leckerli* and *tirggeli*.

As elsewhere in the world, the start of Lent is a time of indulgence before fasting. In Basel look for *Zibelewaie*, a type of creamy onion quiche. Calorie-laden treats include the *Fasnachtskiechli*, or *merveilles*, sugary fritters, and *Zigerchugeli* and *Zigerchröpfli*. These deep-fried turnovers, stuffed with cinnamon and hazelnut-flavoured soft cheese, are delicious eaten fresh from the baker. In Ticino local variations include *ravioli di carnavale*, pastries stuffed with prune purée. The Ticinesi also have a communal feast, featuring *luganiga* (Lugano sausage) served with enormous vats of saffron-yellow risotto.

cookies) or *Mailänderli* (shortbread). Look for regional specialities, such as *Zimmetstern* (cinnamon stars) from Chur, almondy *Biberli* from Appenzell and *Brunsli* (chocolate "brownies") from Basel.

SWISS WINES

Despite being produced since Roman times and enjoying an ever-improving reputation, wine is still one of Switzerland's best-kept secrets. Only one percent of Swiss wine leaves the country (mostly to Germany), which means that the Swiss drink most of the annual output themselves.

About 15,000 hectares (37,000 acres) – less than 0.4 percent of the country – is under vines.

On 6 January, a family epiphany treat is the three king's cake, Dreikönigskuchen, a crown of sticky buns with a hidden prize. If you find the small plastic king in your bun, you will be crowned king for the day.

it sounds negligible, that places it tenth in the world in terms of country size to vineyard ratio. The Swiss are major wine drinkers, downing 33

Chasselas is a very old native Swiss grape variety, sprung from the shores of Lake Geneva. In the Valais it's known as Fendant, an easy-drinking, fresh white. The second white drunk in the Valais is Johannisberg, made from the Sylvaner grape, which the rest of French-speaking Switzerland call Gros Rhin. The dominant red wine is Dôle, a light blend of Pinot Noir and Gamay. Vintners have their own recipes, juggling the balance between these grapes and adding others including Syrah and Merlot. If natural sugar levels are not sufficient to classify

Tins of Lindt chocolate.

litres per capita a year – double that of France and placing it well ahead of Italy, Spain and the rest of Europe.

Fortunately for visitors, you are never far from a vineyard, whose best wines are always showcased proudly by local restaurants, bistro and bars.

Of more than 200 grape varieties grown in Switzerland, the most popular are the Chasselas, used for whites, and Pinot Noir, accounting between them to nearly 60 percent of total production. They're followed by Gamay and Merlot, then by other more marginal varieties such as Gamaret, Müller-Thurgau, Garanoir, Chardonnay, Sylvaner and Pinot Gris. The six main grape-growing regions are headed up by the Valais and the Vaud.

⊘ CHOCOLATE

When it comes to fine chocolate, the Swiss and Belgians vie for top honours, though the Swiss tend to excel in milk chocolate, the Belgians dark. Many of the world-famous Swiss brands were innovators, dreaming up delights we now take for granted: Charles-Amadée Kohler (hazelnut chocolate), Tobler (Toblerone bar), Daniel Peter (milk chocolate) and Lindt (chocolat fondant). Chocaholics may flock to Zürich and indulge at stores on the glamorous Bahnhofstrasse such as Sprüngli, Teuscher or Läderach, but all small towns have specialist confiseries and artisan chocolatiers who invent their own signature goodies. Many have an adjoining café, with rich pastries and coffee.

as a Dôle, the wines instead are called Goron, a lighter, fruitier quaffing wine often drunk in little *Stübli* and *Wirtshaus* (pubs and inns).

The sloped vineyards of the Valais, representing a third of Switzerland's total wine production, extend over 100km (62 miles) along the Rhône, from Salquenen in the east, west to Martigny.

In 2017, up to 40 percent of the Valais harvest was wiped out by an extreme cold snap in late April. Usually, climatic conditions here are ideal; protected by the Alps, this is the country's sun-

light white wines that make for convivial evenings. While to the south, bordering on Italy and following its viticultural traditions, is the Ticino, whose premium, rich, dark Merlots

> *In the Valais, everyone seems to have a private wine plot. The vast areas under vines are split among 22,000 owners. As locals quip, "It's impossible to marry a girl who has no vineyard."*

Swiss wines.

niest, driest region, though the steep, dry hill-sides demand intense manual labour for both irrigation and maintenance.

The vertiginous vineyards of the Vaud, stretching up the hilly northern shores of Lake Geneva, are all planted with Chasselas grapes, producing crisp, often heady and fruity whites. Most come from the adjacent La Côte, Lavaux and Chablais, three of the Vaud's winegrowing subregions. The Lavaux, extending from Lausanne to Vevey-Montreux, includes the canton's most famous appellation, Dézaley, whose terraces cling to the abrupt Unesco-classified slopes overhanging the lake.

Circling the lakes in French-speaking western Switzerland are patches of vines producing

rarely leave the region. Mature Merlots from Mendrisio are powerful yet smooth full-bodied reds. Hoarded in the deep cellars of restaurants great and small, they are a revelation to most visitors. Everyday wines, vino da tavola, also provide drinking pleasure. Take a seat in a rustic grotto-bar and order a carafe of red, produced from the host's own plot, and a plate of his home-cured salami: gustatory memories are made of this.

Sweet Swiss wines are a perfect foil for foie gras or dessert. Gemma, for example, made in Salgesch, Valais, is matured in barrels from October to June high in a cave in the Rhône glacier. With its high acidity, this is the sort of wine where you really want a second glass.

CHEESE

The quintessential Swiss cheese with holes – as featured in countless *Tom and Jerry* cartoons – is Emmental, just one of some 450 cheeses.

Contrary to the idea those cartoons created, the holes are not made by mice nibbling their way through the cheese. Nor it seems do they come down to carbon dioxide released by bacteria during the fermentation process, as was thought for more than a century. In recent years, scientists noticed that the holes – known as eyes – were getting smaller. And in 2015 a Swiss laboratory said they had found out why – and discovered the true cause of the holes. Hay. Tiny hay particles would fall into buckets collecting milk, and develop into bigger holes as the cheese matured. Old-fashioned barns and buckets allowed more and larger hay flecks into the process, hence bigger eyes.

The Swiss were making cheese before their written history began, and Roman records indicate the cheese they imported over the Alpine passes had holes in it, probably a kind of Emmental.

Today Emmental is imitated all over the world, but even identical processing can't achieve the flavour imparted by the Alpine herbs which the cows graze on in the high pastures during summer months.

With the end of the Pax Romana, the Swiss must have relied on goat's milk for their cheese because only goats would have survived winters at the altitudes to which herdsmen were pushed by hostilities below. It was only 14th-century military victories at Morgarten and Sempach that brought safe grazing to cattle in mountainous regions such as Schwyz, the Bernese Oberland and Gruyère.

Down the line, herdsmen had to decide between growing cereals for their own consumption or devoting the acreage to grazing. The cows won.

After Emmental, Gruyère and Appenzeller, one of the best-known cheeses is Sbrinz, an extra-hard variety, often likened to Parmesan, though less salty. Alongside these biggies are other notable delicacies – pungent Schabziger from Glarus,

Vacherin Fribourgeois and soft Tomme Vaudoise, Tête de Moine from the Jura, Appenzell Rässe and many Ticino cheeses such as Formaggini and Piora.

Two of the most popular Swiss dishes would not exist without cheese. A genuine fondue is made of three melted cheeses – Emmentaler, Gruyère and Vacherin – combined with kirsch. This communal

Raclette.

dish is shared among friends, using chunks of bread to scoop up the hot, creamy liquid. Next comes the famous *raclette*. The traditional preparation starts with a wheel of cheese from the Valais, placed before a fire. As the cheese melts, it is scraped onto boiled potatoes and eaten with gherkins and pickled onions. Both *raclette* and fondue are more than a meal, they are rituals, enjoyed by locals and by visitors, particularly those on skiing holidays.

Both are ancient dishes. Dairymen stuck in the Alps used to melt their cheese and mix it with milk. Valaisans first refined the method by pouring it over potatoes.

Purists rightly insist on making it only by an open fire or large charcoal oven. While fondue burners may have become a global trend, this is still the best way to experience it when in Switzerland.

Sure-footed Alpine ibex.

FLORA AND FAUNA

From the emblematic edelweiss to soaring eagles, the Swiss landscape has an unexpectedly wide range of wildlife.

Switzerland's varied landscape creates ideal conditions for a diverse collection of plants and animals, much of which can be seen against spectacular forest backdrops or mountain vistas. From the snow-tipped Alpine peaks of western Switzerland to the warm lakeshores of Ticino, few European countries can boast such a range of vegetation – palm trees and other tropical plants in the east; edelweiss, gentians and abundant wild orchids and other delicate flowers in the Alpine pastures – and natural life. While many of the most remarkable species are shy, live predominately in woodlands or are nocturnal, in a short period of time visitors can still see a host of wildlife. Bearded vultures now again grace the skies over the Alps, while in western Switzerland re-introduced species such as the lynx and ibex are making a strong comeback.

Edelweiss.

CHANGING FACE OF WILDLIFE

A combination of forces has resulted in some major changes to the flora and fauna of Switzerland and neighbouring Alpine countries. Glaciation and changing climate patterns wiped out the last of the dinosaurs many millions of years ago. Traces of this remarkable era can still be found in rock outcrops in the central Valais. Less accessible are a collection of 200 footprints thought to have been made by prosauropods and theropods in the Swiss National Park in the canton of Graubünden. Skeletons of giant lions, panthers and bears have been recovered from many parts of the country – witness to a rich former fauna.

These species died out largely from natural causes, but human interference has more recently caused the demise of many other wildlife species, among them the wolf, brown bear, lynx and ibex, largely as a result of overhunting. Through careful

conservation and management programmes many of these species have now begun to appear again – although some of the re-introductions have been, and continue to be, quite controversial. Nevertheless, it is hoped that the return of these native species will eventually restore some of the country's former natural diversity.

INTO THE WOODS

Switzerland's forests are a haven for much of the country's most spectacular wildlife. Although highly managed for commercial purposes – as well as serving as important barriers to avalanches – forests cover some 30 percent of the country. While the last vestiges of its old-growth forests have all but disappeared, much of the forest and woodland one sees today, while managed, is composed of an interesting mixture of species which is far more beneficial to wildlife than pure stands of monoculture.

Among the many species to be seen is the remarkable capercaillie, the largest bird you are likely to spot in Switzerland's forests. Most people's first encounter with this species is through its raucous cry, which starts with a resonant rattle and ends with a noise that resembles a cork being pulled and liquid poured from a long-necked bottle, followed by a crashing sound made by the bird scraping its wing feathers along the ground.

If you want to trace the source of this startling performance – the purpose of which is to alert other capercaillies to its presence – you should look for a blackish-grey, turkey-sized bird with a distinctive green throat, chestnut and white patches on the side and wings, and a large, black tail.

WILDCATS

Another woodland dweller along the Jura of western Switzerland that makes a rare appearance

European wildcats are bigger than domestic cats, with a heavier build.

⊘ LAST OF THE BIG CARNIVORES

The years 1871 and 1904 supposedly marked the end of an era for Switzerland's wolf and brown bear populations that once roamed the countryside. In this traditionally pastoral country, domesticated species were prioritised, and hunters gradually wiped out the wild predators.

Ironically, the Val Mingèr, where the last bear was thought to have been shot way back in 1904, is now part of the conservation-zealous Swiss National Park in the southeastern Graubünden canton. All of a sudden, more than a century down the line, bear sightings and incidents are occurring again.

Switzerland's bears, which have been sighted on numerous occasions since 2005, are believed to be the descendants of ten Slovenian bears that were released into an Italian national park between 1999 and 2002. Sadly, many of these animals have been classified as posing a risk to humans and have subsequently been shot by the authorities. With sightings becoming more common, people continue to work on strategies to promote coexistence between humans and bears, including preventative measures such as electric fences and more effective waste disposal.

Meanwhile, sightings of wolves are reported occasionally and a debate is under way – fuelled by conservation and animal-welfare movements – concerning possible re-introduction programmes for these two species.

is the wildcat. Substantially larger and far more aggressive than the average domestic cat, these superb hunters are mainly nocturnal and feed primarily on small rodents and ground-nesting birds.

Slightly larger than the wildcat, but equally secretive, is the European lynx, which is again making a comeback to Switzerland following a re-introduction programme in 1970. With an increasing population, sightings are becoming more frequent along the Jura, in central Switzerland and the Valais, in the southwest, although you should take care not to approach if you are lucky enough to spot one of these animals, especially in spring and early summer when female lynx might be guarding cubs.

THE NUTCRACKER

At higher altitudes, in pine forests, look out for the nutcracker. The presence of this characteristic brown and white spotted bird is often betrayed by heaps of broken pine cones on the ground. One of this bird's most curious acts is its food-hoarding behaviour. Each autumn, nutcrackers pluck mature cones from the pine trees and extract the nutritious seeds at the base of the soft outer scales. With up to 90 seeds in its gullet, the bird then flies to another part of its territory, where it proceeds to bury the seeds by digging small holes in the forest floor and embankments. What is remarkable is that around 85 percent of these stored seeds are recovered: nutcrackers depend on this food source from October to June, when snow covers the soil and when no other foods are available. At any one time an individual nutcracker may have up to 100,000 pine seeds hidden within its territory. Those they fail to recover often germinate, and grow into new trees.

LIFE IN RIVERS AND LAKES

River banks and lake shores make great birdwatching sites: considerable numbers of resident and migratory species, including black and white storks, red- and black-throated divers, kingfishers, ring ouzels, dippers, little bitterns, little- and great-crested grebes, together with many wildfowl species, are all commonly seen.

Strolls along some of the quieter backwaters of rivers in western Switzerland, as well as the lower reaches of the Rhône, might be rewarded by sightings of the European beaver – or at least their homes. Large mounds of logs and branches

are hauled into place and built into an almost impregnable dam by hard work and abundant applications of mud. Because beavers actually live in chambers beneath these "huts", the

Top places for birdwatching include: Verbois (Geneva), Lac de Pérolles (Fribourg), Grangettes (Vaud), Erlimoos (Bern), Barrage de Klingmann (Aargau) and Bolle di Magadino (Ticino).

The distinctive capercaillie.

entrance is underwater, and your best hope of a sighting is when they are swimming to and from the hut, or when grooming or undertaking the regular maintenance to the outside of the mound.

Strange encounters may arise with two introduced species, the coypu, a native of South America, and the muskrat, from North America. These species are found in northwestern Switzerland and along the River Aare, respectively.

Although otters are occasionally spotted in streams in western and northwestern Switzerland, sadly, this animal, which was once abundant in Switzerland, can no longer be considered a resident, following severe persecution in the first half of the 20th century.

Keep an eye out also for some of Switzerland's

smaller aquatic fauna such as the water shrew, a small insect-eating mammal which is characterised by its pointed snout, long tail and striking colour contrast of black fur on its back and a white

underside. Water shrews are widespread throughout the country – except at high altitudes – and are most often seen scurrying along riverbanks or eating or grooming on exposed rocks midstream.

> Many of the species of Alpine wild flowers are protected by law, so the policy of "leave only footprints and take only memories and photographs" should apply here.

ALPINE PASTURES

Between the mountains and the valleys, the Alpine pastures lying at 800 to 3,000 metres (2,600 to 9,800ft) are havens for wild plants. As the spring snows melt away, carpets of low ground plants such as wild crocuses and gentians poke through the still boggy soil, waiting to erupt in a profusion

Crocuses at sunset.

The marmot, a close relation of the squirrel.

⊘ THE SWISS NATIONAL PARK

The Swiss National Park is one of the last unspoilt areas of Europe. Officially founded in 1914, the park grew from a desire to establish a wilderness area in eastern Switzerland first expressed in 1907 – a commission was duly established by the Swiss Society of Naturalists to pursue this vision. Starting with a lease on 21 sq km (8 sq miles) of land in 1909, the park has grown over the years to its current 172 sq km (66 sq miles).

Rigorously preserving its original declaration, the park provides a safe home to many species of flora and fauna, including some that are either endangered or extinct elsewhere in the country, as well as some

recently re-introduced species.

It is now clear, however, that this area is too small to allow adequate conservation of such a wide range of species: further expansion is being seriously considered.

Visitors to the park are required to remain on the more than 80km (50 miles) of well-defined paths throughout, but there's a range of interesting walks to enjoy a varied landscape and learn more about the natural systems of this enchanting region. You can organise a private guided walk in English. For practical details about visiting the Swiss National Park, see page 215.

of colour that transforms pastures almost over-night. Species to look out for are blue and yellow gentians, lilies, Alpine snowbells, Alpine columbine, Alpine asters, cyclamens and the edelweiss.

A rare inhabitant of Alpine meadows, woodlands, rubble slopes and quarries of northern Switzerland is the Alpine salamander. After wintering below ground for 7–8 months, the totally black salamander generally emerges in May and disappears again in October. Early morning, especially during moist, cool conditions, is the best time to look for this rare species. On exposed rocky, scree slopes you might have chance encounters with some of Switzerland's other native reptiles, such as grass snakes, smooth snakes and adders.

UP TO THE TREE LINE

Most often heard before they are seen, the shrill, high-pitched whistles of marmots in the Alps serve as warning calls of danger – usually from eagles or foxes, but also the occasional walker that ventures too close to their colonies. Hibernating in underground burrows and chambers for the winter months, marmots give birth during the spring, but the young only emerge around June–July, when their playful antics are a joy to watch.

Usually found in groups of anything from 5 to 50, Alpine ibex, easily recognised by their large, ridged, backward-curving horns, are found as high as 4,000 metres (13,000ft), preferring cliffs and sheer rock areas above the tree line. In summer, ibex graze on the rich high-Alpine flora, descending in winter and spring to lower, south-facing cliffs. At the onset of the rutting season, solitary males are often seen duelling – rising up on their hind legs and crashing down against each other with resounding cracks of their horns – for the right to breed with females. Exterminated in Switzerland in the 19th century, the ibex has made a spectacular comeback thanks to careful management. The largest groupings of ibex – which in total number more than 16,000 today – are found on Mont Pleureur and Aletsch (Valais), Graue Hörner (St Gallen) and Albris (Graubünden).

Other, even more abundant, ungulates to watch for are chamois, characterised by their short pointed horns and nimble footwork as they perform movements along sheer mountainsides. Two small groups of mouflon – another type of mountain goat, originally from Corsica and Sardinia – occur in Morgins and around Champéry.

THE HIGH FLIERS

Lofty peaks are also the empires of many species of raptors, including spectacular golden eagles and bearded vultures. Feeding on anything from small mice and marmots to birds such as grouse, ptarmigan and partridge, golden eagles may also prey on sick, weak animals such as roe deer and chamois fawns – a service which contributes to the maintenance of healthy populations of wildlife.

Bearded vultures (or *Lämmergeier*) perform an equally important clean-up service. This vulture feeds mainly on bones from animal carcasses –

Bearded vulture in the Swiss National Park.

unusual for such a large bird: their wingspan can reach almost 3 metres (10ft). Few other carrion-feeders bother with such an unappetising meal, but by breaking open the bones – which they do by dropping them onto scree slopes from great heights – they can reach the soft inner marrow. Driven out of the Alps by 1913, the re-introduction programme under way to bring this majestic species back to its former haunts is proving that such initiatives can be possible. Under the programme, bearded vultures were first released into the Swiss Alps in 1991, yet it was not until 2007 that the first pair succeeded in breeding in the wild. Since then, two to six individuals have been born annually. For best viewing opportunities, contact the park's information centre.

A kayaker navigates a drop in Ticino.

OUTDOOR ADVENTURE

Whether you are after white-knuckle thrills or a gentle, pastoral meander, Switzerland is one of Europe's great outdoor playgrounds.

Unless you happen to be addicted to surf, there is no better destination in Europe for sporting pursuits than Switzerland, which is, in many ways, the original outdoor destination, certainly as far as winter sports and mountaineering are concerned. Whether your interest lies in gentle walking or diving headlong into heart-pumping adventure sports, you will not be short of choice, and with such a remarkable array of beautiful natural settings, a healthy climate and world-class facilities it is small wonder that huge numbers of Swiss are active, outdoor people.

Before plunging into the Swiss sporting experience, be sure that your insurance covers you fully, particularly for sports like mountaineering and skiing, where your policy should cover helicopter rescues. In addition, always try to minimise your environmental impact, and remember that mountain ecosystems are especially fragile: if hiking or mountain biking, stay on the paths and do not pick Alpine flowers; skiers should stick to the pistes or designated off-piste areas.

SKIING

Switzerland cannot claim to be the birthplace of skiing – the Scandinavians had been using skis for cross-country transport for thousands of years before skis first came here in the late 1850s – but it was here, from the 1880s, that skiing grew up to be a glamour child, developing into a downhill sport. As with so many of the winter sports, the pioneers were British (either holidaymakers or recovering convalescents), whose activities were viewed at the time as rather eccentric. Nevertheless, the fledgling sport soon spread in popularity,

Ice climbing is not for the faint of heart.

numbering the likes of Sir Arthur Conan Doyle among its aficionados. During those early years, practitioners would labour up the slopes on foot, but the situation improved once funicular railways started operating winter services, and then with inventions like the T-bar drag lift in the 1930s, the chairlift and, by the 1960s, the cable car. The first downhill race was staged in 1911 in Montana in the Valais, and, in 1921, the Briton Arnold Lunn invented the slalom in the small mountain village of Mürren in the Bernese Oberland, arranging the first race the year after.

Lunn also organised what some see as the true ancestor of all ski races, the mad Inferno, first held here in 1928, covering almost 15km (9 miles; not all of it downhill) from the summit of the Schilthorn to the village of Lauterbrunnen. It is still an annual event, open to all comers, and is held in mid-January. Even more challenging, and better known, is the annual Lauberhorn race at Wengen (see box).

Nowadays, more than 2 million people ski the Swiss Alps annually. There are hundreds of places you can visit, ranging from small villages offering nothing more than a couple of beginners' drag lifts over local cow pastures to world-famous resorts in Graubünden, and

on the invitation of a local hotelier, Johannes Badrutt, in 1864. Famous for its sunny climate and chic designer boutiques, it also has some great skiing as well as a host of other winter sports. **Davos** and the more sedate **Klosters** are two similarly well-heeled resorts, the latter being favoured by the British royal family. Both of these resorts use the large Parsenn skiing area around the Weissfluh, and they are famous for long, cruisy pistes, up to 12km (7.5-miles) long. **Arosa** is popular as an attractive family resort with plenty of intermediate

The scenery and skiing around Verbier are stunning.

the higher ones of the Valais and the Bernese Oberland.

Swiss resorts are typically scenic, village-based places, with more traditional chalet-style hotels than the type of purpose-built high-rise resorts to be found in France – and though the sport is not cheap by the time you have hired equipment and bought yourself a lift pass, you will get some of the best skiing in the world for your money.

THE TOP SKI RESORTS

In eastern Switzerland you will find perhaps the most famous resort of all: **St Moritz**, the patriarch of winter sports ever since the first party of British tourists wintered here for free

⊘ THE LAUBERHORN RACE

The most famous high-speed ski race in Switzerland is the blue-riband Lauberhorn race held in the Bernese Oberland resort of Wengen in early January. In the competitive downhill calendar, only Kitzbühel's Hahnenkamm in Austria can rival this terrifying descent in terms of both prestige and fear, and the cacophony of cowbells and hollering that accompanies Swiss competitors lends atmospheric charge to the thrilling spectacle. To win, racers attempt to complete the 4.2km (2.6-mile) course in under two-and-a-half thigh-burning minutes. Except for the period just before the race, you can, if you are a confident skier, try the course out yourself.

runs, and up-and-coming **Flims-Laax-Falera** is carving out a reputation for some first-rate snowboarding, good-value accommodation and a relaxed atmosphere.

Every March, Verbier is home to the international O'Neill Xtreme Snowboard Contest, one of the world's most prestigious events for this activity, held on the mountainside of Bec de Rosses.

Verbier, to the east of Martigny in the Valais, has one of the finest interconnecting networks in the country, the Four Valleys, with over 400km (250 miles) of marked pistes. Its lifts run right up to Mont-Fort (3,329 metres/10,922ft), with its sensational views of most of the grandest peaks in the Alps, including Mont Blanc, the Weisshorn and the Matterhorn (here called by its French name, Cervin).

Verbier, where accommodation is based more around self-catering chalets than hotels, is also one of the best bets for fine late-season skiing, plus world-class off-piste and snow-boarding options.

Northeast of Verbier, near the town of Sierre, is **Crans-Montana**, which hosted the 1992 skiing World Championships: though a famous name, it is not the most attractive of resort developments. You will get some fine panoramic views when skiing, and there is good boarding, but it offers less challenging pistes than either Verbier or the Valais' third major skiing destination, **Zermatt**. This charming, car-free resort village has unbeatable views of the Matterhorn and neighbouring Alpine giants. Other bonuses about Zermatt are that there is some great eating in the piste-side restaurants, and a healthy (or unhealthy) dose of nightlife in the village. Just to the east of Zermatt is the resort of **Saas Fee**, with plenty of glaciers nearby that make it an ideal destination for summer skiing. Summer glacier skiing is likewise available in Zermatt, Verbier and other high-level resorts.

BERNESE OBERLAND RESORTS

Skiing in the Bernese Oberland centres on the majestic Jungfrau region, with connecting

resorts such as the carless village of Mürren, set high up on a plateau above the Lauterbrunnen Valley, and whose skiing commands wonderful views of the Eiger, Mönch and Jungfrau; busier **Grindelwald**, surrounded by savage mountain peaks; and Wengen. Trains from the last two will sweep you up to Kleine Scheidegg, where you can find dramatic skiing at the foot of the Eiger's north face. Another famous Bernese ski centre is the chic little village of Gstaad, renowned less for its skiing (which is scenic but comparatively tame), than

Learning to ski, Ticino.

for being a playground for Europe's rich aristocracy, who take up residence for the season in its opulent hotels.

SKI SCHOOLS

All Swiss mountain resorts have ski schools, staffed by extremely professional instructors, many of whom are multilingual. If you want to escape the pistes and have both the money to seek out high-altitude virgin powder and the skill to ski it, you can arrange heli-skiing at any of the major resorts. You will be whisked up as high as 4,000 metres (13,000ft) and dropped off to ski with your guide – mandatory on all such trips to ensure that you do not get caught out by the very real danger of avalanches.

> For daily, up-to-date reports on the weather, snow conditions and avalanche alerts, check the Swiss Tourism website at www.myswitzerland.com.

For those who would prefer to appreciate the mountain scenery at a more sedate pace, Switzerland has wonderful options for cross-country skiing (called *Langlauf* in German; *ski de fond* or *ski nordique* in French). Graubünden is a popular

mid-February, the run is opened up to guests of members of this British-run club (the St Moritz Tobogganing Club), who pay a sizeable whack for the privilege of making five runs. Non-members can book online as a beginner (www.cresta-run.com). It is most definitely not for the faint-hearted, and, in a touch of old-boy chauvinism, women are not allowed.

Do not confuse the toboggan (also called the skeleton) with the luge (which is similar, but riders travel feet-first) or the bobsleigh, also invented in St Moritz. Both are practised at the

Mountain biking in the Valais.

destination, but there is a huge network of trails: some of these are free, but for the majority, you will need to purchase a reasonably priced pass from the local ski centre.

OTHER WINTER SPORTS

In addition to ice-skating, the frozen waters of St Moritz's local lake play host to skijoring, a risky sport whose competitors get dragged on skis by a galloping horse: experienced skiers only might like to give it a try. St Moritz's most famous site is the Cresta Run (see page 106), the world-famous toboggan track, founded in 1884, and where the fastest daredevils have touched speeds of 150km (90 miles) an hour. Once the last big race of the season is over in

resort's famous 1,600-metre (5,250-ft) Olympic bob track. For a thrill, you can hail the four-man "bob taxi", for one 130kph (80mph) run. It books up fast and they start taking reservations in July (tel: 081 830 02 00).

CYCLING

The idea of making Europe's most mountainous country a destination for a cycling holiday might, at first, seem ludicrous. However, travelling Switzerland by bike is one of the most rewarding ways of exploring the country, and, if you are concerned that your fitness is not up to the mountains, stick to the lowlands and valleys, or jump on a train with your bike for a difficult stretch. Swiss roads are fantastic, its drivers are generally very respectful of cyclists, and the country's acute environmental awareness is characterised by encouraging the activity at all turns. Cities such as Züg and Zürich, for example, have free bike-loan schemes: all you need is your passport and a small deposit. There are nine national cycling routes, which form part of an interlinking, 3,300km (2,050-mile) network of regular road routes and mountain-bike trails, all of which are marked on maps called *Velokarten* (available in bookshops or online; 1:100,000 scale). Make use, too, of the wonder-

Oberland. There is a trail that crosses the entire range of low, forested Jura Mountains; or you can explore the exquisite valleys of Ticino – areas near Locarno, for example, like **Maggia**, **Verzasca** or **Centovalli** – with their tiny stone-built villages and thick forests.

You can walk around the steep, wooded shores of **Lake Uri** (Urnersee), the nation's historical core, on the highly recommended 35km (22-mile) Trans Swiss Trail, developed to celebrate the 700th anniversary of the birth of the Swiss Federation in 1291, and best done as a two-day

Switzerland offers some awesome hiking.

The Preda to Bergün sledging route.

ful national scheme whereby you can rent well-maintained bikes from most railway stations. Choose between a touring bike or a slightly more expensive 21-speed mountain bike, and for a small charge (family rates also available), you can return your bike to any other recognised station, which allows you tremendous flexibility in planning a route.

HITTING THE TRAILS

Switzerland is the kind of country that makes the feet of even confirmed couch potatoes begin to itch. You might like to hike the rugged mountain scenery of the Swiss National Park in Graubünden, looking out for ibex, or trek around the high peaks of the Valais and Bernese

⊘ CROSS-COUNTRY SLEDGING

If you fancy a gentler ride than St Moritz's bob sleigh or toboggan circuits, there is a delightful alternative, to the northeast of the town. This is the classic 5km (3-mile) sledging route through the spectacular Albula (or Alora) Valley from Preda to Bergün.

Rent a sled in Preda and set off without fear: the road is closed to cars and its specially banked corners prevent mishaps. At the other end, buy a day pass for the Rhätische Bahn train and jump aboard to be ferried back up to the start. The route is flood-lit, so you can carry on well into the night, staving off the cold with a hot chocolate or Glühwein while you wait for the train.

walk. Alternatively, check out the dramatic **Churfirsten**, a sheer-sided limestone range that rises in jagged peaks from rolling hills near Appenzell's Walenstadt, in the northeast of the country. Switzerland's network of hiking trails, marked with a clear and reliable system of sign-posting, is second to none. Yellow signs designate normal hiking trails (*Wanderweg*, *chemin de randonnée* or *sentiero*), for which you do not need anything better than decent walking shoes. Yellow signs tipped by a white-red-white direction pointer designate higher mountain trails (*Berg-*

Schools (Verband Bergsportschulen Schweiz; tel: 027 948 13 45; www.bergsportschulen.ch) has a list of these and registered private guides. Centres offer guided hikes in their locality as well as short courses for those interested in rock- and ice-climbing. The service between centres does vary, so if you are planning your holiday around such a trip make arrangements well in advance. Always ensure you get a full list of the equipment and clothing you will need for your proposed activity and where you can rent this: ice axes, crampons, harnesses

Mountain hiking on the Blümlisalp Massif.

Climbing above the azure-blue Öschinensee.

weg, *chemin de montagne*), and though trails are well marked you will need at least hiking boots with decent ankle support for these. Check the weather before setting out, and when up in the mountains never underestimate the need for proper outdoor clothing, sun protection and water: day-hikers tend to be caught out more often by dehydration, exposure or hypothermia than more serious mountaineers.

MOUNTAIN-CLIMBING SCHOOLS

If you are keen to stretch your limits or learn techniques to progress beyond the normal hiking trails, head to one of the many mountain-climbing centres across Switzerland. The Swiss Association of Mountain Climbing

and helmets are often rented by the respective mountain centre, but you may find it easier to bring items like karabiners, rucksacks, gaiters, boots and clothing with you. In addition, follow the centre up to ensure that they have indeed contracted the services of a guide for your dates, as demand often outstrips supply at peak times of year. Even the best-laid plans, however, can be thwarted by poor weather in the mountains.

From the Bergsteigerzentrum in Grindelwald, you can arrange challenging treks in the region of the **Eiger**, **Mönch** and **Jungfrau** massif. The Eiger's brooding North Wall (2,000 metres/6,600ft) remains one of the world's classic technical rock-climbing challenges, despite having been first successfully negoti-ated as far back as 1938. Tragically, ice- and rock-falls down its face claim several climbers'

> *The Alps' main hiking season lasts from May to mid-October, and late May and early June are generally excellent times for enjoying the glorious Alpine meadow flowers that appear after the spring thaw.*

lives every year. Hikers who merely want a look at this rock face from close up can hop on the train to Alpiglen and take the trail that leads to its foot.

Other famous Swiss destinations for moun-taineers and climbers are Pontresina near St Moritz and, naturally, Zermatt with its Matter-horn (see page 178).

SAILING AND WATERSPORTS

The lakes of Switzerland provide marvellous venues for a whole host of watersports, rang-ing from diving and waterskiing to windsurfing and sailing, whereas several rivers are being touted for their white-water rafting and canoe-ing potential. Some of the best sailing lakes are **Lake Thun** in the centre of the country, and lakes **Silser** and **Silvaplaner** in the east, between St Moritz and Maloja. Beautiful lakes like Lake Luzern and Lake Lugano are better suited to motorboats than to sailing, as condi-tions are less regularly windy. In midsummer, even some high Alpine lakes reach swimma-ble temperatures, but you will need a wetsuit if you are going to be staying in for long.

HIGH-ADRENALINE ADVENTURE SPORTS

If all else fails to satisfy your craving for an adrenaline buzz, do not lose hope. Track down the 45-metre (150ft) canyon jump at the spec-tacular Gletscherschlucht ravine in Grindel-wald, or plunge 120 metres (395ft) on a bungee cord from the Stockhorn cable car, also in the Bernese Oberland, near Thun.

Other cable-car jumps exist across Switzer-land, but the most hair-raising bungee jump of all – and, at 220 metres (720ft), reputedly

the world's highest, is just to the northeast of Locarno, made famous by the death-defying opening scene of the James Bond film, *Gold-eneye*. Here is the spectacular **Verzasca Dam**, where you can take a bungee jump down its sheer concrete face, between the months of April and October, either during the day or by full moon (contact Trekking Team; tel: 091 780 78 00; www.trekking.ch). In addition, you will find a host of places across the country advertising hot-air ballooning, tandem skydiving, hang-gliding, paragliding and parascending.

Kite-surfing on Lake Silvaplana.

⊘ MOUNTAIN REFUGES

Mountaineers, climbers and experienced trekkers who want to make longer hikes in higher Alpine terrain can use the fantastic network of reasona-bly priced mountain refuges (*Berghütten, cabanes de montagne*), found at altitudes usually well over 2,000 metres (6,560ft). They are run by the Swiss Alpine Club, which operates 152 huts providing 9,200 beds. The huts have communal bunks with plenty of blankets (but no sheets), and basic meals are usually available. For more information, visit www.sac-cas.ch/en. During the busy summer sea-son, make sure to book your sleeping berth at least a month in advance.

THE CRESTA RUN

Before the motorcar and aeroplane, the fastest men on earth were an amiable group of eccentrics including the author and literary critic John Addington Symonds who, strictly speaking, should have been tucked up in bed in the Swiss hospital in which he was staying.

Riding the Cresta run, 1914.

Instead, Symonds and company, some of whom were also in Switzerland on doctors' orders, begged and borrowed *Schlitten* (which the Swiss used as their ordinary means of winter transport) and, hurling themselves down a hill near the Belvedere Hotel in Davos and down the Clavadel Road leading to Klosters, invented the sport of tobogganing and hence its offspring, bobsleighing.

By 1903, the year in which the Wright brothers nursed Kitty Hawk into the air, they were attaining speeds of some 130km (80 miles) an hour. This was at a time when motorcars were still being preceded by pedestrians waving red flags.

An entry in Symonds's diary is one of the earliest references to how the sport started. After a dinner which lasted until two in the morning, complete with a zither and guitar player, he and two friends "descended on one toboggan in a dense snowstorm. It was quite dark and drifty beyond description." They got down all right, the diary notes, but not so "Miss I" who was on another toboggan. She completely lost control, flew over a photographer's hut and landed "on the back of her head on the frozen post-road. I fully expected to find her dead. She was only stunned, however."

The original *Schlitten* was simply a pair of flat iron runners screwed to a wooden frame on which riders sat upright. Canadian settlers discovered that the native peoples used something similar, and in 1870 they were tearing down Mt Royal in Montreal.

The English invalids founded the Davos Tobogganing Club in 1883 and in that year issued a challenge to all other nationalities to a race down the twisting road from Davos to Klosters. Two Australians, one Canadian, two Germans, one Dutchman and 12 Swiss accepted. The race was a dead heat between the Australian, one George Robertson, and a Swiss bus conductor, Peter Minsch.

In the meantime, the St Moritz invalids had also made a rough-and-ready run alongside the Kulm Hotel. The general standard of behaviour among these invalids was very open to reproach: "A good deal of gambling and drinking took place at times and flirtation led to many scandals, all of which used to stop when the spring came and the invalids scattered with the melting of the snow."

Realising the commercial potential of the new craze, the owner of the Kulm Hotel contributed towards the cost of building a better run to woo custom away from Davos. The result was the most famous toboggan run of all, the Cresta, and competitions between the two fledgling resorts were soon being organised on a regular basis.

The 1886 competition provided a sensation. Up until that year riders had invariably sat upright on the toboggan but, as the local Alpine Post newspaper dramatically reported: "Mr Cornish... lay his body on the toboggan, grasping its sides well to the front, his legs alternating between a flourish in mid-air and an occasional contact with mother earth... To see him coming head first down the leap is what the Scotch call uncanny... Unfortunately, however, he came to grief more than once during the race, though the extraordinary quickness of his recovery astonished the onlookers."

The following year provided an even greater thrill. A New Yorker, a Mr L.P. Child, "who had considerable experience of tobogganing in the United States", asked a local carpenter to run up a toboggan to his own specifications. He named it America. It was long, low, built of solid wood and had spring steel runners attached fore and aft.

Mr Childs thrashed the opposition down the Clavadel road. The shocked regulars wanted the device banned, but others could see the writing on the wall and rushed off to see their carpenters. The genesis of the bobsleigh was produced by a blacksmith on behalf of a Mr Wilson Smith.

Tobogganers seemed routinely to die, but it was from tuberculosis or whatever complaint had brought them to Switzerland, rather than the sport, in the first instance. The first death to occur on the run was that of a 27-year-old British Army captain, Henry Pennell, who had ironically won the Victoria Cross on the Indian North West Frontier. The second death followed less than a month later and involved another heroic character, Count Jules de Bylandt, a Dutch big-game hunter. De Bylandt crashed into the level crossing which controlled traffic where, before a tunnel was built, the run crossed a road.

The scene of Captain Pennell's accident was a particular curve, known as Shuttlecock, which caused so many horrific tumbles that in 1934 a club was formed, and an annual dinner given, by those who survived. As is the custom of such clubs in other spheres, members instituted their own peculiar rites, and wore elbow pads over their dinner jackets.

The 1928 Winter Olympic Games were held in St Moritz and six nations took part in the toboggan event. The British regarded the Cresta as their pet invention and entered two lords, Brabazon and Northesk, but the former was eliminated by a crash at Shuttlecock during practice which left him with broken ribs and a badly bruised face. In the end the event was won by two American brothers, Jennison and Jack Heaton.

Over the years since the 1928 Olympics, the Cresta Run has been tackled by any number of celebrities, some of them lulled into trying by an oleaginous veteran who would sidle up to visitors to St Moritz and say: "Let me introduce you to a sport that requires no work at all. All you have to do is lie on a toboggan..."

There is a story that Errol Flynn stopped at Shuttlecock, knocked back a glass of champagne proffered by an astonishingly beautiful blonde, and continued to a chauffeur-driven Rolls-Royce at the bottom. Brigitte Bardot used to be a familiar sight at the Cresta while she was married to Gunther Sachs, the industrialist and pillar of the club in more recent years.

The Cresta is not all about fabulous wealth and glamour, however. The most successful rider of the

The Cresta today.

run's history, and therefore by definition the most absurd, was Nino Bibbia, who hailed from St Moritz and was a greengrocer. It's possible for absolute beginners to ride the Cresta, but you need to book well in advance (www.cresta-run.com).

Vineyard above Sion, the Valais.

Basel's Old Town and cathedral
across the Rhine.

View from the Castelgrande over Bellinzona, Ticino.

The Julier Pass above Bivio, Graubünden.

INTRODUCTION

A detailed guide to the entire country, with principal sights clearly cross-referenced by number to the maps.

Skeleton rider statue in St Moritz.

Switzerland is an attractive destination at any time of year, and its dramatic divisions of landscape and major differences in elevation mean different regions can be rewarding in different ways, depending on the season. Eastern Switzerland and the lowlands, with their blossoming orchards and forested hills, are at their best in spring, while in summer visitors tend to gravitate towards the banks of the country's numerous Alpine lakes, or to the walking trails of the Alps. Serious outdoor lovers, hikers and bikers should head to the Alpine slopes and challenging mountain passes of the south on the border with Italy. Windsurfers and yachtsmen are fond of western Switzerland, the ice-cold yet always breezy Alpine lakes of inner Switzerland and the Grisons.

Autumn, with the promise of crisp, misty mornings and clear afternoon skies, can be enjoyed in many ways: in the vineyards of the Valais or the Vaud, in the bright-yellow larch forests of the Engadine or the southern valleys of the Grisons. In Ticino, autumn – as winter – can be significantly warmer than in the rest of the country, and this, combined with the absence of summer crowds, makes it the perfect time to visit. Winter provides innumerable possibilities throughout the Alpine region for winter sports or trekking through the snow. It is also an excellent time to discover the atmospheric wintry delights of cities such as Zürich, Bern and Lausanne.

Autumn colours and crystalline waters, Preda.

Switzerland may be small, but it is packed with history, culture and nature. Many visitors make the mistake of sticking to the through-routes and zipping around the most obvious sights without taking due time to explore the hidden gems.

In contrast to tourists of the past, who were compelled to explore the still undiscovered Alpine country of Switzerland on foot, on the backs of mules, or in buses with little if any suspension, today's travellers have an astonishingly thorough and comprehensive traffic system at their disposal. Thanks to the many and varied means of travel available – whether rail, bus, cable railway or boat – it is very tempting to leave the car at home, and to get to know really large areas of the country in a relatively short time.

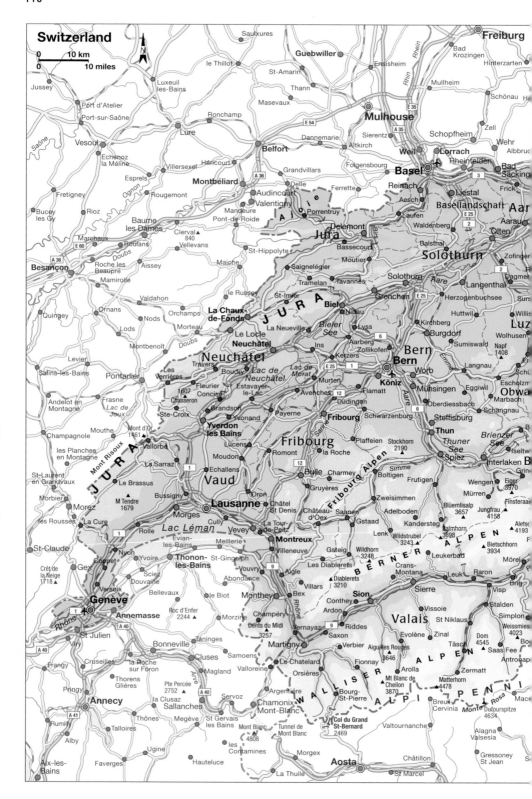

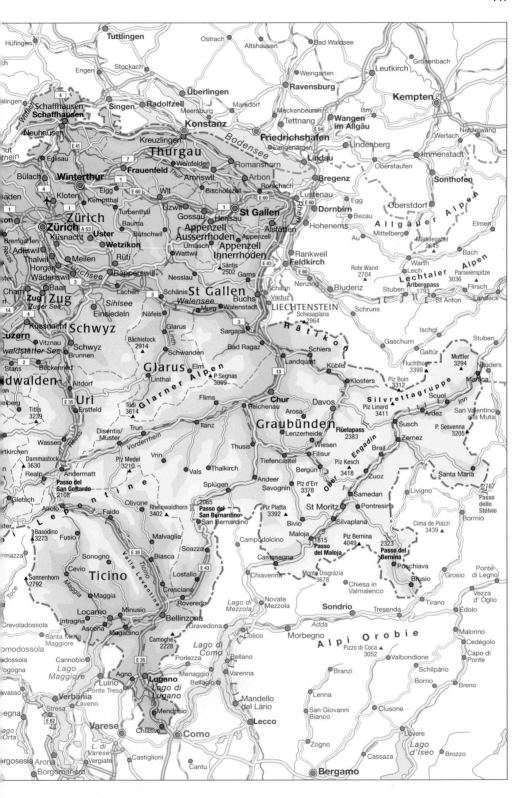

Recharging the batteries at a traditional chalet.

THE BERNESE OBERLAND

With its massive peaks, typified by the craggy Eiger, immaculate villages and indefatigable mountain rail network, this central region is Switzerland's Alpine holiday heartland.

The region to the southeast of Switzerland's capital of Bern, extending up to the Bernese Oberland and its famous Alpine peaks, is characterised not just by great mountains but all three types of Swiss topography: the lowlands, Alpine foothills and Alpine massif. The region reflects the economic strengths of each of these landscapes – travelling south from Bern, industry becomes less important and agriculture and tourism more so. Further east Alpine meadows dominate; cattle and dairy farming are still big business in the Oberland. About a 40-minute drive southeast of Bern, the famous Jungfrau region begins in Interlaken, on the Jungfraustrasse. The backdrop is the great wall of the Bernese Alps, dominated by three iconic peaks, the Mönch, the Eiger and the Jungfrau.

THE FEDERAL CAPITAL

The charming city of **Bern ❶**, in contrast to most other European capitals, is not obviously international in any way. The complexities of Swiss history have not left the country with any one centre where the nation's greats forged their and their country's destiny. There was never a unifying, inspiring personality around whom the upper echelons of society would gather, as there was, say, in the case of Europe's monarchies. Rather, Bern is the result of the

hegemony of a few patrician families who managed to retain their claim to a leading role for centuries.

The Unesco-classified Old Town can be visited no matter what the weather: even in torrential rain, you will not get too wet because the old streets are lined with covered arcades 6km (3.5 miles) in length. The main streets run roughly parallel with the end of the rocky outcrop skirted by the **River Aare**. Outside these rows of buildings in the city centre, the land falls off steeply on three sides down to

⊙ **Main Attractions**
BärenPark
Bern Münster
Bernisches Historisches
 Museum
Zentrum Paul Klee
Gurten
Emmental Region
Thun

⊙ **Maps on pages
120, 124**

An ibex takes in the view.

A happy BärenPark resident.

the Aare. This area beneath the town forms the "lower town", where the level of life was once lower socially as well as topographically. The view from the **Münster-Plattform** illustrates the point perfectly: deep below, at the foot of a mighty retaining wall, lies the area known as the **Matte**. Once a workers' and artisans' quarter, it is now particularly favoured by the arty set.

Bern was founded in 1191 by Duke Berchtold V of Zähringen. When the Zähringen dynasty died out the town became free. Bern's compact structure is an accurate reflection of its single-minded spirit. Its victory over Burgundy and the ensuing policy of expansion transformed Bern into the largest city-state north of the Alps. Even internal unrest could not bring the absolutist rule of the patricians to an end. It was only in 1798 when the French Army marched in that the old Bernese power structure finally collapsed. This political consistency has left its mark on the enclosed, unified-looking streets of the Old Town. Medieval and Baroque facades blend harmoniously. Today, the arcades are given over to rows of shops and, even if you are not keen on shopping, you may still appreciate the architectural details of the arcades, both by day and also when illuminated at night.

The city contains numerous restaurants; note, though, that their doors are quite often disguised as cellar entrances, with steep flights of steps leading down from the street.

You do not need to visit museums or art galleries to enjoy Bern. The streets themselves hold plenty to interest visitors, including 11 historical fountains from the mid-16th century, from which figures such as Justitia (Justice) and the dreaded Kindlifresser (child-devourer) peer down on the bustling streets below. Bern's most recent, and controversial, fountain (1983) was the creation of a famous artist, Meret Oppenheim.

BERN'S BEARS

There is much to see in Bern, including plenty of bears. The city and canton emblem, the beloved bears are found on flags, candy boxes, crests, clocks,

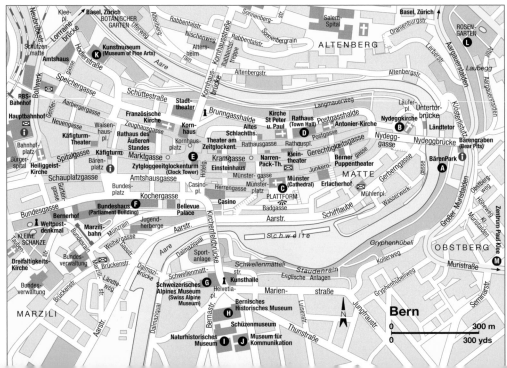

local teddy-bear-shaped cookies, statues and the sides of buildings. Legend has it that the city's founder pledged to name the city after the first animal he hunted in the woods in 1191. The forest was subsequently chopped down to build Bern. In 1857 Bern's bears were allocated a special home. The famous 150-year-old bear pit, the Bärengraben, located on the edge of the old city, closed in 2009 after the euthanasia of its last resident, Pedro, a 28-year-old brown bear who was suffering from incurable arthritis. It has since transformed into the **BärenPark Ⓐ** (Grosser Muristalden 6; tel: 31 357 15 15; www.tierpark-bern.ch; daily 24 hours; free), stretching over 6,000 sq metres (65,000 sq ft) from the old pit to the River Aare, giving its family of resident brown bears a greater chance to roam, hide in grottos and catch fresh fish. The new area has tried to respond to concerns from the public and animal-rights activists about the bears' need for adequate space. The pits are still there and can be seen, but the park has stolen the limelight as a healthier and happier place, despite the history of the former. A free inclined elevator offers access to the park between the hillside end of the enclosure and the riverbank.

The bear park falls under the umbrella of the small, mostly open-air public zoo, **Tierpark Dählhölzli** (Tierparkweg 1; tel: 31 357 15 15; www.tierpark-bern.ch; open daily late Mar–late Oct 8.30am–7pm, winter 9am–5pm). Here you will find deer, bison, bears, wolves and snow leopards in enclosures in a mixed-beech forest, carriage and pony rides, a lovely children's playground and a BBQ/picnic area.

THE OLD CITY CENTRE

Situated on a nose-shaped bend in the River Aare is Bern's Old Town, the Altstadt. From the Bear Pit, cross the old Nydeggbrücke bridge to the spired **Nydeggkirche Ⓑ**, a 14th-century church built over the ruins of the original city fortifications (Mon–Sat 10am–noon and 2–5.30pm, Sun 2–5.30pm).

A few blocks west is the city's spiritual centre, the **Münster Ⓒ** (tel: 031 312 04 62; www.bernermuenster.ch; Easter–Oct Mon–Sat 10am–noon and 2–5pm, Sun 11.30am–5pm, rest of the year Mon–Fri 10am–noon and 2–4pm, Sat until 5pm, Sun 11.30am–4pm; free). This is the most important late-Gothic cathedral in Switzerland; the three-aisled pillared basilica, begun in 1421, was designed by Matthäus Ensinger of Ulm. The tower, however, was not completed until 1893. Inside, its most notable features include finely carved choir stalls (1523), and a Gothic font. Over the main portal is a wonderfully intricate sculpture of the Last Judgement. From here, detour due north via the lanes, almost to the river, to see the early-15th-century **Rathaus Ⓓ** (Town Hall), which unfortunately is not open to the public. Its fine facade is worth a closer look, however, with columns decorated with figures such as St George, dating from 1406. Much was reconstructed after World War II.

Bern's Old Town looking festive.

Back on the main street (**Kramgasse**), walk west past the **Einsteinhaus** (tel 031 312 00 91; www.einstein-bern.ch; daily Feb–Dec 22nd 10am–5pm), where the great scientist lived from 1903 to 1905 as he worked out the Theory of Relativity.

From here it's a short walk uphill to the **Zytgloggeeitglockenturm** E (Clock Tower), another important symbol of the city. The astronomical clock, dating back to 1530, was once the main city timekeeper. Try to be there four minutes before the clock strikes the hour, when its mechanical figures are set in motion – the whimsical procession has to be seen to be believed. Just a block north is the city **Kornhaus** (Granary), now an intriguing exhibition centre with art galleries and a restaurant.

Another important stop in Bern's old city centre is the copper-domed parliament building, the **Bundeshaus** F, overlooking the River Aare. This is where the national parliament meets, built after Bern was declared the capital in 1848. To reach it from the clock tower, walk two blocks south and turn

The Kunstmuseum.

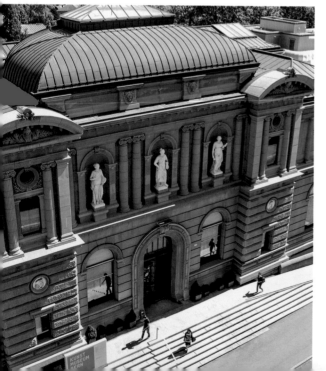

west for two more. Outside parliamentary sessions, free daily tours are given in various languages. (tel: 58 322 9022; tour in English Sat 2pm).

MUSEUMS GALORE

Being the capital, Bern has plenty of museums. Most are concentrated in a complex south of Kramgasse across another bridge. Walking south across the **Kirchenfeldbrücke**, you come to **Helvetiaplatz**, home of the **Schweizerisches Alpines Museum** G (tel: 031 351 04 40; www.alpinesmuseum.ch/en; Tues 10am–8pm, Wed–Sun 10am–5pm), which displays detailed maps and models of the Alps, mountain-rescue history and famous summit ascents. It also boasts temporary exhibitions. Opposite is the **Bernisches Historisches Museum** H (tel: 031 350 77 11; www.bhm.ch; Tues–Sun 10am–5pm), which also contains an Einstein Museum, made up of hundreds of objects, dozens of audiovisual elements and an imaginative look at the person behind the genius. Themes such as the horror of the Holocaust and the atomic bomb are sensitively treated. Other highlights of the permanent exhibition include part of the booty acquired after Bern's conquest of Aargau and Vaud and an excellent 16-room display of local history.

Leaving Helvetiaplatz, but just a two-minute walk south, is the **Naturhistorisches Museum** I (Bernastrasse 15; tel: 031 350 71 11; www.nmbe.ch; Mon 2–5pm, Tues–Fri 9am–5pm, Wed until 6pm, Sat–Sun 10am–5pm), whose collection of rocks, minerals and wildlife diorama includes the stuffed body of a Saint Bernard dog that made more than 40 mountain rescues. In the parallel Helvetiastrasse, the refurbished **Museum für Kommunikation** J (tel: 031 357 55 55; www.mfk.ch; Mon–Fri 10am–3pm), shows the development of the Swiss postal service into the country's remote and near-inaccessible corners.

North of the old city, near the northern bend of the Aare, is Switzerland's oldest fine-art museum, the **Kunst-museum** Ⓚ (Hodlerstrasse 8–12; tel: 031 328 09 44; www.kunstmuseumbern. ch; Tues 10am–9pm, Wed–Sun 10am–5pm). The incredible Masterpieces collection includes 175 works by Swiss and international artists, from Impressionism to Expressionism, Cubism to Surrealism. The artists represented here include Hodler, Picasso, Giacometti, Rothko, Oppenheim, Chagall, Monet, Manet, Pissarro, Renoir, van Gogh, Rothko and Pollock.

The **Rosengarten** Ⓛ (Alter Aargauerstalden 31b), north of the BärenPark, is a garden with a beautiful viewing platform over the Altstadt and River Aare loop from a small plateau. Its 200-plus rose varieties, 200 iris and dozens of rhododendrons bud up from a former cemetery. Reach it from the city centre on bus Nos 12 or 15.

Well to the east, via bus No. 12 from the town hall or No. 10 from the railway station, is the **Zentrum Paul Klee** Ⓜ (tel: 031 359 01 01; www.zpk.org; Tues–Sun 10am–5pm), dedicated to the work of the great Swiss artist. The stunning building, designed by Italian architect Renzo Piano, contains some 40 percent of his life's oeuvres – 4,000 paintings, watercolours and drawings as well as archives and biographical material.

SOUTH TO THE GURTEN

Nature lovers can follow the local droves and head to the resident mountain (well, the closest of them), the **Gurten** ❷, just south of the city. Its 860-metre (2821ft) high peak may be child's play compared to what you're headed for, but bigger is not always better. The views over the city, the countryside and the Alps are fabulous. There is also a children's playground and miniature railway, a restaurant and a winter toboggan run. You can reach the mountain by taking the S-Bahn Line 31 followed by the Gurtenbahn funicular in 20 minutes, beating motorists who have to tackle the steep winding road.

BERNESE CASTLES

The whole Bernese region is full of castles that the canton's gracious lords either had built or restored as country

Sunset over Bern.

⌖ Eat

If you are in the Emmental region and want a good, strong cheese, ask for one that is "Reif, Gelagert und Gepflegt".

seats. Many are still in private hands, sometimes those of the original patrician families.

Approximately 27km (17 miles) north of Bern is the **Schloss Landshut** ❸ (Schlossstrasse 17, Utzenstorf; tel: 32 665 40 27; mid-May–mid-Oct Tues–Sat 2–5pm, Sun 10am–5pm), the only moated castle in the canton of Bern. It houses the **Swiss Museum for Wildlife and Hunting**, part of Bern's Natural History Museum. Its wood-panelled rooms and banqueting hall are richly decked with paintings, including still lifes by Swiss artist Albrecht Kauw.

Another interesting trip northwest of Bern will take you to **Seeland**, the so-called Land of Three Lakes, also known as the canton's vegetable garden. It contains the lakes of Biel, Neuchâtel and the Murtensee, all benefitting from the impressive backdrop of the Jura mountain foothills.

THE EMMENTAL REGION

Less than an hour's drive east of Bern is the **Emmental** region, home to Emmentaler, the ultimate (and holey), Swiss cheese. Today Emmental, as the cheese is more widely known outside of Switzerland, is sold and imitated worldwide. All through the undulating valley, streams have cut their way into the deposits left by glaciers, meaning the landscape is only suitable for small farmsteads and family cheese producers. Many have disappeared over recent years in the face of

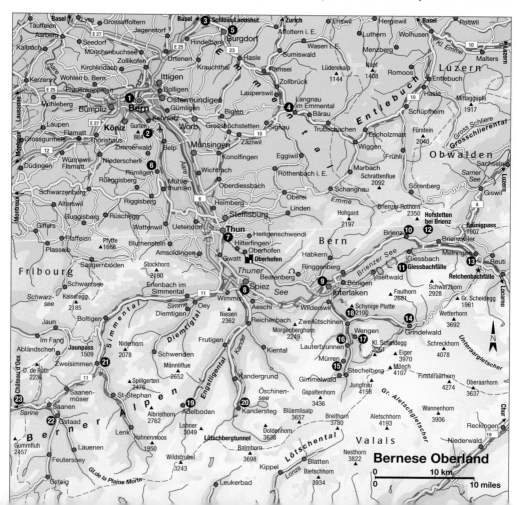

competition from bigger farms. Along the small backroads of the Emmental cheese route you will encounter dozens of dairies that have not. Many have shopfronts selling Emmentaler AOP cheese – aged for at least four months and a protected appellation.

Emmental's sedate regional capital, **Langnau im Emmental** ❹, has one of the most beautiful village squares in Switzerland. But its real value lies in the many nearby hiking trails, which lead to mountains with wonderful views.

Half an hour's drive to the northwest amid the hilly countryside and cliffs, is the medieval market town of **Burgdorf** ❺, with its 12th-century castle looming over the River Emme from a sandstone outcrop. The castle is home to a local history-packed Schlossmuseum (tel: 034 423 02 14; closed for renovation until further notice). Though not the capital, Burgdorf is the largest hub and is frequently advertised as the gateway to the Emmental. Its Altstadt, comprising an upper and lower town, is graced by several late-Baroque patrician houses, and a museum dedicated

to the works of the contemporary Bern-born artist Franz Gertsch (Platanenstrasse 3; tel: 34 421 40 20; www.museum-franzgertsch.ch; Wed–Fri 10am–6pm, Sat–Sun until 5pm). The striking minimalist building also doubles up as a contemporary art space for other temporary exhibitions. Hiking enthusiasts can meanwhile enjoy a loop walk through the idyllic rural surrounds, taking in the Gisnauflüe rock wall, sandstone outcrops and views over the town and River Emme.

Twelve kilometres (7.5 miles) east, in Affoltern im Emmental, is the **Emmentaler Schaukäserei show dairy** (Schaukäsereistrasse 6; tel: 034 435 16 11; www.emmentaler-schaukaeserei.ch; daily Apr–Oct 9am–6.30pm, Nov–Mar until 5pm; free), where you can see the cheese-making process first hand.

THE NAPF REGION

The hilly Napf region, lying on the border of Bern and Luzern cantons, is also one of small-scale farming, riven by deep valleys radiating out from Napf Peak (1,411 metres/4,630ft). Its

⊙ Tip

Bike lovers can hit the 1–2-day (35–78km/21–48-mile) circular cheese trail by taking the Emmentaler Käseroute (www.kaese route.ch/en) from Burgdorf, guided by the e-Bike app. E-Bikes can be hired from stations in Burgdorf and Langnau.

The road to Burgdorf in the Emmental region.

slopes provide popular walking and hiking trails, accessible by road from the pretty village of **Trubschachen** to the south.

RIVER LANDSCAPE

To the southeast, the River Kleine Emme flows in the direction of the Reuss, which it eventually joins below Luzern. The people here, like those from the nearby Emmental, were accurately portrayed by the novelist Jeremias Gotthelf (1797–1854), who was pastor at Lützelflüh. Even today they are well known for their unmistakably independent streak.

It is via the valley of the Aare that the **Bernese Oberland** proper is finally entered. The path of the river between Bern and Thun, with its meadows, forests, reed grasses, sedge and backwaters, is one of Switzerland's most precious river landscapes, much of it a nature reserve. The longest wholly Swiss river, the Aare is 295km (183 miles) long.

The course of the Aare and its tributaries determined the regional layout of the Bernese Oberland. It can be broadly defined by the east-west course of the Aare with its two basins, **Lake Brienz** and **Lake Thun**. South of this line, the lateral valleys run almost parallel to each other, from north to south: the **Simmental**, **Frutigtal**, **Engstligental**, **Kandertal**, **Lauterbrunnental** and **Haslital** – far over to the east – where the Aare has its source.

To the west of the Aare, and separated by a small range of hills, lies the **Gürbetal**. The gateway to this side valley is formed by **Kehrsatz**, 5km (3 miles) south of Bern. The neoclassical **Lohn Country House**, now owned by the Confederation, is situated here. It is often used for official receptions, and for accommodating guests of the Swiss Government. Another 15km (9 miles) south along the valley, we reach **Rümligen 6**. This little village prides itself on having had a real Bernese patrician among its denizens; Elisabeth de Meuron (1882–1980), a famous Bern eccentric, inhabited Rümligen Castle. She once locked up a suspected thief in a tower, claiming ancient legal rights to do so.

Thun reflected in the Aare.

⊘ NAPF VALLEY FARMING

The intensely steep, mountainous landscape of the Napf region has forced the locals to adapt to survive. The main peak, the Napf, is the highest mountain between Entlebuch and Emmental. Long, steep and forested rift valleys radiate out from here, sporting a dense coverage of spruce, silver fir and beech trees, with Alpine meadows on the flatter sides. Down below, waters collect in an almost circular valley. Because of high rainfall, the Napf is suited to pasture-based cattle farming and some crops.

The farmsteads often look like small hamlets from afar. Each has a farmhouse, barn and smaller, richly decorated wooden storehouse once used for food supplies and valuable objects. Keeping the buildings well apart minimised the danger of spreading fire. Nowadays the storehouses often serve as lodgings or retirement homes.

The real gateway to the Oberland is **Thun ❼**, 25km (15 miles) south of Bern. Lying at the point where the River Aare flows out of the Thunersee (Lake Thun), the late-Medieval Old Town is dominated by its multi-turreted hilltop castle, **Schloss Thun**, now a history museum (tel: 033 223 20 01; www.schlossthun.ch; Apr–Oct daily 10am–5pm, Nov–Jan Sun 1–4pm, Feb–Mar daily 1–4pm). The 12th-century castle, with its four corner towers and the impressive Bernese Alps behind it, is reminiscent of a Norman castle. Behind its milky stone facade, the charming interiors include a neo-Gothic dining room and a Grand Hall where regular cultural events take place. Outside, the gardens are splendid, and contain interesting interpretation panels on the castle's construction. There are numerous other castles in the area, and the Thun-Thunersee tourism office (Seestrasse 2; tel: 033 225 90 00; www.thunersee.ch) provides a handy brochure describing them all, as well as the wonderful lake activities available.

Alongside the attractive Old Town are military barracks and the **Wocher-Panorama**. This circular picture, painted between 1808 and 1814 by Marquard Wocher, is a lifelike representation of Thun in the Biedermeier period, and is situated in a round building in the park of **Schloss Schadau**.

The landscape of the southern side of Lake Thun is dominated by the 2,360-metre (7,700ft) -high **Niesen**, which separates the entries of the Simmental and Kandertal Valleys. It can thus be circumnavigated on three sides. There is a good view of the entire Lake Thun region from the top. At the foot of the mountain, right next to the lake, is **Spiez ❽**, with its harbourside castle **museum** (tel: 033 654 15 06; mid-Apr–mid-Oct Mon 2–5pm, Tues–Sun 10am–5pm) and adjacent **Church of St Columba** (open daily dawn to dusk; free). Both buildings are more than 1,000 years old and still retain many of their Romanesque features.

On the opposite side of the lake, beneath the sunny slopes of the village of **Beatenberg**, are the St Beatus Höhlen caves (tel: 33 841 16 43; www.beatushoehlen.swiss; Mar 18–Nov 12 daily 9.45am–5pm; 75-min guided tours depart every 45 minutes), where visitors can venture along 1,000 metres (3,300ft) of underground walkways. At the St Beatus Caves Museum there are modern interactive displays about the flora, fauna and geology of the Jungfrau region. You will also learn the story of the hamlet's namesake, St Beat, who, legend has it, once drove a dragon from its cave. The saint probably belonged to a group of Irish monks who came and settled in Switzerland in the 6th century.

A REGION RICH IN TRADITION

From Spiez, the River Aare continues eastwards, connecting Lake Thun with Lake Brienz. In between these two great lakes sits the aptly named town of **Interlaken ❾**. This popular resort town is noticeably full of splendid hotel buildings. They serve as a reminder of the health-spa-oriented, cosmopolitan

⊘ Tip

Performances of Schiller's William Tell are held in the open air in Rugen Forest, on the outskirts of Interlaken, from mid-June to early September. Tickets are available from Tellspiel-buro (tel: 033 822 37 22; www.tellspiele.ch).

View across a vineyard to Spiez.

lifestyle of the upper classes in both Europe and the rest of the world in the second half of the 19th century.

That is not surprising once you learn that this may be the place where modern-style tourism all started. Lord Byron and Felix Mendelssohn Bartholdy both stayed here as guests, and the cultural tradition has continued; today the town is famous for its William Tell outdoor theatre, its classical music festival, a casino and droves of young backpackers who bunk down here before setting off into the overhanging mountains.

What would Byron think of all this? Local adventure companies specialise in packages of extreme adventure sports such as bungee jumping into gorges, paragliding off cliffs and canyoning.

For those who are not up to such white-knuckle extremes, quite a few of the fin-de-siècle hotels are now used as retirement homes or congress centres. There is also quite an active nightlife in the town centre, plus several good museums and some splendid ivy-covered holiday cottages tucked away from the tourist excess.

The small town of **Brienz** at the eastern end of Lake Brienz is famous for its woodcarvings, which can be bought in every souvenir shop in the Oberland. There is a glut of souvenir shops selling carvings, which are mostly of people and animals, but you can also see the artisans in action, which does at least prove that they are not mass-produced abroad. Brienz can be approached by bicycle, boat, train, car or even on foot, but tourists traditionally take the boat. A trip around this mountain lake, which is 14km (9 miles) long, takes some 2.5 hours. The best means of transport to choose for this is the *Lötschberg*, a paddle steamer every bit as good as its Mississippi counterparts, and the pride of the Brienz fleet.

TOURISM IN THE OLD DAYS

Elisabeth Grossmann, the "boatwoman of Lake Brienz", was depicted in countless paintings. More than 150 years ago, she wept bitter tears over her unrequited love for a young professor. The grieving woman was immortalised by the painter Johann Emanuel Locher (1769–1820). His picture of La Belle Batelière was one of the bestselling colour etchings of its time.

She was one of the local girls who used to row the tourists to **Giessbach**, and who were always mentioned in accounts of the journey. The German physicist and astronomer Johann Friedrich Benzenberg, who visited Giessbach in 1810, had this to say: "The maidens who acted as our guides were also skilled in the art of song, and did not take much prompting. The maidens here have the reputation of being the best singers of all the farm-girls in the Haslital."

The real promoter of Haslital Valley turned out to be Hans Kehrli, a teacher from Brienz, at the beginning of the 19th century. In 1818 he built a footpath to waterfalls above the lake's southern shore, the **Giessbachfälle** , and erected a simple mountain hut there.

Giessbach's falls.

On pleasant days the whole family would take up position and sing songs for the visitors, with father Kehrli himself playing along on an alphorn. The family became so famous that one of the many landscape painters of that time captured them in a picture entitled *The Giessbach and the Singing Family on its Alp*. In those days, landscape painting was a thriving industry, and there were studios in which employees would copy masterpieces or colour etchings, and these were the forerunners of today's picture postcards.

Giessbach's falls became one of the major attractions for 19th-century visitors to Switzerland and gradually Giessbach began to be developed to accommodate tourists more comfortably. In 1840 a guesthouse appeared; 1872 saw the opening of the first hotel, which was replaced by a larger, more lavishly furnished building after a fire in 1883. Franz Weber, the environmentalist, managed to save it from destruction in 1983 and had it restored to its former glory. It prospers under the motto "Giessbach belongs to the Swiss". Today,

people cross the lake in a steamer, and the funicular, commissioned in 1879, still provides tourists with a comfortable ride from the docking area to their hotel.

The 2,350-metre (7,700ft) **Brienzer Rothorn** towers above the town of Brienz. The Brienz-Rothorn-Bahn, the only steam-operated rack railway in Switzerland, travels up to an altitude of 2,240 metres (7,300ft) in one hour. The line was built at the end of the 19th century and copes with an average gradient of 22.5 percent. The railway operates only in the summer, but anyone who wants to enjoy the view from the Rothorn in winter can get there by cable car from the town of **Sörenberg** in the canton of Luzern to the north.

FOLLOWING THE COURSE OF THE AARE

En route to the area where the Aare has its source, you might like to drop by the **Ballenberg** Freilichtmuseum der Schweiz (Swiss Open-Air Museum; tel: 033 952 10 30; www.ballenberg.ch; mid-Apr–Oct daily 10am–5pm) at **Hofstetten bei Brienz ⑫**, 5km (3 miles) east of Brienz.

The Brienzer Rothorn steam-powered rack railway is open during the summer months.

SHERLOCK HOLMES: THE FINAL DRAMA

The Reichenbach Falls were – in part – made famous by Sir Arthur Conan Doyle, who chose the spot to "kill off" fiction's most famous detective.

The falls, near Meiringen, were described by Arthur Conan Doyle in *The Final Problem* as "a fearful place. The torrent, swollen by the melting snow, plunges into a tremendous abyss, from which the spray rolls up like the smoke from a burning house. The shaft into which the river hurls itself is an immense chasm, lined by glistening coal-black rock, and narrowing into a creaming, boiling pit of incalculable depth, which brims over and shoots the stream onward over its jagged lip. The long sweep of green water roaring forever down, and the thick flickering curtain of spray hissing forever upward, turn a man giddy with their constant whirr and clamour..."

Engraving of the death of Sherlock Holmes, 1893.

Thus was recorded the scene of one of the most dramatic moments in Victorian English literature. Here, at the Reichenbach Falls, Sherlock Holmes apparently met his end in a fatal fight with Professor James Moriarty, "The Napoleon of Crime".

The Final Problem, the story which should have been the last word on the world's greatest detective, appeared in *The Strand* magazine in 1893 and was based on a trip Conan Doyle had just made to the falls. In the story, Dr Watson was not present, but had been sent away on a ruse to treat a consumptive woman in Davos.

In real life, Conan Doyle's wife, Louise, had been diagnosed as consumptive, and the author, who was also a doctor, blamed himself for not spotting her condition before they had embarked on what had been a gruelling journey. According to Conan Doyle's biographer, Charles Higham, the consumptive Louise brought about the death of Holmes, simply because she required Conan Doyle's attention, and the scene of his "death" was deliberate, as the visit to the falls had aggravated her illness and he had soon afterwards taken her to Davos.

Although Conan Doyle confessed he had had an "overdose" of his hero, as in the best soaps the hero was brought back to life by popular demand. Yet the site of the fight is still remembered by hundreds who make a pilgrimage to it every year. A rack railway goes by the falls and a bronze plaque at the bottom of the chasm commemorates the desperate struggle.

In nearby Meiringen, meanwhile, a complete replica of the fictitious 221B Baker Street, London, lodgings of Sherlock Holmes, forms a museum to the illustrious detective (tel: 033 972 50 00; www.sherlockholmes.ch; 29 Apr–29 Oct daily 1.30–6pm, 30 Nov–26 Apr Wed–Sun 4.30–6pm). The **Sherlock Holmes Museum**, in the basement of the former English Church, was inaugurated in 1991 on the centenary of Holmes's "death" and the square outside has been named Conan Doyle Place.

In the town, there is also a statue of Sherlock Holmes, by John Doubleday, which contains clues to each of the 60 Holmes stories, and gives visitors and members of the world-wide Sherlock Holmes Society, of whom there are more than 1,000, an opportunity to use their sleuthing skills.

Some 100 traditional rural buildings from all over Switzerland can be seen in this idyllic 66-hectare (163-acre) site – old farmhouses, stables, bakehouses and barns, set up as small hamlets. They have all been dismantled, transported and rebuilt here, starting in the 1970s, saving many historic buildings from demolition. The museum provides a snapshot of Swiss rural life and old customs, complete with 250 native farmyard animals, indigenous plants and crops, and demonstrations of rural crafts. Afterwards, you can sample some hearty typical Swiss fare in one of the three inns on the premises.

Haslital Valley, on the eastern edge of the Bernese Alps, is where the Aare has its source, and it ends at the catchment basin formed by the **Grimsel Pass**, the only adequately surfaced road between the Upper Valais and northern Switzerland. The higher one goes in the valley the rougher the landscape becomes, and it leads into the largest continuous glacier region of the Alps, covering a surface area of 300 sq km (190 sq miles); among the many glaciers here are the

Aare, **Rhône** and **Aletsch**. They are all conservation areas. Their water not only supplies the surrounding region but also flows into the Mediterranean via the Rhône and into the North Sea, too, via the Aare, in combination with the Rhine from the nearby Graubünden Alps.

Like everywhere else in the Swiss Alpine region, the plentiful water supply is put to good use. Reservoirs and pressure pipes collect huge masses of seething mountain water with which to drive mighty turbines and generators, providing Switzerland with much of its hydroelectric power. The power stations themselves are situated inside the mountains and are an important source of employment in the mountain areas where they help to stem the emigration of the local population.

HOLIDAY DESTINATIONS

One of the best-known holiday areas in the Haslital is the region around **Meiringen** ⑱ and **Hasliberg**. High up here on the Hasliberg, on the **Mägisalp** and in the **Justistal Valley** above Lake Thun, a special festival has developed: the

Tip

Meiringen is a starting point for a road tour by postbus, known as the Three Alpine Pass Tour, a circular day trip crossing the Susten, Furka and Grimsel passes. The tour runs on Tuesdays from July to September.

Winter hike through powdery snow near Hasliberg.

Chästeilet (cheese-sharing). The cheese produced on an Alp has to be divided up among the various farmers in relation to the "milk-efficiency" of the cows that grazed on the Alp. In the old days this took place without any great ceremony, but the farmers of today have turned the whole thing into a small folk festival. Sales booths are set up on the Alp and tourists and locals alike have the opportunity to buy the cheese directly. The food, drink and music add an extra dimension to the view of the mountain peaks around the Alp.

If you are in Meiringen, it is worth making a trip to the 200-metre (650ft) deep Aareschlucht or **Aare Gorge** (tel: 033 971 40 48; www.aareschlucht.ch; daily 8.30am–5.30pm, West entrance mid-Apr–Oct, East entrance mid-May–Oct, floodlit illumination July–Aug Thur–Sat until 10pm). Between **Innertkirchen** and Meiringen the river has to cut its way through a rocky ridge 1,600 metres (5,250ft) in length. The footpath through the high and narrow rocky walls runs partly via suspended walkways and partly via galleries hewn out of the rock.

If you choose to take the path through the gorge in only one direction, you can return to the carpark by bus. From the West (Meiringen) entrance to the middle, it is wheelchair accessible.

If you follow the **River Lütschine** upstream (that is south) from Interlaken you will find that the valley divides after only 10km (6 miles) or so, leading eastwards to Grindelwald and southwards to the **Lauterbrunnental**. The whole valley is separated from the Haslital by rocky massifs, some as high as 4,000 metres (13,000ft), and they all form part of the glacier conservation area. The **Finsteraarhorn** (4,274 metres/14,022ft), situated at the centre of this glacier region, is the highest point in the Bernese Alps.

Here we leave the valley of the River Lütschine and arrive at **Grindelwald** ⑭, in the valley of the Schwarze (black) Lütschine, so called because the river's water is the colour of slate from the Black Mountain. It is possible to get to Grindelwald by public transport; better still, you can make a rigorous but enjoyable full-day hike over the Grosse

Mürren and its gondola in summer.

Scheidegg from Meiringen. It is a walk for the physically fit, but transportation – via the occasionally passing, bright yellow postbus – can help out along the way if you find the thin air daunting; these are the only motorised vehicles allowed to use the road across the pass. Views of the surrounding glaciers are splendid.

The town of Grindelwald has sold its soul to tourism, no doubt about it. This has been true for quite some time: after the village burned down in 1892 – the wooden houses provided the flames with more than enough fuel – the new buildings were adapted to suit economic factors, which had changed since the original settlement was built. As was the case in most of the mountain regions, the first tourists had been the English, who paid their first winter visits here in 1860. In 1891 an Englishman amazed the people of Grindelwald by bringing a pair of skis along with him. The area would never quite be the same.

Still, it is exceptionally well located. A day visiting the ice grottoes or glacial gorges, and the spectacular sight (when the clouds of mist part, that is) of the three peaks towering high above, is almost enough to make you forget the sprawl of chalets, bars and souvenir shops spilling along the main street.

THE ALPINE REGION

A whole series of mighty mountain peaks lies directly on the border separating the cantons of Bern and the Valais. Foremost among them are the **Eiger**, **Mönch** and **Jungfrau**; these are perhaps the most famous and are almost always thought of as a trio. Since 1912 there has been a railway line leading up to the **Jungfraujoch**. Information is provided in several languages during the journey and the train covers most of the distance inside the mountain itself, although intermediate stations with panoramic windows provide views of the mighty scene. A modern restaurant at the end of the line, 3,454 metres (11,332ft) above sea level, provides food and drink.

The summit of the Jungfrau is 4,158 metres (13,642ft) above sea level, and averages temperatures below zero even at the height of summer. The weather station up on the Jungfrau collects important data for meteorologists.

The cable-car ride up past **Gimmel-wald** to the **Schilthorn** begins near the high car-free resort village of **Mürren** ⓰, below the Jungfrau group and at the upper end of the Lauterbrunnental. To get to Mürren from Grindelwald by rail you have to return down the line towards Interlaken and change trains at Zweilütschinen, where the Lutschine Valley divides. Traditionally uniformed and bewhiskered station guards are on hand to direct lost passengers to the correct platform. From the top of the Schilthorn there is a magnificent all-round view of the Alpine region – a panorama that can also be lapped up during a meal. The revolving restaurant at the top takes an hour to go full circle. All the cable-car scenes and ski-chase sequences from the James Bond film On Her Majesty's Secret Service were shot on the Schilthorn, which brochures

Skiing heaven.

> **Fact**

Goethe was inspired by the Staubbach Falls to write his poem "Song of the Spirits over the Water."

still refer to as "Piz Gloria" – the peak's name in the film. The swivelling restaurant, the Schilthorn Piz Gloria, shares the name too.

Heading back up the Lütschine Valley towards Interlaken, the astounding Staubbach Falls are another spectacle, outside the picturesque village of **Lauterbrunnen** . So impossibly tall that they appear to be a trick of the eye until you get closer, the water crashes over a wall of rock 280 metres (920ft) high, dissolving almost entirely into fine spray as it does so. When there is a lot of water in the summer, this spray hangs suspended in the air and can often be felt as far away as the village itself.

WENGEN AND THE SCHYNIGE PLATTE

Wengen 🅱, another village without cars, lies just to the north of Lauterbrunnen up a branch rack railway line. Wengen's main claim to the tourist market is in the winter when it hosts the annual international skiing contest on the **Lauberhorn**. This popular event attracts the crowds, who pay to watch the race and for the practice sessions. Being car-free, Wengen is an especially quiet place for the rest of the year but for the pleasing racket of cowbells and the frequent clanking and braking of the rack railway grinding its way up and down the steep gradient to the valley. For a small town, it is well supplied with amenities, including a cinema, tennis courts and a pool hall. After dark, Wengen's nightlife gets going – more so in the winter, when the glitterati show up for the ski event. It is possible to follow marked trails just uphill from the little station for a bit of pleasant walking through pastures and past rustic, log-heated homes, or you can walk back downhill to Lauterbrunnen in about one hour. Get a good trail map if you will be going further into the backcountry.

Returning to Interlaken, a rack railway line leads up to the **Schynige Platte** 🅱, a glorious rocky plateau at the entrance to the Lütschinen Valley. The **Schynige Platte Botanical Alpine Gardens** (tel: 33 828 73 76; www.alpengarten.ch; May 27–Oct 22 8.30am–6pm; admission included in train ticket) located here contain more than 650 species of plants native to the Swiss Alps, planted in over 8 hectares (20 acres) of velvety meadows. If you do not want to read all the information provided, you can simply admire the visual beauty of these plants. Beware of picking any of these wild flowers, as they are protected by law.

THE WAY TO THE VALAIS

Another key traffic junction in the Alps, in addition to the St Gotthard, is the **Lötschberg Tunnel**. It provides a connection with the Valais that is passable even in winter and saves having to go the long way round the Alps via the Lower Valais. The chance to load their cars onto a train also provides motorists with a well-earned break on their journey towards the south. This stretch of railway opened in 1913.

Train travel is a rewarding way to take in the arresting Swiss landscape.

The route to the Lötschberg leads south from **Spiez** and through the **Kandertal**, the third of the four huge valleys of the Bernese Oberland. (The others are the **Frutigtal**, **Kiental** and **Engstligental**.)

The valleys are flanked to the west by the Niesen range. **Reichenbach** is a rather inconspicuous little village on the lower reaches of the **River Kander**, in the Frutigtal. Most of its houses were built in the 18th century, and are examples of the fine carpentry that has been a feature of the Bernese Oberland for centuries. The village's main street is lined with solid-looking wooden houses, each decorated with richly carved and painted facades.

RIVERS AND WATERFALLS

Frutigen, the main town in the Engstligental area, stands at the junction of the Kander and the Engstligenbach rivers. The strong erosion of the currents has given the valley its "V" shape, as powerful torrents of water have cut deeply into the soft rock layers of the Niesen range. Despite these obstacles, the industrious

Swiss have built bridges and flights of steps right next to the rivers, some of which provide spectacular views of the frothing action. The numerous local waterfalls and dramatically eroded rocks form a superb natural spectacle.

Adelboden ⑲, a resort occupying a sunny position at the head of the Engstligental, some 15km (9 miles) from Frutigen, is an exceptionally popular holiday resort and offers a broad range of winter and summer activities including over 300km (186 miles) of walking trails. Buildings such as the church, constructed in 1433, are consequently often disregarded, but are worth a look. Its exterior wall has a late-Gothic painting of the Last Judgement dating from 1471, and inside there is modern stained glass by Alberto Giacometti (see page 78).

Kandersteg ⑳, a beautifully situated resort and mountaineering centre of long standing, lies at the entrance to the Lötschberg Tunnel about 12km (8 miles) south of Frutigen. In the 18th century considerable trading took place here, with the north exchanging

⊙ Tip

Kandersteg has plenty of seasonal activities on offer, including 750 metres (2,500 ft) of summer toboggan run.

A waterfall plunges into the Öschinensee, near Kandersteg.

Simmentaler calf.

cattle for spices from the south. The porters involved in this trading gradually adapted to the increasing needs of tourism, and whole dynasties of mountain guides arose. The **Blümlisalp Massif** is an ideal destination for mountaineers. Water sports are also possible: the **Öschinensee**, which lies 1,578 metres (5,180ft) above sea level, is just the place for an Alpine swim. This lake was produced by a landslide in the latter part of the Ice Age. The water flows out from the lake underground, and is used to produce electricity.

THE SIMMENTAL

The last of the large valley communities in the Bernese Oberland, the **Simmental** has belonged to Bern since 1386. At the end of the 14th century, the city-state of Bern took over political control of the region from the monastery at Interlaken. The inhabitants of the valley were, however, far from convinced by the Reformation in the 16th century, and most of them remained loyal to their Catholic faith. Despite this, the Simmental did not become alienated from Bern. One conspicuous illustration of this is the Bern coat-of-arms that can be seen at **Schloss Wimmis**, marking the entrance to the Simmental.

The **Lower Simmental River** winds its way westwards through the mountain ranges and then describes a large bend before heading off southwards again as the **Upper Simmental**. The observant traveller – shortly after having entered the **Diemtigtal Valley** (noted for its *Papierschnitzerie* – richly decorated paper cutouts depicting scenes of forests and animals) – will have already noticed the typical Simmental houses in **Erlenbach** as well as in **Därstetten**. The **Knuttihaus**, built in 1756, is considered one of the finest farmhouses in Europe. With its whitened cellar and first storey and loft above it, it is the archetypal Simmental house.

The village of **Bad Weissenburg**, beyond Därstetten, flourished thanks to a mineral spa. It was here, shortly before the outbreak of World War II, that Juliana, later to become Queen of the Netherlands, became engaged to Prince Bernhard. The water is still bottled and sold today, but the spa itself stopped operating long ago. Further up the valley, the road forks off at **Boltigen** (itself 35km/22 miles southwest of Thun), west into the **Jaun Pass**. This leads off into the French-speaking region of Gruyère. Further along the Simme, the valley changes from the Lower into the Upper Simmental.

Zweisimmen ㉑ is, from the point of view of transport at least, the most important town in the Upper Simmental – it is right on the main lines stretching to Spiez, Interlaken and even Geneva via the attractive Golden Pass line, which runs through these hills several times a day (though only once nonstop). From here one can either follow the Simme further up to the spa town of Lenk, or go off westwards into the Saanetal, the easternmost projection of the canton of Vaud. The **church** in Zweisimmen is all that remains of the old village, for the town was destroyed by fire in 1862, just as Grindelwald would be 30 years later. The 15th-century church, consecrated to the Virgin Mary, is decorated both inside and out with late-Gothic frescoes which survived the conflagration. On the 12km (8-mile) drive south to **Lenk**, note the preponderance of finely crafted, painted and decorated wooden homes; this is known as the Simmental House Trail, and makes for a pleasing diversion along the road. Lenk, like Zweisimmen, lives mainly from tourism, but it also has a sulphur spring that has been in commercial use since the 17th century.

GSTAAD

Just to the west, the **Saanetal** has the town of **Gstaad** ㉒, also on the Golden Pass route, to thank for its fame. High society from all over the world meets up here in the winter months. Gstaad, as for **Gsteig** 10km (6 mile) south, is also a summer resort and despite its snooty image, is as keen on receiving year-round visitors as any other town. The local Gstaad Alpine Centre carries a staff of guides who lead rafting expeditions on the River Saane, maintain a tricky ropes course and run a programme of other pulse-pounding adventures in the surrounding mountains and rivers.

From **Saanen** – more of a country town and without much of the overbearing wealth of its showier neighbour Gstaad – the **River Saane** continues west as the Sarine (its French name) into the Pays d'Enhaut in the Vaud, later to flow into the Swiss-French lowlands and eventually into the Aare. However if, south of Château d'Oex, you cross one of two passes – the **Col des Mosses**, or the **Col du Pillon** – from Gsteig, you find yourself in the Rhône basin heading for the Mediterranean. If you leave the Pays d'Enhaut in a northerly direction and go up the Sarine you reach the canton of Fribourg.

Château d'Oex ㉓ does make a fine last stop in the area. Not technically part of the Oberland, it is nonetheless a breath of fresh air – literally – with the popular annual International Hot-air Ballooning Week that brings in the visitors every January, offering rides and some spectacular race events.

Christmas in Gstaad.

📷 SWITZERLAND'S ALPINE RAILWAYS

Trains snake their way through picturesque valleys and up steep mountains, offering views of lush green hillsides and snowcapped peaks.

Switzerland's expertise in railway construction was already fairly proven before the opening of the Gotthard Base Tunnel in 2016. The 57km (35-mile) twin-bore tunnel runs through the Swiss Alps, connecting northern and southern Europe. Taking 17 years to build, the tunnel shot to the top of world Alpine rail technology, overtaking Japan's 54km (33-mile) Seikan rail tunnel as the world's longest.

No other country in the world is so dependent on its mountain railways as Switzerland, whether it be to take milk down from the Alpine pastures or to ferry skiers to the pistes. To help trains climb steep gradients on conventional railways, a "rack" between the rails allows the pinions of a cog on the train to engage the rack and claw its way up the slope – or brake its descent. Although the rack system was pioneered in the United States, it was Swiss engineers who developed it and exported equipment all over the world, from Sumatra to North Wales. Another means of mountain climbing was the funicular, using a cable to balance ascending and descending cars.

SPECTACULAR ALPINE VIEWS

To travel on Switzerland's extensive mountain rail network is one of the greatest pleasures. Most famous of all journeys is the *Glacier Express*, which conveys passengers in generously glazed, air-conditioned splendour between St Moritz and Zermatt. Though an 8-hour journey, there is barely a dull moment, and the lunch served in the restaurant car is astonishingly good. Wine is served in glasses with angled stems to compensate for the steep slopes.

For those who relish the bracing Alpine air, some trains on the spectacular *Bernina Express* route between Chur and Tirano in Italy via Davos and St Moritz have open carriages from which to enjoy the glacial blue-green of Lago Bianco and the mountains surrounding the highest rail crossing of the Alps.

Switzerland has one of the densest railway networks in the world. Its trains are able to navigate the challenging Alpine landscape.

The Bernina Express embarks upon a legendary train journey. Here it is seen crossing the Landwasser Viaduct, with its 65-metre (200ft) limestone arches.

The Gotthard Panorama Express.

Up Mount Rigi on the rack railway

Long before the opening of Europe's first Alpine railway up Mount Rigi in 1871, the peak, known as "the Queen of Mountains", was one of the Swiss summits to climb. Hikers enjoyed watching the sun set and rise over the magnificent panorama of peaks 805km (500 miles) in circumference.

To cater for these visitors, the first hotel close to the summit opened in 1816. It was progressively enlarged, resulting in the Hotel Schreiber, which opened in 1875 with accommodation for 300 guests. Both César Ritz and Auguste Escoffier worked at the Schreiber, as head waiter and chef respectively, before becoming famous.

The idea for the first rack railway in Europe was apparently suggested by the Swiss Consul-General in Washington, John Hitz, during a visit to the works of Niklaus Riggenbach in Olten, a small engineering town in the Jura. Using a rack system he had patented in Paris, Riggenbach began building work in September 1869, and after delays in the delivery of rails and passenger vehicles caused by the Franco-Prussian War, it opened in 1871 with Riggenbach at the controls of the first train.

train crosses a viaduct on the international Centovalli ne, which runs between Locarno and Domodossola.

regional train passes icy Lago Bianco in Graubünden uring winter.

The Rigi railway, Europe's original Alpine railway. Pictured in the late 19th century.

Winter panorama over pretty Fribourg.

THE WEST

Tucked between Lake Geneva and Lac de Neuchâtel, this region is characterised by small-scale dairy villages, the Alps, wines and Gruyère cheese.

The cantons of **Vaud** and **Fribourg** spread between the lowlands and Alpine foothills of French-speaking western Switzerland, and play host to two rivers: 68km (42-mile) Broye and 128km (80-mile) Sarine. The jumbled borders in the **Broye Valley** and its three Catholic enclaves date to 1536, when Swiss Confederation members Bern and Fribourg captured the Savoy-controlled Vaud.

At the time of the revolution, those areas captured by Catholic Fribourg during the Reformation did not want to be melded with the Protestant canton of Vaud. This region, with its gentle hills and low mountains, fields of waving corn, green meadows and spick-and-span towns, has been largely spared from mass tourism.

Despite industrialisation, Fribourg remains the most markedly rural of Switzerland's cantons: one in six employed people works in agriculture (the figure was closer to 39 percent in 1950), more than three times the national average. The canton has its own breed of cattle, patriotically sporting the black-and-white colours of the canton, and two types of cheese: Gruyère and Vacherin, a fondue cheese. The language border is also a "cheese border": the French-Swiss part of Fribourg produces Gruyère, the Swiss-German part produces the large-holed Emmental.

Nature reserve on Lac de Neuchâtel.

FRIBOURG, THE BRIDGE TOWN

Within a loop described by the River Sarine lies the cantonal capital, **Fribourg ❶**. The fine townscape is dominated by the tower of the Cathédrale St Nicholas (St Nicholas' Cathedral), which has the Last Judgement depicted on its western portal. The Sarine marks the linguistic border. Fribourg is – both literally and metaphorically – a bridge town; for nearly a millennium it has formed a bridge between German- and French-speaking Switzerland. Its

Main Attractions
Fribourg
Gruyères
Aventicum Roman Site & Museum
Murten
Lac de Neuchâtel
Château de Grandson

Map on page 142

⊙ Fact

The Moléson Cheese Factory, dating from 1686, is open to visitors (tel: 026 921 10 44; www.moleson.ch; daily 9am–7pm mid-May–Sept).

setting is spectacular. At the end of the 18th century, the English historian William Coxe was so impressed by its aspect that he was driven to one of his not infrequent flights of fancy: "Many [of the buildings] overhang the edge of a precipice in such a manner that, on looking down, a weak head would be apt to turn giddy...."

Fribourg, founded as a *Freie Burg* in 1157 by Berchtold IV of Zähringen, on a peninsula in the River Sarine, was bigger than both Bern and Zürich when it entered the Confederation, and in terms of prosperity it was easily on a par with Basel and Geneva. Trade and business flourished; the woollen cloth and leather the town produced were sought-after commodities.

After the Reformation – Fribourg stayed with the "old faith" and became an island of Catholicism in a Protestant land – its economic power declined, even though the town managed to extend its dependencies. It wasn't until the second half of the 20th century that Fribourg emerged from its somnolence and rapidly industrialised.

THE GRUYÈRE REGION

To the south of Fribourg is the Valley of Gruyère, through which the River Sarine flows. The valley is a microcosm of Switzerland: a plateau surrounded by mountain peaks, and right in the middle, in a commanding position, a small town with a château, whose lords have ruled the region for centuries. The whole Gruyère region is steeped in history.

Every year over a million people visit the small town of **Gruyères** ❷ and its 13th-century château, some 30km (19 miles) from Fribourg. Between its ramparts, guard room, salons and formal *jardins à la française*, the treasures at the **Château de Gruyères** (rue du Château 8; tel: 026 921 21 02; www. chateau-gruyeres.ch; Apr–Oct 9am–6pm, Nov–Mar 10am–5pm) include ornate stained-glass windows, frescoes commissioned by the bailiffs under the Old Swiss Confederacy and paintings by 18th-century French landscape painter Jean-Baptiste Camille Corot. This is a major tourist attraction complete with restaurants and souvenir shops.

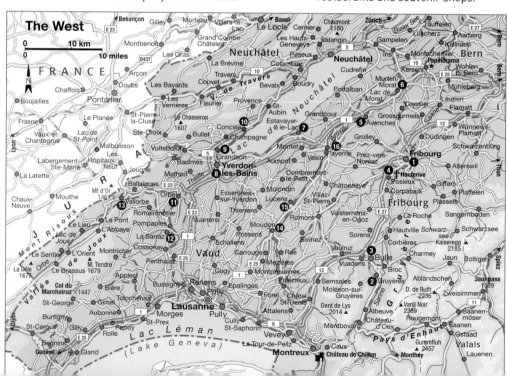

West of the town centre, near the railway station, is **La Maison du Gruyère** (Place de la Gare, 3; tel: 026 921 84 00; www.lamaisondugruyere.ch; daily June–Sept 9am–6.30pm, Oct–May until 6pm, market daily June–Sept 7.30am–7pm, Oct–May until 6.30pm), with its demonstration *fromagerie* (cheese dairy), so clean it looks more like a laboratory than a true rural dairy, and an interactive cheese exhibition. It also has a cheese market, the Marché Gruérien, where you can stock up on Gruyère AOP, fondue, Gruyère cream, Vacherin Fribourgeois AOP, sweets and souvenirs, as well as a large, bright warehouse restaurant – with plenty of fondue.

As in German-speaking Switzerland, a rich cow-herding culture has developed in the Alpine foothills. Folk artists immortalised the *Poya* – the ceremonial driving of livestock to the summer pastures – in colourful paintings (especially from the 18th century onwards), which decorated crossbeams and barn doors. Many depict the cows, along with a horse piled high with luggage, a pig and several goats, zigzagging their way up the mountainside, accompanied by herdsmen with rucksacks and walking-sticks on their way to the Alpine hut. A fascinating collection of this farm art, so typical of the Gruyère region, can be found in the **Musée Gruérien** (tel: 026 912 72 60; www.musee-gruerien. ch; Oct–May Tues–Fri 10am–noon and 1.30–5pm, Sat 10am–5pm, June–Sept Tues–Sat 10am–5pm, Sun 1.30–5pm) in **Bulle** ③, a rewarding place to visit a few kilometres to the north of Gruyère on the road to Fribourg; the museum's exhibition of costumes and farm tools is also worth a look.

Alongside the River Sarine just to the south of Fribourg is the Cistercian **Abbaye de Hauterive** ④ near **Posieux**. The 12th-century monastery is Switzerland's only remaining abbey belonging to Cistercian monks. Also unique is the 13th-century **Monastère de La Valsainte** near **Charmey**, to the east

of Bulle, the only Carthusian monastery in Switzerland, inhabited today by members of this austere order who live as semi-recluses in rows of individual cells, each with its own garden.

A LANDSCAPE STEEPED IN HISTORY

Most Swiss lakes were formed during the Ice Age; as it ended the glaciers gradually melted and their basins filled with water. After the Rhône glacier had receded, an area of water 100km (60 miles) in length, covering the base of the Jura all the way to Solothurn, formed northeast of the continental divide of La Sarraz. This "Lake Solothurn" finally split up into three distinct parts: Lac de Morat, Biel and the lakes of Neuchâtel. After the lake had receded, the Orbe Plateau developed, and today this plateau provides fertile agricultural land.

In **Avenches** ⑤, to the northwest of Fribourg, are the extensive and well-preserved Roman ruins of the Helvetian capital of *Aventicum*. The **Aventicum Roman Site & Museum** contain an amphitheatre, temple, baths, theatre

⊙ Tip

Fifteen minutes' drive to the northeast of Gruyères, in Broc, is a chocolate wonderland, the Maison Cailler (7 rue Jules Bellet; tel: 026 921 59 60; www.cailler.ch; daily Apr–Oct 10am–5pm, Nov–Mar until 4pm). This is one of the country's finest artisan chocolatiers and offers award-winning tours in a startlingly white mansion.

Producing cheese by hand near Gruyères.

⊘ Tip

On 1 October, Murten holds a road race to Fribourg, in memory of an army messenger who collapsed and died in Fribourg after relaying the news of the German victory at Murten in 1032.

and museum, making for a very pleasant short walk from the town (daily; free entry to the Roman site). While here, you might wish to visit the adjacent **Musée Romain d'Avenches** (tel: 026 557 33 00; www.aventicum.org; Apr–May and July–Sept Tues–Sun 10am–5pm, June daily 10am–5pm, Oct and Feb–Mar Tues–Sun 2–5pm, Nov–Jan Wed–Sun 2–5pm).

To the north of Avenches, on the shore of the Lac de Morat, is the town of **Murten ❻**. This exceptionally well-preserved town has walls topped with towers, a castle, 15th-century churches and a good little **museum** in what was once a windmill, which displays interesting prehistoric artefacts found in the lake and lots of medieval history (tel: 026 670 31 00; www.museummurten.ch; Mar 19–Dec 10 Tues–Sat 2–5pm, Sun 10am–5pm).

East of Murten, the **Papiliorama** tropical plant and butterfly house in Kerzers (tel: 031 756 04 61; www.papiliorama.ch; summer 9am–6pm, winter 10am–5pm) features a heated dome with butterflies, birds and fish, and another for nocturnal creatures.

LAKE NEUCHÂTEL

West of Morat, lying in the shadow of the rugged Jura range, is the large Lac de Neuchâtel, whose shores boast an eclectic range of historic sites including more Roman settlements. Halfway down the lake's eastern side, in **Estavayer-le-Lac ❼**, is the 14th-century **Château de Chenaux**. Although the home is now in private hands, you can stop by for a look and to visit the dungeon. The town also has a bizarre **Musée des Grenouilles** (Frog Museum; tel: 026 664 80 65; www.museedesgrenouilles.ch; Mar–Oct Tues–Sun 10am–noon and 2–5pm, Nov–Feb Sat and Sun 2–5pm), with a collection of 108 stuffed amphibians arranged in scenes portraying daily 19th-century life from political dinners to schoolrooms.

At the lake's southern tip lies **Yverdon-les-Bains ❽**, a small industrial town with thermal baths fed by sulphur springs. Between 1805 and 1823, the famous teacher Heinrich Pestalozzi ran his world-renowned education institute from the Savoy

Murten's Old Town beside Lac de Morat.

castle here. Today, Le Château houses the **regional museum** (tel: 024 425 93 10; Tues–Sun, June–Sept 10am–noon and 2–5pm, Oct–May 2–5pm), which includes prehistoric items recovered from Lac de Neuchâtel.

Another castle awaits just to the north in the historic town of **Grandson ❾**, where the Confederate army defeated Charles the Bold of Burgundy in 1476. The mighty **Château de Grandson** (tel: 024 445 29 26; www.chateau-grandson.ch; daily 8am–5pm) is a repository of ancient armour, crossbows and other weapons, as well as vintage cars. No less fascinating a building is the Romanesque church of **St John the Baptist**.

Further up the west bank of Lac de Neuchâtel, beyond the centre of **Concise ❿**, lies the Roman quarry of **La Lance**. Wooden stakes were once hammered into the unworked limestone and soaked with water until they cracked the rock, and traces of this technique can be clearly seen today. Ships would then transport the stone across the lake to **Yverdon** (*Eburodunum*) or via the Broye over to the Helvetian capital of *Aventicum*, today's Avenches.

To see what are heralded as the most beautiful Roman mosaics in the northern Alps, head to the **Boscéaz** site, part of the town of **Orbe ⓫**, about 15km (9 miles) south of Lake Neuchâtel. The figurative and geometric motifs once decorated the floors of a 35-room Gallo-Roman villa dating to the 2nd century AD (tel: 024 442 92 37; June–Sept Sat–Sun 10am–6pm).

LA SARRAZ

Located strategically between lakes Léman/Geneva and Neuchâtel is the small town of **La Sarraz ⓬**. The name La Sarraz is presumed to come from the Latin *serrata*, meaning saw-shape: the road here squeezes its way tightly between the mountains and hills. Up on a rocky knoll, nearly 1,000 years ago, the lords of Grandson built a castle, from which they could supervise this route. One of their descendants turned the **Château de La Sarraz** into a museum in

Estavayer-le-Lac and the Château de Chenaux.

⊙ Fact

Vacherin Mont d'Or, one of Switzerland's most popular cheeses, available only in the winter months, takes its name from the Mont d'Or, overlooking Vallorbe.

1911; on his death, his widow made it a centre where people in the arts could meet and find inspiration. She invited Russian film director Sergei Eisenstein, German painter Max Ernst and Swiss-French architect Le Corbusier to the castle, organised an architects' conference and, in 1929, hosted the first congress of independent film makers. Reopened in 2017 after a three-year renovation, the Château currently shows impressive furniture and painting collections (tel: 021 866 64 23; www.chateau-lasarraz.ch; June–Oct Wed–Fri 1–5pm, weekends 11am–5pm). The castle stables house an interesting Horse Museum, **la Musée du Cheval** (June–Aug Tues–Sun 1–5pm, Apr–May, Sept–Oct weekends only 1–5pm).

Near the castle there is a Gothic **chapel**, containing the tomb of Franz of La Sarraz, on which his decaying corpse has been rendered in stone. It is a very graphic depiction of the transition from this world to the next: worms are crawling through the body and the face and genitals are hidden by toads.

THE CANAL OF LA SARRAZ

In the 17th century, La Sarraz Pass was chosen to become a major European traffic route, part of a canal linking the North Sea and the Mediterranean. The idea behind the scheme was to provide The Netherlands with an easy route to India, avoiding not only the Straits of Gibraltar but also their Spanish enemies and the Moorish pirates who plagued the North African coast. Canals already led through Belgium and the County of Burgundy, both under Spanish control.

Elie Gouret, a British Huguenot in the service of the Dutch, handed the council in Bern a memorandum with the plans of the ship canal and most of the capital he needed. He also brought with him technicians and carpenters to build the sluices and boats. The plan was to connect Yverdon, on Lac de Neuchâtel, with Lac Léman/Lake Geneva. After two years' labour, construction workers reached **Entreroches**. There, they built a harbour and a harbourmaster's house, which can still be seen today. Eight years later, they had got as far as **Cossonay**.

It was at this point that they ran out of money, and the dream of a trans-European canal through Switzerland was shelved. Yet stretches of the canal were used right up to the 19th century. Ships with wine, salt and grain (the Vaud trinity) travelled via the Canal d'Entreroches into Lac de Neuchâtel, and then via the Zihl and the Aare up to Solothurn. Still today it is easy to make out sections of the old waterway. From the station at Eclépens a signpost points the way to the **Canal d'Entreroches**. In a beech and oak forest lies a ravine between some limestone rocks. The deep trench between Cyclopean walls is the ship canal.

THE VAUD JURA

Vallorbe ⑬, a strategic border town located 21km (13 miles) west of La Sarraz on Autoroute 9, is the gateway to

Swiss flag in La Sarraz.

Vaud's section of the vast Jura Mountains. One of the town's top attractions is the **Musée du Chemin de Fer** (Iron and Railway Museum; tel: 021 843 25 83; www.museedufer.ch; Mar–Oct Tues–Sun 10am–6pm, Mon 2–6pm, Nov–Feb Tues–Fri 10am–noon and 2–6pm), housed in the riverside **Grandes-Forges** building. International TGV rail traffic speeds through here from Paris via Lausanne to the south of France or Italy via the Simplon Pass. The **River Orbe**, which once provided power for mills, has its source at the top of La Dôle, the second-highest mountain in the Jura.

The **Dôle** (1,677 metres/5,502ft) is one of the cornerstone peaks of the Jura, where there is a weather station that serves all of western Switzerland. Tourists, however, tend to prefer the **Col du Marchairuz** (1,447 metres/4,747ft), just south of Le Brassus, which has Nordic skiing runs. A pass road leads over the Marchairuz from Lac Léman/Lake Geneva into the Jura. Here, at the end of a long and tiring hike, you can relax in a natural paradise, the huge (40 sq km/15 sq miles) and many-faceted **Parc Jura Vaudois** (Jura Vaudois Nature Park), which stretches south as far as the Col de la Givrine. The park has a 523km (325-mile) network of well-signposted trails. Along the way you might stop and savour some Alpine Gruyère AOC cheese, which is made using traditional methods in many of the mountain huts.

To the north, the River Orbe forms the **Lac de Joux**, an elevated basin hemmed in by **Mont Tendre** (1,679 metres/5,508ft) on one side, and the wooded crest of the Jura's **Mount Risoux** on the other, along whose ridge runs the Swiss-French border. The Jura's biggest lake is popular for windsurfing and yachting, rowing and swimming. The short 2.5km (1.5-mile) nature trail from Le Brassus at the lower (northwestern) tip of the lake leads into one of Europe's largest forests: the Grand Risoux, renowned for its tonewoods, used to manufacture premium violins and guitars, and its diverse fauna and flora, pointed out with information panels.

About 20 minutes' drive to the northeast are the **Grottes de Vallorbe** caves (1 Chemin de la Résurgence; tel: 021 843 22 74; grottesdevallorbe.ch; daily Mar and Nov 1.30–4pm, Apr–May and Sept–Oct 9.30am–4.30pm, June–Aug 9.30am–5.30pm), particularly famous for their stalactites.

MEDIEVAL BROYE

Finally, returning north again to the Broye Valley (the main route from Lausanne to Bern) there are a clutch of picturesque medieval towns: **Moudon** ⑭ has a delightful old quarter; **Lucens** ⑮, with its château and its Sherlock Holmes Museum (see page 130); and **Payerne** ⑯, which has a Romanesque **abbey** and a parish church with the tomb of the legendary Burgundian queen, Bertha. On a hill east of Lucens, lies **Romont**, whose château contains a museum of stained glass.

A chamois in the Parc Jura Vaudois.

☉ THE SONG OF SWITZERLAND

As in German-speaking Switzerland, a rich cow-herding culture developed in the western Alpine foothills, producing a long-standing tradition of folk music. The cowherd's melody became known as the Song of the Swiss and became famous around the world. The song with the dialect refrain "Lioba, lioba, por ario" recalls the Poya, driving the cattle up to the Alpine pastures.

It is supposed to be so evocative of life on the Alps that in former days it provoked an uncontrollable feeling of homesickness in Swiss mercenaries. So strong was their nostalgia on hearing the song that they would burst into tears. In 1621, a minister of the King of France is said to have banned Swiss mercenaries serving in France from singing the cowherd's melody. But the melody proved so popular that it found its way into operas and operettas, which were performed across Europe and the United States throughout the 19th and 20th centuries.

Today, there are innumerable arrangements and piano renditions, libretti and arias containing the cowherd's melody. They all sing the praises of the rural Switzerland that the homesick mercenaries longed for, a way of life that in today's Switzerland is best summed up by picturesque Swiss dairy towns such as Gruyères.

Sea horse sculpture in Vevey on Lake Geneva.

LAKE GENEVA

Known to the French as Lac Léman, this is one of the most famous lakes in the world, instantly recognisable for the soaring Jet d'Eau fountain on its banks and, of course, its lakeshore mansions.

The train journey from Zürich and Bern towards Geneva rewards travellers with a stunning view of the vast, light-blue expanse of **Lake Geneva** – and the mountains surrounding it – as they emerge from a tunnel just before Lausanne. The sloping vineyard next to the railway line here is jokingly referred to as the "Clos des Billets", for Swiss-Germans overcome by the beauty of the landscape reputedly fling their return tickets (*billets*) out of the train windows. While a likely exaggeration, ever since the days when English poet Lord Byron and his romantic compatriots sang the praises of the region, guests have been arriving en masse.

The French name Lac Léman derives from the Roman Lacus Lemanus, first referred to in the 1st-century BC *Commentaries* of Julius Caesar. One legend attributes its origins to Lemanus, son of Trojan prince Paris (who started the Trojan War by abducting the beautiful Helen), who conquered the area and named the lake after himself. Others say it pre-dates the Romans and owes its name to the Celts, for whom it meant "water between the mountains". Yet another version says the Greeks for centuries called it "limnê" – lake – which the Gallo-Romans transformed to Lemanus.

The Romans also transformed the area by introducing vines. Later on,

Christian monks took over from them, and cultivated the slopes by the lake.

The perfect spot for vines, Geneva is the third-largest wine-producing canton in Switzerland after the Valais and Vaud. It is said that the steep vineyards of Lavaux on the northern shores of Lake Geneva, between Lausanne and Montreux, benefit from the sun's rays in three ways: when it shines from the sky, when it reflects off the lake, and at night-time when its warmth, absorbed during the day, radiates from the vineyard walls.

Main Attractions

Cathédrale Saint-Pierre
Patek Phillipe Museum
Jet d'Eau
The Palais des Nations
Museé Olympique
 Lausanne
Chaplin's World
Château de Chillon

Maps on pages 150, 158

Lake Geneva steamer.

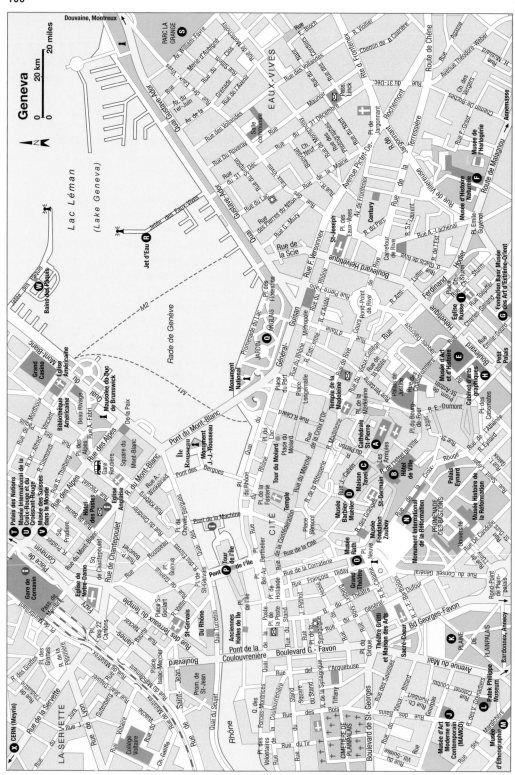

Along the Côte (north shore) between Lausanne and Geneva the vineyards form a gentler slope.

WESTERN EUROPE'S LARGEST LAKE

The largest of the Swiss lakes, croissant-shaped Lake Geneva is 72km (45 miles) long, 13.5km (8.5 miles) at its widest point and 310 metres (1,000ft) at its deepest. Its total surface area is a staggering 582 sq km (225 sq miles); 348 sq km (134 sq miles) of that belong to Switzerland, the rest to France. Lake Geneva, which contains 89 billion cubic metres (3,143 billion cubic feet) of water, is the largest freshwater reservoir in Europe, with twice as much water as Lake Constance, six times that of Lake Neuchâtel and 22 times the capacity of Lake Zürich.

Within its 167km (104-mile) coastline, Lake Geneva is divided into three zones: the narrowest being Petit-lac between Geneva and Nyon; the Grand lac from Lausanne across to Évian-les-Bains in France; and the upper Haut-lac, around Vevey and Montreux in the east. The Rhône, which supplies the bulk of its water, joins the lake here at Villeneuve. The second major source is the Dranse, on the French side, near Thonon-les-Bains.

It was in 1823 that the steamer *William Tell*, belonging to an American named Church, first crossed the lake (initially horrifying many of the locals, who thought it was an invention of the devil). Traditionally, freighters with lateen sails were used to bring construction material for the two towns across the lake from Meillerie (Savoy). Unfortunately, there are only two remaining examples of such vessels, the *Vaudoise* in Lausanne and the *Neptune* in Geneva, but it is still possible to experience something of the flavour of lake travel in the early days: paddle steamers take passengers over to the French side of the lake, to Evian-les-Bains (with its casino, Olympic-size swimming pool and a mineral-water

source) and Thonon-les-Bains. There are also regular sailings to the flower-bedecked French village of Yvoire and the Château of Chillon, on the Swiss side, as well as a selection of half- or full-day round trips.

Geneva ❶ (Genève/Genf; city pop. 202,000; canton pop. 493,000) has an international airport from which it takes only 6 minutes to reach the centre of the city. Yet it really needs to be approached from the lake, ideally on an old-fashioned steamer, to appreciate its magnificent location: nestled among hills and gardens, surrounded by mountain ranges and cradling its broad harbour "La Rade". A superb fountain spouts heavenwards at the mouth of La Rade – the Jet d'Eau.

In its proud history, the city-republic of Geneva has never laid claim to any other regions, which isn't to say that gains of a different kind are not highly desirable. Indeed, money has great importance here. The British actor Robert Morley described Geneva as "this city of wealth by stealth", and there is no doubting the pioneering role

Swimming deck near the city of Rolle, Lake Geneva.

Geneva has played in the creation of the capitalist credit system. Lausanne-born writer Charles-Ferdinand Ramuz concluded towards the mid-1900s: "Geneva based itself on abstract thinking quite early on; and trading and banking really are abstractions if one compares them to the concrete activity of farming." Nowhere else in Switzerland are arguments indulged in so eagerly, and words bandied about so assiduously as here in Geneva; nowhere else is there so much political discussion.

THE CITY-REPUBLIC

Geneva is a cosmopolitan city of great influence, profound thought and famous personalities. In the 16th century the reformer, Calvin, turned Geneva into a "Protestant Rome", the effects of which were felt worldwide. Two centuries on, in the city's "Golden Age", writer-philosopher Jean-Jacques Rousseau paved the way for human rights and the French Revolution. In the 19th century, engineer and Swiss army chief, Guillaume Henri Dufour, became a confederate peacemaker and helped to establish the Red Cross at the Geneva Convention in 1864. Alongside him – naturally – was Red Cross founder and co-recipient of the first Nobel Peace Prize, Henri Dunant, who made his home city headquarters of his organisation and elevated the Swiss flag – or at least an inverted form of it – into an international symbol of humanist ideals.

For centuries, the tiny city-state was surrounded by regions controlled by enemy princes – Savoy and France – and was completely cut off from the lands in the Confederation. The most important transport connection was across the lake. It was only at the Congress of Vienna of 1814–15 that the border came down and Geneva was finally provided with land access to Switzerland. The umbilical cord is slender: the canton's border with France is 102km (63 miles) long, while the boundary with the rest of Switzerland measures just 4km (2 miles).

The German magazine *Stern* once came to the conclusion that Geneva contained "more millionaires than unemployed people". Even Voltaire, who lived in Geneva and nearby Ferney (where his house is now a museum), remarked derisively that the city had "very little else to do but earn money". It is said that the older inhabitants of Geneva grew rich by saving their money. Geneva also has its poor, the victims of prosperity, but they do not make the headlines of the international press. Neither are they that visible, at least not in the places frequented by visitors.

AMERICAN LINKS

Since the Reformation the coat-of-arms has borne the inscription *Post tenebras lux* (light after darkness). The same words appeared on the title pages of the English Bibles printed in Geneva that the pilgrims took on the *Mayflower* (1620) to America. Calvin's teachings had a worldwide effect: American president Woodrow Wilson, a Calvinist,

Rue du Marché, Geneva.

suggested Geneva as the seat of the League of Nations after World War I.

Geneva makes a great show of championing freedom. In December every year the city celebrates the "Escalade", commemorating the Duke of Savoy's vain attempt to capture the city in 1602. His troops used ladders to climb the city walls but were repelled by the population. In the 19th century, Geneva bankers financed the Greeks' struggle for freedom.

SIGHTS AND MUSEUMS

The centre of Geneva's Old Town, *Vieille-Ville*, sits on a small rise on the left bank of the Rhône. Here you will find the cathedral, the Town Hall, shopping streets and excellent museums. International Geneva – the Palais des Nations, the International Labour Organisation, the International Committee of the Red Cross and other institutes – lies on the right bank. Magnificent parks line the edge of the lake.

A good place to begin a walking tour of the city centre is at the Place de la Taconnerie, whose centrepiece

Cathédrale Saint-Pierre (tel: 022 311 75 75; June–Sept Mon–Sat 9.30am–6.30pm, Sun noon–6.30pm, Oct–May Mon–Sat 10am–5.30pm, Sun noon–5.30pm; free but fee to climb the South Tower) was built between 1160 and 1252 but sports an 18th-century neoclassical west facade.

Protestant since 1536, the church is where John Calvin (1509–64) famously preached. It also has an impressive **archaeological site** (tel: 022 311 75 74; daily 10am–5pm) displaying mosaics, artefacts, sculptures, tiles and other remnants of former churches that have stood here, including a monk's cell and Roman crypt. The excellent, high-tech presentation includes reconstructed models and audio-visual "spectacles" to illustrate the former churches, dating to the 4th century BC. In a 13th-century Gothic side chapel on Rue Guillaume-Farel, the **Auditoire de Calvin**, you can see the triangular stool where Calvin apparently used to sit, just next to the Pulpit, while preaching his historic Protestant reforms. Around the corner is the **Musée Historique de la Réformation**.

Geneva's Cathédral Saint-Pierre.

A couple of minutes' walk away is the grand 15th-century **Hôtel de Ville** (City Hall; free), also home to the Canton executives. Behind its Renaissance facade, added in the early 1600s, the first Geneva Convention was signed in 1864 – an international treaty to bring wartime relief to injured soldiers. Until the 1930s when the Palais des Nations building was finished, this was the place to hammer out international decisions. From its arched courtyard, the "monumental ramp" – a cobbled spiral staircase – leads upstairs; 17th-century statesmen used to mount it on horseback.

It was outside the City Hall in 1762 that the public executioner burnt Rousseau's polemical novel on education, *Emile*, condemned as "reckless, scandalous, impious and heretic", forcing him to flee Geneva.

Back towards the cathedral, at Rue du Puits-Saint-Pierre 6, is the **Maison Tavel** , the oldest house in the city, originally built in the 13th century but destroyed by fire and rebuilt in 1334. Inside at the **Musée du Vieux Genève**

View from the Cathédral Saint-Pierre over Geneva and the Jet d'Eau.

(tel: 022 418 37 00; daily 10am–5pm; free, except for temporary exhibitions), visitors can learn about the city's fascinating history through a variety of (mostly medieval) artefacts, multimedia displays, and a 3D map of 19th-century Geneva, still within its city walls.

A few steps further north bring you to the **Musée Barbier-Mueller** (10 Rue Jean-Calvin; tel: 022 312 02 70; www.barbier-mueller.ch; daily 11am–5pm), an important private collection of tribal and classical artefacts, art, sculpture, fabrics and ornaments from different civilisations.

Heading southeast of the cathedral quadrant, you will come to the fountained **Place du Bourg-de-Four**, the city's oldest square and a lively shopping and dining district, flanked by tall houses, café terraces and the walls of the law courts, the Palais de Justice.

Just to the east of here is the city's largest art museum, **Musée d'Art et d'Histoire** at Rue Charles-Galland 2 (tel: 022 418 26 00; Tues–Sun 11am–6pm). Among its 7,000 exhibits is the famous 1444 altar painting *The*

Miraculous Draught of Fishes by Konrad Witz, depicting Christ on Lake Geneva with Mont Blanc in the background. As well as important collections of fine art, ranging from the Middle Ages to the 20th century – including Ferdinand Hodler, Félix Vallotton and Jean-Baptiste Camille Corot – the museum has an interesting Egyptology section.

About 10 minutes' walk further east, beyond the Old Town, is the well laid-out **Musée d'Histoire Naturelle**  (Route de Malagnou 1; tel: 022 418 63 00); Tues–Sun 10am–5pm; free). This museum has permanent displays on regional fauna and animals of the world, an interactive palaeontology exhibition and a zoology collection with 15 million specimens.

Working your way back to the Old Town, drop by the **Fondation Baur Musée des Arts d'Extrême-Orient**  (Museum of Far Eastern Art; Rue Munier-Romilly 8; tel: 022 704 32 82; www.fondation-baur.ch; Tues–Sun 2–6pm) to view a fascinating private collection of Chinese and Japanese art gathered in the 1920s and 30s by fertiliser tycoon Alfred Baur. Less than five minutes' walk away, at Promenade du Pin 5, is the **Cabinet d'arts graphiques**  (tel: 022 418 27 70; Tues–Sun 11am–6pm; free) – a precious collection of some 375,000 drawings, pastels and prints, which is part of the Musée d'Art et d'Histoire. It houses one of the largest assemblies of art by Ferdinand Hodler, the world's biggest collection of works by Jean-Étienne Liotard and an invaluable set of prints by Félix Vallotton, John M Armleder and Hans Hartung.

Also nearby is the domed **Église Russe** , at the end of rues Lefort and François d'Ivernois, more interesting from outside than inside due to its nine gilded domes.

If you still have an appetite for art, head west to the **Musée d'Art Moderne et Contemporain**  (MAMCO; Rue des Vieux-Grenadiers 10; tel: 022 320 61 22; www.mamco.ch; Tues–Fri noon–6pm, Sat–Sun 11am–6pm). MAMCO has many fine examples of late 20th-century art displayed in a stark modern building which was once a physics laboratory. Tram lines 12 or 15 will get you there,

alighting at **Plaine de Plainpalais** Ⓚ (the stop is officially called Plainpalais). This fine plaza is the site of an outdoor flea market on Wednesdays and Saturdays, as well as a farmers' market on Tuesdays, Fridays and Saturdays. It also has a skatepark, roundabouts and rollercoasters, and has become a bit of a nightlife hub for a young crowd over recent years. You will also find free Wi-Fi, lots of park benches and picnicking tables, bike lockers, grocery stores, and plenty of cafés, restaurants, pubs and takeaway food outlets nearby.

Neighbouring MAMCO is the **Patek Philippe Museum** Ⓛ (Rue des Vieux-Grenadiers 7; tel: 022 807 09 10; www.patekmuseum.com; Tues–Fri 2–6pm, Sat 10am–6pm), a watchmaking timeline from antique Genevese, Swiss and European creations of the 1500s to the company's own gold-lined, bejeweled and mechanical masterpieces produced since its founding in 1839. Showcased in a four-floor industrial Art Deco building, the man behind it is Philippe Stern, whose family have owned and operated Patek Philippe for

80 years, and for whom watchmaking is a consuming passion.

A couple of blocks south, at Boulevard Carl-Vogt 65, is the **Musée d'Éthnographie** Ⓜ (MEG; tel: 022 418 45 50; Tues–Sun 11am–6pm), recipient of the 2017 European Museum of the Year Award. Its permanent exhibition, "The Archives of Human Diversity", includes 1,000 global cultural artefacts – from a collection of 80,000.

PARC DES BASTIONS TO THE LAKE

If you fancy relaxing in a park for a while, head east and cross through the Plaine de Plainpalais, and continue back towards the old quarter. Within ten minutes you will come to the **Parc des Bastions** and its **Monument International de la Réformation** Ⓝ (Reformation Wall), a tall and long stone wall erected in 1917 and incised with the images of the leading members of the Reformation: Farel, Calvin, de Bèze and Knox. It stretches nearly 100 metres (330ft) and commemorates the key historic events of the Reformation.

Displays at the Musée d'Éthnographie.

A few paces to the north, on Place Neuve, is the little Greek temple-like **Musée Rath** (tel: 022 418 33 40; Tues–Sun 11am–6pm), used for temporary exhibitions curated by the Musée d'Art et d'Histoire about three times a year.

Continuing north up Rue de la Corraterie you will arrive at the **Pont de l'Île** ⓟ. This bridge spans the two riverbanks across a little island on the Rhône. A plaque commemorates the bridge's destruction by Julius Caesar in 58 BC. Later the bridge was rebuilt and the city became a major European trading centre; it was once the site of the only checkpoint on the route linking northern and southern Europe. The **Tour de l'Île** tower is all that remains of a 13th-century fort that once stood here. Visitors crossing to the north bank, Rive Droite, will discover some good restaurants around the Place de l'Ile, on the nose of the island, and around its girth of quais, de l'Ile and des Moulins.

For now, stay on the southern Rive Gauche instead. It is less than 1km (0.5 miles) to the lakeside **Jardin Anglais** ⓠ, Geneva's largest park and the unofficial gathering place for everyone from disaffected youth to the well-to-do on lunch breaks. This is also the spot to catch the CGN steamer for scenic rides around the lake and even to France. From the park, you get an especially close view of the gushing **Jet d'Eau** ⓡ. The original fountain was designed in 1886 as a safety feature to reduce pressure on the city's water system. Its touristic potential was subsequently seized upon and today it jets up to 140 metres (460ft) high, at a force of around 200kph (120 mph).

To visit another park, continue east to the **Parc la Grange** ⓢ (Apr–May and Sept–Oct 7am–9pm, June–Aug 6am–10pm, Nov–Mar 7am–6pm), the biggest and arguably most beautiful of the city's parks and gardens, built on the site of a Roman settlement dating to 50–60 AD. Pivoting around a geometric rose garden brimming with some 200 varieties and 10,000 flowers, the park has two theatres; the Théâtre de Verdure (nicknamed the Ella Fitzgerald stage) gives over to regular free summer concerts during the July–August festival, Musiques en été. Unusually, the park closes at night.

You can cross the lake to the Rive Droite at two main points: via the busy **Pont du Mont-Blanc** or the more delightful little **Pont des Bergues**, which falls onto Île Rousseau with its statue of the philosopher. From here it's a serious hike (of over 40 minutes) to get to the hub of Geneva's international community and political life. In half that time, Tram 8 will get you from the Mont-Blanc stop (just over the Pont du Mont-Blanc) to the **Palais des Nations** ⓣ (14 Avenue de la Paix; tel: 022 917 48 96; tours only Apr–Aug Mon–Sat 10am–noon and 2–4pm, Sept–Mar weekdays only; passport required). Inaugurated in 1936 as the headquarters of the League of Nations, three decades later it became the European headquarters of the United Nations.

Parc la Grange.

The Broken Chair Sculpture at the Place des Nations.

The Palais sprouts up from the 46-hectare (113-acre) **Ariana Park**. These immense gardens contain all kinds of areas – pretty, prestigious and wild – with populations of peacocks and sheep, several villas, 100-year-old-trees and a total of 800 plant species. It's more a nature reserve than a garden.

A few steps away, at Avenue de la Paix 17, the **Musée International de la Croix-Rouge et du Croissant-Rouge** (International Red Cross and Red Crescent Museum; tel: 022 748 95 11; www.redcrossmuseum.ch; Tues–Sun Apr–Oct 10am–6pm, Nov–Mar until 5pm) houses some of the city's most moving displays. The museum is dedicated to human compassion and suffering, highlighting some of history's greatest tragedies – and heroes – through the use of photographs, video footage, a reconstructed cell used to hold prisoners of war, and other exhibits.

Have a walk around this esteemed area, with its ensemble of elegant gardens and spacious squares. On its western side in the Place des Nations is the monumental **Broken Chair**

Sculpture, an Alice in Wonderland-scale chair 12-metres (nearly 40ft) high, by sculptor Daniel Berset. It was installed here in 1997 by Handicap International in a call for all nations to sign the Ottowa treaty for the banning of landmines. It symbolically stands on just three legs, dignified nonetheless, and almost as tall as the classical columns on the building behind it.

The handsome **Penthes de Château**, in a magnificent park nearby, houses the **Musée des Suisses dans le Monde** (Museum of the Swiss Abroad; Chemin de l'Impératrice 18; tel: 022 734 90 21; www.penthes.ch; Tues–Sun 1–6pm), with military memorabilia and cultural artefacts that recall the history of the Swiss who left the country to find their fortune and sometimes their death too: "Pas d'argent, pas de Suisses" (no money, no Swiss), was a popular saying during the days when the Swiss fought in foreign wars as mercenaries.

In the heat of summer, if you feel like taking a dip, or submitting to a hammam, Turkish bath or massage, head

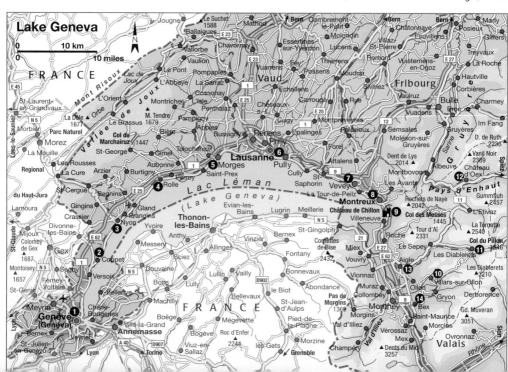

back towards the northern shores of the lake, and do so at the public baths, **Bains des Pâquis ⓦ**, at Quai du Mont-Blanc 30. On a jetty sticking into the lake, the 1930s baths are a lively and cultured meeting place with free classical music and a host of other activities.

Finally, for something different, take Tram 18 west from Geneva Cornavin train station to **CERN ⓧ** (European Laboratory for Particle Physics; tel: 022 767 76 76; call ahead to join guided tours Mon–Sat 11am–1pm and 1–3pm, in summer possible additional tours 8.45–10.45am and 3–5pm; free) and its big golden globe building, located in Meyrin. It has the world's largest ring tunnel (Large Electron Positron Storage Ring; 27km/17 miles long), used to explore matter. Using this in 1996, scientists at CERN made history as the first people to create antimatter.

THE VILLAGES ON LAKE GENEVA

The countryside around Lake Geneva's northern lakeshore, La Côte, is dotted with pretty, historic villages. Vineyards dominate this area, producing the popular wines of the Vaud.

One of the highlights of La Côte is **Coppet ❷**, about 14km (8 miles) north of Geneva, and its magnificent dusty-pink 18th-century **château** (rue de la Gare 2; tel: 022 776 10 28; www.chateaudecoppet.com; Apr–Nov daily 2–6pm; 45-minute guided tours). The Château de Coppet was originally owned by Geneva banker Jacques Necker, whose daughter Germaine de Staël (1766–1817) was one of the most important figures in European intellectual and literary life. The Baron of Coppet, Louis XVI's Minister of Finance, married off his daughter to Sweden's ambassador in Paris, the Baron of Staël-Holstein. First an admirer, later a critic, of Napoleon, she was forced into exile in Switzerland by Bonaparte. The leading minds of the age used to meet in the Château de Coppet. Madame de Staël's autobiographical novels are as striking today as they were then in their advocacy of women's emancipation, and her political tracts such as *De l'Allemagne* are pleas for European reconciliation.

> **⊙ Tip**
>
> For one of the best views over the lake and Canton Geneva, head to Mont Salève in France, which Geneva claims as its own. Spend a day hiking there and back, or take Train no. 8 to the border at Veyrier-Pas-de-l'Échelle and walk or cable car (www.telepherique-du-saleve.com) from there. On a clear day you can see all the way to Mont Blanc.

Coppet's pier encased in ice.

🔍 HOME OF THE UN

International Geneva is like a city-state all to itself, thanks largely to the United Nations' offices.

The UN's offices in Geneva are located at the Palais des Nations (guided tours daily) – a workplace for 3,500 international civil servants – which has its own postal service as well as its own stamps, just like Monaco, Liechtenstein or the Vatican. Larger than the Palais de Versailles, it is also the leading congress centre in the world, with more than 8,500 meetings every year.

The 40-plus international organisations provide some 22,000 jobs; the diplomats and civil servants (numbering over 30,000 including their families) live tax-free, admittedly, but they also spend over 1.2 billion Swiss francs a year in Geneva, thus providing a catalyst for the city's prosperity. More than 170 countries, including Switzerland itself, have diplomatic missions in Geneva; the Swiss Embassy in Geneva represents the country in the various international organisations.

Geneva's rise as a famous conference centre began in 1871: a court of arbitration was held in the Town Hall

The well-kempt Palais des Nations.

during the row about the sinking of the battle cruiser *Alabama* in the American Civil War. On the first centenary of American independence in 1876, in memory of the arbitration award, US officers handed in their swords, the metal of which was recast into the form of a ploughshare; it can be seen in the "Salle Alabama" in the Town Hall. Geneva's international mission, however, dates back to Calvin and his "Protestant Rome".

Geneva's big moment came in 1919, when it was chosen as the seat of the League of Nations. With the advent of World War II the International Labour Organisation moved to Montreal and New York was chosen as the seat of the United Nations, and it was only thanks to the efforts made by several diplomats that Geneva became the European seat of the UN. Then a whole series of organisations started moving to Geneva: the UN possesses several special institutions, including 14 intergovernmental and 108 non-governmental organisations, and it is now considered the done thing for organisations' headquarters to be based in Geneva. Cardiologists, university chancellors, the World Council of Churches, the Women's League for Peace and Freedom, the World Wildlife Fund, the YMCA and the Boy Scouts all have a base here.

Scarcely any other city in the world receives so many visits from foreign heads of state. Geneva has been the scene of many historically important conferences:

1954: The Indo-China conference ended France's intervention and decided, fatefully, on the division of Vietnam.

1955: The Big Four summit: Eisenhower (USA), Bulganin (USSR), Eden (Britain) and Faure (France). The first meeting of The Conference for the Peaceful Use of Atomic Energy.

1983: Conference on Palestine.

1985: Summit meeting between Ronald Reagan (USA) and Mikhail Gorbachev (USSR) paved the way for the arms reduction agreements and the end of the Cold War.

2003: Unofficial peace proposal, the Geneva Accord, launched in an attempt to resolve the Israeli-Palestinian conflict.

2017: UN engagement in political talks between Syrian government and opposition leaders to try to forge a peace agreement.

Further along the shore 9km (6 miles) north of Coppet is another delightful little town, **Nyon** ❸, originally a Helvetian settlement named Noviodunum, then a Roman fortified town founded by Julius Caesar, Colonia Iulia Equestris. On Rue Maupertuis, at No. 9, is the **Musée Romain** (tel: 022 316 42 80; www. mrn.ch; Tues–Sun, Apr–Oct 10am–5pm, Nov–Mar 2–5pm). Housed in the ruins of an ancient basilica, behind a bright strawberry-red facade, it documents life in the town during Roman times. The museum is also behind many cultural events including Roman Days, and a biennial International Festival of Archaeology Films (www.fifan.ch), held over four days in March; the next is due to be held in 2019.

Note that a ticket to the Musée Romain also includes entry to Nyon's other two museums, valid for 12 months. The first of these is the **Musée du Léman** (Quai Louis-Bonnard; tel: 022 316 42 50; Tues–Sun Apr–Oct 10am–5pm, Nov–Mar 2–5pm), which has exhibits on the flora and fauna of Lake Geneva and an aquarium, as well as paintings, a display of steamships and other lake history.

With the same ticket you can enter the **Château de Nyon** (Place du Château; tel: 022 316 42 73; Tues–Sun Nov–Mar 2–5pm, Apr–Oct 10am–5pm), which shows hundreds of pieces of locally made porcelain, dating from 1781 to 1813. Once occupied by the Counts of Savoy, Bern's leaders ousted them and gave the turreted castle its current look in the late 1500s. After the Vaudois Revolution of 1798, the castle was bought by the City of Nyon in the newly created Canton of Vaud.

You can really feel the French presence at the 18th-century **Château de Prangins**, just to the west of Nyon. It has impressive French-style gardens constructed in the 1730s around a large courtyard and, for a while, it was home to Voltaire and Joseph Bonaparte. The castle houses part of the **Swiss National Museum** (tel: 058 469 38 90; www.nationalmuseum.ch; Tues–Sun 10am–5pm), a showcase of daily life and customs in the 18th and 19th centuries with various exhibitions and

Bird's-eye view of Nyon.

a replica kitchen garden of an 18th-century palace.

The attractive little town of **Rolle** ❹, situated on the lakeside about 11km (7 miles) beyond Nyon, developed around the 13th-century château (closed to the public) built by Savoy Count Amadeus V. The small offshore island called **Île de la Harpe** was created in 1835 from surplus earth during the construction of the harbour. On the island is an obelisk, a monument to Vaud freedom-fighter Frédéric César de la Harpe, who was also a tutor at the court of the Tsar.

Another 14km (9 miles) along the lakeshore road, the town of **Morges** ❺ also has a huge Savoyard fortress, Château de Morges, which houses the **Musée Militaire Vaudois** (tel: 021 316 09 90; www.chateau-morges.ch; July–Aug daily 10am–5pm, Mar–June and Sept–Dec 3 Tues–Fri 10am–noon, 1.30–5pm, Sat–Sun 1.30–5pm), the old arsenal, a collection of 10,000 lead soldiers and other remnants of war. The Château also hosts temporary exhibitions on a range of topics, such as the relationship between Audrey Hepburn and fashion

designer Hubert de Givenchy. The iconic actress lived near this medieval town from 1963 until her death in 1993, at her home in the hamlet of **Tolochenaz**.

At Grand-Rue 54, in Morges, the **Musée Alexis Forel** (tel: 021 801 26 47; www.museeforel.ch; Mar 17–Dec 5 Wed–Sun 2–6pm) is named after the artist, engraver and collector who lived here in the early 1900s and restored the 16th-century house, with its splendid Renaissance Hall and Italianate gardens. Today it contains collections of furniture, dolls and tapestries.

A little further around the lake, just 3km (2 miles) before Lausanne, **St Sulpice** has a lakeside Romanesque church originally constructed in the 11th century and rebuilt a century later; it is now the site of summertime concerts.

COSMOPOLITAN AND RURAL MIX

Before you arrive in the centre of **Lausanne** ❻, the capital of Vaud canton, you might like to start your visit where Lausanne itself started: at the Roman

Football sculpture in the Musée Olympique garden.

settlement of Lousonna. Near the lake in the district of Vidy, the **Musée Romain de Lausanne-Vidy** (Chemin du Bois-de-Vaux 24; tel: 021 315 41 85; July–Aug daily 11am–6pm, Tues–Sun rest of year) sits on the former site of one of Lousonna's grandest villas. It explains Roman life through archeological finds, models and reconstructions. In the lakeside parklands opposite is the Château de Vidy, the seat of the International Olympic Committee. The Promenade Archéologique de Vidy leads about 1km (0.6 miles) east past ruins of the Roman forum, temple and harbor wall to the **Port de Vidy**, the actual site of the Gallo-Roman merchant port in the late 1st century AD, which had important links with other Roman towns on the lake, such as present-day Geneva, Nyon and Villeneuve.

A decent walk eastwards along the lake will take you to the Quai d'Ouchy and the Parc Olympique. Within it, the **Musée Olympique** (tel: 021 621 65 11; www.olympic.org; mid-Apr–mid-Oct daily 9am–6pm, Nov–Mar Tues–Sun 10am–6pm) has a lively programme, with special exhibitions as well as those on the Games' history and golden moments, told through archive material and multimedia displays. The grand views, good food and fun activities (for the young and old alike) make it a rewarding stop.

Also in parkland near the waterfront is the **Musée de l'Elysée** (tel: 021 316 99 11; Tues–Sun 11am–6pm, Thur until 9pm). Dedicated to photography, this museum is worth a visit for its stunning visiting exhibitions.

Beyond it is the port-resort of the former fishing village of **Ouchy**, Lausanne's harbour, which bustles with boating, windsurfing, bathing and other sports during the daytime, then pulses at night with revellers in a string of bars and dance clubs. Sunset is wonderful here, as is the view of the distant twinkling lights across the lake.

Down by the pier, the *embarcadère*, where steamers have been mooring since 1823, is a drinking fountain decorated with three donkeys' heads. The inscription, *En souvenir de l'Académie d'Ouchy*, honours the donkeys and pack mules that carried stone blocks, sand and other construction material from the freighters up to town. As the animals and their guides made their way through the vineyards, townspeople shouted in jest, *"Voilà l'Académie d'Ouchy!"* in mocking reference to the professors who went in a similar procession through Lausanne.

The rack railway is somewhat ambitiously referred to as the Métro (the former funicular is still popularly referred to as *la ficelle*, the string), but another way up to the **Cathédrale de Notre-Dame** (tel: 021 316 71 61; daily Apr–Sept 9am–7pm, Oct–Mar until 5.30pm) in the Old Town is on foot. It is not for the faint-hearted and the people of Lausanne are kept fit by all the stair climbing up the Escaliers du Marché required to reach the cathedral. Climb higher still, up the southwest tower, for a breathtaking view of the city.

Tip

Don't plan a visit to the Cathédrale Notre-Dame on a Sunday morning, unless you wish to attend the service.

Escaliers du Marché leads up to Lausanne's cathedral. Beware – it's a steep climb.

From 10 in the evening until two in the morning, just after the cathedral bell rings the hour, the voice of the night watchman up in the tower echoes through the vicinity as he announces the time like a foghorn in the dark: "Il a sonné douze" (it has struck 12). The cathedral itself, consecrated in 1275 in the presence of both the emperor and the Pope, is considered one of the most beautiful early-Gothic buildings in Switzerland.

Inside the cathedral, visitors can admire the stained glass of the **rose window**, which was built around 1240, the choir ambulatory and the elegant pillars. The last king of Burgundy, Rudolf III, was crowned here. A sarcophagus contains the mortal remains of Jean Abraham Davel, who tried to start a religious uprising against Bern in 1723 and was later executed.

To the north of the Old Town is an urban forest, the **Bois de Sauvabelin**, the upshot of an incredibly avant-garde stab at nature protection in 1888. Today, there's resident deer and an increasing return of wildlife. At its heart is a lake, and the Tour de Sauvabelin tower, a far more modern addition, where good views over hilly Lausanne can be had from its 35-metre (114ft) viewing deck.

Nearby, on Route du Signal, is the **Fondation de l'Hermitage** (tel: 021 320 50 01; www.fondation-hermitage.ch; Tues–Sun 10am–6pm, Thur until 9pm), an art gallery that has a fine permanent collection of Impressionist and post-Impressionist treasures and a varied schedule of temporary exhibitions.

Head west to Avenue des Bergières and the **Collection de l'Art Brut** (tel: 021 315 25 70; www.artbrut.ch; 11am–6pm, July–Aug daily, Sept–June Tues–Sun), well worth a visit for its fascinating and provocative collection of works by fringe artists. It is housed in the Château de Beaulieu, an 18th-century patrician's residence. French painter Jean Dubuffet coined the term Art Brut in the mid 1900s when he assembled a collection of objects created by the inmates of various psychiatric hospitals and prisons. In their creations, he saw "an entirely pure, raw artistic operation" fully reinvented

St Saphorin vineyards.

by the accidental artists through impulse and spontaneity.

If you visit Lausanne in September, look out for the 10-day food and wine fair known as Le Comptoir Suisse, held at the exhibition space of the Palais de Beaulieu. On top of the traditional activity of parading cattle and bulls around, today it is a far more modern occasion to show off the regional *terroir* and wines of the Vaud, and indulge in some delicious street food.

THE LAVAUX

Continuing east around Lake Geneva beyond Lausanne, the steeply pitched wine region of **Lavaux** comes into view. The picturesque villages and small towns of the region nestle among vineyards on the terraced slopes or down by the lake itself. In fact, to get to Vevey, there is a choice of two routes: either along the lake, or further up, along the side of the valley. In the two large wine-growing regions of La Côte and Lavaux, carefully plotted vineyard routes and hiking trails lead to winegrowers' cellars *(caveaux)* and village inns *(pintes)*. In the *caveaux*, whether in Mont-sur-Rolle, Aubonne or elsewhere, winegrowers will offer wine accompanied by *saucisson* (sausage) with pickled onions and cheese. In the village inns one can find delicious ham, sausage with cabbage *(saucisses aux choux)* and fresh trout from the lake, or – in Vinzel – *Malakoffs*, a kind of cheese doughnut made to a recipe said to have been brought back by veterans from the Crimean War.

VEVEY AND CHAPLIN'S WORLD

Lying some 20km (12 miles) around the lakeshore from Lausanne, the town of **Vevey ❼**, founded in the Middle Ages, is the base for wine-seeking trips and headquarters of the giant food corporation, Nestlé. On the waterfront is the Nestlé's food museum, **Alimentarium** (tel: 21 924 41 11; www.alimentarium. org; Tues–Sun Apr–Sept 10am–6pm,

Oct–Mar until 5pm) at Quai Perdonnet 25, an attractively laid out exploration into the theme of food and nutrition, with demonstrations, a junior academy, kitchen garden and café, which does wonders for their image. A visit to the **Musée Historique de Vevey** (tel: 021 925 51 64; Tues–Sun 11am–5pm) on Rue d'Italie, a charming town museum with a massive Bernese-style timber-frame roof, is also highly recommended.

The neighbouring town of **Corsier-sur-Vevey** contains the grave of Charlie Chaplin, where he lived for 25 years until his death in 1977. In 2016, after 15 years in the making, **Chaplin's World** (Route de Fenil 2; tel: 0842 422 422; www.chaplinsworld.com; daily 10am–6pm) opened here, dedicated to the London-born comedian and Hollywood icon. The museum is located on the vast Manoir de Ban estate where he lived with his wife Oona and their eight children. You can also get here by bus 212 from Lausanne (or boat to Vevey quay and then the bus), alighting at the Chaplin stop.

Exhibit in the Alimentarium.

Recreated scene from The Great Dictator at Chaplin's World.

In The Studio, an immersive experience allows you to teeter on the edge of a cliff in a cabin, as Chaplin did in *The Gold Rush*. It also contains replicas of giant machinery from his 1936 film *Modern Times*, iconic personal items such as his bowler hat and cane and various film costumes. Thirty wax figures created by the Grevin wax museum in Paris include film characters, colleagues and politicians: Gandhi and Churchill, Buster Keaton and Sophia Loren; and those inspired by him – Roberto Benigni, Federico Fellini and Michael Jackson.

To celebrate what would have been Charlie Chaplain's 128th birthday, more than 650 fans dressed as Charlie Chaplin's The Tramp character descended upon the museum.

From Vevey, you can hop aboard the *Train des Vignes* (vineyard train; www.lavauxexpress.ch) and voyage across the terraced vineyards of Lavaux above Lake Geneva, a World Heritage Site since 2007. It chugs along the Chemin des Vignes, starting near the cornice road then looping inland through several winegrowing towns such as Cully, cute St Saphorin – perhaps the most atmospheric of them all – Chardonne and Rivaz, before returning to Vevey. What started as a concerted effort by local winegrowers during the mid-1990s to boost tourism has borne fruit. In each town growers are on hand to sell their wares.

MONTREUX AND THE CHÂTEAU DE CHILLON

Back on the lakeshore, the journey continues to **Montreux** ❽, the world-famous spa. The climate here is exceptionally mild, as the palm trees and camellias lining the lake's promenade testify. The town draws people from all over the world. The busiest time to be here is during the annual jazz festival in July. Mountain cable railways lead to Caux, and to the Rochers de Naye – both have magnificent panoramic views of Lake Geneva.

The big attraction for most visitors is, without a doubt, the **Château de Chillon** ❾ (tel: 021 966 89 10; www.chillon.ch/en; daily Apr–Sept 9am–7pm, Oct and Mar 9.30am–6pm, Nov–Feb 10am–5pm). Fortified by the counts of Savoy and captured by Bern in 1536, beneath the château lies the underground dungeon of François de Bonivard, a lay prior from Geneva who was set free when the Bernese arrived. His story inspired swooning English Romantic poet, Lord Byron, to write *The Prisoner of Chillon* in Lausanne in 1816. The château is Switzerland's most visited monument. Perched on a tiny islet jutting into the lake, actually in Veytaux, 3km (2 miles) from Montreux, visitors can approach on foot by coastal trail, or by boat in the summer.

From Montreux, one splendid day-trip option is to take any of a number of narrow-gauge railway lines up the sharply ascending mountains overhanging the lake. Rail enthusiasts prefer the weekend steam train up to **Blonay**, while sightseers tend to go for the MOB

⊘ THE PRISONER OF CHILLON

The plight of François de Bonivard, who was imprisoned by the Duke of Savoy for several years in the 16th century at a rocky fortress on Lake Geneva, moved British poet Lord Byron (1788–1824) to immortalise him in *The Prisoner of Chillon* in 1816.

From 1530, Bonivard, who came from Saint Victor's priory in Geneva, was held in the dungeon of Château de Chillon and chained to a pillar for preaching about the Reformation against the explicit wishes of the duke. He was freed after the arrival of the occupying forces of the Bernese in 1536, who remained in Vaud until its independence in 1798.

Several other writers from the 19th-century Romantic era, such as Jean-Jacques Rousseau, Victor Hugo and Alexandre Dumas, wrote about the château. It is a spectacular structure, with lofty towers, subterranean vaults, courtyards, a striking chapel, many rooms full of beautiful furniture and frescoes on the walls and on the ceiling of the Great Hall.

Take a walk around the château independently, or join a guided tour available in eight languages. Visitors should allow at least a couple of hours to explore, and can even visit the dungeon where Bonivard was held.

(Montreux-Oberland-Bernois) railway (some trains have panoramic coaches) which climbs to the Les Avants ski area and offers excellent views back down over the lake. Really, any one of the lines brings you to superb meadow walking and inns serving hearty, rustic fare.

SKIING AND SALT MINES

The Vaud Alps contain a number of winter health spas, most notably **Villars-sur-Ollon** ❿ (an excellent hiking area in the summer) and **Les Diablerets** ⓫, a trés-chic resort area with a cable car leading up to the **Diablerets Glacier**, 2,940 metres (9,600ft) above sea level. There is also the **Château d'Oex** ⓬, a mountain cheese-dairy town. Less health-conscious visitors may prefer the winemaking centres along the Rhône Valley, such as **Aigle** ⓭ (a château with its own winemaking museum) and **Yvorne**. Most of the region – the town and dominions of Aigle (or Älen in German) – was captured by the city-republic of Bern in 1475 during the Burgundian wars and was the first French-speaking part of Switzerland.

Such towns became particularly valuable when salt was discovered in the region in the 16th century. The saltworks of **Bex** ⓮ (pronounced "bay") and Aigle are still in use today, contributing to the town's wealth. They provide the salt for the canton of Vaud and the chemical industry in Monthey, in the Valais.

Today the Bex Saltworks is a tourist attraction: visitors travel on a narrow-gauge railway through the tunnels, halls and corridors through which the brine (rock salt solution) is pumped out of the mountain. The salt deposits are estimated to amount to 10 million tonnes.

In the Middle Ages, salt was as important a natural resource as oil is today. An imperial decree bestowed on princes the right to manufacture salt (the so-called *Salzregal*), and Switzerland's cantons have had a virtual monopoly on the salt trade to this day. Before the salt deposits in Bex were discovered, the republic of Bern used to import its salt from Venice and from saltworks in the Franche Comté region of western France.

The romantic Château de Chillon.

The Zinalrothorn with the
Matterhorn behind.

THE VALAIS

This large, predominantly French-speaking canton in southwestern Switzerland has some of the country's best ski resorts, and is crowned by the mighty Matterhorn.

The name of the most mountainous region of Switzerland comes from the Latin word for valley; the Valais unfurls for about 130km (80 miles) along the River Rhône to Lake Geneva. Nestling in the chain formed by the Valaisan and Bernese Alps, it contains some 47 peaks over 4,000 metres (13,000ft). A landscape of stark contrasts, here you will encounter glaciers, mountain plateaus, vineyards and almond trees within a relatively small area, against the immense backdrop of the Alps. In Goms, the loftiest valley along the Rhône, the scenery has an awe-inspiring breadth, panning out from a valley floor of just 500 metres (1,600ft) above sea level towards a sweep of the Alps' highest peaks.

The Valais lies on the Simplon rail line (Paris-Milan) and is connected to the north via the Lötschbergbahn (Bern-Brig). The famous *Glacier Express* between Zermatt at the foot of the Matterhorn and the fancy ski resort of St Moritz is one of the most scenic rail journeys in Switzerland. Billed as "the slowest express train in the world", the narrow-gauge train takes about eight hours to cover 290km (180 miles) at an average speed of 39kph (24mph).

From Martigny, the Mont Blanc Express travels into France, winding up in Chamonix, while the *St Bernard Express* excursion heads up to the St Bernard Pass, ending at the historic Grand St Bernard Hospice.

The A9 motorway links Lake Léman/Geneva with Sierre in the heart of the valley. Eventually, it will extend another 32km (20 miles) through the Upper Valais to Brig, about half of the journey via tunnels. In 2017, 80 percent of the trip was still along Route 9. The latter also links Sierre to Täsch, 280 metres (920ft) from Zermatt where the Gornergrat Bahn, another historic Alpine railway – and Europe's highest open-air rack railway – departs for the

Main Attractions

Fondation Pierre Gianadda
Barryland – Musée et
  Chiens du Saint-Bernard
Verbier
Pyramides d'Euseigne
Leukerbad Therme
The Matterhorn
Goms Valley

Map on page 170

Mont Fort restaurant, Verbier.

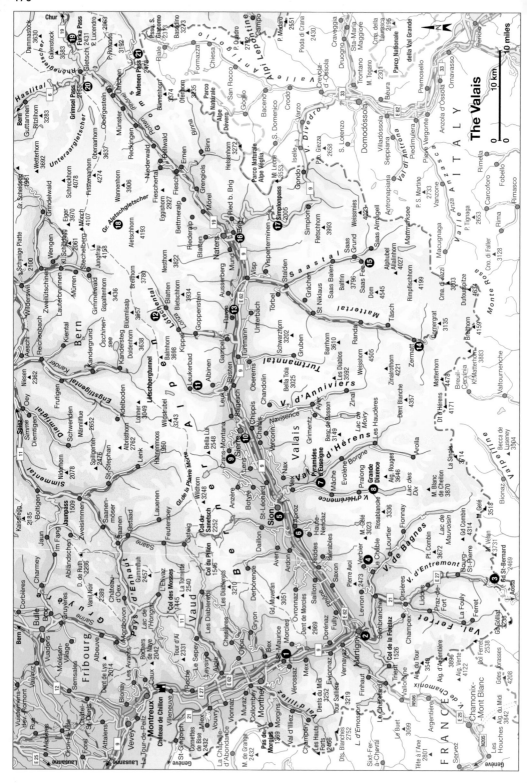

The Valais

peak-surrounded Gornergrat viewing platform 3089 metres (10,134ft) above.

The cantonal roads in the main valley as well as those leading off into the side valleys are also in very good condition and make it easy to get around.

A BIT OF HISTORY

"Individualists" is the word usually used by the Swiss to describe the people of the Valais, the area lying between the Rhône Glacier and Lake Geneva. Even the German-speaking people of the Upper Valais, who form a quarter of the canton's population, are markedly different from other German-speaking Swiss. Centuries of rule by the Upper Valais over the lower part of the canton ended when Napoleon's troops marched in and created the Revolutionary Republic of Valais in 1798, absorbed into the larger Napoleonic puppet state, the Helvetic Republic. After that collapsed in 1802, the Valais was eventually fully absorbed into France in 1810 as the "Département du Simplon". With the end of the Napoleonic Empire, its independence was restored in 1813. By then, impoverished, plundered and burned, it could take only one course of action: joining the Swiss Confederation in 1815.

Travellers arriving from Lake Geneva make their first acquaintance with the Valais in **St-Maurice ❶**, some 27km (17 miles) south of Montreux on the A9 toll motorway. After visiting the splendid 3rd-century **Abbaye de St-Maurice** (19 Avenue d'Agaune; tel: 024 485 15 34; www.abbaye-stmaurice.ch; Tues–Fri 10am–5.30pm, Sat–Sun 1.30–5.50pm), founded in 515 by the martyred Burgundian King Sigismund, it is worth spending some time in the centre of the Rhône River town, which also takes its name from a martyr. Maurice was a Coptic officer, who – along with 6,600 fellow soldiers – was killed by Emperor Maximian and died for the sake of Christ. The old Roman burial site of Agaunum became an important pilgrimage stop on the Via Francigena, linking Canterbury with Rome, after the death of St Maurice in the late 3rd century AD. The local tourism office, on Avenue des Terreaux, can provide you with plenty of information on those major European cultural routes.

St-Maurice's city hall.

⊘ **Fact**

Octodorus was the Roman name for Martigny, which in the 1st century BC was developed into a fortified outpost by General Servius Galba under Julius Caesar's orders.

There is also a castle to see, the rebuilt 15th-century **Château de St-Maurice**, just north of the abbey by the Rhône, whose exhibition space hosts some interesting themed round-ups of drawings, cartoons and comic strips. Directly behind it, off the Route du Chablais, is the **Grotte aux Fées**, an enchanting little fairy cave, whose café-restaurant offers good views over the town rooftops. You will also find a picnic ground here and children's play area.

The cultural and historical centre of the Lower Valais lies 10km (6 miles) further south, up the valley in **Martigny** ②, where the narrow hollow formed by the lowest part of the Rhône Valley suddenly opens out. This ancient town has developed into an internationally celebrated cultural centre in recent years, capping its role as an industrial centre and an important site of Roman-era archaeological finds.

The town has attracted travellers for centuries. Close to the main square, Place Central, is the former inn Grande-Maison (9 rue Marc Morand), where an incredible list of dignitaries and writers stayed during their travels: Jean-Jacques Rousseau, Johann Wolfgang von Goethe, Stendhal, François-René de Chateaubriand, Lord Byron, Franz Liszt, George Sand, Richard Wagner and even Jules Verne.

Today the main cultural hub is the **Fondation Pierre Gianadda** (Rue du Forum 59; tel: 027 722 39 78; www.gianadda.ch; daily 10am–6pm or 9am–7pm – times vary according to exhibition), recalling a member of the Gianadda family who died in an aeroplane accident. It rolls the ruins of a Roman amphitheatre, an art museum and an automobile museum into one, as well as enjoying a striking sculpture-decked garden and a café. The temporary art exhibitions are a highlight, showcasing works by Hodler, Monet and Munch, Rodin, Toulouse-Lautrec, Picasso and Giacometti. Permanent exhibitions include the **Musée Gallo-Roman**, displaying finds from local excavations and bronze statues from Octodurus, discovered in 1883. **La Cour Chagall** contains a monumental mosaic commissioned in 1964 to decorate a Parisian residence, while the **Musée de**

Martigny and its surrounding vineyards.

l'Automobile holds some 50 vintage cars dating from 1897 to 1939, most of them still roadworthy, including the first-generation vehicles of such prestigious names as Rolls-Royce, Mercedes-Benz and Bugatti. The **Parc de Sculptures** is a marvel, dotted with bright fibreglass works by Niki de Saint-Phalle, Henry Moore's bronze Reclining Figure, and George Segal's bronze Woman with Sunglasses on Bench. The other museum attraction in Martigny is the St Bernard Dog Museum (Barryland; see box).

ST BERNARD PASS

Closely linked to the fate of Martigny is the **Col du Grand St-Bernard ❸**, some 38km (23 miles) south via the E27. Since the road tunnel opened, this route across the Alps, used by Napoleon as a gateway into Italy for the decisive battle against Austria at Marengo, might have been all but forgotten – but, ironically, that has helped save the Great St Bernard Pass.

A quick trip to **Aosta** in Italy, via the **Val de Bagnes**, **Val d'Entremont** and **Val Ferret**, makes a delightful detour at this juncture – you will reach Italy within 90 minutes. From Martigny, small side-roads (Route 9/Rue du Simplon) lead northeast within 15 minutes to the medieval castle-town of **Saillon**, the setting for many tales and legends.

HEADING FOR THE SLOPES

A 30-minute train ride (as by car) from Martigny on the *St Bernard Express* (www.sbb.ch), then a cable-car ride from Le Châble (www.televerbier.ch), will deposit you at **Verbier ❹**. This is the fashionable heart of the four Vallées ski resorts, Switzerland's largest ski area, and particularly popular among intermediates and pros, snowboarders and off-piste aficionados, plus those with a thirst for the luxury skiing scene. Events like April's long-running Xtreme Verbier, considered the hardest freeride competition on earth, bring an excited crowd here to gawk as the world's best freeskiers and snowboarders, who shoot down the rocky, nearly 45-degree pitch of **Mont Fort's** 3,330-metre (10,920ft) north face – known as the Bec des Rosses. Other high-adrenaline events include the Verbier High Five, pitting amateurs against world champs, and the Patrouille des Glaciers, a gruelling biennial ski touring race from Zermatt in which military and civilian teams compete.

Skiing is spectacular here, and not as congested as many similar Swiss resorts, thanks to one of Europe's largest lift systems, and its more out-of-the-way location. You can lose yourself in the backcountry for a few hours or even days at a time; there are many kilometres of trails of all different sorts, and local outfitters will guide you, provide maps and equipment, and even lift you in a helicopter to a remote location (for a hefty price) if you are so inclined. Several schools in and around the town also promote summer adventure sports, such as rugged hikes and daring hang-glides, and the Verbier Bikepark is a hit with mountain bikers, who can ride its various downhill

Hitting the slopes, Verbier.

⊘ THE GREAT ST BERNARDS

In 1049, an Augustine monk, St Bernard de Menthon, established a monastery and hospice for travellers and pilgrims at the highest point of passage between the Swiss and Italian Alps, the 2469-metre (8100ft) high Great Saint Bernard Pass. Beloved mountain rescue dogs, Saint Bernards, were bred here from the mid-17th century, and helped save the lives of some 2,000 travellers in the following two centuries. Their sturdy bodies and broad chests helped them force a path through the snow, while their reliable sense of direction enabled them to find their way home even in the midst of the heaviest storms. Today the dogs have been entrusted to the Barry Foundation, and can be seen at mealtimes and play at Barryland – Musée et Chiens du Saint-Bernard, about an hour's drive south in Martigny (tel: 027 720 49 20; www.fondation-barry.ch; daily 10am–6pm). Located upstairs, the museum that tells the history of the dog and the Saint Bernard Pass. Meantime, back up near the monastery in Bourg-Saint-Pierre, you will find another little museum: the Grand Saint Bernard Hospice Museum (tel: 027 787 12 36; June–Sept daily 9am–6pm), which relates the history of the monks as well as the region's natural history through objects from Gallic coins to a bronze statue of Jupiter. The latter was found during late-19th-century excavations on the Col du Grand-Saint-Bernard, in a temple dedicated to Rome's mightiest deity.

trails at set times from June through October (www.verbier.ch).

Classical music and poetry festivals are other summer favourites.

CULTURAL SION

Presided over by two hills, like lumps of the Loch Ness monster, **Sion** ⑤, 30km (20 miles) northeast of Martigny via the A9, is the canton's capital. Despite its reputation among some Valaisans for being a boring town full of civil servants, it is in fact blessed by significant cultural and historical heritage – and sunshine. Surging up in the midst of the town is a pair of rocky hillocks, the Collines de Valère and Tourbillon, upon which are perched the **Château de Valère** and **Château de Tourbillon** respectively. Jutting up behind them are the domes and beaked peaks of the Alps, often iced in snow.

In the Old Town, a visit to the **Cathedral of Notre-Dame-du-Glarier** (Mon–Sat 7am–6pm, Sun 10.30am–6pm), the last medieval episcopal church in Switzerland and one of the most impressive religious edifices in the Valais, is highly recommended. Its carved 17th-century choir-stalls, magnificent St Barbara altar and 15th-century bishops' tombs are its most notable treasures.

At the foot of the two hills lies the town hall, **Hôtel de Ville**, and the cantonal museums: the **Musée de la nature** in Rue des Châteaux, and the **Musée d'art** on Place de la Majorie, which frequently hold interesting exhibitions of local natural history and art. The 15-minute walk up to the castle-church of the Château de Valère is worth it, if only to take a look at one of the world's oldest functioning organs, dating from the early 15th century, found inside the castle's **Musée d'histoire**. A few ruins consisting of hewn grey stone are all that remain of the Tourbillon fortress, erected in the Middle Ages by the once-mighty prince-bishops of the Valais.

What is undoubtedly a unique Swiss custom, cow fighting, takes place every spring and autumn all over the canton. Around mid-May, in **Aproz** ⑥, just southwest of Sion, the great cantonal championship cow fight is held. It is a popular spectacle in which the

Aproz is famous for its cantonal championship cow fight.

most belligerent representatives of the Eringer breed – not large, but they can be suitably aggressive – are brought face to face. The fights developed from the natural sparring by which hierarchies were established within cow herds in the Alps, and the cows fight only when they feel like it, regally avoid chasing their rivals after they have beaten them, and scarcely ever injure one another.

Further south of Sion, a little way down the **Val d'Hérens** (which eventually leads to the quiet ranges and towns that mark the Italian border), is a striking range of jagged peaks known as the **Pyramides d'Euseigne ❼**, which have been carved by millennia of wind, water and ice into a formation that resembles a jester's crown. Formed during the last Ice Age, which eroded the surrounding rockscape, these dramatic fangs remained, thanks to their protective caps of hard rock, formed by piles of debris containing boulders. A protected national monument, the pyramids are a sight to behold from the road, though it's more enjoyable to walk to them if you are staying in the area.

GRANDE DIXENCE DAM

Continuing south from Sion down the **Val d'Hérémence**, you come to another, more recent monument: the concrete dam of **Grande Dixence ❽**. More than 50 years after its construction, which took 14 years from 1951, this is still one of Europe's highest dams, and the world's highest gravity dam, towering at 285 metres (935ft). A statistic-lover's paradise, 400 million cubic metres (14 billion cubic ft) of water lie within the 700-metre (2,200ft) long concrete leviathan. 200 metres (650ft) wide at the bottom but only 15 metres (50ft) wide at the top, it weighs 15 million tonnes. Construction of this dam – unlike the Mattmark Dam in the Saas Valley where 88 people died in a glacier accident in 1965 – was largely disaster-free.

WINE AND SPA WATER

Golf and skiing are the main attractions for the fashionable visitors to **Crans-Montana ❾**, a fancy resort where almost everything comes at a price. This is not the place to find Alpine quiet – you will be amazed by the sprawl,

The impressive Pyramides d'Euseigne.

traffic and nightlife in such a tiny valley – but the glacier skiing here is terrific, if not terrifically challenging: the local glacier is nearly level, and it is normal to traverse it on cross-country skis. In late summer, the annual Swiss Open event at the resort's course brings Europe's finest golfers to town.

The **Val d'Anniviers**, 15km (9 miles) west near Sierre, is one of the valleys of the Central Valais in which nomadic mountain people were still moving between the valley floor and the Alps with the seasons as recently as the mid-20th century. The Austrian poet Rainer Maria Rilke called **Sierre** a mixture of Provence and Spain – heady praise indeed.

The rocky, chalky vineyards just east of Sierre, on the edge of the Pfyn-Finges nature park and the French-German linguistic border, produce a fine drop, the AOC Pinot Noir de Sierre, and a new Sierre Grand Cru, which is top-shelf wine. With its plentiful sun and almost Mediterranean feel, the neighbouring village of **Salgesch** also has wine in its veins, with some 30 wineries to around

A terrifying Tschägättä.

1,400 inhabitants. The small vintners here and the tourism office of Sierre Salgesch (www.salgesch.ch) are intensely oriented to wine tourism. The latter can provide all the information required on winery visits, wine-tastings and the terroirs here, and the well-marked wine trail between the two towns. The 4km (2.5-mile) route takes in vineyards, 80 information boards and the impressive Gorges de la Raspille, as well as linking the two sites of the **Musée Valaisan de la Vigne et du Vin**. The first, located opposite the Château de Villa in Sierre (Rue Ste Catherine 6; tel: 027 456 35 25; www.museeduvin-valais.ch; Mar–Nov Wed–Fri 2–6pm, Sat–Sun 11am–6pm), hosts temporary exhibitions, while the **Maison Zumofen** in Salgesch (Museumplatz; hours as above) is a permanent museum space focusing on all aspects of the Valais wine-producing tradition.

On the small, narrow road that leads from Salgesch 15km (9 miles) north in the direction of Leukerbad, the impressive-looking **Pfynwald** comes into view; it is the largest continuous forest of Arolla pine in central Europe, and much of it is now protected. There is a warm microclimate here, with a rich abundance of flora and fauna.

In the Leukerbad Valley basin, surrounded by the rocky walls of the **Gemmi** region (these impressed Goethe even more than the fleas in his tent), are the healing hot springs of **Leukerbad** . As its name suggests, the town is famous for its thermal baths, which can be enjoyed at the wellness paradise of the **Walliser Alpentherme & Spa Leukerbad** (www.alpentherme.ch) complex on the village square, Dorfplatz. They are open year-round, both indoors and out in the open, at their natural 50°C (122°F) or cooled in pools down to a more tolerable 25°C (77°F). Refreshing, to say the least – particularly when you take the treatment that alternates steam, hot water and ice-cold water. The springs not only nourish the expensively furnished bathhouses, but also keep the steep part of the street near the church completely free of snow and ice in winter, thanks to a system of pipes laid under the road surface. The Leukerbad Tourism office is a great source of information on the region; you can find it at the **Rathaus** (Town Hall; tel: 027 472 71 71; www.leukerbad.ch).

The historic pass walk from Leukerbad into the Bernese Oberland via the gigantic rocky peaks of the 2350 metre (7,6961ft) **Gemmipass** require reasonable fitness and about 4 hours to reach Kanderstag where you can take a cable car to Sunnbüel, and either walk out 3.5 hours or drive back to Leukerbad and ease out your muscles in the soothing therme. (For timetables visit Kanderstag Tourism, www.kandersteg.ch).

If you are less keen on walking, the Gemmirail cable car will whisk you up to the viewing platform at the Berghotel Wildstrubel (www.gemmi.ch; free for guests), with its panoramas over the Mischabelgruppe, Monte Rosa, Weisshorn, Matterhorn and Berner Alps. If you can't tear yourself away from them, you might bed down a night.

THE LÖTSCHENTAL

Branching off to the north near the twin towns of **Gampel-Steg**, east of Leukerbad, is one of the most beautiful and unsophisticated lateral valleys in the whole Valais – the **Lötschental ⑫**. Bordered by a mighty circle of mountains, this valley has managed to preserve not only its villages but also some pre-Christian customs, such as the winter tradition of the *Tschägättä*. With their frightening masks carved from Arolla pine and their shaggy sheepskins, the *Tschägättä* can send quite a shiver up your spine.

A stay in the Lötschental would not be complete without a visit to the local history museum in **Kippel** (15km/9 miles north of Gampel-Steg), the chapel in nearby **Kühmatt** or the place of pilgrimage in **Blatten**, with its impressive votive offerings.

Further up the Rhône Valley you can visit the grave of famous Austrian poet Rainer Maria Rilke (1875–1926). It is next to the south wall of the impressive-looking church in **Raron ⑬**, a few kilometres/miles east of Gampel-Steg. The

Walliser Alpentherme & Spa Leukerbad.

🔍 THE MATTERHORN

On 14 July 2015, the authorities declared the 4,478-metre (14,730ft) -high Matterhorn off-limits for a day to mark the 150th anniversary of the first ascent, and to honour more than 500 climbers who have died trying to reach the top.

Both terrifying and beautiful, the Matterhorn – Switzerland's most famous peak and one of the most recognisable on the planet – breaks the horizon south of Zermatt like a giant canine tooth. The archetypal chocolate-box mountain, it has inspired everyone from the Victorian aesthete and art critic John Ruskin, who called it "the most noble cliff in Europe", to the inventor of pyramidal Toblerone.

The Matterhorn's limestone and serpentine mass stands sentinel over a tough Alpine pass on the Swiss-Italian border, used before Roman times. However, it was not until 1858 that anyone had the temerity to

Scaling the daunting peak.

attempt to scale a peak that was feared by some locals as the abode of giants or even the devil, who, in a rage, was wont to hurl rocks down from the heights.

The early attempts all ended in failure, with the result that the Matterhorn became the last of the major 4,000-metre-plus Alpine peaks to remain unconquered: it was indomitable, the ultimate mountaineering challenge of the day. In the end, it was the British engraver-cum-mountaineer, Edward Whymper (1840–1911), and six comrades (three fellow Brits; the Chamonix-born guide Michel Croz; and a father-and-son team of Zermatters, both called Peter Taugwalder), who first reached its summit, on 14 July 1865, narrowly beating a team led by the famous local Italian climber Jean-Antoine Carrel. Triumphalism turned to tragedy, however, on the descent, when four of the victorious party slipped to their deaths, as recounted graphically in Zermatt's Alpine Museum.

Of course, the Matterhorn did host many subsequent feats of heroism: Lucy Walker became the first woman to reach the summit in 1871; the fearsome north face was first scaled in 1931; and, in more recent decades, Jean-Marc Boivin skied down the east face, and then solo-climbed the north face in a mere four hours.

Today, it remains an extremely popular climbing destination. The most straightforward season to climb runs from mid-July to mid-September, depending on snow conditions and, all being well, as many as 200 climbers can reach the summit every day via Whymper's classic Hörnli route, using the fixed ropes up this northeastern ridge (your time at the top will be restricted if it is busy). However, over 500 people have died on the mountain, so do not underestimate the dangers of weather, rockfalls and inexperience. A guide is essential, plus you will need to be in excellent physical shape and to have some prior rock-climbing experience. It is also worth acclimatising by ascending some of the less challenging high peaks in the area.

"The time may come", wrote Edward Whymper, "when the Matterhorn shall have passed away, and nothing, save a heap of shapeless fragments, will mark the spot where the great mountain stood. That time is far distant … and generations unborn will gaze upon its awful precipices, and wonder at its unique form."

Burgkirche was built between 1508 and 1517 at the request of Cardinal Matthäus Schiner, and contains the remains of Rainer Maria Rilke, as well as a fresco depicting the Day of Judgement, with devils dressed in the clothing of the notorious Swiss mercenaries of that time.

ZERMATT AND THE MATTERHORN

Further east, at Visp, the valley branches off southwards, and separates much like a wishbone into the Mattertal and the Sasstal valleys. Tucked within each are the ski resorts of Zermatt and Saas Fee; both are accessible from the fork in the road at Stalden. If Zermatt did not have the most original and thus most famous rock formation in all the Alps, it might have to compete for visitors more with its neighbour in the adjacent valley. **Zermatt** ⑭ covers a large winter and summer skiing area with its Klein-Matterhorn cable railway, and Saas Fee does much the same with its Metro Alpin. Looming over this busy resort, the **Matterhorn** (4,478 metres/14,692ft) is the very obvious drawing card to Zermatt, although at 4,634 metres (15,203ft) the nearby **Dufourspitze** is the highest peak in Switzerland, named after General Henri Dufour, who made a name for himself in the Swiss Civil War of 1847 (between the old Catholic cantons and the reformed ones). It is the photogenic Matterhorn, however, that is instantly recognisable to most visitors – and, if its crooked peak can be seen (clouds are frequent), it is certainly an impressive, almost unbelievable, sight of sheer rock in perfect proportions. Much of the walking here is scary and challenging, and the climbing – well, that is for serious experts only. Despite – or perhaps because of – its quite remote position, Zermatt is also becoming something of a haven for action-adventure junkies. They sign up with one of the numerous hiking, climbing or biking outfitters, then drink hard in the bars lining Bahnofstrasse before crashing to sleep.

SAAS FEE

The car-free resort of **Saas Fee** ⑮, at the end of the Saastal Valley, is set

⊙ Tip

Near Brig is the mountain village of Mund, which is the only remaining place in Switzerland where they still cultivate the saffron plant.

Zermatt lies at the foot of the Matterhorn.

in even more splendid surrounding mountains, and nearly touched by the icy tongue of the Feegletscher. **The Ice Pavilion**, at the top station of the funicular leading up to the glacier, is well set up for children with educational exhibits on glacial activity (entrance fee). The town itself has retained much of its sedate village character, especially at night.

Returning north, and back to the east of Visp, **Brig** ⑯, the capital of the German-speaking Valais, is dominated by the **Stockalper Palace** (tel: 027 921 60 30; May–Oct Tues–Sun for guided tours at 9.30 and 10.30am, 1.30, 2.30 and 3.30pm; book through the tourist office), former residence of one Kaspar Jodok von Stockalper, a 17th-century merchant whose industrious zeal played a large part in the city's rise to power. The palace is more generously proportioned and more imposing than any other building in the canton. It was purchased from the impoverished Stockalper family in 1948 by a foundation and the municipality of Brig-Glis, and restored at great expense.

For Stockalper, just as for the French some time later, the **Simplonpass** ⑰ south of Brig – and the connection it provided with Italy – was vital to strategic planning. Under orders from Napoleon, forced-labour convicts upgraded the road between 1801 and 1805. The first crossing of the Alps by aeroplane is also closely associated with the Simplonpass. Jorge Chavez, from Peru, won the competition in 1910 by flying his monoplane over the Alpine pass, which lies 2,000 metres (6,500ft) above sea level. Unfortunately, he crashed as he landed in Domodossola and was killed.

If you are travelling further east into the **Goms Valley**, it is worth a detour to look at the mighty **Grosser Aletschgletscher** ⑱ and the **Aletsch Forest** – a wonderland of ancient pine trees and interesting Alpine vegetation. Get there by taking the cable car from **Mörel**, just east of Brig, up to either the **Riederalp** or the **Bettmeralp**. This mighty river of ice, the largest (surface area: 118 sq km/45 sq miles) and the longest (nearly 24km/15 miles) in Switzerland, which is nearly 800 metres

Snow-capped peaks near Brig.

(2,500ft) thick in places, extends in an elegant arc from the Konkordiaplatz at the foot of the **Aletschhorn** to below the **Riederfurka**. On its northern slopes it has one of the finest forests of Arolla pine in the country, which has been strictly protected since the 1930s.

The Nature Conservation League has renovated the **Villa Kassel** in Riederalp. This building, in which Sir Winston Churchill used to spend his summers as a boy, now hosts courses in botany and conservation, under expert supervision.

IN THE GOMS VALLEY

The highest of the Rhône valleys, stretching from Lax to Gletsch – the village at the foot of the Rhône Glacier – Goms is popular in winter for cross-country skiing, in summer for off-the-beaten-path hiking. Beyond their winter closure, three high mountain passes connect it with the rest of the country: the 2,429-metre (7,969ft) **Furka Pass** ⓳, linking Gletsch to Andermatt and Canton Uri in the northeast; the tortuous **Grimsel Pass** ⓴ (2,164 metres/ 7,100ft), leading north from Goms to Interlaken in the Bernese Oberland; and the 2,478-metre (8,130ft) **Nufenen Pass** ㉑, the country's highest road passage, spiralling down to Airolo in the northern Ticino's Val Bedretto (Bedrettotal), at the foot of the St Gotthard Pass.

Year-round, the Furka car train (Furka Basistunnel or base tunnel) between Realp in Canton Uri and Oberwald in Goms means you can reach the area from Central Switzerland in 15 minutes, with a departure every half hour. (The same line continues to Visp and Täsch, near Zermatt; for timetables see www.matterhorngotthardbahn.ch.) That said, the experience of driving – or even cycling – one of the passes in summer is out of this world. From the Valaisian side of the Furka Pass for example, you can view the **Rhône Glacier** – the source of the great river, which has shrunk a little with climate change. In the 19th century, this vast sheet of

ice extended way down into the valley basin; today it ends at the height of the Hotel Bélvèdere, about 3km (1.8 miles) below the ridge of the Furka Pass.

The breadth of the high Goms valley and the villages in its upper part – still intact, with their dark wooden houses and slender-spired Baroque churches – give the magnificent landscape its distinctive appearance.

Niederwald, one of the smaller villages, some 25km (15 miles) northeast of Brig, was the home of the "king of hoteliers and hotelier to kings", César Ritz. The Valais is rich in ecclesiastical buildings, but the nearby churches at **Ernen** and **Münster** are considered particular jewels.

Many visitors who dislike the hectic pace of life in the larger winter sports resorts are attracted to the northernmost parts of the canton. The carefully tended cross-country ski trail in the Goms is nearly 40km (25-miles) long, while in summer the Upper Valais is considered an absolute paradise for hikers, encircled by many 3,000-metre-plus (10,000ft) peaks.

The famous Hotel Belvedere lies on the winding Furka Pass.

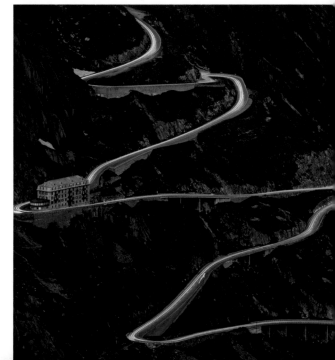

Picturesque harbours dot the shores of Lago Maggiore in Ticino.

TICINO

Switzerland's southernmost region has more than a little dolce vita flavour; tourists are drawn by the Mediterranean climate, glittering lakes and medieval Italian-style architecture.

Bound on the west, east and south by Italy, and separated from the German regions to the north by the Alpine massif, the Italian-speaking canton of **Ticino** is a country within a country; a breezy, sunny province that in some respects is more Italian than it is Swiss. Travelling by road or train from the north, you emerge from one of the sub-Alpine tunnels that have linked the two regions since the late-19th century into a lake-studded land of pizzerias, animated piazzas, gorgeously perfumed Mediterranean gardens, brightly stuccoed Catholic churches and erratic drivers who talk with their hands. The people here are markedly different too. Germanic reserve and orthodoxy give way to typically Italian spontaneity and gaiety.

The main attraction for visitors is the sunny Mediterranean climate coupled with watery splendour. The annual average temperature here is some 3°C (5.5°F) higher than in the north of the country and spring often begins in March. Autumn ends later too, with the warm days sometimes extending into November. It is not unusual for the Ticinesi to eat outdoors in short sleeves at Christmas, as the rest of Europe huddles indoors. The temperate climes are ideal for the Merlot grape, used to make increasingly popular Ticino reds.

Many tourists head straight for the chic lakeside riviera towns of Locarno

Chiesa di San Carlo Borromeo, Gambarogno.

and Lugano, with their medieval piazzas, pizzerias and gelato stores.

Up in the sparsely populated mountains in northern Ticino, between Airolo and Biasca at almost 1,500 metres (4,900ft), the winters are harsh. Even in summer, the weather in the valleys in the northern part of Ticino never gets as hot as it does in the south, making it excellent trekking country. This was actually an advantage in the days when people went to mountain health resorts for the summer rather than to the Adriatic: the first hotels in Faido

Main Attractions
Bellinzona
Locarno
Santuario della Madonna del Sasso
Val Verzasca and Valmaggia
Ascona
Lugano
Museo Hermann Hesse

Maps on pages 185, 196

⊙ Tip

The new Gotthard Base Tunnel (opened in 2016) cut the north-south train journey by around 30 minutes. On the northern side of the tunnel you may well spot deep piles of snow, on the other palm trees blowing in the breeze.

and in the hills of the Val Blenio were built around the beginning of the 20th century for wealthy visitors from Milan and Lugano, who came here looking for an opportunity to cool down and see the thundering waterfalls, a common natural feature in Ticino.

TICINO'S GEOGRAPHY

Ticino is bisected south–north by the River Ticino, which runs south from the Alps around Airolo before draining into Lago Maggiore. The Ticino flows through a valley peppered with traditional settlements and pastoral farming villages, many of them rarely visited by tourists. Romanesque churches and small Baroque chapels cling to the high slopes, well beyond the reach of the floodwaters that sometimes cause havoc in the area as a result of spring meltwaters and summer thunderstorms. In October 2000, several people were killed in Ticino when torrential rain led to floods and landslides that washed away whole villages.

At the region's southernmost tip, where a finger of fertile land reaches

Pino on Lago Maggiore.

out to the Italian border, the hills around Mendrisio were once planted with tobacco; there are many unspoiled villages in the area that are never overrun by tourists and are a pleasure to explore. Further south still, the Magadino Plain, which spills over into northern Italy near the town of Como, used to be swampland before it was drained for agriculture. It remains one of Ticino's few flat and fertile areas of cultivable land.

QUIET VALLEYS

Ticino is, first and foremost, a canton of spectacular lakes and mountains. Its two biggest and most popular lakes are at the foot of the Alps where Ticino borders on Italy. **Lago Maggiore**, broad and majestic, nestles among the southern Alpine foothills, while the contorted **Lago di Lugano** lies between the majestic peaks of Monte Bré, San Salvatore, San Giorgio and Monte Generoso. Away from the lakes, but just a few kilometres from the motorways and railways that have opened up the region to tourism, it's still possible to find wonderfully

quiet valleys filled with sunshine and sub-Alpine vegetation, and crisscrossed by idyllic footpaths meandering through the hills to rarely explored villages that have hardly changed in hundreds of years. Here, south of Lago di Lugano, the gentle hills of Mendrisio give way to the fertile plain of the Po as you cross into northern Italy.

A LAND OF EMIGRANTS

Northerners may envy Ticino's copious sunshine, nonchalant ways and earthy cuisine, but the lifestyle long idealised by Swiss-Germans is characteristic not only of a people predisposed to a certain Italian-like godersi la vita (enjoyment of life), but of those who have endured long periods of poverty and

hardship, with dignity and grace. For centuries this turned the regions south of the Alps into a land of emigration.

Industrialisation from the mid-19th century onwards made German and French-speaking Switzerland relatively prosperous but bypassed the remote rural valleys of Ticino, and when a comparatively modest tobacco and silk industry was established in the late 1800s it was mainly due to the area's large pool of cheap labour. Even the opening of the first Gotthard railway tunnel in 1882 did little to change things in the short term, though it did gradually help turn Lugano and Locarno into tourist resorts.

For most of the population, nothing really changed for the better. Between

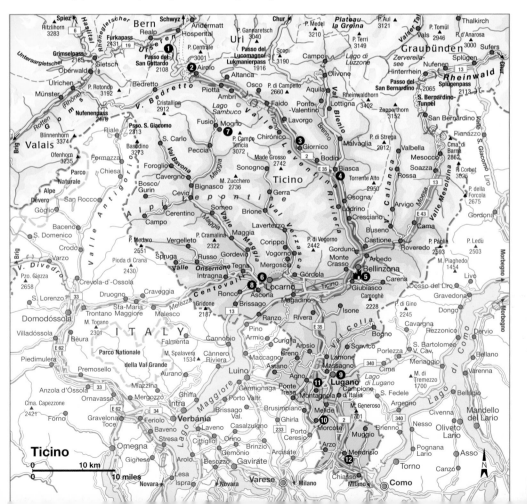

1881 and 1930 alone, a total of 25,300 inhabitants emigrated abroad. Right up until the 1950s, a trip to Ticino was still considered to be a trip back into a different era.

Now all that has radically changed. The villages in the valleys are still there, romantic and sleepy, but many of their inhabitants have resettled in crowded industrial areas around Lugano, Locarno, Bellinzona and Mendrisio-Chiasso. About 80 percent of the Ticino's 350,000 residents and 90 percent of jobs are concentrated into less than a fifth of the canton, close to the main traffic axes heading all over Europe.

Meanwhile, German-speaking Swiss, as well as Germans and other foreigners, have progressively ventured into the mountain villages and valleys, and have converted deserted houses and stables – the so-called rustici – into smart holiday homes, used for only a few weeks of the year. In fact, second homes account for over 30 percent of Ticino residences. As a result, a Swiss law introduced in 2012 limits the construction of second homes, which must not count for more than a fifth of any municipality's housing. The aim is to relieve the fallout on locals, who find it increasingly hard to secure inexpensive homes because of the inflated property demand and massive rise in the cost of land.

CUTTING TRAVEL TIME

Many factors have transformed Ticino into a centre of tourism and finance, backed by fast-growing services and new technology sectors, pharmaceutical and biomedical industries. Transport is the main catalyst. The AlpTransit project which saw the launch of the new Gotthard rail tunnel (baptised the Gotthard Base Tunnel) shaved 30 minutes off the Zurich-Lugano train trip, and an hour off Zurich-Milan (via Lugano). The Lugano-Agno international airport links the region to the world via Zürich and Geneva, while the A2 motorways hook up the sunny region with the rest of Switzerland and Milan, Italy. Four road passes underpin the Northern connections: St Gotthard (known here as the San Gottardo), Nufenen, St Bernhard and Lukmanier; and even when closed in winter, there is the famous year-round Gotthard Tunnel, with plans afoot to overhaul and expand it.

FORGING A MODERN IDENTITY

After all the years of postwar emigration of the Ticinesi to Australia in particular, and earlier in the late-19th century to America, the past few decades have been characterised by migration to the region, driven by a steady need for labour. While the area's character has long been shaped by thousands of frontier commuters coming back and forth, mostly from Italy, as well as the foreigners who moved in, times are changing. The Ticino, along with the rest of the country, is cracking down on migrant and foreign work quota laws. In September 2016 the canton enraged Italians by voting in favour of limiting the access of

Boating across Lago di Lugano.

cross-border workers, with a referendum – promoted by the ultra-conservative Swiss People's Party – obtaining 58% of the vote against 39.7%.

Rapid development, combined with a vague feeling among the people of becoming more dependent on Zürich and Milan, has led to many long disputes about Ticino's actual identity. One response to the threat of cultural colonisation has been the emergence of a unique form of Ticino architecture, which has even become something of an export commodity. The "La Tendenza" movement sprang up thanks largely to the architect Mario Botta, who in 1986 was commissioned to rebuild the 17th-century chapel in Mogno in the hills of northern Ticino when it was destroyed by an avalanche (see page 194). What he built instead was a futuristic granite and marble structure, topped with a glass roof. It caused apoplexy among the local gentry at the time, but the people of Ticino have come to see it as being in perfect harmony with the traditional buildings and Alpine landscape. Botta's home

town, Lugano, has become a showcase for his work. Some of his greats, influenced no doubt by Le Corbusier for whom he worked briefly in 1965, include the Museum of Modern Art in San Francisco, and the Cathedral of the Resurrection in Évry, France.

Luigi Snozzi performed similar wonders restoring a former convent in the village of Monte Carasso near Bellinzona.

RUGGED MOUNTAIN TOWN

One of the most dramatic entrances to the Ticino is through the northwestern **St Gotthard Pass ❶** (St Gotthard Pass). One of the best-known Alpine journeys, the pass runs 2,108 metres (6,916ft) along the route through the lush valley, offering wonderful views of the mountainous countryside and lakes.

The town of **Airolo ❷**, once the staging-post where travellers took a rest and changed horses after the rigours of crossing the St Gotthard Pass, and today the place where drivers emerge into the fresh air after 17km (10 miles) inside the Gotthard road tunnel, is an

Sunrise washes over the famous St Gotthard Pass.

example of the rugged side of Ticino, and of the tough living conditions still faced by many of its inhabitants even today. One can also reach Airolo by taking the visually rewarding route over the pass along well-surfaced roads, and visit the museum dedicated to the history of this route, the **Museo Nazionale del San Gottardo** (June–Oct daily 9am–6pm). It's housed in a former customs house and coaching hotel at the top of the pass and contains a collection of old documents and models which plot the development of the pass and the tunnel construction.

A monument by Ticino sculptor Vincenzo Vela erected near the railway station in Airolo is a reminder of the 177 people who lost their lives while the Gotthard rail tunnel was being built. In winter the snow here can be a metre (3ft) or more deep; the devastating winter of 1951–52, when avalanches caused death and destruction, is still remembered today.

To guard against damage by storms and floods the villages are built high up on the slopes of the valley of the River

Ticino, or huddled against the mountainside: **Quinto**, **Rodi Fiesso**, **Ambri** and **Piotta** and, further down, **Faido** and **Bodio**, are all examples of villages deliberately built away from the threat of natural disasters. One level higher up are the farming villages, often consisting of only a handful of houses and a church, some free from ornamentation, and some richly decorated like the one at **Rossura**.

Today, all these villages are connected by the **Strada Alta**, a hiking trail (with modest overnight accommodation) that leads from Airolo high above the valley to Biasca. Unfortunately, some of the mountain trails and paths along it have been asphalted over. A somewhat more attractive prospect is the path that runs along the top of the right-hand side of the valley (one can be transported to exactly the right height via cable car from Airolo). The route has no real gradients, passes through extensive woods, and takes in the unspoilt villages of **Prato** and **Dalpe** near Faido and also **Chironico**, near Giornico, with its remarkable church.

Looking out to Airolo town from the St Gotthard Pass.

STEEPED IN HISTORY

The centre of the **Valle Leventina**, the second-highest valley in Ticino, is picturesque **Giornico** ❸; it is here that the canton's history is most comprehensively illustrated. High up among the ruins of a Milanese castle that was destroyed in 1518 stands the 12th-century **Chiesa di Santa Maria di Castello**, with its frescoes dating from 1448.

Only a few steps away from the church lies another, and what is probably the most important – and moreover practically unaltered – Romanesque building in Ticino: the **Chiesa di San Nicolao**. Built in the first half of the 12th century, the church has a baptismal font dating from the same period and an impressive series of frescoes from 1478. It was in Giornico that the Swiss gained their first decisive victory over the Milanese, and thus began to establish a lasting grip on Ticino. A monument in the town serves as a reminder of the successful battle.

Up until the capture of Bellinzona in 1503, the *balivo* (lord) of the Leventina had his seat here, in the **Casa Stanga**, now the **Museo di Leventina** (Apr–Oct Tues–Sun 2–5pm). The coats-of-arms on the outer wall remind us of the famous visitors who stopped here on their way over the St Gotthard Pass.

Further southeast in **Biasca** ❹ is an old church, which is just as important as those of Giornico from the point of view of art history. The **Chiesa di San Pietro e Paolo** was built between the 11th and 12th centuries at a safe height above the village, and for a long period was the mother church of the whole of upper Ticino. The frescoes (12th–17th century) inside the building are particularly fine. If you want to visit the church you should ask for the key from a house nearby – check at the parsonage in the village.

Biasca is positioned defensively at the entrance to the **Val Blenio**, to the north, and thus also to the **Lukmanier Pass** (Passo del Lucomagno), which along with the St Gotthard is one of the most important north–south routes across the Alps. A northern excursion from Biasca provides good opportunities for country hikes through the unspoilt

⊙ Fact

Visitors touring Biasca may want to look around inside the beautiful Chiesa di San Pietro e Paolo. Ask for the key at one of the nearby houses or at the parsonage in the village below.

The historic town of Giornico.

valley. Though still a rural haven, Val Blenio has seen some homes converted into holiday cottages.

There are many reminders of the strategic importance of this traffic route, including the ruins of the once-mighty **Castello di Serravalle** at **Semione**. In **Lottigna** the Swiss showed the right instincts when they erected their lords' seat high above the valley. The building, richly decorated with coats-of-arms, houses a museum of local history and an important weapon collection.

In fact, a whole series of fine churches more than justifies an extended stopo-ver in the Val Blenio: **San Martino** in **Malvaglia**, **San Remigio** near **Dongio**, **San Martino** in **Olivone**, and above all the remote Romanesque church of **San Carlo** in **Negrentino** near **Prugiasco**, with its extraordinary and very well-preserved frescoes and wall paintings dating from the 11th–16th centuries.

Today, the valley is a popular holi-day, recreation and skiing area. The mighty heap of rubble at the entrance to the valley is the only reminder of the enormous landslide in 1512 that

The Romanesque church of San Carlo in Negrentino surrounded by lush meadow.

dammed up the **Biaschina**, creating a lake that, upon bursting the following year, caused a flood that extended as far as Lago Maggiore.

A MEDIEVAL BARRIER

Half an hour south (the efficient trains get here even quicker) is the canton's capital, **Bellinzona** ❺, the most Italian city in Switzerland, its famous castles set against the foothills of the Alps. Though prior to 1878 Bellinzona alter-nated the job and responsibilities of capital every six years with Lugano and Locarno, its geographical position, close to three of the major Alpine passes con-necting the Ticino with the rest of the country and beyond, makes it an ideal hub. Furthermore, the town has been a centre of government authority for cen-turies, and the settlement of Ticino's Alpine valleys began here.

Evidence suggests that the **Castel-grande** (tel: 091 825 81 45; Apr–Oct 10am–6pm Nov–Mar until 5pm), the mightiest and oldest of its trio of Une-sco-classified medieval bastions, was settled as early as 5200 BC by small groups of farmers, at a time when only hunters and gatherers roamed the for-ests of German-speaking Switzerland. From then on, Neolithic settlers, then the Celts, Romans, Lombards, Franks and native chieftains, are presumed to have occupied the hilly stronghold. Looming from a rocky peak over the Ticino valley, the citadel switched identity several times over the centu-ries: from Castel Magnum in the 14th century, to Burg Uri in the 17th and San Michele in the 19th.

This strategically important site then grew across the marshy val-ley, bolstered by other fortifications of generous dimensions – the neigh-bouring castles of **Montebello** and **Sasso Corbaro**. Milanese dukes, Visconti and Sforza, who in the 13th century extended their dominion over the whole of Ticino, were responsible for the construction. The Castello di

Montebello, originally based on a keep, is a particularly interesting example of fortification. In the long run, however, the castelli could not withstand the repeated attacks from the Swiss, and in 1503 they succeeded in capturing Bellinzona. The three inner provinces of Uri, Schwyz and Unterwalden set up their lords' seats in each of the three, thereby ensuring that this most impressive example of medieval fortifications remained largely intact.

Further edifices of note, both inside and outside the confines of what has since become a rather sleepy and sober-looking town full of civil servants, include three remarkable churches. **Chiesa di San Biagio** in **Ravecchia**, **Chiesa di San Bernardo** on **Monte Carasso**, which can only be reached on foot and, in Bellinzona itself, the former Franciscan **Chiesa di Santa Maria delle Grazie**. The latter has noteworthy Renaissance paintings – including a picture of the Crucifixion – and one of the few rood screens still in existence in the country, making it one of the most valuable churches in south Switzerland.

Continuing south, travellers have a choice between Locarno, on one side of Bellinzona, or Lugano, on the other, with **Monte Ceneri** forming the dividing line between the two in the southern Ticino. Their inhabitants live in two different worlds – and not just in the geographical sense.

In Lugano, people prefer to read the *Corriere della Sera* in addition to the local papers, and are culturally oriented towards Milan and Lombardy; in Locarno, *La Stampa* from Turin is the most widely read Italian newspaper, and here one feels a great deal closer to Piedmont, Novara and Turin. One explanation for this cultural division could be the historic transport route across Lago Maggiore: the narrow-gauge railway leads from Locarno through the **Centovalli** to **Domodossola** and then into Piedmont.

LOCARNO

Travel on from Bellinzona's castles to the lakeside splendour of **Locarno ❻**, half an hour due west. You won't mind leaving ancient history behind once

⊙ Tip

Visitors in town for the Festival del Film Locarno, an international film festival in early August, can buy daily tickets, or festival passes, giving access to most screenings (tel: 091 756 21 21; www.pardolive.ch).

Montebello castle illuminated at night.

you've feasted your eyes on the town's stunning setting by the northwestern shores of Laggio Maggiore, its flower-brimming gardens, palm-lined boulevards and pretty piazzas. Locarno, Ascona and the numerous small villages on the banks of Lago Maggiore can claim to enjoy the mildest climate in Ticino. This has nourished tourism, and has led to large numbers of Germans and Swiss-Germans coming here to build second homes or retirement homes, in many cases renovating old *rustici* in the valleys.

The influx has had some negative fallout on local life, however, with lakeside campsites packed year in, year out; at times unbearable traffic congestion; and a fair share of property blights around the lake shores in the form of housing estates or second homes which stand empty through the winter months. Many hotels close off-season, adding to the impression that the palm-lined area lives only for tourists.

In summer it is far more spirited, particularly around the colourful piazzas of the **Città Vecchia**. Alongside you will find the **Castello Visconteo** watching over the old city. Today only a fifth of the 15th-century fortress remains (and the floor of an earlier 12th-century castle). The erstwhile residence of the Visconti Dukes of Milan now houses the **Museo Archeologico** (Apr–Oct Tues–Sun 10am–noon and 2–5pm).

Perched on a crag above the town is the **Santuario della Madonna del Sasso** in **Orselina**, an important stop on the pilgrimage route. Founded in 1487, though rebuilt in the early 17th century, legends says the Franciscan church here was founded by Fra Bartolomeo, a friar from the local convent who wanted to build a place of worship on the "Rock" of Locarno after an apparition by the Virgin Mary. It contains Bramantino's *Flight into Egypt* (1536) and an entombment by Ciseri (1865). One of the Ticino's most important religious and historical sites, the "Sacred Mount" has been mooted for world heritage. The climb up here through little vineyard plots on the Sentiero delle Vigne is steep – very steep in parts – but very rewarding.

Piazza Grande, Locarno's main square.

Other church buildings of merit include the former **Monastery** and **Chiesa di San Francesco** (1528–72), west of Castello Visconteo, which serves the German-speaking Catholics of the town. The **Collegiate Church of San Vittore** in nearby **Muralto**, east of the station, along with San Nicolao in Giornico, numbers among the most important Romanesque churches in the whole of Ticino. Ecclesiastical splendour apart, Locarno's main claim to fame is its International Film Festival. Held over 10 days in early August, it claims to be among the top five in the world. Some of the new films are displayed on a large screen set up in the main square, the Piazza Grande, where thousands of people enjoy the open-air shows.

If you are looking for a refreshing change of scene after sightseeing, visit the **Lido Locarno** open-air swimming pool on the nose of land just south of the city at Via Respini 11. It is hard to imagine a more idyllic setting for a pool; set at the end of the lake in moss green lawns, this is one of the best swimming complexes in the canton, with games, spas, a fitness centre, kiddies paddling areas and an indoor pool for training as well.

Just a few minutes' walk further south, at the end of the coastal Parco della Pace, is a glorious little camellia garden, **Parco delle Camelie**. Another garden of some note is found on the Isola di Brissago: the canton's **parco botanico** (tel: 091 791 43 61; www.isole brissago.ch; 22 Mar–15 Oct daily 9am–6pm) on a little island in the middle of the lake, whose 7,000 plants come from far-flung destinations including Australia, California and Chile. You can reach it by boat from Locarno (30mins), Ascona (15mins) or Brissago (10mins). If you want to stay overnight there's a hotel, the Herman Hesse Montagnola.

A TRIP INTO THE VALLEYS

Locarno is the base point for excursions into the incredible wild river valleys surrounding it, where cascading azure rivers meet deep ravines, antiquated stone-roofed houses and grotto taverns. The two most beautiful are the **Val Verzasca**, poking inland from Locarno like a long finger, and reached within half an hour by car, then deeper in the **Valmaggia**. These and the **Valle Onsernone** are the main trio of some 12 lateral valleys in the Ticino, and you can also get to them by postbus service. It might take a little time but you will be greeted by one of Europe's most beautiful wild rural valleys, with houses huddled together in narrow village streets, picturesque slopes populated by goats and haystacks, forests of chestnut trees and slender little bridges spanning wild mountain streams of crystal-clear water.

The area has a long history of hardship: poverty and natural catastrophe forced local men to work in Milan, Venice and Turin as chimney sweeps or builders, often not returning home for years. In Val Blenio, locals made up the bulk of emigrants to Australia and California. The few rich people in the

Hillside village in the verdant Valle Onsernone.

valleys capitalised on the trend, lending migrants money for their journeys and taking their land as a guarantee for repayment. Very few were ever able to, and so their houses and estates invariably fell into the hands of the moneylenders.

This – and the fact that some who did manage to make their fortunes abroad returned to their villages and valleys – explains why even the remotest villages usually have some majestic *casa*, and why churches too are often of an unexpected size and splendour for such a wild region. That is certainly the case in **Cevio**, the capital of the Valle Maggia, with its cluster of 17th-century bourgeois houses such as the **Palazzo Franzoni** and the **Casa Respini**, which used to be the seat of the rich Swiss lords, the Franzoni, and their families during the domination by the Swiss Confederacy from 1503–1798. Between them, these two sites make up the fascinating little **Museo di Valmaggia** (Apr–Nov Tues–Sun 1.30–5pm).

You have to drive deep into the Valle Maggia to get to the architect Mario

Botta's incredible play on rustic Ticino architecture at the cylindrical **Chiesa di San Giovanni Battista** in **Mogno** ➐, which he completed in the 1990s after an avalanche ruined the original 15th-century church, but it's worth it, and the waters flowing over the smooth stone of the Val Verzasca riverbeds and massive rocks are almost mint green.

WEST TO ASCONA

Barely 2km (1.2 miles) southwest of Locarno is the well-heeled little resort of **Ascona** ➑, where one or two narrow alleyways in the old part of the town still hint that this was once one of the most ancient settlements on Lago Maggiore. The houses along the promenade, too, are a reminder – from afar, at least – that fishermen once lived there.

The church of **Santa Maria della Misericordia** (1399–1442) contains one of the most extensive late-Gothic fresco cycles in Switzerland. The **Collegio Papio** surrounds Switzerland's finest Renaissance courtyard, and the **Casa Serodine** features the most richly decorated stucco facade on a secular building that Switzerland has to offer.

In the hills above Ascona, at Strada Collina 84, is the somewhat legendary **Monte Verità**, an early-20th-century magnet for writers, artists, hippies, spiritualists, vegetarians, nudists and esoterics of all kinds. From 1901 to 1920 it attracted a steady stream of people interested in alternative lifestyles and natural healing, and photos show some of them as happy as a clam at high tide, gardening their biodynamic vegetables in the nude. This was also a meeting place for artists and writers including Hans and Hermann Hesse and later became an oasis of tranquillity for those in search of rest. Today it runs various cultural activities, and has a museum complex made up of a pavilion and two smaller casas (tel: 091 785 40 40; www.monteverita.org; Casa Anatta 20 May–Oct Tues–Sun 1–5pm; Casa Selma Apr–Nov Tues–Sun 9am–7pm). There's also a

Ascona and Lago Maggiore.

restaurant, a bookshop and a glorious historical park, open (on demand) to the public. Guided visits take place in the gardens, or you can follow the "Chiara's Rainbow" route, taking in the views of the Ticino valleys and Lago Maggiore. If you feel like sleeping over, there is also a hotel. The hills behind give way to the lovely **Centovalli** region, with its rolling hills and Alpine streams.

Much further inland, at the end of a small side valley of the Valle Maggia, lies the small village of **Bosco Gurin**. Here, unlike the rest of Ticino, German has been spoken for centuries – an unusual and traditional kind of vernacular German, known as "Ggurijnartitsch", imported here by 14th-century settlers from the German-speaking upper Valais.

SOUTH TO LUGANO

Those in Lugano were sucked into Switzerland's political whirlpool much later than their northern Ticino neighbours. For a long time, the whole region between Monte Ceneri and the Italian border at **Chiasso** was like an outlaw unto Switzerland. For even

longer, **Mendrisio**, near the southern tip of Lago di Lugano, was vaguely considered to be Italian anyway, despite its inhabitants declaring their Swiss allegiance in 1803 with the slogan *Liberi e Svizzeri* – Free and Swiss.

Mendrisio's residents frequently felt political developments in Italy; the border is, after all, just a few minutes' drive away. The municipality's liberal and conservative factions fought each other so fiercely they nearly resorted to using arms – a tactic seen as decidedly Italian in the eyes of the rest of Switzerland. Even in the 19th century it was possible for travellers to be attacked and robbed by brigands on the heights of Monte Ceneri. It was only when the railway was built across Lago di Lugano between Melide and Bissone that Mendrisio was brought closer to the canton, and a long-lasting bond established.

Since the launch of the Gotthard railway tunnel in 1882, **Lugano ⑨**, frequently described as "the pearl of Lake Lugano", has been deluged with tourists from all over the world. Arriving in the city by rail – particularly at night

Piazza della Riforma, Lugano.

– is something to behold, with the lights shimmering around the lake like a halo set deep in the mountain silhouettes.

Unlike the flat and rather unexciting landscape around Locarno, the bay of Lugano between the two mountains of **Monte Brè** and **Monte San Salvatore** can almost compete with Rio de Janeiro and its famous Sugar Loaf in terms of grandeur. Both Monte Brè and Monte San Salvatore can be scaled by funicular. From their summits, in fine weather, one can see the plain of the Po all the way to Milan in one direction, while enjoying a panoramic view of the whole of the Bernese and Valais Alps in the other.

Understandably, this lake region has long been used as a trade route; traces of the Etruscans and Gauls as well as the Romans, Franks and Lombards have all been found around Lake Lugano.

Modern Lugano has been greatly influenced by the many big banks based in the city. The imposing-looking buildings housing the prestigious financial institutions seem to compete with one another in terms of splendour. Ticino architect Mario Botta set

the pace with two buildings, the **Banca del Gottardo** and the **Palazzo Ransila**.

Rapid construction in the town has spared many of its arcaded alleyways. Another building to survive modernisation is the **Cattedrale di San Lorenzo** Ⓐ, situated on a steep slope between the railway station and the lower part of the town. Originally Romanesque, it was enlarged in the 14th century and renovated in the 17th and 18th centuries. A notable feature is its facade, a masterpiece of the Lombardy Renaissance.

But the true religious gem in Lugano is the **Chiesa di Santa Maria degli Angioli** Ⓑ on Piazza Bernardino Luini, built in 1499 at a former Franciscan monastery. Just south of the centre along the lakeshore, the church contains the most famous Renaissance fresco in Switzerland: the vivid and richly coloured *Passion and Crucifixion of Christ* by Bernardino Luini (1529), which covers the whole wall of the nave. Actually it depicts two main scenes – the Last Supper and Virgin Mary with Baby Jesus – in which the influence of Leonardo da Vinci, with whom the painter worked, can be seen.

Ancient gate, Parco Ciani.

CITY OF THE ARTS

With its healthy clutch of museums, Lugano has made a name for itself as a city of the arts. Opposite the church on the same square is a new cultural centre, the state-of-the-art **LAC Lugano Arte e Cultura** **G** (www. luganolac.ch; Tues–Sun 10am–8pm, Thur until 10pm). It is only fitting that this visual arts, music and performing arts centre, which aspires to become one of the country's best, takes a commanding lakeside position alongside the city's main historic attraction. On top of a high-tech 1,000-seat concert and theatre venue, the striking building is also home to the **Museo d'Arte della Svizzera italiana** (MASI; Art Museum of Italian Switzerland; tel: 058 866 42 30; www.masilugano.ch; Tues–Sun 10am– 6pm, Thur until 8pm), formed in 2015 by the merging of the old Museo Cantonale d'Arte (the Cantonal Art Museum) and the Art Museum of the City of Lugano. Their collections have been moved here to form the permanent exhibition of the three-floor gallery. Meanwhile, MASI will continue to stage exhibitions at the

Palazzo Reali, the historic seat of the Museo Cantonale d'Arte, due to reopen following 2017 renovations. It's in town at Via Canova 10.

PIAZZAS, PALAZZOS AND PARKS

Walk back either along the Via Nassa, the city's elegant shopping boulevard, or along the Riva Vincenzo Vela lake promenade to **Piazza della Riforma** **D**. The generously proportioned square next to the Municipio di Lugano (Town Hall) offers outstanding views. This is the place to laze in the sun or relax in one of the convivial cafés. Just to the east is the Palazzo Reali.

A short stroll further along the lake leads to **Parco Ciani** **E**, a pretty park dotted with various villas and palazzo, including the busy Palazzo dei Congressi and the handsome flamingo-pink Villa Ciani. Villa Ciani, which once housed an impressive art collection, now hosts congress-goers in its 30 salons.

East of Lugano in **Gandria** is the delightful little **Museo delle Dogane Svizzere** (Swiss Customs Museum;

⊘ WINE COUNTRY

The small Ticino vineyards which dot the landscape over some 1,000 hectares (2,470 acres) benefit from the region's mild temperatures, varied *terroirs* and microclimates. The Monte Ceneri Pass effectively splits the Ticino into two wine-growing areas: the high-altitude Sopraceneri in the north and the lower Soltoceneri in the south.

Across the eight winegrowing districts, about 88 percent of vineyards are planted with Merlot, nurtured by warm days and cool nights, and with just enough rainfall to ensure a fruitful annual harvest. Introduced from Bordeaux, France in 1907, today Merlot has become something of a trademark of the canton. The grape is used to produce a full-bodied red wine, and also rosé wine and a white Merlot.

In the early 20th century, Ticino was home to more than 7,000 hectares (17,300 acres) of vine, but the grape phylloxera disease ruined many of the indigenous grape varieties, as it did across Europe. Local authorities have vigorously promoted the cultivation of Merlot, boosted by an oenological revolution in the 1980s driven by a group of Swiss-German winemakers.

Also look out for Nostrano – a table wine made from a combination of grape varieties – and white wines made from Chasselas, Sauvignon and Sémillon grapes. These are just a drop in the ocean, given that red wine accounts for 98 percent of production.

Apr–Oct daily 1.30–5.30pm), which can only be reached by boat. It documents the ingenious schemes of generations of smugglers. Clinging to a steep slope above the lake, Gandria itself is a charming village, and worth visiting for the day to wallow among its Baroque church, narrow alleyways and terraced vineyards.

AWAY FROM THE CITY CENTRES

Anyone keen to venture out of the towns and cities and get close-up with a genuine piece of Ticino is sure to appreciate the **Val Colla** northeast of Lugano, and the villages of **Tesserete**, **Bigorio**, **Cimadera**, **Sonvico** and **Dino**. To the northwest there is also the **Malcantone**, where picturesque villages such as **Bedigliora**, **Astano** and **Breno** nestle in the hilly landscape.

The trip to **Monte San Salvatore** (www.montesansalvatore.ch) is undoubtedly the most popular, and the hiking opportunities up here, like the views, are seemingly endless. You can get to the mountain in about half an hour with a mix of train and funicular, or drive south

Taking in Lago di Lugano and the Swiss Alps from a viewpoint on Monte Generoso.

for a few minutes to reach the funicular station. It's a charming trip. At the top, sheets of glassy lake and ice-cream coned peaks spread in every direction. Much further, hovering over the southeastern part of the lake, **Monte Generoso** can be reached from **Capolago** via a rack railway. It affords magnificent views far across the plain of the Po. Nearby, the narrow, deep **Valle di Muggio** is a wonderful place for hiking.

West of Monte Generoso is **Morcote** ❿, on the Ceresio Peninsula. Once a sleepy fishing village, it is now a popular tourist spot. Visitors come to see the pretty architecture including the **Chiesa di Santa Maria del Sasso**, which sits high up in the hills. On the outskirts of the village are walking trails from which to enjoy the scenery and views over the lake.

From here, it's a 20-minute drive north to the **Museo Hermann Hesse** in **Montagnola** ⓫ (tel: 091 993 37 70; www.hessemontagnola.ch; 10.30am–5.50pm Mar–Oct daily, Nov–Feb Sat–Sun). A pretty museum, in a pretty place, one can understand why the Nobel Prize-winning writer chose this as his haven. The museum is located in the medieval Torre Camuzzi, part of the mansion in which Hesse lived from 1919 to 1931, where his study had marvellous views of the Lago di Lugano. Books, typewriters, photos, watercolours and other personal belongings, laid out through the tower's airy loggia, bring to life Hesse's 40 years in Montagnola (up until his death in 1962). Afterwards, follow the lovely Herman Hesse trail from the cemetery where he lies through the woods to his "local", the **Grotto del Cavicc** (Via ai Canvetti 19a; tel: 091 994 79 95; www.grottocavicc.ch).

If you are in the mood for wine tourism and tasting, head much further south towards the Italian border, where the gentle hills of the Mendrisio district are named after the area's largest town, **Mendrisio** ⓬. This is wine country, and the climate and fertile land have made it a major producer.

THE SOUTHEAST

Switzerland's largest and easternmost canton, Graubünden, is home to the Swiss National Park and the swish resorts of St Moritz, Davos and Klosters.

The canton of Graubünden (Grisons in French, Grishun in Romansh) is most people's view of Switzerland in microcosm – a picturesque region of rolling valleys, emerald lakes and chic ski resorts. It was in St Moritz in 1864 that winter sports had their origins as a mass tourism activity in Switzerland when a hotelier seeking extra income during the unprofitable cold months invited some of his more illustrious guests to stay on for free. Today, more than 50 percent of the canton's population is allied to the tourism industry.

A CONSERVATIVE PEOPLE

Despite the riches brought to Graubünden by tourism – "snow business" in particular – it remains a traditional and conservative area, with its people seen by the rest of the country as the quintessential *konservativ* Swiss. The Bündner – the people of Graubünden – have a reputation for rejecting nearly everything new out of hand. They were the last people in the Western world to accept cars on their roads: motorised traffic was banned in the canton until 1925. Graubünden was also among the last Swiss cantons to grant women the right to vote. Some of this resistance to change stems from the traditionalism that still exists among the small pockets of population in many of the canton's isolated valleys; some neighbouring

The Castello di Mesocco.

valleys speak different dialects. This was once a largely Romansh-speaking province, further setting it apart from the rest of the Confederation, which it joined in 1803. But German speakers now account for 64 percent of the population, with those speaking Romansh down to 13 percent. Italian speakers represent 11 percent of the population in Switzerland's only trilingual canton. The remaining 12 percent use a mix of other regional dialects.

Traces of the Roman legacy are evident everywhere in Graubünden. The

Main Attractions

Chur
Arosa
Kirchner Museum
Swiss National Park
Kloster St. Johann Müstair
St Moritz
Bernina Express

Map on page 202

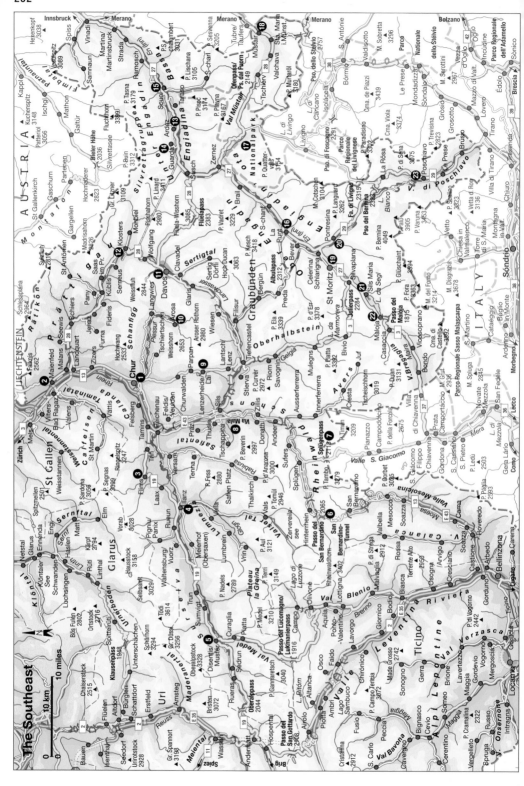

The Southeast

children of the Engadine celebrate the New Year *Chalandamarz* on 1 March, just as the pagan Romans did, chasing away winter by parading through the streets cracking whips, singing songs and ringing bells. The Romans were also responsible for giving the canton the foundations of its existing road infrastructure, with many roads in the Graubünden Alps still following old Roman routes.

THE CANTON'S CAPITAL

In an amphitheatre of the Alps, **Chur** ❶, the canton's capital, is the best starting point for any Graubünden holiday because of its excellent road and rail network. Some visitors treat Chur as an obstacle on the way to their destination resort, but it is worth taking time to look around this lovely river-swept city, which has one of the country's best preserved old quarters, the Altstadt, which is entirely car-free.

The oldest town in Switzerland was settled by the Celts 5,000 years ago, who no doubt admired its location and views. You can do the same from the cone-shaped local mountain above the city, the **Dreibündenstein**, reached by a combination of a cable car and hike.

The tourism office at the railway station (Bahnhofplatz 3; tel. 081 252 18 18) can provide you with plenty of information and trail maps on this and other mountain excursions, as well as the self-guided tour through the medieval heart of the so-called Alpenstadt, "Alpine City".

CITY WALKING TOUR

Allow a couple of hours at least for this route. Starting from the station, red signs lead, not as rumour has it from pub to pub, but from historical highlight to highlight: the Gothic **Rathaus**, (Town Hall) and four-storey **Obertor** (church tower); the Baroque Altes Gebäu (city palace; Poststrasse 14); and the **Arcasplatz**, the town's loveliest square, down by the *Plessurquai* skirting the river of the same name. From here, it's a ten minute walk up Hofstrasse to the fortified **Bishops Palace**, whose **Hof**, courtyard, contains the 12th-century mainly Romanesque

Chur, the pretty capital of Graubünden canton.

⏺ THE FATE OF THE PASSES

Graubünden's Alps contain no fewer than 14 different passes, all very close to each other, but this was far more of a curse than a blessing for the inhabitants of Graubünden over the millennia since the Romans marched through the Julier Pass in 15 BC.

Half of Europe fought over the most important through-routes across their territory, dividing the population's loyalties on several occasions. During the Thirty Years' War it found itself at the heart of bitter wrangling between the supporters of France and the Habsburgs. Even when calm finally descended on the European political scene, and Graubünden had joined the Confederation – albeit as late as 1803 – and begun their 100-year-long task of transforming the medieval gravel-covered mountain tracks into thousands of kilometres of navigable road, the region's luck failed to change: the new Austro-Italian Brenner railway and the Swiss St Gotthard railway snatched away the entire north-south traffic.

With this, the classic pass region of Graubünden was relegated to the status of a poor border region almost overnight. Whole valleys of people who had lived off the north-south traffic for centuries suddenly emigrated to California and Australia.

🔍 ROMANSCH

Romansh – still spoken by anywhere between 30,000 and 100,000 people in Switzerland – can be broken down into a number of different dialects.

Unterländer, the name the people of Graubünden give to anyone in Switzerland who lives in the valleys and plains below them, and any foreign visitor interested in the Romansh language, are faced with a confusion of languages. Romansh, the general term applied to the Rhaeto-Romanic dialects, is a mixture of the language spoken by the original Rhaetish inhabitants of Graubünden and the Latin spoken by the Roman conquerors.

Because of the region's topography, however, five main dialects developed over the centuries in what used to be Rhaetia. The *Bündner Oberländer*, the largest group, speak *Sursilvan* (from *Surselva*,

Romansh sundial in Ardez.

meaning "above the wood"). In the Lower Engadine they speak *Vallader* and in the Upper Engadine *Puter* (the two are also known collectively as *Ladin*). In the Oberhalbstein and Albula valleys, as well as in parts of central Graubünden, they speak *Surmiran*. In the rest of central Graubünden, *Sutsilvan* (from *Sutselva*, meaning "below the wood") is spoken.

All five dialects are considered standard Romansh languages; in addition to these five there are also dozens of local dialects that make the Romansh region an area of extreme linguistic confusion. In the Upper Engadine, for example, the inhabitants of some neighbouring villages can be recognised from the way they pronounce the letter "e". In Zuoz, the word for bread is *pem*, while in Samedan it is *päm* (and, when written, *paun*). In the Lower Engadine, the word, both written and spoken, is *pan* – but that belongs to another dialect altogether, *Vallader*.

The shadowy origins of the first Rhaetians might shed some light on these linguistic oddities. According to the latest research, the Rhaetians – who also include the early inhabitants of the south Tyrol and of Friuli, where Rhaeto-Romanic dialects also exist – are, in essence, not Indo-Germanic. One thing is certain: Etruscans living in the Po Valley influenced the Rhaetian language.

The Celts, too, an Indo-Germanic tribe from middle and western Europe, left their mark on pre-Roman Rhaetia. Research also indicates Semitic origins, which would mean that the mysterious original language was related to Arabic, Hebrew and Accadian.

To begin with, around the year 300, the Emperor Diocletian divided the province of Rhaetia into *Raetia prima* (with Chur as its capital) and *Raetia secunda* (Augsburg being its capital), both of which fell into the hands of the Teutons at some point during the 5th century. Later, in the Middle Ages, the economic problems of the mountain valleys forced many young neo-Latins to emigrate. Then the tourists finally arrived.

Step by step, Romansh was pushed aside. The flowering of Rhaeto-Romanic literature, which began in the 19th century, hardly provoked a Romansh linguistic renaissance. Whether the standard language *Rumantsch grischun* developed by Romansh scholar Heinrich Schmid will survive, or prompt a new surge of interest, is doubtful.

Kathedrale, plainish from the outside but with many hidden gems within (tel: 081 252 92 50; daily 8am–7pm), including a magnificent late-Gothic carved High Altar by Jakob Russ.

The city's fine arts **Bündner Kunstmuseum** (Bahnhofstrasse 35; tel: 081 257 28 70; www.buendner-kunstmuseum.ch; Tues–Sun 10am–5pm, Thur until 8pm), a couple of minutes from the bustling main square, **Postplatz**, is worth a visit for work by such artists as the Giacometti family, Angelika Kaufmann and the Italian artist Giovanni Segantini, as well as contemporary art and photography. All the artists have some kind of connection with the region – the name Bündner means people from Graubünden.

With the River Plessur running before it, Chur's **Altstadt** (Old Town) is exceptionally beautiful when snow lies on its mighty roofs, and the grey squared-stone masonry of the houses seems more intense and powerful than ever. In the autumn, by way of contrast, when the *Föhn* wind whips south and colours the sky Prussian blue, the smell of new wine forces its way out of the few remaining wine-presses in localities like **Lürlibad**, and every restaurant in town serves venison from the hunt.

On mild summer evenings people sit out of doors in Chur's old quarter, enjoying the warmth of the day radiating from the walls of the houses. On nights like these, Chur becomes the most Italian town north of the Alps. One delicious dish to sample in town is the Capuns: noodles wrapped in beet leaves and boiled in stock, a traditional and very filling Graubünden speciality. Try the Restaurant zum Metzgertor on the Arcasplatz (Arcas 3; tel: 081 250 41 79). Also order a glass or two of Churer Schiller rosé, a typical local wine.

COUNTRY OUTINGS

From the city, the Brambrüesch cable car, or Bergbahnen, will whisk you up to the Alpine meadows, the tinkling of cowbells and the pure mountain air of the high plateau area (the station is at Kasernenstrasse, 15). From here, between June and October, you can launch out on the Dreibündenstein Rundwanderungen, a 12.5km (7.8-mile)

⊙ Fact

Bündner Herrschaft is Graubünden's most important wine region, unfurling between Maienfeld, Fläsch, Jenins and Malans. Some 45 grape varieties are grown here, predominantly Pinot Noir (Blauburgunder), representing 78 percent of crops. Many vineyards and wine cellars – *Torkel* – can be visited, and there's a lovely hiking loop through the vineyards east of Malans.

Ochsenplatz, Chur.

⊘ Fact

Excavations of Roman remains at Welschdorfli near Curia have even revealed oyster shells imported from Burgundy, suggesting that life for some of the imperial forces was far from harsh.

circular trail between the 2,160-metre/ 7086ft Dreibündenstein and Feldis, from where you can take a cable car to Rhäzüns, then train to Chur. Allow at least four hours for the "panorama trail", as it's christened.

You can also follow the people of Chur on one of their typical autumn outings, into Heidi land. Take the A13 north into the most far-flung corner of Graubünden, the Bündner Herr- schaft. The Rhine town of **Maienfeld** ❷ (also 20 minutes by rail from Chur) is famous for its Heidi-Hüsli, where the heroine of Zürich-born Johanna Spyri's famous novel is said to have lived. Since 1999 the house has been a museum, the **Heididörf** (Oberdörfli- gasse 15; tel: 081 330 19 12; www.heidi dorf.ch; mid-Mar–Nov daily 10am–5pm) with an outside area set aside for farm animals. You can also hike there in about half an hour, following the red markers up from the Städtliplatz.

THE BÜNDNER OBERLAND

Much originality – alongside a few con- cessions to modernity – is provided west

The Rhine Gorge near Laax is sometimes known as the "Swiss Grand Canyon".

of Chur by the **Surselva**, which was dis- covered by tourism only a short while ago. It is here that you can find those white-bearded individuals so loved by photographers, and houses burned dark by the sun; bread is still baked in some of the public ovens in the village squares. A particularly fine example can be found in **Luven** above Ilanz, dec- orated with the rather apt saying: *Nies paun da mintg gi* (our daily bread).

Tourism has still only reached the entrance to the Surselva and the **Vorderrhein**, 20km (12 miles) west of Chur – above all at Flims and Laax. In the summertime white-water enthu- siasts go rafting here, down into the ravine of the wildly foaming Rhine. However, the Rhine is developing into more of a thin trickle than a torrent since Graubünden allowed itself to be done out of its water rights – for a pittance – by lowland power stations. River-rafters on the River Innen in the Lower Engadine (Unterengadin) are also familiar with this problem.

Flims ❸ (a postbus stop on the road from Chur, thus more built-up) and **Laax** (a somewhat quieter, more rus- tic town) have long since turned their attention to wooing skiers: within the so-called "**White Arena**", the brain- child of a master butcher from Flims, which covers an area of 140 sq km (85 sq miles); even the most ener- getic skier cannot hope to cover all the descents in a single day. Unfortu- nately, the ski lift reaching the summer ski resort on the glacier is no longer in regular operation, but other offer- ings have taken up the touristic slack. A young backpacker set is thronging here for the spectacular hiking, biking and snowboarding.

At the very top of the valley, too, near the source of the Rhine at the **Tomasee** (incidentally, there is a very attractive walk which can be taken along its banks), the locals are trying to attract as many tourists as possible. Some 40km (25 miles) west of Ilanz in

Sedrun – on the **Oberalp Pass**, which leads onward to Andermatt in the canton of Uri – snowfall is reliable, even when other health-spa managers are wringing their hands in despair.

It is also worth pointing out that no other valley in Switzerland contains quite so many Baroque churches and chapels. Many of them were built at the time of the ravages of the Plague, when people were frightened of being infected in the bigger churches. The finest examples – some of them Gothic – can be found in **Falera** outside Laax (the Church of St Remigius), **Sevgein** (just southeast of Ilanz), Ilanz (St Margarethen) and **Waltensburg**, 8km (5miles) west of Ilanz off the main road (the Reformed church).

The wild **Safiental** can only be reached via 365 hairpin bends; head 10km/6 miles east from Ilanz, then turn south at Versam. In the **Valser Tal**, due south of Ilanz, you can drink the mineral water of the same name and swim in it too, in open-air thermal baths (at the Hotel Therme – open to non-residents).

THE SURSELVA'S FAITH AND POLITICS

In no part of Graubünden are politics so closely tied to the church as they are in this Surselva region: when votes are taken on Sundays, the ballot boxes stand in front of church doorways. The priests' sermons tend to be far more political than they are in other parts of the country. It is not only ethical issues – such as refugee problems or abortion – which concern the priests; even such seemingly secular matters as proposed nuclear power stations and highway construction projects are likely to come under fire from the pulpit.

Centuries of religious apartheid and conflict between Catholics and Protestants have certainly left their traces in the region. The differences are already evident in the language itself. In the Romansh-speaking Surselva, one confession writes *de* while the other uses *da* in preference – this is still a consequence of the Reformation, when anything that had been written or printed in the heretical neighbouring valleys was totally ignored. It was only very

The world's first solar-powered ski lift was opened in 2011 in the Safiental.

gradually that the barriers between the Catholic and Protestant areas crumbled.

Today things have progressed so far that, when the expression "mixed marriage" is mentioned in conversation, the first thing that crosses most people's minds is not their religion but the language that the couple speak.

For art and nature lovers, **Ilanz** ❹ – some 30km (19 miles) west of Chur along the Rhine, beyond Laax – is the best base to choose: everywhere is within easy reach – by car, on foot, or by postbus. In the lateral valleys of the Surselva, far from the through-routes and their filling stations, it is possible to take a journey back 100 years into the past.

Farther west still, past Trun and just east of Sedrun, is **Disentis** ❺ (in Romansh: Mustér) – with its **Benedictine Monastery**, the finest Baroque edifice in Graubünden. Its reputation now rests on its lawn tennis courts, facilities that have inspired the tourist office to label it the "Wimbledon of the Alps".

MAGNIFICENT PASSES

Everyone who wants to cross the passes in Graubünden these days has to take the route used 2,000 years ago: through the narrow gap formed by the Bündner Herrschaft and Chur. For real pass enthusiasts, here are two particularly attractive routes.

The first is ideal for motorists with relatively little pass experience: it leads from Chur (via Lenzerheide and Tiefencastel or via Landquart and Klosters) to Davos, and then on over the **Flüela Pass** – which has a barren landscape of stone and water – to **Susch**.

PASSO DEL SAN BERNARDINO

Another trip into the southern part of Graubünden provides the possibility of going over a pass on the journey there and travelling back via a road tunnel. This is the **San Bernardino Pass** ❻, the alternative to the St Gotthard for road traffic travelling through Switzerland. The pass is named after the 15th-century San Bernardino of Siena, who used to preach here. The tunnel, at 6.6km (4 miles) long, is only about half as long as

Roads negotiate the Alpine landscape, often featuring hair-raising hairpin turns.

the road over this ancient pass, if you are in a hurry. If you do opt for the tunnel, you will be missing some excellent views from the road over the Rheinwald Valley and its northern peaks – although negotiating the 18 hairpin bends demands careful attention.

It is worth taking this route if only to meet with the Val Mesolcina, making your way from Chur through the valley of the Hinterrhein, then up over the pass (which is dotted with Alpine roses in the summertime) to the mountain resort of **San Bernardino**, just beyond the southern entrance to the tunnel, a popular base for local hiking and cross-country skiing activities. The mountain pass also skirts an enchanting moor, and the mountain lake of Lago Moesola, before arriving at its 2,065-metre (6,775ft) crest.

The main village in the region is **Mesocco**, another 40 minutes' drive south, with a solid-looking cluster of stone houses. The ruins of the **Castello di Mesocco**, dating from the late 15th century, dominate the valley from the heights of its rocky ridge below the

village. By following a route through the villages in preference to the *Autobahn*, you will see the picturesque stables built from rubble dotting the fields outside the villages, and you will not miss **Roveredo** either, where the road branches off towards the **Val Calanca**, high in the mountains. The entry to it is guarded by a 13th-century pentagonal tower and the lavishly decorated **Church of Santa Maria Assunta** (17th century) in **Santa Maria di Calanca**.

Then there is a whole series of tiny villages nestling in a delightful landscape. Many of these look almost deserted, and not without reason: people have emigrated from this high valley since the 16th century. Able-bodied men traditionally went off to seek their fortunes in Italian cities, first as master builders and as artists, later as chimney sweeps.

Anyone who finds these routes too tame could even try a third option, known to send a shiver up the spine of even daredevil travellers. This too starts in Chur, and continues via **Thusis** along highway A13 to Splügen, before

⊘ Tip

Arosa is divided into two parts: Ausserarosa has the main resort facilities, based around the railway station by the shores of the Obersee lake, and Innerarosa is the older part of town.

launching on to the cross-country **Splügenpass ⑦**, down several wildly romantic hairpins into the Italian town of **Chiavenna**. You can return to Switzerland via the Bergell. The mountains here are so high that some villages remain without sunshine for months at a time. It continues over the **Maloja Pass** into the Engadine, then back to Chur via the Julier, a route once used by the Romans and child's play compared with the route covered so far. If you would rather let others do the driving, you can do the whole round trip on the comfortable postbus rural service (switching between the Thusis-Splügen–San Bernardino and Julier Pass routes, with changes in Splügen, Chiavenna and Silvaplaner; www.postauto.ch; tel: 081 651 55 77).

INTO THE ABYSS

If you are driving south from Thusis, detour from the A13 motorway and take the old Route 13, **Via Mala ⑧**. The main reason for doing so is to visit the **Viamala Gorge**, once loathed because the ravine was an obstruction on the

journey through the Alps. Thus the mountainous road leading to it was named the "bad path", winding deep into the Hinterrhein Valley, through tunnels that are still crudely hewn. The sensation is similar to being on a particularly scary ghost train; you can even feel the moist air wafting up from down below. Black and forbidding, the crumpled-looking layers of slate, 300-metres (985ft) high, tower to left and right.

In Roman times there was no road, only a narrow trail; the first road was built towards the end of the 15th century. Today, a well-signposted path also leads down 321 steps to the thundering river. Walk across the small bridge and through a tunnel and you'll reach a viewing platform with spectacular views of the southern end of the gorge. Though the gorge is relatively short, just a kilometre (a little over half a mile) in length, what makes it so impressive is its extreme narrowness in parts, no more than a metre wide. When meltwater rushes through in spring, it's a memorable sight.

Canyoning in the Viamala Gorge.

Looking up you can see the famous arched **Wildener Brücke** high above, looking exactly as it did when Goethe sketched the bridge in 1788. It also appears in several plays, and books such as John Knittel's *Via Mala*, filmed several times, which locals still have not forgiven him for writing, for portraying them as a bunch of drunkards and rowdies. Perhaps he drew inspiration from the fact that the Romansh language contains more expressions for fighting and brawling than any other in the world.

AWAY FROM THE BUSTLE

Alongside the two brightest stars in the Graubünden holiday firmament, St Moritz and Davos, its less dazzling resorts have quite a hard time of it. Approximately 16km (10 miles) south of Chur, on the Julier Pass route, **Lenzerheide 9** prides itself on being a family resort, while **Parpan** and **Churwalden,** en route, are said to have introduced Graubünden *Bindenfleisch*, air-dried beef. The dish is known all over Switzerland by its local name, *Bündnerfleisch*. Gourmets, and people who are in search of some peace and quiet, are liable to feel a lot more at home in such places than avid downhill skiers and celebrity-spotters.

ISOLATED AROSA

Another place almost isolated from the outside world is **Arosa ⑩**, a classic Graubünden family holiday resort with extensive sports facilities, summer bathing in the local lake, the Untersee, and lots of short hiking trails. One of these, right near the village, is the "Squirrel Trail", where the critters are happy to be fed by visitors. Best known in winter for its moderately difficult downhill skiing and ice-skating on the lake, year-round it offers the pleasurable feel of being far removed from civilization; lying at the end of a valley with no through traffic, it is reached from Chur via a very scenic narrow-gauge railway or a twisting 30km (19-mile) road, with hundreds of serpentines. This is a romantic trip, most attractive in the summer when the Arosa train also has a special roofless observation car. With the wind in their hair, passengers travel over deep ravines, through quiet forests and finally over the famed viaduct at Langwies.

It is a wonderful journey, and though the town itself may not live up to expectations of the perfect Swiss village, the views are splendid, as is the skiing, snowshoeing, walking, cable-car rides and crisp air.

One hiking highlight leads to the little hillside church, **Bergkirchli** (June–Oct, for guided tours only, at 2.30pm), whose wood-planked tower and steeple prod up among the Alpine peaks.

MAGIC MOUNTAIN

The **Prättigau**, running southeast from Landquart, shares the same fate as many other valleys with famous resorts at the end of them, in this case **Davos** and **Klosters**: it is treated as merely an access route and most visitors

A new summit restaurant crowns the Weisshorn, Arosa.

⊘ Tip

For cycling enthusiasts, many handy bike services are available under the Rhaetian Railway's RhB scheme, offering everything from self-service bike transport to unlimited travel with a graubündenPASS Bike.

Davos once functioned as a retreat for people with breathing complaints.

drive through it quickly, sparing no time for a closer look. In the autumn, though, the magnificence of the huge beech woods here can be captivating, and the region's Romansh villages are renowned for their festivals.

It was through the Prättigau in 1889 that the Rhätische Bahn (Rhaetian Railway) transported the first tuberculosis patients to the sanatoria of **Davos** ⓫, which today publicises itself with the slogan "Davos – famos". With a resident population of over 10,000, it is a town that pulsates with life all year round. The mountain air was thought to be particularly beneficial to people with lung complaints. The forbidding buildings of former days have long since become five-star hotels, one example being today's Steigenberger Hotel Belvedere, on which Thomas Mann based his *Magic Mountain* sanatorium.

It is the **Parsenn Mountains** that have made Davos famous: 200km (125 miles) of Davos' 320km (200 miles) of piste lead down into the valley below. The slopes here are so gentle that they do not even worry beginners. Anyone keen on avoiding waiting time at the crowded ski lifts on weekends and public holidays should do as the natives do and take the **Schatzalp-Strelabahn** to the top of the slopes. At night, there are plenty of clubs (though some are dear and clique-ish) in which to drink your cares away with the jet set. In summer, there is just as much – probably more – to do in the area, including inexpensive luge runs (they operate year-round) and some testing mountain biking and hiking up into the surrounding mountains.

KLOSTERS

Some visitors, which traditionally includes the British royal family, prefer quieter **Klosters** ⓬ next door, sharing the same ski slopes but a more authentic Alpine charm. A rail tunnel has opened up Klosters to the north, allowing quicker passage from Landquart and Chur. Once here, you could hit the slopes with skis or, increasingly popular, a snowboard; in addition to some world-class half-pipe on **Jacobshorn**, there are several recently opened

snowboard-theme hotels around town as well. However, these are definitely *not* the places to go to for peace and quiet.

Another option from Klosters is to take a pricey mountain railway ride up the **Gotschna** for views back down into the valley, or up the **Madrisa** to begin a hike. Locals also recommend hikes in the Jöri lakes – you get there from Berghaus, a postbus ride away from town. Still another fine idea, if you have the time, is to take a leisurely walk into the two quieter adjacent valleys to the southeast, the **Sertigtal** and the **Dischmatal**. The German Expressionist painter Ernst Ludwig Kirchner depicted these landscapes in many of his works. Kirchner, one of the founders of the renowned artistic group, die Brücke, spent his last 20 years here from 1917 to 1938 before taking his own life – provoked in part by the confiscation of his works in Nazi Germany. His grave and that of his partner Erna Schilling are in the forest cemetery in Davos, while the **Kirchner Museum** (tel: 081 410 63 00; www.kirchnermuseum.ch; May 28–Oct 29 Tues–Sun 11am–6pm) **in Davos** contains oil-paintings, sketches and assorted documents.

THE LOWER ENGADINE VALLEY

The **Unter Engadin** is particularly conscious of its ancestral heritage. The village of **Ardez** ⓭, for instance, 35km (22 miles) east of Davos via highways 27 and 28, was chosen as a model municipality in Europe's year of preservation; the "Fall" depicted on the double-oriel facade of the **Haus Claglüna**, the most richly decorated house in the whole of the Engadine, is worth stopping to admire.

From Ardez a small road, also good for hiking, leads 5km (3 miles) up to **Guarda** ⓮, which clings dramatically to the sunny slope; it has been painstakingly renovated with the help of national funds. The village's houses and inns are typical of a style prevalent in the Lower Engadine since the 14th century, combining living quarters and stables under one roof. The window openings slope inwards and many of the houses feature the elaborate *sgraffiti,* which originated in Italy.

Skiing in the Parsenn Mountains.

You will discover a way of life that is still largely unspoilt in the nearby municipality of **Sent**, 15km (9 miles) back east on highway 27, with its decorated gables, as well as on the **Panorama High Path**, lying on the former route through the Lower Engadine. En route, the hamlet of **Ftan** has gained a reputation as a centre for excellent food.

The best starting point in the Engadine is **Scuol** ⓑ (Schuls in German), a romantic and pretty spa town nestling down in the valley below, whose attractions include an 11th-century **castle** and a picturesque old quarter, featuring cobbled alleys, bubbling fountains and old bakery ovens. Scuol's mineral water, known as the "Champagne of the Alps", can be drunk from the village fountain or soaked in at the thermal baths, such as the Bogn Engiadina Roman-Irish baths, offering a wide range of steamy therapeutic indulgences. You might appreciate these after more energetic activities. On an architectural note, most of the town's older houses

Schloss Tarasp.

feature a *balcun tort*, an oriel window from which the street can be observed from both sides. Unique to this region, they were a means by which members of the community kept a close eye on each other.

POPULATION DRIFT

Such close supervision has made life in Graubünden too claustrophobic for many of its inhabitants and the town has witnessed a steady stream of emigration over the centuries. It was often the brightest who upped and left; philosophers and idealists never really felt much at home under the watchful gaze of their neighbours in Graubünden.

Architects who had built such castles as **Schloss Tarasp** (tel: 081 864 93 68; www.schloss-tarasp.ch; daily, for tours only: 20 May–10 July at 2.30pm, 11 July–20 Aug at 11am and 2.30, 3.30 and 4.30pm, 21 Aug–20 Oct at 2.30 and 3.30pm), just to the south of Scuol were also attracted abroad.

The Bavarian castles of Nymphenburg and Schleissheim were built by Graubünden architects from Roveredo. Powerful Graubünden merchants traded in Italy, Russia and Spain, and ran the most famous cake shops in Venice. Meanwhile, the vacancies they left at home were filled by foreigners: the German Hennings and the Dutchman Holsboer planned the most difficult stretches of the Rhätische Bahn; the German doctor Alexander Spengler turned the Davos area into the international health spa that it is today. The annual "Spengler Cup" ice-hockey tournament is named after him.

If you are after more tranquil outdoor pursuits, you can find more room to move and as much wild and romantic natural scenery in the **Val Scharl**, which can be reached easily from Scuol either on foot, by car or by postbus heading due south. There are no hotels here, but it is a popular area with hikers, with good summer walking as far as the Ofenpass and the Val Müstair.

THE SWISS NATIONAL PARK

Those after gentler scenery, as they head towards the Swiss National Park, may take the road from Tiefencastel, about half an hour's drive south of Chur, then drive east via **Bergün** and the **Albula Pass** (open to cars only in the summer). This route features exceptionally attractive vegetation, and less stony desolation – but the 40km (25-mile) stretch to **La Punt ⑯**, is very narrow, so drive with care, even if there is a lot less traffic.

Continuing north up highway 27, you soon come to **Zernez**, the gateway to the **Swiss National Park ⑰**. Here, in a rugged mountainous area covering 1,700 sq km (660 sq miles), nature has been left largely to its own devices since the park was founded in 1914. Strict rules restrict visitor access to certain areas, while campfires and flower picking are punishable by large fines levied by unsmiling rangers. Visitor information is provided at the **Nationalparzentrum** (tel: 081 851 41 41; www.nationalpark. ch; June–Oct daily 8.30am–6pm, Dec 26–Mar 10 Mon–Sat 9am–5pm, Mar 12–May 10 Mon–Fri 9am–noon and 2–5pm) in Zernez, where a 3D model of the national park prepares you for the experience ahead. With the help of a touchscreen, laser beam and a large screen projection, you can map out your visit to the park, and its top 20 sights and 21 walking tours. Fifteen minutes' drive to the northeast is the **Schmelzra Museum** (mid-June–mid-Oct Tues–Fri and Sun 2–5pm), with its bear and mining museums, and a bear trail.

The park is intersected by the **Val Müstair**, which you can cross by taking highway 28 southeast to the village of Santa Maria Val Müstair. Here, at the fork in the road, head a bit further north to the staunchly Romansh village of **Müstair ⑱**, the easternmost village of Switzerland, lying on the Italian border. The big attraction here – unmissable even for those in a real hurry – is the world heritage Kloster St Johann Müstair, an 8th-century convent containing the best-preserved and most extensive collection of Carolingian wall paintings in the Alps. According to legend, Charlemagne, after being

Beautiful scenery in the Swiss National Park.

The Diavolezza cable-car.

St Moritz without its snowy covering.

crowned King of the Lombards, was caught in a snowstorm here while travelling over the Umbrail Pass. Being unharmed, he founded the convent as a sign of gratitude. The convent itself is closed to the public but the church can be visited (daily 8am–7pm), and a **museum** (www.muestair.ch; daily May–Oct 9am–5pm, Nov–Apr 10am–noon and 1.30–4.30pm), with guided tours, tells the history of the convent.

Before leaving the area you might fancy a *piccolo viaggio* onto Glurns, the smallest town in Italy's South Tyrol. South of the fork, the road leads over the Umbrail Pass (open only between June and October) and the sinuous Passo dello Stelvio into northern Italy's enormous national park of the same name.

A WORLD APART

The **Unter Engadin** and **Ober Engadin** (Upper and Lower Engadine) valleys are not divided by any visible border, but are worlds apart in attitude. In the Unter Engadin tradition is still considered a private, local affair. In the Ober Engadin it has blatantly been adapted to meet the demands of tourism. For example, the *Schlitteda*, the traditional winter sledge outing of the village youth, uses horse-drawn buggies in summer to oblige visitors. In the Unter Engadin, valuable Romansh artefacts stand unobtrusively in parlours. In the Ober Engadin, they are more likely to be found prominently displayed in chic establishments such as the Chesa Veglia in St Moritz.

St Moritz ⑲ is the Ober Engadin's jetsetter's winter resort *par excellence*, and though it costs a pretty penny to eat and stay here, it undeniably makes an excellent base for outdoor sporting. The place claims to be the oldest winter resort in the world, and once hosted the Winter Olympic Games.

It all began in 1864 when Johannes Badrutt, owner of St Moritz's Kulm Hotel, invited some English summer guests to spend the winter there, promising they would be able to sit outside in short sleeves in December. Various other St Moritz premières followed: in 1880, Europe's first curling

tournament took place in the town, and in 1884 the first toboggan run was built here. In the case of the latter, the daring participants plunged down the run, reaching speeds of up to 140kph (85mph). It was also in St Moritz that the bobsleigh came to life, in 1891. Occasionally a visitor will pluck up the courage to go down the famous St Moritz-Celerina Olympic bob run – albeit usually in the passenger seat.

The Ober Engadin lives up to every cliché of the moneyed Alpine playground. Here we see the beautiful people stepping out of Rolls-Royces, and members of Europe's aristocracy at play. There is always something astonishing going on – beautiful women draped in furs and being transported in a horse-drawn sledge, Champagne parties and carriage rides on frozen lakes are reality, not fantasy. Up on the sun terrace on **Corviglia**, St Moritz's local mountain, which can be comfortably reached via cable railway, VIPs and would-be VIPs greet one another like castaways who have just been rescued. After several schnapps on the dazzling slope-side sun terrace of the Alpina Hütte the welcoming kisses tend to be aimed rather less accurately.

FUN AND GAMES

This is when the fun really starts. Bolstered by schnapps and feeling positively foolhardy, revellers are suddenly willing to participate in the most dangerous sports. One of the most popular activities is hang-gliding or paragliding down to the **St Moritzer See**, where the range of sports on offer seems to multiply every year: golf and polo in the snow (using red balls) are both popular. In the evening, the bars are full of tourists sporting injuries: tobogganists with plaster casts and skijoring gladiators whose chests are covered in livid bruises (caused by the lumps of ice flying off the horses' hooves). As Art Buchwald said of St Moritz in *I Chose Caviar*, it is "the heart of the broken-limb country, where a man must prove himself first on skis and then on a stretcher".

No one can dodge the bustle in St Moritz or avoid all the frantic activity. That is why there should be somewhere

The Snow Polo World Cup, St Moritz – the only polo tournament played on snow.

in the resort where you can retire. Luckily, the Upper Engadine is just like all other "in" places frequented by the rich and fashionable: take only a few steps off the beaten track and the roar of Ferrari exhausts and the cloying scent of perfumes and aftershaves fade away.

Only then can the visitor get a glimpse of the Upper Engadine as the Austrian poet Rainer Maria Rilke described it in 1919: "How demanding these lakes and mountains are, there is a strange abundance about them, the moments they provide are far from simple. The astonishment of our grandfathers and great-grandfathers seems to have had much to do with this place: they travelled here from their own countries, which apparently had 'nothing', while here there was 'everything' in plenty. Nature with its ups and downs, full of abundance, full of increase, its outlines starkly emphasised."

However, tourism has arrived in full force to see this grandeur and the results have not always been good. Parts of the town resemble city blocks of ugly concrete-box hotels, and in recent years St Moritz has even been compelled to hold its village festival on the roof of its multi-storey car park because all the other open areas have now been built up.

EVENING DELIGHTS

What about evenings in the Engadine? Shortly before dinner is the best time in the day to catch a glimpse of the rich and famous. However, anybody who is anybody tends to prefer cocktail hour in the privacy of their villa on the **Suvrettahang**. This area sloping to the west of St Moritz is the most exclusive part of the town. A tabloid newspaper once made the exaggerated claim that it contained some 50 multimillionaires.

A more rewarding way of spending the twilight hours is to travel to Punt Muragl, 5 minutes by car, 10 by direct train, and take a cable car up to **Muottas Muragl**. From no other observation point is the sheer breadth of the Upper Engadine lake landscape so impressive as when the silvery light starts eddying on the mountainside towards evening. Those who have experienced it once are always drawn back: the early twilight permeates the broad expanse of the plateau until both earth and heaven become a single supernatural shimmer – then suddenly, dusk falls.

If you are looking for less of a crowd, take the narrow-gauge trains or one of the postbus fleet to the surrounding towns, most of them quieter than St Moritz. But if you cannot tear yourself away from St Moritz's party scene, at least make time for a day trip into the hills via one of the many cable cars ascending Piz Nair, and other ski slopes and peaks. High among them, in every respect, is the Diavolezza – not as diabolic as it sounds, in views at least, which are peerless from the mountain top station over the Bernina Massif. The cable car station is at Pontresina, southeast of St Moritz on Route 29; it takes 20 minutes by car or about an hour by train.

Funicular on Muottas Muragl.

THE MORTERATSCH GLACIER

To the east of St Moritz, and branching south off the **Val Bernina** are the two valleys of **Val Roseg** (accessible from the station in **Pontresina** ⑳, where horse-drawn sledges can be hired) and **Val Morteratsch** (which can be reached from the railway station of the same name), both of which are equally pretty in summer or winter. The footpaths here are not steep, and if you walk quietly enough you might just see some young and fearless ibex on the mountain slopes, or a few chamois rooting about in the snow for grass; and in summer maybe even a herd of deer. If you are lucky, the wind might part the clouds suddenly and – for a few glorious minutes only – reveal the **Morteratsch Glacier** lying ahead, covered in fresh snow and bathed in sunlight, and the **Bernina Massif**, towering more than 4,000 metres (13,000ft). The Morteratsch Glacier provides skiers with pretty demanding and varied downhill runs from the **Diavolezza Pass**, and can be reached from the Bernina Pass road via cable car; through binoculars from here, you can see the mountaineers on the Piz Palü, the Bianco Ridge or the Bernina, whatever the time of year.

Pontresina also offers the option of horse-drawn carriage rides up the Bernina Valley, and is another potential jumping-off point for the spectacular *Bernina Express* train-and-bus ride into Italy or the *Glacier Express* west all the way to Zermatt. Alternatively, for those who crave a two-wheeled experience, without doubt the finest cycle route in the canton is a 60km (37-mile) stretch in the Upper Engadine, where every holiday resort is directly connected to the cycle route network. The way leads along the edge of the **Oberengadiner See**, through forests and across broad meadows.

LAKES SILVAPLANER AND SEGL

Another spectacular region to find natural tranquillity is to the southwest of St Moritz where a string of lakes forms the final link in the

Hikers tackle the Morteratsch Glacier.

Ice-Age chain of glacial erosion. The route down the right-hand side of the valley from St Moritz is not too busy. It leads perhaps 20 km (12 miles) southwest across wooded, sheltered slopes, past bog lakes and special stands containing food for the deer, through an idyllic landscape with wonderful views over **Lej da Silvaplaner** below; continue past the foot of the **Corvatsch**, considered by many to be the best mountain for skiing in the world. It is shady and cool here in the summer, and in winter the cross-country skiing routes are prepared and freshened up every day. These are particularly recommended for people wishing to avoid the thick columns of cross-country skiers on the frozen lakes and who want a bit more excitement and exercise.

Beyond Lake Silvaplaner, linked by the town of Sils Maria (Segl in Romansh) is **Lej da Segl**. Nietzsche wrote his *Zarathustra* in **Sils Maria** ㉑ in 1888. Plagued by almost unbearable migraines, his eyes aching, and totally exhausted, he felt transported by nature on this plateau "which has piled itself up fearlessly close to the terrors of the eternal snows, here, where Italy and Finland form a pact with one another and seem to play host to every silvery colour nature possesses – happy is he who can say: 'Nature certainly has bigger and better things to offer, but this is something truly close to my heart'."

Nietzsche Haus (mid-June–mid-Oct and Jan–mid-Apr Tues–Sun 3–6pm), where Nietzsche lived in the summers from 1881 to 1888, is now a museum. Be aware that the exhibits are all captioned in German, although it has some interesting photographs of the man throughout his life.

From the village square of Sils Maria, you can climb aboard a horse-drawn sledge and travel due south into the car-free **Val Fex**. With luck, there may be just enough daylight left to visit the pretty little church in **Crasta** in the valley and admire its wall paintings, dating from 1500. They have only recently been uncovered, but they look almost as good as new.

Romantic sleigh ride in the Val Fex.

VAL BREGAGLIA VILLAGES

Reaching Maloja is like reaching the edge of the world: the pass road plunges 300 metres (1,000ft) into the depths, in 12 steep curves. The villages in Val Bregaglia are agreeably intact; the valley is mainly attractive to mountaineers (the Sciora and Bondasca ranges to the southeast are particularly popular), and hikers, too. The hamlet of **Grevasalvas**, situated high above the **Lej da Segl** up a mountain track just east of the Maloja Pass on the northern side of the lake, can be reached on foot only in summer months, from Maloja.

Thanks to the enterprising spa director of St Moritz, large numbers of tourists have been making the pilgrimage to this unspoilt Alpine hamlet for some years now. Impressed by the number of foreign tourists in St Moritz asking about Heidi – heroine of Johanna Spyri's children's book (who inconveniently had her home in Maienfeld, way to the north of the canton) – he took advantage of the fact that one of the innumerable Heidi films had been shot in Grevasalvas and declared the whole of the Engadine "Heidiland".

Maloja ㉒ itself is extremely small, quiet and Italian-flavoured – a wonderful antidote to the excesses of its famous neighbours Davos and St Moritz – and the stroll to Silvaplaner is breathtaking.

The Val Bregaglia has produced at least one famous artistic family: the village of **Stampa**, further down highway 3 towards the Italian border was the home of the Giacometti family: glass painter Augusto, his cousin Giovanni, the Impressionist, and last but not least Giovanni's son Alberto, whose sculptures can be found in the world's top museums.

SPECTACULAR RAIL JOURNEYS

In the aftermath of World War I, when Graubünden picked itself up out of the dust by spending 26 years building its very own 375km (235-mile) narrow-gauge railway network, the rail was used to transport not the wealthy nobility they had expected, but war refugees instead. The first-class carriages went quietly rusty. Today the Rhätische Bahn (Rhaetian Railway) plays on people's nostalgia and has come full circle as a favoured means of travel into the Alps. The old trains have progressively been made railworthy again, and dolled up. They rock their passengers to and fro on velvet cushions, through 115 tunnels and across 485 bridges. A train such as the *Glacier Express* takes eight hours to reach Zermatt in the Valais from St Moritz, via Andermatt, Chur and Davos.

Most tourists are so enchanted, they don't realise the little red trains and picturesque Alpine stations are not a specially laid on tourist experience, but a real part of everyday life. No other railway in the world alternates between such extremes. Even when the champagne is bubbling and caviar being spread in the

Aerial view of the Maloja Pass.

A train crosses the Val-Mela Viaduct.

⏱ Tip

While the Chur–St Moritz section of the *Bernina Express* is famous, lesser known but spectacular is the looping ride down from the Bernina Pass, Europe's highest railway Alpine pass at 2,253 metres (7,392ft), to the remote Val Poschiavo, in the far south of Graubünden canton.

The Bernina Express.

walnut-panelled, lavishly upholstered restaurant car with its shiny brass fittings, three carriages down, farmers are travelling to market and children to school.

Between Christmas and the New Year every single seat is occupied, and even the most dilapidated-looking wooden carriages groan over the rails, transporting passengers to the skiing resorts. In May and November, on the other hand, the carriages are often near empty.

THE BERNINA PASS

In 2008, the *Bernina Express* stretch between Thusis and Poschiavo was designated a Unesco world heritage landscape for its spectacular railway architecture, deep gorges and icy glaciers. The journey is composed of two historic Rhaetian Railway lines: Thusis to Albula in the north, and Bernina south to Poschiavo. In total, the 128km (80-mile) trip across Canton Graubünden countryside features an astounding 55 tunnels and covered galleries, and 196 viaducts and bridges.

For many years, the whole route starting in Chur and ending up just over the border from Poschiavo in Tirano, Italy, has been considered a showpiece stretch of the legendary rail journey, winding its circuitous way southeast through gorges and over the famous Landwasser Viaduct – a curved single-track overpass composed of several 65-metre (200ft) high limestone arches – reaching Tirano roughly 4 hours later. The most thrilling part awaits passengers at the **Bernina Pass**, where in winter and spring the locomotive ploughs through metre-high snow at an altitude of 2,257 metres (7,400ft), flanked on all sides by many of Switzerland's highest peaks. Then, in the Mediterranean climes of its southern destination, it comes to a halt among palm trees and magnolia. The gradient achieved in the first part of the journey is about 7 percent, which makes it one of the steepest conventional rail routes in the world.

Railway enthusiasts will also enjoy the stretch between **Bergün** and **Preda**. In order to gain height, the railway line

performs a series of five loops and two tunnels through the mountainside, thus avoiding the more typical Alpine cogwheel system. In this section alone, the line climbs 416 metres (1,365ft) over a distance of only 12.6km (7.8 miles), and goes through the **Albula Tunnel**, at 1,820 metres (5,970ft), the highest rail tunnel in Europe. In winter, the trip can also be done by sledge. Then the 5km (3-mile) stretch of road between Preda and Bergün is closed to cars, and turned into the most popular sledge run in the whole Graubünden Alps. Sledges can be hired from a shop at the station in Preda; a ride through the snow during a full moon is particularly recommended. The train shuttles the sledge parties from Bergün back to their starting point until 1.30am.

The Rhätische Bahn runs several tourist trains on this route throughout the year, all equipped with modern comforts and panoramic observation carriages (Bahnhofstrasse 25 Chur; tel: 081 288 65 65; www.rhb.ch).

Beyond the Bernina Pass, at the heart of Val Poschiavo, is the picturesque town of **Poschiavo** ㉓, with several remarkable churches, and the colourful, richly ornamented facades of the *quartiere spagnolo*, built around 1830 by emigrants returning from Spain.

The Vereina (road) tunnel allows travel to the Unter Engadin, year-round, connecting Prättigau near Chur to Engadin in about 20 minutes. Prior to its 1999 opening, vehicles had to rely on the Flüela Pass linking Susch in the lower Unter Engadin with Davos – a road that is closed in winter. The Lower Engadine is a paradise for incorrigible mountain-pass cyclists, who come for the climb to the 2,383 metre/7,818ft crest. Catering to them, the Bahn also offers a very unbureaucratic bike service. If you book two days ahead, online or by phone, you can pick up a hire bike from many stations on the Rhätische Bahn/Rhaetian Railway network, ride off and hand it in at the station of your choice at the end of your tour. There are bicycles for hire – as well as mountain bikes – at most local tourist offices too.

Mountain bikers on the Suvretta Loop.

📷 TOURING THE SWISS LANDSCAPE

Switzerland's tourist industry has an enviable reputation for excellent facilities, reliability and cleanliness. But it was not always so...

Until relatively modern times, travellers shunned the Alps, regarding them as dangerous and inhospitable, and as little more than "considerable protuberances", thinly populated by suspicious and hostile mountain peasants. Hotels were non-existent and inns dirty and flea-ridden. Yet by the late 18th century peaks and glaciers were being explored and studied, less for their beauty than for their scientific interest. Then came the literary Romantic movement, and its cult of wild nature, which endowed the mountains with a quasi-religious, mystical meaning, appealing to the upper-middle classes of Victorian Britain. Professional people flocked to the Alps, some to boldly scale the summits. The first climbers were Swiss, but most peaks were conquered by Britons, notably the Matterhorn by Edward Whymper in 1865. Huts were built high up for climbers, and grand hotels and modest pensions at lower altitudes for an increasing number of ordinary tourists, some of them brought here on Thomas Cook's pioneering tours, whose vintage posters of Swiss Holiday Tours are priceless classics.

Switzerland is not just a winter-sports tourist destination. Walking trails can be found all over the country, making the most of its exquisite and diverse scenery.

Poster advertising the Montraux–Bernese Oberland railway, 1922.

TOURIST CHIC

By the early 20th century a stay in an elegant Swiss resort such as Interlaken or St Moritz was the ultimate in chic. Few tourists came to an isolated Switzerland during the two world wars (1914–18 and 1939–45), but post-war affluence opened up the country to a wider public. Today more visitors come here than ever before, staying in anything from a self-catering chalet to a luxury hotel.

Tourists relax on the Wetterhorn, 1890.

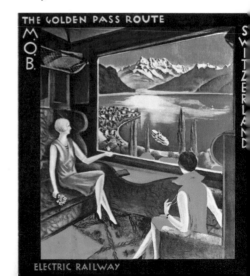

Hikers traverse a karst formation on the ascent of Mount Schrattenfluh.

Switzerland on foot

A glance at a large-scale map of any part of Switzerland, lowlands or Alps, will reveal a dense mesh of footpaths – a paradise for walkers. The country's paths are not only comprehensively mapped, but they are impeccably waymarked – mostly with cheerful yellow signs – indicating destinations and approximate walking times required to reach them. One important distinction is that between an ordinary hiking path, *Wanderweg*, and a mountain path, a *Bergweg*. The first can be attempted by anyone, while a mountain path may involve tough terrain, and steep and exposed places, with particularly difficult sections secured by ropes or chains. Or they may involve crossing a river. The *Wanderweg* have plain yellow signs; the mountain paths have the same, but with a red and white tip. Then there are seriously heavy-duty Alpine routes marked by deep blue signposts with a blue and white tip, which cross mountain passes or tackle other extremely challenging high Alpine routes by day (or over several). Along the way, blue and white painted stripes mark the route, while information panels at the start spell out special requirements and cautions. Many visitors content themselves with day walks, but it can be great fun to ramble from place to place. Staying overnight in Alpine huts makes it possible to cover long distances at high altitude. Enthusiasts could try one of the great cross-country walks, like the historic Gotthard route, which starts in Basel and ends up in Lugano, in the Ticino, via the St Gotthard Pass. An indispensable source of information on all things hiking is Wanderland.ch, the website of the Switzerland Mobility Foundation, which manages a national network for "non-motorised traffic", including walking, cycling, mountain biking, skating and canoeing.

ypically Swiss accommodation can be found at the Hotel afleralp in the Valais.

he Historic Railway Trail is a hike with information oards on the Albula section of the Rhaetian Railway.

Hiking signpost on Mount Säntis.

The Limmat River and Zürich's Roman-Gothic Grossmünster.

ZÜRICH

The Swiss banking capital has relaxed, with a flourishing arts scene and some arresting new architecture capping off its stunning Alpine and lake setting.

Zürich in many ways could be taken as the Swiss capital. For a start, it's the largest city in Switzerland, with a population of more than 380,500. Secondly, it is located in a dominant position in the north of the country, well above the actual capital, Bern, and the international one, Geneva. And finally, it is big, dazzling and wealthy.

The City of Zürich alone represents nearly 10 percent of Switzerland's workforce, and over 40 percent of the country's banking institutions have their headquarters here, sweeping up 85 percent of the total value of the assets held in Switzerland. But Zürich is not just about banks. Art and culture is a burgeoning sector that has grown in recent years as the city has let its hair down and embraced public art and a zany river lifestyle, experimental post-industrial architecture and fabulous design hotels. In fact, one in five jobs in the creative economy are located in Zürich, accounting for CHF 9.2 billion – 15 percent of Switzerland's entire revenue.

Even linguistically the city can claim some dominance. Zürich's own form of Swiss German (Schweizerdeutsch) is called Zürideutsch (locals call it Züritüütsch). It has a wider audience than other regional dialects, is understood countrywide and is even spoken on national radio programmes, most of them produced in Zürich.

Strolling along Utoquai.

ARRIVAL IN ZÜRICH

Travellers who approach the city by air will land at **Zürich Airport**, which is the largest in Switzerland – everything Swiss, apart from the mountains, is bigger in Zürich. From the airport, the train takes no more than 15 minutes to reach Zürich's main railway station; you can also take the tram.

Zürich is divided into 12 different districts, the Kreis: the equivalent of Paris's *arrondissements*. The Old Town, the Altstadt, falls into Kreis 1 and encompasses the historical core of the

Main Attractions

The Altstadt
Zürich-West
Landesmuseum
Kunsthaus
Grossmünster
Opernhaus Zürich
Schauspielhaus Zürich
Uetliberg

Maps on pages 228, 242

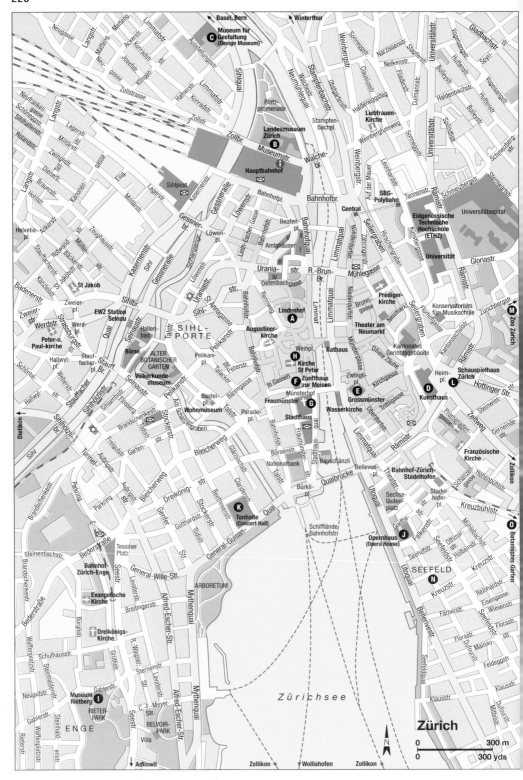

↓ Basel, Bern   ↓ Winterthur

Museum für
Gestaltung
(Design Museum) C

Neugasse

Langstr.
Matteng.
Ackerstr.
Konradstr.
Josefstr.
Klingen-
Neu-
gasse
Zollstrasse

Limmatstr.

Ausstellungstr.

Sihlquai

Platz-
promenade

Stampfenbachstr.

Sonneggstr.
Weinbergstr.
Nelkenstr.

Universitätstr.
Vogelsangstr.
Spyri-
str.

Gladbachstr.

Neufrankeng.
Schöneggstr.
Schönegg-
str.
Sihlfeldstr.

Langstr.
Lagerstr.
Militärstr.
Zwinglistr.
gasse
Dienerstr.
Brauerstr.
Hohlstr.
Langstr.

Limmatstr.
Hafnerstr.
Konradstr.
Zollstr.

Zollbr.

Landesmuseum
Zürich B

Museumstr.

Walche-

Stampfen-
bachpl.

Liebfrauen-
Kirche

Weinbergstr.
Weinbergfussweg

Clausiusstr.
Fliederstr.
Haldenbachstr.

Universitätstr.
Hüttenstr.
Bolleystr.
Hüttenstr.

Haldenbachsteg

Culmannstr.

Universitätstr.
Vogelsangstr.
Bolleystr.

Schmelzberg-
str.

Neugasse
Eisg.
Kanonen-
str.
Kasernenstr.

Sihlpost

Hauptbahnhof ✉

i

Bahnhofpl.

Bahnhofbr.

SBG-
Polybahn

Central

Eidgenössische
Technische
Hochschule
(ETHZ)

Universitätsspital

Gessnerallee
Lagerstr.
Kasernenstr.
Gessner-
br.
Schanzenstr.

Löwenstr.

Beaten-
pl.
III
Bahnhofstr.

Bahnhofpl.

Bahnhofquai

Leonhardstr.

Zähringerstr.

Seilergraben

Hirschengr.

Kunststrasse

Rämistr.

Universität

Gloriastr.

Helvetia-
pl.
Ankerstr.
Rotwand-
str.
Müllerstr.
Zeughausstr.
St Jakobstr.

St Jakob

Gessner-
str.

Löwen-
pl.

Amtshausen
Urania-
str.
Oetenbachgasse

R.-Brun-
Br.

Mühlegasse

Prediger-
kirche

Neumarkt

Konservatorium
für Musikschule

Zürichbergstr.

M
Zoo Zürich

Badenstr.
Zweier-
pl.
Zweier-
str.
Werdstr.
Kanzleistr.

Sihlstr.

Kasernenstr.

Sihl

Gessnerallee

Löwenstr.
Sihlbr.

St Annagasse

Rennweg
Lindenhof A

Limmat

Brunn-
gasse

Theater am
Neumarkt

Kantonales
Gerichtsgebäude

Kantonsschulstr.

Rämistr.

Hirschengr.

Strassburgstr.
Schöntal-
Werd-
str.

EWZ Station
Selnau

Hallen-
bad

Talstr.

Uraniastr.

Sihl

SIHL-
PORTE

Augustiner-
kirche

Weinpl.
H
Kirche
St Peter
Zunfthaus
zur Meisen F

Rathaus

Münstergasse
Obere Zäune

Schönberg-
str.

Heim-
pl. L

Schauspielhaus
Zürich D

Hottinger Str.

Zeltweg

Peter- u.
Paul-kirche

Hallwyl-
str.

Stauf-
facher-
pl.
Stauff.
Br.

Börse

ALTER
BOTANISCHER
GARTEN

Pelikanstr.

St Peterstr.
Pelikan-
pl.

In Gassen

Bärengasse
Talacker

Münsterhof
G
Fraumünster

Fraumünsterstr.

Zwingli-
pl. E

Grossmünster

Wasserkirche

Kirchgasse

Oberdorfstr.
Trittligasse

Promenadengasse

Rämistr.

D
Kunsthaus

L

Schöntal.
str.
Hallwyl-
str.

Völkerkunde-
museum

Bastei-
pl.

Wohnmuseum

Stadthaus

Parade-
pl.

Börsenstr.

Limmatquai

Bauschänzli

Bellevue-
pl.

Theaterstr.

Französische
Kirche

Hohenbühlstr.

Schänzen-
gasse

Zollikon
O

Brandschenkestr.

Selnaustr.
Sihlamtstr.
Sihlhölzistr.
Sihlhölz-
br.
Tunnelstr.
Aurorastr.
Freigutstr.
Garten-
str.

Brandschenkestr.

Parking

Bleicherweg
Dreikönig-
str.

Stockerstr.
Beethovenstr.
Claridenstr.

Nationalbank

Bürkli-
pl.

Quaibrücke

Utoquai

Bahnhof-Zürich-
Stadelhofen

Stadel-
hofer-
pl.

Kreuzbühlstr.

Kreuzstr.

Botanischer
Garten

Dietikon
←

Stauffacher-

Genferstr.
Gotthardstr.
Todistr.
General-Guisan

Quai

Tonhalle
(Concert Hall) K

Schiffländer
Bahnhofstr.

Sechse-
läuten-
platz

Goethe

Falkenstr.
Seefeldstr.

Opernhaus
(Opera House) J

Mühlebachstr.

Zollikon

Bahnhof-
Zürich-Enge

Evangelische
Kirche

Dreikönigs-
Kirche

Tessiner
Platz

General-Wille-Str.
Lavaterstr.
Breitingerstr.

Alfred-Escher-Str.

Mythenquai

ARBORETUM

Seestr.

Steinentischstr.
Brandschenkestr.
Bederstrasse

Bürglistr.
Schulhausstr.

Steinenstr.

C.F.-Meyer-Str.

Sternenstr.
Lavaterstr.
R.-Wagner-Str.

Bederstr.

Museum
Rietberg I

RIETER-
PARK

BELVOIR-
PARK

Villa

Gablerstr.
Neugutstr.
Gablerstr.
Steinhald-
enstr.
Waffenplatzstr.
Rieterstr.

ENGE

Kreuzstr.

SEEFELD
N

Seefeldstr.

Dufourstr.
Florastr.
Mainaustr.

Hohlstr.
Ithastr.

Feldeggstr.

Wiesenstr.
Eisengasse
Reinhardstr.

Färberstr.

Hottinger Str.

Zollikon

Bellerivestr.

Utoquai

Seefeldquai

Dufourstr.
Mittelstr.
Klausstr.

Zürichsee

Zürich

N

0   300 m

0   300 yds

↓ Adliswil   ↓ Zollikon   ↓ Wollishofen   ↓ Zollikon

city as it was prior to 1893 when the districts gradually began to be swept into the city area.

The busiest place in Zürich every morning is the main **Hauptbahnhof** railway station, or simply Zürich HB. A sea of bankers, business people and cultural industry movers and shakers flows into the city from the suburbs, which spread into the green and hilly outlying areas all around. Whatever the residents of Bern or Geneva might say, Zürich remains Switzerland's main commercial and cultural centre. It has also repeatedly been elected the city with the best quality of life in the world – little wonder so many people want to live and work here, and that the population is steadily on the rise.

It was here, on Bahnhofplatz, on a nose of land between the Sihl and Limmat rivers, that Zürich first began to improve its links with the rest of Europe. The large, bright railway station hall was considered a significant architectural achievement at the time it was built, between 1865 and 1871. Since then it has been extensively renovated. The colourful guardian angel sculpture by Niki de St. Phalle hanging from the roof of its main hall in bright papier-mâché is particularly striking.

BAHNHOFSTRASSE AND BEYOND

Bahnhofstrasse is the buzzing commercial centre of the city. Some call it the finest street in Europe, and the people of Zürich are particularly proud of it. Curving its way round from the Hauptbahnhof to the lake, it extends almost a mile to the Bürkliplatz and Quaibrücke, where the Zürichsee kisses the Limmat.

Along its length is an impressive display of wealth: the dazzling consumer temples of the Manor, Globus and Jelmoli department stores, the head offices of the "Gnomes of Zürich" (as the big bankers are referred to) and all the major luxury fashion brands, both local and international. The chic shopping enclave bordered by Bahnhofstrasse, **Storchengasse** and the **River Limmat** offers every kind of fancy couture and jewellery shop, with some contemporary creative influences thrown in as well. Everything you can never afford to buy can be found here; this is the centre of Switzerland's opulence, as luxurious as anything you will find in Tokyo, London or New York.

Ultra-glamorous but also an embodiment of everything Swiss, Bahnhofstrasse has all the typical virtues of order, cleanliness and punctuality. An everyday pair of trousers or a simple shirt is displayed in the shop windows like a masterpiece at the Louvre. Banks line the strip all the way through to **Paradeplatz** – a small square home to the headquarters of all the main banks and the largest financial transaction site in the country. Paradeplatz's trading history dates back to the 17th century, when it was known as Säumärt, doing a lively trade in pigs and other livestock.

⊙ Tip

If you plan to do a lot of travelling around, purchase a 24 or 72-hour ZürichCARD, providing all bus, train and cableway travel in the city and the surrounding region, plus free or reduced admission to most museums. Buy online or at the tourist office in the main station (tel: 044 215 40 00; www.zuerich.com; Mon–Sat 8am–8.30pm Sun 8.30am–6.30pm).

Christmas on Bahnhofstrasse.

Zürich cityscape by night.

RIVERSIDE TREASURES

The architecture on Bahnhofstrasse is also worth closer inspection: in particular the Art Nouveau facades of the department stores of Manor and St Annahof; the early iron construction of Jelmoli (Zürich's first glass palace, dating from the 1660s); the **Bank Julius Bär**, modelled on an Italian palazzo, and the head office of the **Credit Suisse Bank**, which takes up one whole side of the **Paradeplatz**.

At the south end of Bahnhofstrasse, modern architect Arnold Bürkli used the excavated material from the city's many new building sites to fill in the large quay area at **Bürkliplatz** by the lake. Here is unquestionably the finest **post office** building in all Switzerland, and beside it the Renaissance *palazzo* of the **Fraumünsterpost** and the Renaissance-style **Stadthaus**. The area is also home to some of the city's most luxurious hotels, notably the sumptuous **Bar au Lac**, not only one of the city's best hotels, but the world's, its gardens rolling down to the lakeside. Crossing the Quaibrücke to Bellevueplatz, an important tram hub, takes you to the lower part of the Altstadt and Kreis 1, which ends at the adjacent Opernhaus Zürich. Between the opera house square and Bellevueplatz the avenues are wider and more open, with many elegant restaurant terraces where you can eat outside on summer evenings, or sip, see and be seen, while consuming *coupes* (ice cream) and *Cüplis* (glasses of champagne).

ALTSTADT: ZÜRICH'S OLD TOWN

Zürich's Old Town, the **Altstadt**, falls within Kreis 1, and takes in a whole circular area straddling the banks of the river, and from the Zürich HB area south to the lake.

A charm magnet, and a good launch pad for exploring Zürich, is **Niederdorf**, named after the long sinewy street that runs through it, Niederdorfstasse. Locals refer to the whole area on the right bank of the Limmat as "Dörfli", the village. This narrow street in the old town, intersected by more than 30 other streets, is traffic free and lined

with narrow Gothic houses, some perennially dingy, occupied by bakeries, delicatessens, tobacconists, second-hand bookshops and antiques shops. It is also a thriving residential area populated by some 5,000 people: many young and fashionable who have injected new life into the heart of the city; others, elderly residents who were born here and who have chosen to stay, keeping their original "village spirit" alive for as long as they can.

Niederdorf is also Zürich's oldest entertainment district, and hoards are attracted here by its nightlife. The place does not really pick up momentum until about eight in the evening. Until then there are still empty tables in the restaurants and at pavement cafés, street musicians are busy tuning up and club dancers are drinking coffee at the bar. Soon, however, everything is in full swing. Crowds fill the streets, beer flows Munich style, and the bars throb with music. Most of the activity stops at around midnight, but continues on a smaller scale until at least 2am in a number of select nightclubs.

HISTORIC ZÜRICH

Take in historic Zürich on the left bank of the Limmat, firstly with a climb up to the **Lindenhof** Ⓐ, a small hill with splendid views over the river, the Old Town, the Grossmünster church and Rathaus (city hall), stretching all the way to the university and Swiss Federal Institute of Technology in the distance. It was here that the Celts settled in around 80 BC and then later the Romans, from around 15 BC onwards, with their customs station on the Limmat, "Turicum" (a byword for Zürich used in many names here, even their locally brewed gin).

In the 9th century, the grandson of Charlemagne built a palatial residence on the same site, which has been such a crucial historical meeting place – this is where the Helvetian Constitutional oath sealing Swiss unity was taken in 1798.

Nestling around the Lindenhof is the most ancient part of the medieval town, its small streets lined with tall, narrow houses, blended in with Baroque and Rococo facades.

⊙ Tip

Highlights of the Kunsthaus Zürich include Rodin's *The Gates of Hell* on its facade, the largest set of works by painter Edvard Munch outside Scandinavia, plus many pieces by Alberto Giacometti.

POST-INDUSTRIAL ZÜRICH

The redevelopment of the old industrial area of Zürich-West has put the city on the map as a daring new international design hub, fusing bold architecture with heritage, nature and community.

The old breweries, railway viaducts and soap factories that once dotted the Kreis 5 district, unfurling over a 2.5km (1.5-mile) stretch west of Zürich HB along the River Limmat, have gradually been transformed into new cultural and performing-arts spaces, jazz clubs and striking mixed developments featuring luxury hotels and spas, spanking new apartments and retail heavens.

The old shipyard, **Schiffbau**, was one of the first developments. The restaurants, shops and bars under its soaring ceilings, metal structure and glass walls are typical of these striking labour-yard conversions. As well as being a major secondary location for the Schauspielhaus Theatre, it also houses the city's best jazz venue, Moods (www.moods.

Frau Gerolds Garten.

ch), Restaurant LaSalle and lofty NietturmBar, which has great views over the district.

By night, the surrounding square, **Turbinenplatz** – whose name gives away its industrial past – lights up colourfully, highlighting the stark mix of concrete, glass and greenery. Like much of "Züri West" the space often gives over to festivals and public art – here you will encounter sculptures, installations, handcrafted benches and colourful fibreglass cows (the now international CowParade).

Opposite, the former metal foundry **Giessereihalle Puls 5** is used for contemporary art fairs. Towards the river, on Limmatstrasse, is the **Löwenbräu-Areal**, a silo-topped 1897 brewery housing two art spaces, the Kunsthalle (http://kunsthallezurich.ch) and Migros Museum fur Gegenwartskunst (http://migros museum.ch), as well as a residential tower and smaller galleries. The Kunsthalle was one of the earlier signs of the arty improvements in store for this former workers' district, and has made a name for itself with a high-quality and packed programme of local and international contemporary art shows.

Curving round between the railway and the river is the charming **Viaduktstrasse** (http://im-viadukt.ch), whose old arches house clothing boutiques, craft stores and cafés. It passes by the **Josefwiese**, a delightful garden with a community feel, a playground and a café. And almost nestled under the railway tracks is the unbelievably novel bike-filling station-cum-restaurant and garden, **Frau Gerolds Garten** at Geroldstrasse 23.

Finally, for relaxation, Züri West has its amazing free river bathing spots. The almost Olympic length channels of the **Schwimmbad Oberer Letten** (Lettensteg 10; daily excepting bad weather, mid-June–Aug 7am–8pm, May–mid-June and Sept 9am–8pm, rest of year 9–11am) near the Sihlquai are located on a long concrete pier in the middle of the river. Quite a bit downstream but well worth the river stroll – or cycle – is the historic wooden river bath **Flussbad Unterer Letten** (Wasserwerkstrasse 141; daily excepting bad weather May–Sept 9am–8pm, rest of year 9–11am), which has a large pool, a wading pool and a playground for kids, a diving board, picnic tables, a river bar and even an open-air cinema in July. The water temperature at both hovers around 19°C/70°F in summer.

ART GALLERIES

Just behind the station, on Museumstrasse, is the excellent **Landesmuseum Zürich B** (Swiss National Museum Zürich; tel: 058 466 65 11; http://nationalmuseum.ch; Tues–Sun 10am–5pm, Thur until 7pm; free). A castellated building erected in 1893, an arresting new concrete extension was added in 2016. Like many cultural projects in the city, the upgrade was funded by private sponsors as well as national and local government, which helps make culture a big value-added business.

The labyrinthine gallery comprises a collection of artwork and exhibits in more than 100 different rooms. There are archaeological finds, Roman relics, cultural artefacts dating from the Middle Ages, heraldic shields and a whole series of rooms and halls furnished in the styles of the 15th–18th centuries. Inside, you will notice the enormous fresco by Ferdinand Hodler, showing the defeat of the Swiss Army by the French at Marignano in 1515.

Do not miss the nearby design museum, located in the old milk-factory redevelopment known as Toni-Areal, the **Museum für Gestaltung C** (Pfingstweidstrasse 96; tel: 043 446 67 67; www.museum-gestaltung.ch; Tues–Thur 10am–8pm, Fri–Sun 11am–6pm). The minimalist cubic structure puts on dynamic and cutting-edge temporary shows, hinging on design, graphics, posters and applied art, which dip into its extensive collections of some half a million objects from the everyday to the creative and the industrial.

From here, a small stint on public transport (change from train to tram No. 3 direction Klusplatz at Central Station) will take you to the seriously impressive fine arts museum, the **Kunsthaus D** (tel: 01 253 84 84; Tues–Thur 10am–9pm, Fri–Sun 10am–5pm) on **Heimplatz**. Race through two millennia of European art history in the best gallery in the country, whose collection grew from 1787 and has been boosted by generous endowments from private collectors as well as its own major purchases. Only Paris can boast a better exhibition of French painting, which joins other highlights including works by Giacometti and Munch, and

The Landesmuseum Zürich.

collections of Swiss painting, classical modernism, 17th-century Dutch painting and Italian Baroque. Due for completion in 2018, an award-winning extension designed by British architectural firm David Chipperfield will add 15,000 sq metres (160,000 sq ft) of new exhibition space, as well as an art garden and recreation zones.

NIGHTLIFE

Zürich has long shaken off its reputation for having a rather Swiss, conservative and restrained nightlife. In recent years Zürich has loosened its shackles and dozens of chic new bars, cocktail lounges, restaurants and clubs have opened. Many of the more traditional places – Teutonic pubs serving frothy Pilsner and smoky little cellar bars – have remained, providing something for everyone's taste for a night on the town. A good place to start the evening is Niederdorf, where you can wander from café to café before choosing a restaurant for dinner. Or a stroll along Langstrasse, the once seedy, now hip, former red-light street.

Zürich's rooftops seen from the Polyterrasse.

The city's nightlife reflects its cosmopolitan nature, with bars and restaurants that take their inspiration from Morocco, Brazil and Vietnam. Sit sipping a Mai Tai in a bar like Acapulco in trendy Neugasse and you'll forget you're in Zürich at all. Some of Zürich's uber-chic nightlife is expensive, but a good night out doesn't have to bankrupt you. In the fashionable district behind the Hauptbahnhof there are eastern European restaurants serving goulash and local bars where you can drink alongside budget-conscious students. Nestling alongside it is Zürich-West (see page 232), a post-industrial hub stretching along the Limmat with a thriving cultural and bar scene by night.

If you're looking more for night views than nightlife, take a walk after dark (or if that's too much, a short trip on the Polybahn funicular from Central) to the **Polyterrasse**, a lookout point next to the city's polytechnic university. Here you will see Zürich nestling below, its brightly lit landmarks towering out of the sea of lights. The **Predigerkirche**, a Gothic church, is in the foreground;

behind it is the Romanesque-Gothic **Grossmünster** Ⓔ, with its twin towers, cut down to size somewhat after an 18th-century fire. Back on the west bank of the Limmat, the rococo **Zunfthaus zur Meisen** Ⓕ, a jewel-box of a building, contains a ceramics collection from the National Museum, highlights of which include faïence-style ceramic stoves. Alongside is the slim Gothic grandeur of the **Fraumünster** Ⓖ, once part of a convent; its stained-glass windows were created by famous Russian-born artist Marc Chagall (1887–1985). Also nearby is the tower of **Kirche St Peter** Ⓗ, with its eye-catching clock face, which, at 8.7 metres (28ft in diameter), is Europe's largest.

AROUND THE ZÜRICHSEE

Zürich's lake is part of the city centre. Its northern tip comes right up to greet the Altstadt, at the lake-crossing **Quaibrücke**, where the west and east banks of the Limmat collide. From there, the rest of the lake can be reached via shady shoreline walks. Down the Mythenquai, which skirts its western shore, you can continue until you reach the city's largest and beautifully landscaped **Rieterpark**, in the Enge district. Here, on a small rise, is **Villa Wesendonck**, where composer Richard Wagner set his famous *Wesendonck Lieder* to the words written by his beloved Mathilde. Not only Wagner, but also Franz Liszt, Gottfried Semper, Johannes Brahms and the Swiss poet Conrad Ferdinand Meyer were guests at this villa, which today houses the **Museum Rietberg** Ⓞ (tel: 044 415 31 31; Tues–Sun 10am–5pm). It contains more than 2,000 cultural artefacts from far-flung countries.

Equally exotic in its own right is the curious and quirky **Sukkulenten-Sammlung Zürich**, situated on Mythenquai, whose collection of over 5,000 cacti and other succulents includes some truly magnificent plant specimens from Africa and South and Central America. It's right alongside the Mythenquai Strandbad, a sandy open-air beach, if you feel like a dip.

Alternatively, stroll west for about 15 minutes to **Sihlcity**, a glittering retail and leisure space in a former paper mill in the Wiedikon district. Another of Zürich's post-industrial marvels, a 65-metre (213ft) brick chimney and three other buildings were integrated into the development to maintain a sense of the past – when people worked, not shopped, here 12 hours a day. The same historical sensitivity, and the industrial chimneys, mark the River Sihl area, such as the amazing Hürlimann brewery a bit further downstream, which houses the B2 Boutique Hotel + Spa.

CLASSICAL MUSIC AND OPERA

Two buildings worth visiting, whether for a performance or not, are the **Opernhaus** Ⓙ (Opera House) on Sechseläutenplatz, and the **Tonhalle** Ⓚ (Concert Hall) in Gotthardstrasse, with its magnificent organ and unusually clear acoustics. Both buildings contain so much stucco and painting that the eye can happily take over from the ear during any (rare)

The Museum Rietberg now occupies Villa Wesendonck.

⊙ Tip

If you fancy a breath of fresh air while watching a film, the is the city's open-air lakeside cinema, showing about 30 films, from latest releases to vintage slapstick, from mid-July to mid-August.

boring stretches of a musical performance. Both of Zürich's orchestras are so generously supported by public funding that quality is assured. The operas are world-renowned, with a number of new productions each season.

Zürich's thriving alternative arts scene can be found at the **Rote Fabrik**, a former factory turned grassroots cultural centre, run by a collective, which stages concerts, solidarity parties and experimental theatre. Find it down the west side of the lake at Seestrasse 95 (take Tram 7 to Wollishofen).

MUSIC AND DRAMA FESTIVALS

Biennially, the **Festspiele** or Zürich Festival (www.festspiele-zuerich.ch) kicks off the city's vivacious show of summer events. Held for four weeks from 1 June, major cultural institutions including the Opera House, Schauspielhaus Theatre, the Tonhalle concert hall and Kunsthaus come together to put on an amazing show, with the Museum Rietberg and Gessnerallee, Neumarkt and Rigiblick theatres also involved. Each time it focuses on a different theme, explored

through theatre, opera, concerts, dance, exhibitions, readings and discussions. There are also outdoors events.

But the highlight of contemporary musical and theatrical life for many is the performing arts festival, **Theater Spektakel** (www.theaterspektakel.ch), which takes place in August and September, when the very best in experimental productions from all over the world can be seen at the alternative culture venues.

ROCK MUSIC, TECHNO, JAZZ AND CINEMA

The event that really launches Zürich's summer, ahead of the (relatively staid) traditional cultural events, is the end of August techno **Street Parade**. Truly wild – particularly when set against the city's traditionally buttoned-down past – it is an incredibly fun time to be in town. Billed as Europe's biggest technoparade, up to a million youths and techno and party fans of all ages descend upon the city for an afternoon parade and all-night dance session. The event lights up the city as the throngs follow some 26 floats, known as "lovemobiles", through the streets, often under a powerful sun, with the high-decibel electronic beats blaring out over the lake.

A major entertainment venue for concerts, shows and parties is the **Maag Halle** (www.bymaag.ch) in Zürich-West, just behind the Hardbrücke train station. Billy Idol, Kid Rock and Lady Gaga have all performed here. Also in Zürich-West, you will find the city's top jazz venue, **Moods** (www.moods.ch), at the Schiffbau centre. The club hosts over 300 concerts a year, ranging from jazz to electro, and you can dance the night away here on Fridays or Saturday. Pop and jazz concerts are also staged at the community-run Rote Fabrik centre, while the huge rock concerts that are held in the **Hallenstadion** in Oerlikon attract coachloads of fans, many travelling from Germany and Austria.

Zürich's annual Street Parade is noisy and colourful.

Then there are the clubs. Once they were staid, but everything has changed in blazing fashion: Zürich now counts itself among a handful of cities in the world at the centre of the house, techno and trance music scene. Whether or not the throbbing bass lines and endlessly repetitive synthesised beats are to your taste, they have brought an unprecedented surge of youthful energy to the city. All-night rave parties are the norm and nightclubs have popped up everywhere. Possibly the most famous club is **Kaufleuten** (www.kaufleuten.ch/anfahrts plan) on the Pelikanplatz, where house music and Ibiza-style beats lure along with red velvet lounges and strobes.

For those who want more sedate diversion there is always the cinema. The most popular are those that show films in the original language, from the latest Hollywood box-office hits to the established classics, all the way to the outermost fringes of the avant-garde. Despite the distinct lack of cinemas, the city is still very much a cinema city, where seeing the latest film is a must

if you want to keep up with the cultural and social scene.

THE SWISS STAGE

Zürich is a city alive with theatre, from traditional to cutting-edge. Beyond the conservative facade, the city has always concealed an avant-garde underbelly. One local institution, Cabaret Voltaire, hosted the first ever Dada event, a subversive and unorthodox art movement in the early 20th century that paved the way for Dalí, Picasso and a host of other artists trying new ideas and forms. The institution is still putting on exhibitions and jazz in Spiegelgasse.

Just outside the Altstadt, east of Grossmünsterplatz, is one of the most important playhouses in German-speaking Europe, the **Schauspielhaus Zürich** ● (Rämistrasse 34; www.schauspielhaus.ch). A bastion of anti-fascist resistance during World War II, star-studded premieres of Bertolt Brecht plays, modern classics by Swiss authors such as Max Rudolf Frisch and the epic theatre pieces of Friedrich Dürrenmatt, focusing on his

The Schiffbau centre, a popular event space.

war experiences, were staged here during the post-war years. Having celebrated its centenary anniversary in 2018, the Schauspielhaus has helped carve out a deep culture of theatre among the locals.

In 2000, the Schauspielhaus expanded across to the other side of the river, to the old shipbuilding yard turned performing arts centre, the **Schiffbau**, in the Escher-Wyss district. The eye-catching redbrick building, lit up in neon, is a symbol of the transformation of Zürich's west side. The three auditoriums – the Halle, the Box and little Matchbox – amount to Switzerland's largest performance space, and there are also jazz clubs and restaurants.

Several small established theatres are also nearby: west towards the Münster is the atmospheric Theater Stok, which stages drama and music; north in the Altstadt is the Theater am Neumarkt, with its contemporary takes on classics as well as varied explorations on a theme; and the neighbouring experimental Theater Winkelwiese.

Sechseläuten folk festival.

FOLK FESTIVALS

The high point in Zürich's folk calendar is the **Sechseläuten** (Sächsilüüte in local dialect) in April. During the festival, the medieval order of the guilds is celebrated in just as exaggeratedly idealistic a manner as it was in the 19th century, when the festival was first celebrated. All the city's notables, dressed in a range of historical costumes representing the various artisans, take part in a procession. On horseback or in carriages, they parade through the crowded streets. The idea is to represent "permanency in change", as the official definition has it. The guilds then ride around a snowman, made of cotton wool, known as "Böögg" – an allegorical symbol of winter. In similar fashion to England's Guy Fawkes, he is perched on a funeral pyre, which is subsequently ignited, symbolising the end of winter.

Much the same is true of the **Knabenschiessen** held in September, when schoolboys and girls take part in a shooting competition, using live ammunition at a range of 300 metres (1,000ft). The winner of the contest

is proclaimed Champion Marksman. However, the main attraction on the Albisgüetli shooting range is a miniature town of booths and sideshows, the largest *chilbli* (fair) in Switzerland. The **ZüriCarneval** – the city's answer to the national Fasnacht carnival is a far more subdued affair, held for a couple of days in March, and not a patch on the one in Basel.

ZÜRICH'S MANY FACES

Though they may be less in number than a few decades ago, magnificent villas still populate the genteel lakeside district of Enge on Zürichsee's western shore, and the hilly district on the opposite shore. There is a pleasant walk that leads up from the lakeside south of Bellevueplatz, through the upmarket residential district of Kreis 8 to the Art Nouveau **Dolder Grand Hotel**. Those who live in the area usually inherit their houses and possess a considerable personal fortune. In the silence that hangs over these town houses and villas you can almost hear the interest and dividends piling up, assuring children and grandchildren of a decent standard of living. Up here on the sides of the **Zürichberg** hill the view stretches for miles across the city. The suburban sprawl has progressively nudged its way along the lake towards Rapperswil.

One of the highlights on top of the Zürichberg, and a fun day trip, is the **Zoo Zürich**  (tel: 044 254 25 00; www.zoo.ch; daily 9am–5pm, Mar–Oct until 6pm) at Zürichbergstrasse 221. It is reached by Tram 6 in under half an hour. On the way in, take a peek at **James Joyce's gravesite**, on the right as you get off the tram. The Irish writer, who made the city his home, died here in January 1941. A statue of Joyce tops the memorial that marks his grave.

Down below is Kreis 8's trendified waterfront area known as the **Seefeld**, which starts just south of the opera house and stretches down the lake along the Seefeldquai. Here, many of the old traditional *Beizen* (inns) have become popular meeting and eating places. But nature also has a presence here. All the way along the strip are pretty gardens, culminating in a host of

⊘ Tip

Zürich's hillside Dolder Grand Hotel is an architectural attraction in its own right: a sumptuous 19th-century turreted palace and historic home to European royals, complete with butler service, Michelin-starred restaurant, an outdoor whirlpool and sprawling grounds.

The fairytale Dolder Grand Hotel.

parks around the Zürichhorn, the river delta on the Zürichsee. Within them you will find a casual fish diner with a beer garden (the Fischstube), a cinema and several other restaurants and cafés. Among the gardens is the **Chinagarten Zürich** (19 Mar–Nov daily 11am–7pm), a so-called Chinese temple garden with gorgeously garish-coloured pavilions, a small island and a lake. Beyond it is the lakeside pool **Strandbad Tiefenbrunnen**, a closed in area of lawns and a lido, and just another of Zürich's incredible places to saunter and swim. Another of them is back towards the opera house, the historic wooden **Seebad Utoquai** swimming baths.

Nature lovers might also like to visit the **Botanischer Garten** ⓞ (Botanical Garden), also in Kreis 8, at Zollikerstrasse 107. Its greenhouses and the university's herbarium house 1.5 million plants and offer a real oasis of tranquillity after an eventful day.

For plenty of street colour, head to the former red-light district of **Langstrasse** on the west side of the Limmat, in Kreis 4, which despite considerable

The Chinagarten Zürich.

gentrification over recent years still retains its vibrant social mix and diversity of ethnic restaurants and shops. A lively hub round-the-clock, by day there are Turkish and Italian delicatessens and second-hand clothing stores alongside chic boutiques; by night, restaurants serve exotic specialities and traditional inns, the *Beizen*, sit alongside modern eateries and trendy clubs.

LOCAL ISSUES

It is hard to believe that beyond Zürich's squeaky-clean image once lay a city besieged by crime, a critical drug problem and serious pollution. Within a couple of decades Zürich turned itself around to become one of the most desirable places to live in the world, for locals and immigrants alike. In the early 1990s, the city had a notorious open drug scene, Europe's biggest, with up to 3,000 drug addicts a day frequenting "needle park", the Platzspitz, near Central Station. Heroin users headed to the city in droves, rising to a population of 30,000 users by 1992.

Today the Platzspitz is a spiffy public park, and heroin addiction is rare, thanks to the pioneering response of prescribing the drug to addicts. (Though Zürich ranks high for cocaine usage, together with five other Swiss cities including Geneva and Basel, which rank among Europe's top-20 coke-using populations).

All the once-seedy parts of the city, from parks to riverside zones, have turned into hubs of creative cool and flourishing communal life. In that remaking there are probably grains of the student "Globus Riot" of 1968, and the "Movement" of 1980, when young people hurt by the recession showed a new creativity, coming around again.

Beyond the glamorous, fun lake surrounds there are residential and working areas on the city limits, in the north and west of the city, such as Spreitenbach, stretching along the Limmat to the northwest towards Baden, with its large shopping centres such as Tivoli and big brands including the likes of Ikea. This is where the lower to middle classes live out their T-shirted *Gemütlichkeit* (comfortable life) with their families. These concrete housing estates, which were built in the 1960s and 1970s, contain more yodellers, accordion players and wearers of traditional local costume than all of the mountain cantons put together.

But even those in the most far-flung suburbs benefit from those things that frequently see Zürich nominated as having the world's best quality of urban life. The Mercer index bases its results on factors including leisure and recreation, safety, cleanliness and political and economic stability, as well as public transport and medical care.

WINTERTHUR: CITY OF ART

Typical Swiss countryside – that of the popular image – lies close to Zürich. The American writer F. Scott Fitzgerald commented on this quality in *Tender is the Night*: "In Zürich there was a lot besides Zürich – the roofs upled the eyes to tinkling cow-pastures, which in turn modified hilltops farther up – so life was a perpendicular starting off to a postcard heaven". The citizens of Zürich tend only to dream of the country. They seldom actually go there, and when they do they tend not to stay for long.

Not more than a half-hour's drive or express train away from Zürich, the city of **Winterthur** ❶ makes an easy day trip. Winterthur was founded in 1170 by the Kyburgs, but had its origins in the Gallo-Roman camp of Vitudurum. It has been unlucky more than once in its history: in 1467 the Habsburgs pledged this market town to Zürich, and ever since that time it has been in a state of permanent rivalry with its more powerful neighbour, the canton's capital, which lies only 25 km (15 miles) away, and which has jealously guarded its civic privileges. It was, however, this competition that acted as a catalyst for Winterthur's industrialisation during the 19th century, after protectionist trade barriers had been removed.

It all began with the textile industry – Europe's first textile factory was

Contemplating the Fotomuseum, Winterthur.

in Winterthur – which soon extended its sphere of activities to towns in the Zürich Oberland situated beside rivers, using the hydraulic power the water provided. Textile manufacturing then led to the textile machine industry, and diversification followed: Winterthur produced turbines for power stations, ships' propellers and engines, and then locomotives and railway carriages. Paradoxically, it was the planned expansion of the Swiss rail network that ended up isolating Winterthur from the major transport routes so that it was finally beaten by its more successful competitor, industrialised Zürich.

Meanwhile, another facet of the early stage of rapid industrial expansion was the need for a lifestyle and a culture appropriate to individuals' personal standing. This manifested itself in various buildings as well as in private patronage in music and the fine arts, something which has formed the basis of Winterthur's reputation as a centre of culture to this day.

The city has several museums including the Dr Oskar Reinhart collection which takes up two whole buildings: the **Römerholz** collection and the **Oskar Reinhart Foundation**, at Haldenstrasse 95 (tel: 052 269 27 40; Tues–Sun 10am–5pm). The striking thing about both is not only the sheer number of works of art on view but also their quality, ranging from the old masters right through to modern classics. Artists whose work features in the museum include Brueghel the Elder, Rubens, Rembrandt, El Greco and Goya, as well as several 19th-century French artists.

There are three other well-stocked museums: the **Fotomuseum** (Grüzenstrasse 44; tel: 052 233 60 86; Tues–Fri noon–6pm, Sat–Sun 11am–5pm) is the only photographic museum in German-speaking Switzerland; the **Gewerbemuseum** (Museum of Applied Arts and Design; Kirchplatz 14; tel: 052 267 51 36; Tues–Sun 10am–5pm, Thur until 8pm), which houses the Kellenberger Watch Collection, including the world-famous console watches of the Liechti watch dynasty; and the **Villa Flora** (Tösstalstrasse 44; tel: 052 212 99 66; Tues–Sat 2–5pm, Sun 11am–3pm),

The Oskar Reinhart Foundation.

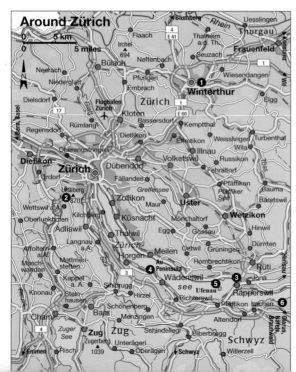

which has works by 19th- and early 20th-century artists such as Cézanne, Van Gogh, Matisse, Renoir, Rodin, Vallotton and Toulouse-Lautrec.

One surviving relic of prosperous 19th-century Winterthur, apart from its industry, is the delightful – and still intact – Old Town, which more than stands up to comparison with that of Zürich. The **Marktgasse**, with its late-Gothic and Baroque town houses, has been turned into a pedestrian precinct, and is so lively in its own provincial way that a gentle shopping trip here can be a lot more enjoyable than one undertaken in its more hectic, neighbouring city.

THE SURROUNDING COUNTRYSIDE

All around Zürich there are excellent hiking and mountain-biking opportunities, crowned by the city's "resident" mountain, the **Uetliberg** ❷ (www.uetli berg.ch), whose 871-metre (2,850ft) peak offers a magnificent panorama of the city, lake and Alps. The view, seen through a blanket of winter fog, is something truly special. Reach it on the S10 train line from Zürich HB in 30 minutes. In finer weather, follow the two-hour Planet Trail from Uetliberg to Felsenegg (Adliswil) via a model of the solar system.

No tour of Switzerland would be complete without a walk through the lowlands around Zürich's lake. You will need a bit of time up your sleeve to complete the entire 115km (71.5-mile) Zürichsee-Rundweg, a circular tour, but at least one of the 10 legs of the walk is highly recommended. Or tackle the Holz-brücke Seedamm-Weg, which stretches between **Rapperswil** ❸, around 40km (25 miles) from Zürich, to Pfäffikon on the other side of the lake dam, Seedamm (allow an hour each way).

This small country town, once so important that it went to war against Zürich, is delightful, with its striking-looking castle and its quay. Hotels

and fish restaurants that have all the charm of establishments on a genuine Italian piazza tempt visitors to stay a night. The Stäfner Clevner and other wines produced around Zürichsee are sure to put you in the right frame of mind. The way back into the city leads along Seestrasse – the "Gold Coast", so called because of its high incomes and low tax brackets.

Reppischtal, the Türler See, the Greifensee, the Forch, the hills of the Albis, the Etzel and the Pfannenstil are other popular weekend excursions for Zürich's residents, but you should not be put off by the thought of crowds.

The country towns of Regensdorf, Grüningen and Eglisau are all close by; as are the Roman citadel of Irgenhausen, the Fahr and Kappel monasteries and the wine villages of Marthalen, Oberstammheim and Unterstammheim.

PAINTERS' LAKE

Zürichsee reaches almost into the heart of the city itself and is therefore considered part of "Zürich Land". With its gentle shores, and the Alps in the

Morning colours on the Uetliberg.

Rapperswil and its quaint quayside.

distance, which tend to look even bigger and closer because of the *Föhn* (a warm southerly wind), it inspired the English artist J.M.W. Turner to paint some of his best skyscapes. Jump aboard one of the lake's nostalgic paddle-steamers, complete with its own restaurant, and take a relaxed ride south to the waterside taverns on the **Au Peninsula**  or, further south still, to the romantic island of **Ufenau** ❺. The numerous and very well-maintained fish restaurants at the waterfront are flanked by the motorboats of the rich – and possibly famous.

The excellent Zürcher Verkehrsverbund transport network, as Swissly efficient as ever, enables you to do all of this even during a relatively short stay. It is important, though, to remember to take plenty of small change along with you: manned ticket-offices – apart from those in railway stations – are relatively thin on the ground, especially in the remote spots, and often you will need to buy tickets from an automatic ticket machine. It is also a good idea to keep a plan of the various transport

Ufenau Island at dusk.

networks handy, because the machines can be difficult to understand.

UNDISCOVERED GLARUS

An hour's excursion southeast of Zürich leads to the canton of **Glarus** ❻, its tiny capital of the same name nestled at the foothill of the limestone Glärnisch mountains and some beautiful surrounding valleys. Head out of Zürich via the Bahnhofplatz and the western side of the Limmat to take the A3 motorway. A train will also get you there in about the same time. Today known for mountain climbing, cycling and winter sports, the canton has a colourful history. The city's uncontrolled hordes managed to defeat a Habsburg army in 1388 and thus secure their independence as part of the Confederation. The valley, almost 40km (25 miles) long, was a harsh environment for those who settled there – the Romans and Germanic-speaking Alemanni tribes.

Despite easier times ahead, residents of Glarus still had to compete with the destructive winds of the *Föhn* (see page 22). The old city was completely burned down in 1861 by a fire fanned by the *Föhn*, and rebuilt according to a grid-pattern with many fine neoclassical buildings.

A deeply curious local tradition upheld for 700 years is the Glarus Landsgemeinde, when hundreds gather in the town square on the first Sunday of May and voice their criticism of the cantonal government. An early expression of Swiss direct democracy, people get to have a say in electing a cantonal Governor, plus judges and a public prosecutor. The governor and a deputy governor are chosen from a council of five senior executive officers already elected into office by ballot vote (who preside over the ceremony in their red cloaks). In a privilege enjoyed only by those in Appenzell-Innerrhoden, each citizen of Glarus can sit in the open-air cantonal assembly, hemmed in by colourful old houses under the conical peaks of the

Glärnisch and help decide on tax and other issues. The 'mob' can even table motions through a mass show of hands. Despite all attempts to abolish it, the tradition survives, and is treated as a day of festivities as much as governance.

Past and present are also on show at the city's attractive **Kunsthaus** fine arts museum located in the Volksgarten (tel: **055 640 25 35**; www.kunsthausglarus. ch; Tues–Fri 2–6pm, Sat–Sun 11am–5pm), which has works from Swiss artists dating from the 19th century to the present day. The museum has an excellent reputation for its visiting exhibitions of modern art.

SKI JUMPING AND HIKING

The first ever ski jumping in Alpine winter sport took place in Glarus, whose ski club, founded in 1892, is Switzerland's oldest. The Pragellauf, a cross-country skiing event that led from the Muota Valley in the canton of Schwyz across to the **Klöntalersee**, a real Alpine gem, and then to the main town of Glarus, was for many years the most popular in Switzerland. In fact, winter sports

and mountain climbing have made Glarus an excellent choice for those in the know. At the little village of **Elm**, at the top of the Semf Valley, a natural spectacle creating a sun window in the rock occurs four times a year. On 12 and 13 March and 30 September and 1 October, the sun shines through the Martin Hole, an opening in the side of nearby Mount Tschingelhorner, and onto the village church steeple.

Before measures were taken to prevent them, the risk of avalanches was once high in the villages of this valley. This was largely because of the vast difference in height between the valley floor (660 metres/2,000ft above sea level) and the highest peak, the majestic **Tödi** (3,614 metres/12,000ft above sea level).

The Tödi seals off the narrow valley. The furthest village inside it is Linthal, and in the mountain above, the River Linth has its source. Further down, it expands in Lake Zürich/the Zürichsee, and continues as the Limmat. The **Klausen Pass**, one of Switzerland's longest alpine passages, leads from

⊘ **Fact**

Over the years, people from this corner of Switzerland have emigrated to all corners of the globe, helping to found settlements in Eastern Europe and further afield – the best known probably being New Glarus in Wisconsin, USA.

Cycling on the Klausen Pass.

Linthal over into the Schächen Valley in the canton of **Uri**. It was here the European Mountain Car Rally Championships were held in 1922 and 1934.

Glarus is also a paradise for hikers, with its gorges, forests, mountains, lakes and over 100km (62 miles) of continuous hiking and cycling trails. **Filzbach** and **Obstalden**, the two villages up here, are largely free of traffic, and because of its remoteness, the region is ideal for hikers.

Any local tourist office can point you in the right direction, offer advice and supply basic maps of the trails.

UNEXPECTED OPULENCE

It is difficult to tell that as recently as the 18th and 19th centuries this canton was the most highly industrialised in Switzerland, and one of the most prosperous, along with Zürich and Basel. The history of the local textiles industry and early phase of industrialisation is well documented at the cantonal **Museum des Landes Glarus** (tel: 055 612 13 78; Apr–Nov Tues–Sun 10am–noon, 2–5pm, Sat–Sun 10am–5pm) in

the town of **Näfels**, which rolls military, sports and textile museums into one. It's housed within the canton's most famous building, **Freulerpalast**, completed in 1648.

It was in the service of the French kings that the Freuler family made their fortune. This in turn enabled Kaspar Freuler (1590–1651) to construct what is referred to modestly as "the big house" in his hometown. Many questions remain unanswered. Who designed the building? Where did the craftsmen who created the stucco ceilings and stone staircases come from? Who furnished the rooms so majestically? And what made Kaspar Freuler build a palace on such a scale in Glarus when he was hardly ever there?

There are several other treats within the canton of Glarus, such as **Braunwald**, a summer and winter resort, built on various rocky terraces with fine hotels and guesthouses, as well as plenty of places to eat and drink. It affords unparalleled views of the area, dominated by the glaciated peak of the Tödi, and hiking opportunities are plentiful.

Hiking in Glarus canton.

Braunwald's gondola offers
unequalled panoramas.

Schaffhausen's 16th-century Munot.

THE NORTHEAST

The rural northeast is somewhat off the map, and visitors can still enjoy tranquil, picturesque medieval settlements and lush green Alpine valleys.

Switzerland, as they say in Bern, Zürich, Basel and Luzern, "ends at Winterthur". In the eyes of many Swiss, the northern and especially eastern parts of the country are of little relevance to the Confederation, and if through some bizarre twist of fate the country were ever forced to relinquish any of its territory, the east would be the first part to go, because it is almost in Germany.

As a border region, eastern Switzerland – Ostschweiz – is seen of secondary importance economically and culturally. Yet in terms of industrial output, Appenzellerland is a strong performer, and those who dismiss the region are missing out on its rich landscapes and cultural history, as well as its hearty hospitality.

Thurgau, with its meadows, forests, fruit plantations and monasteries, has been spared the excesses of industrial expansion. Spreading out from the shores of Lake Constance, many of the small towns and rural villages here still seem draped in history.

The past's presence is strongly felt in the old medieval towns of Schaffhausen, hugged by the Upper Rhine, and nearby Stein am Rhein, with their half-timbered houses and hilltop fortresses.

The monastery town of St Gallen, both Baroque and sober-looking, reflects the two faces of the people of eastern Switzerland: traditional and yet gregarious.

The landscape in the two Appenzell half-cantons, of lush green hills and neat farmhouses set against the imposing backdrop of the Alpine Massif, is delightful. The area encircling the vast expanse of Lake Constance (Bodensee) is a scenic oasis on a scale hardly equalled elsewhere in Switzerland. Here you will encounter vine-covered slopes alternating with reeds and marshes; fields, orchards, forests and meadows; and historic towns and fishing villages.

Main Attractions
Rhine Falls
Munot
Blauburgunderland
    vineyards
Diessenhofen
St Gallen Abbey Precinct
Appenzellerland
Urnäsch

Map on page 250

Traditional milk pails.

People here don't mind being seen as peripheral by their fellow Swiss. They are far more oriented towards their own culture as an historic border region, spilling over into Austria, Germany and Lichtenstein. National borders are almost irrelevant here.

ANCIENT UNITY

Admittedly, there are some historic grounds for the idea that a part of Switzerland with a character all of its own begins beyond Winterthur. At one time all the German-speaking regions of Europe were unified, and vestiges of that political unity survived in central Europe until quite late in history. The eastern Swiss city of St Gallen, for instance, maintained strong alliances

– particularly with southern Germany – until the 14th century. Throughout the 1st millennium AD, the St Gallen abbey played a leading role across the region, and during the Middle Ages was among the most important in the Carolingian Empire, and the Ottonian dynasty of German monarchs. The ties between these frontier regions are so strong that in a referendum in 1919 most of the citizens of Austria's Vorarlberg region voted in favour of annexation with Switzerland. The central governments in Vienna and Bern were not so eager to comply with their wish, and so the dream of unification in the Rhine Valley was never fulfilled. Yet that didn't stop people here continuing to feel a strongly Mitteleuropa culture, shared by those across the way.

AROUND THE RHINE

The city of St Gallen, the largest hub in eastern Switzerland, can be reached quickly and easily from Zürich by the A1 motorway, or by intercity train, but anyone with time to spare might consider heading east and taking in **Rapperswil** on **Lake Zürich** and the **Toggenburg** region en route to St Gallen and Lake Constance. A completely different tack, through historic towns and wine regions neighbouring Germany, is to follow the course of the Rhine north before curving off into the depths of eastern Switzerland. The first stop on this route, taking the A4 from Winterthur in the direction of Schaffhausen, is **Neuhausen am Rheinfall**. The Rheinfallquai is the starting point for a descent to the **Rhine Falls ①** (Rheinfall; www.rheinfall.ch), one of the most spectacular natural sights in the country (also easily reached by train from Zürich).

This grand spectacle of crashing water and flying spray can be enjoyed from many different observation points at the foot of the falls. For an extreme close-up of the thundering mass of water – at peak times it can reach 1,250 cubic metres/sec (37,500 cubic ft/sec) as it crashes over the 150-metre (500ft) wide cliffs – take a round-trip boat ride and climb the rock in the middle of the falls, or through the Rhine Falls basin. Daring visitors can even duck about in hire canoes.

Boats also head to **Schloss Laufen** (Apr–May 9am–6pm), with a visitor's centre, children's playground, interactive exhibition about the falls, a Belvedere panoramic trail, the Känzeli viewing platform beside the falls (fee) and even a panoramic lift for a bird's-eye view.

It's also the launching pad for a gentle, year-round, two-hour circular hike, taking in the falls, then tracing the Rhine to **Wörth Castle**, a former customs house, and other loftier viewing pulpits.

Just a few kilometres northeast is the picturesque town of **Schaffhausen ②**, which boasts a host of nicknames: Rheinfallstadt (Rhine Fall City), because of its proximity to the falls; the Pearl of Eastern Switzerland; City on the Rhine; or Munotstadt, after the 16th-century circular fortress, Munot, towering

The dramatic Rhein Falls.

above the city. In the northernmost corner of Switzerland, on a bend in the Rhine, the settlement sprung up thanks to the Rheinfall, which provided shippers with a place to unload their goods, the rapids being impassable for ships.

A stroll through Schaffhausen reveals that despite industrialisation (watches, textiles and machinery), it has managed to retain many of its historic buildings. A fire almost destroyed the medieval section of the Old Town in 1372; nonetheless it is one of the best-preserved townscapes in Switzerland, with its brightly painted Renaissance facades sporting some 170 bay windows.

The **Haus zum Ritter**, on the corner of Vordergasse and Münstergasse, is worth a visit. On the exterior of the house are copies of frescoes by the Schaffhausen artist Tobias Stimmer. The remains of the original facade, dating from 1570, are preserved at the nearby Museum zu Allerheiligen. The old part of the town is full of Gothic buildings, rows of magnificent residential buildings and guild halls designed in the Baroque and rococo styles. Oriels – richly ornamented

projecting windows on upper floors – ancient fountains, small squares and sleepy corners can be discovered during a stroll in this pedestrianised quarter.

South of Vordergasse, on Klosterstrasse, is the reformed **Münster**, which dominates the town centre. Part of the former Benedictine monastery of **Allerheiligen** (All Saints), it is a masterpiece of Romanesque architecture. The monks left the monastery centuries ago during the Reformation, and now the buildings house the **Museum zu Allerheiligen** (Klosterstrasse 16; tel: 052 633 07 77; www.allerheiligen.ch; Tues–Sun 11am–5pm), which holds interesting historical exhibitions alongside its permanent ones on early advanced civilisations, regional archaeology and cultural history.

A paved path leads up to the **Munot** (www.munot.ch; daily May–Sept 8am–8pm, Oct–Apr 9am–5pm), built on the hilltop to defend Schaffhausen, the Confederation's only estate on the right bank of the Rhine, against Germany. Laid out according to artist Albrecht Dürer's 1527 theory of fortification, the ring-shaped fortress is 49 metres (161ft) in diameter, with a panoramic view of the town from the battlements and a fragrant rose garden below. It is also a bastion of culture, with a lively annual programme of events, including salsa parties and balls, and the **Munot Kino Openair** cinema held over several nights in early August.

BLAUBURGUNDERLAND VINEYARDS

From Schaffhausen you can journey out to wine regions such as the vine-clad slopes of the **Klettgau** plateau to the west, and the hilly region of the **Randen** to the north.

The Klettgau, like many terroirs here, is famed for its Blauburgunder (Pinot Noir) wines, which earn the canton the nickname of Blauburgunderland. Around the smart little village of **Hallau**, nudging Germany, is the largest continuous wine region in

Pastoral bliss in Schaffhausen canton.

eastern Switzerland, covering nearly 500 hectares (1,235 acres). The fresh, fruity Pinot's are the dominant variety here, followed by some other reds and whites, mostly Riesling-Sylvaner (Muller-Thurgau). Romans introduced the grape culture, but monks spread the drinking joy after reading up on the Roman knowledge, and for a time Schaffhausen was the Swiss wine capital. The warm, dry summers, cool winters and the lowest rainfall in eastern Switzerland nurture the vineyard slopes around Oberhallau, Hallau, Osterfingen and Wilchingen. Hallau has a small wine museum, the **Schaffhauser Weinbaumuseum** (Easter–Christmas Mon–Fri 2–6pm, Sat–Sun 11am–5pm), along with a *Vinothek* (wine shop) and *Weinstube* (tavern) on the same site.

You can also learn about winemaking while walking on the one-hour **Trasadingen Wine Trail**, a few minutes south and smack bang on the border. Starting at the local school building, there are 22 information panels along the way. It's also possible to organise a guided tour through the tourism office. This whole area in fact is a hiking haven, known as the **Schaffhausen Nature Park**, set to develop into a protected regional nature park. The park headquarters are in nearby **Wilchingen**.

DISSENHOFEN AND STEIN AM RHEIN

The section of river from Schaffhausen east to Stein am Rhein is considered one of the finest in Europe, with its forested nature reserves, imposing historic sites and pretty medieval villages with covered bridges over the Rhine. One such bridge is found in **Diessenhofen** ❸ whose former Dominican convent, the cloistered St Katharinental with its late-Baroque church, is now a private clinic. The 1814 wooden Rheinbrücke (rebuilt several times from the 13th century original) crosses into Gailingen, Germany, and you can do the same by bike, an extremely pleasant activity in this neck of the woods, peddling along the Rhine's banks. An arched gateway passes beneath the handsome clock tower, or *Siegelturm*, built in 1545 as a place for storing

Lines of vines near Hallau.

Tip

The Rhine Falls is the site of a fantastic firework display, part of the Swiss National Day celebrations on 1 August every year.

manuscripts and the town seal. It's decorated with astronomical symbols representing the 12 signs of the zodiac and a lunar clock showing the phases of the moon. There are also plenty of opportunities here for forest and riverside strolls on well-signed paths, leading in all directions, and you can also hop on one of the boats that ply the passage between Schaffhausen and Kreuzlingen, along the Rhine and into the lower lake of the Bodensee.

Stein am Rhein ❹, near the entry of the so-called **Untersee**, is another gem of medieval architecture, and one of the stops on the Untersee und Rhein cruises, which also venture to the Rhine Falls (for timetables, see www.urh.ch). The town's former Benedictine monastery s considered to be one of the best-preserved medieval abbeys in the entire German-speaking region. Today it houses a small museum, the **Museum Kloster Sankt Georgen** (Apr–Oct Tues–Sun 10am–5pm). Directly opposite, on the other side of the Rhine, is the canton's oldest church, **Kirche Burg**, first mentioned in a document dated 799.

The delightful little white chapel sits amid wall remnants of the 3 AD Roman fortress Tasgetium.

Back in the Altstadt is the striking main town square, the **Rathausplatz**, with its girth of pastel-hued, half-timbered houses sporting magnificent frescos and dainty oriel windows. Look out in particular for the frescos on the **Weinstube zum Rothen Ochsen** (a delightful wood-decked drinking den), the 14th-century merchant's house, **Vorderen Krone** with its Baroque allegories and ornaments, the **Weisser Adler**, with possibly the oldest Renaissance facade frescos in Switzerland, and by its side, the 16th-century **Rathaus** (Town Hall). At the centre of the square is a decagonal-shaped fountain featuring a polychrome and gilded statue of a solider on its column, bearing a sword and coat of arms.

Half-timbered houses, a feature of the Lake Constance region, determine the character of the whole townscape. The heavy oak beams bend beneath the weight of centuries; sometimes entire house facades seem to be on the point of collapse. Nearby is the lower city gatehouse, **Untertor**. Once part of the medieval fortifications, it dates to 1367 but was destroyed and rebuilt after World War II bombings. A five-minute stroll to the north is the frescoed upper gate, **Obertor**, also rebuilt due to fires. South of the Untertor, near the river, is the thieves or witches' tower, **Hexenturm**, at the lower end of Choligass.

Take a break in one of the town's numerous wine taverns, which radiate cheerful *Gemütlichkeit* (cosiness) with their smiling oriel windows and Gothic wooden ceilings.

THE BODENSEE

Observe the landscape from the heights of the **Seerücken** on an autumn day when the light is fading and the Untersee has turned a dull and tired-looking grey: water and sky blend into one another perfectly. The **Höri Peninsula**

Like many Swiss towns, Stein am Rhein puts on a charming Christmas Market.

takes on the appearance of a smudged pencil drawing, and the island of **Reichenau** with its Benedictine monastery founded by St Pirmin in 723, can just be seen in the distance. The sights of the Untersee are not confined to culture and history; the villages on the Untersee also exude tranquillity: **Mammern**, **Steckborn**, **Berlingen**, **Mannenbach** and **Ermatingen**.

On the gentle slopes surrounding the lake, imposing country houses steeped in history will catch your eye. Surrounding the quiet bay in Mammern is the huge park (90,000 sq metres/969,000 sq ft) belonging to **Schloss Mammern**, where knights, and later the abbots of Rheinau once resided. Also forming part of the castle, which today houses a clinic, is a **Baroque chapel** dating from 1749, with noteworthy frescoes.

Salenstein, with its medieval core, rises high over the shores of the Untersee. At one of the lake's finest viewpoints, partially hidden by trees, the **Schloss Arenenberg** sits on top of a steep hill. The park and the imperial bathroom can be visited with entry to the **Napoleon Museum** (10am–5pm Apr–Oct Mon–Sun, Nov–Mar Tues–Sun), and there is also a hotel here and the Louis Napoléon bistro.

The modest exterior belies its historical importance, particularly in the 19th century. After Bonaparte's downfall, Hortense de Beauharnais lived here with her son, who was later to become the Emperor Napoleon III. Following his abdication, the fêted Empress Eugenie spent time at this country seat. The grand furnishings at Arenenberg include royal relics, such as a marble statue of Napoleon, furniture obviously influenced by the Egyptian campaign and court portraits featuring all the finery of the Deuxième Empire.

In contrast, there are simple farming hamlets on the Seerücken, and villages down by the lake, where fishing is still a favourite local pursuit. Many restaurants pride themselves on their distinguished past. The **Hotel Adler** in Ermatingen – an imposing-looking half-timbered building set on a hill over the lake and vineyards – is the oldest hotel in the canton of Thurgau. Alexandre Dumas, Ernst Jünger, Thomas Mann, Graf Zeppelin, Hermann Hesse and Henri Guisan, the general in command of the Swiss Army during World War II, all dined here.

A small detour from **Mannenbach-Salenstein** by solar ferry will take you out to the German island of Reichenau, and its 724 Unesco-listed Benedictine monastery, before continuing east along the Untersee to **Kreuzlingen** ⑤, a suburb of German Konstanz. Here the lake widens, the banks slope more gently, the landscape loses something of its charm and industrialisation increases. Continue southeast to the small town of **Arbon** ⑥, or Arbor Felix as it was known in the ancient world, with its 16th-century fort **Schloss Arbon**, which houses a **history museum** (tel: 071 446 10 58; 2–5pm May–Sept Tues–Sun, Oct–Dec and Mar–Apr Sun only) displaying finds from Neolithic and Bronze Age lake dwellings as well as from Roman

⊙ Eat

Kretzer or *Egli*, (lake fish) fried in butter and baked in oil, and accompanied by a fruity Riesling or Sylvaner from the region, is a typical speciality.

Lake Constance or the Bodensee.

times. The promenade here is an ideal place for a stroll. Southeast is **Rebstein** which has a small castle.

CARTHUSIAN MONASTERY

By branching off to the south of the Untersee and crossing the ridge above the lake, visitors can reach the **River Thur** and **Frauenfeld** ❼, by means of footpaths. The old town of the capital of the canton of Thurgau is dominated by buildings from the period after the fires of 1771 and 1778, which reduced the number of medieval houses in the town to those between the **Town Hall** and the Reformed church. Another relic of medieval times is the **castle**, which stands on a sandstone rock above the banks of the **Murg**. From Frauenfeld, in the centre of the canton, it is a short detour north to one of the finest and best-preserved monastic complexes of northeastern Switzerland.

Set into the hilly landscape near **Uesslingen** ❽ lies the former **Carthusian Monastery of Ittingen**. Founded in 1152 as an Augustinian priory and rebuilt in several stages from the mid-16th century in a unique mixture of styles, in 1982 it transformed into a conference and cultural centre, the **Kartause Ittingen**. As well as restaurant, concert hall, hotel and idyllic gardens, it houses two museums, the **Ittingen Museum** (tel: 058 345 10 60; May–Sept daily 11am–6pm, Oct–Apr Mon–Fri 2–5pm, Sat–Sun 11am–5pm), where you can learn about the lives of the Carthusian monks, and the contemporary art space, the **Kunstmuseum Thurgau**, which also features a collection of naïve art (tel: 058 345 10 60; Mon–Fri 2–5pm, Sat–Sun 11–5pm, May–Sept until 6pm).

Head southeast from Frauenfeld to reach **Wil** ❾, midway between St Gallen and Winterthur. An ordinary little town with next to no tourism, here visitors have the chance to experience genuine Swiss daily life. The new town possesses a faceless agglomeration of houses, and streets that are instantly devoid of people as soon as the shops shut. The Old Town, however, on a hill at the bottom of the valley, is remarkably unspoilt. The Catholic **Parish Church of St Nicholas** can be admired, along with

Morning mist along the River Thur.

the **Dominican convent** and the **Baronenhaus**, the most important neoclassical residence in the canton of St Gallen.

ST GALLEN

According to local history books, it was "the finger of God" which played a decisive role in the founding of St Gallen. This refers to the saga in which the Irish monk Gall, in the year 612, was wandering through the "wild valley of the Steinach" and fell into a thorn bush, interpreting it as an invitation to stay. A bear helped Gall to build a monastery, and thus became the heraldic animal of the city of **St Gallen ⑩**.

There are no other obvious geographical reasons to explain the origins of what is now the economic centre of eastern Switzerland. Not only is there no river – other than the Steinach, which is little more than a stream – but St Gallen lies somewhat in a no man's land, between the Rosenberg hills and the beginnings of the Alps sloping up towards the Appenzell district. Indeed, had a wayward Irish monk not stumbled into a thorn bush, it is hard to imagine how St Gallen would have come into existence, despite the beauty of its setting against the backdrop of the Alpstein Massif.

Thankfully it did, and it's a city packed with architectural treasures, pivoting on the Unesco-classified Abbey Precinct. Here, the most famous landmark is the Baroque cathedral, a treasure chest of sacred art, and the **Abbey Library**, Stiftsbibliothek, which contains some 170,000 documents, many of them hand-written more than a thousand years ago. The library hall, built in 1763, is a fine example of rococo architecture and also contains rare treasures.

In the 15th century, a ring of houses was erected around the newly built monastery precinct following a fire. The town, now famous for its textiles, developed from here, dominated by the Baroque church. The traffic-free old town also contains a series of exceptional burgher houses dating from the 16th to 18th centuries, with colourfully painted oriel windows and decorative woodwork. One of the finest is the early 18th-century **Haus zum Pelikan** (Schmiedgasse 15), whose bay window sports four ornately carved

⊘ Fact

The nave and rotunda of the St Gallen Abbey were built in 1755 by Peter Thumb, while the choir with the twin-towered facade was added in 1761 under the supervision of Johann Michael Beer von Bildstein.

St Gallen.

parapets representing Europe, Asia, Africa and America (Australia is missing), and thus humanity. Crowning the oriel, a pelican stands in a nest modelled after the crown of thorns, symbolising the death of Christ. Angelic representations including winged heads add to the religious imagery.

From the 15th century onwards, St Gallen developed into a prosperous centre of the linen trade, then cotton and embroidery, before teetering on industrial collapse during a world economic crisis. The textiles industry still provides many jobs, with some 1,000 people employed by mostly medium-sized firms throughout the canton, helping to underpin its wealth. West of the cathedral is the innovative little **Textilemuseum** on Vadianstrasse (www.textilmuseum.ch; Mon–Sat 10am–noon and 2–5pm), whose exhibitions look into the global fashion industry and the economic, social and environmental issues behind it. Alongside that excitement, and a textile library, there are more mundane displays of local embroidery and lace dating to the 14th century.

St Gallen, especially its Old Town, is an ideal place for a walking tour to uncover its hidden charms. The town centre has been largely turned into a shopping precinct with innumerable shops and boutiques, as well as restaurants and cafés, tucked behind its historic facades. To get a strong sense of local traditions, beeline one of the wine taverns on the lower floors of the buildings in the old town: the **Weinstube zum Bäumli**, or **Zum Goldenen Schäfli**, the only guild building to have survived. With its sloping floor and late-Gothic beamed ceiling, the "Schäfli", now a fancy restaurant, is one of the oldest taverns in Switzerland.

APPENZELL AND THE APPENZELLERS

The journey south from St Gallen into the canton of **Appenzell** means leaving the lowlands behind and climbing up into a landscape of idyllic mountain scenery. All the way up to the towering **Säntis** (2,502 metres/8,208ft), the regional Alps culminating peak, the hills spread out interminably like

The opulent Abbey Library in St Gallen.

a green carpet. Despite a decline in farming, agriculture is still the primary sector, representing 10 percent of the canton's economy. Small farms are still characteristic of the area. The villages grew up around the churches, many of which were built by members of the renowned Grubenmann family of master builders and engineers who hailed from here.

This region is famous for its traditional arts and crafts: men and women, using brushes and paints, scissors, looms and embroidery frames, have been creating small masterpieces for years on their remote farms, much sought after today by museums and collectors alike. It was here, in this pastoral landscape *par excellence*, that the original and unmistakable peasant art form known as *Senntumsmalerei*, or "herd painting" flourished around the middle of the 18th century (see page 263).

The village of Appenzell is the capital of Appenzell Innerrhoden canton, the smallest canton by population and second smallest after Basel City by area. **Herisau**, the main town of Appenzell Ausserrhoden, has almost double the population, yet is still a small town. Appenzellers prefer to define themselves in terms of their geographical position in the canton. The three main municipalities ribbon out from the Bodensee lake area, with Heiden and its *Vorderländer* a few kilometres from the lake shores, Teufen's *Mittelländer* 18km (11 miles) further inland, and the *Hinterländer* of Herisau almost the same distance again.

The most likely place for regional Appenzellers to meet up is St Gallen, though they do not actually care for the city that much. Nonetheless they have a reputation for welcoming strangers, as long as they bring in the money, and also for a certain obstinacy. All those clichés aside, the people here with their odd nasal dialect and pragmatic minds, are in truth as varied in character as the landscapes that have shaped them.

They also have unique customs, born from a rich and ancient peasant culture, from Appenzeller string music to farm painting. These deep traditional roots have helped keep locals happily immune from contemporary fads.

Anyone visiting Appenzell district should take some time to drive along the winding backroads, or better still, hike along its country footpaths. Though some are almost unheard of outside, Trogen, Heiden, Gais, Urnäsch and Appenzell are all equally representative of Appenzeller culture in their different ways.

FINE VILLAGE SQUARES

Southeast of St Gallen, **Trogen** ⓫ like its southern neighbour Gais, has won several "best-kept village" awards and prides itself on its town square, Landsgemeindeplatz, as a neat and tidy face to the world. Right through until 1997, it was here the men of the canton would gather to vote and help decide on cantonal affairs, alternating the honour every other year with the village of Hundwil.

Alpine herdsmen in traditional Appenzell costume.

For hundreds of years it was local lore for men to wear a traditional sabre or an army bayonet to get access to the event. In 1990 the women of Ausserrhoden were finally allowed to take part, though from then on a somewhat boring voting card replaced the sabre. In these extremely conservative climes, the women of Innerrhoden had to wait until 1991 to get the right to vote, almost a century after women's suffrage came to New Zealand, and only after they battled their case in the Federal Court.

Not to be missed in the square is the pretty 18th-century **Reformierte Kirche**, designed by Hans Ulrich Grubenmann. Other sights include the **Zellweger-Haus** at the entrance to the square, the neoclassical **Gemeindeverwaltung** (Town Hall) and house number 43, the oldest in the square, now a guesthouse.

Continuing south on the trip through Appenzell country, try not to miss **Appenzell** ⓬ itself. Restored at great expense, the village contains delightful, brightly painted patrician houses, as well as a finely preserved village square.

Chocolate-box Appenzell.

ALPSTEIN MASSIF

On Appenzell's doorstep are the Appenzell Alps. Within them is the predominantly limestone **Alpstein Massif**, a popular hiking area with its soft Alpine pastures, emerald-green lakes and numerous peaks. Less than 15 minutes' drive south of Appenzell will land you at **Wildkirchli**, three interlinking caves situated along its flanks, where prehistoric hunters used to seek refuge from bad weather some 40,000 years ago – proven by stone tools discovered here in the early 1900s. A path leads down from the top of Ebenalp summit through the caves. You can also arrive here via a cable car from nearby **Wasserauen**, the last train stop on the Appenzell Railway, then walk 15 minutes to the caves. Across the way is the **Säntis**, the Alpine giant of the canton. Climbing it is your chance to see Switzerland, Germany, Austria, Liechtenstein, France and Italy all at the same time. Less enthusiastic climbers can take a cable car. A 30-minute drive from Appenzell will take you to **Schwägalp** and the Säntis Schwebebahn. The extreme weather conditions have seen a manned weather station in operation here since 1882. There are also cable cars to other Appenzell peaks, including the **Hohen Kasten** and **Kronberg**.

FARMHOUSES AND FOLKLORE

A 30-minutes drive northeast of Appenzell, via Höhi, will bring you to the Hundwiler Höhi, located on the border between Appenzell Ausserrhoden and Appenzell Innerrhoden cantons. The views from this pyramid-shaped 1,306-metre (4,284ft) peak extend from the Alpstein to Lake Constance. You can also gain those heights on an easy, 9km (5.5-mile) circular hiking trial, starting from **Urnäsch** ⓭ 10km (6 miles) west of Appenzell. Up top you will find a mountain restaurant named after its incredible location, the **Bergrestaurant Hundwilerhöhe** (tel: 071 367 12 16), housed in a century-old farmhouse on the crest of a hill. You will see a lot more of these rustic buildings scattered though the Appenzellerland as you descend through Alpine meadows to the accompanying sound of cowbells. According to legend, a giant once wandered about here with a sack full of farmhouses – not realising there was a hole in it.

Urnäsch's village square, Dorfplatz, is also lined with fine-looking colourful timbered buildings, laden with geranium boxes. It is famous throughout the region for its New Year processions which still take place according to the Gregorian calendar, as they have done for a couple of centuries. On December 31 and January 13, during the Silvesterkläuse in Urnäsch, the *Schöne* (beautiful) and *Wüeschte* (ugly) *kläuse* (hobgoblins) march through the streets brandishing pine branches, moss and frightening masks, and go from house to house in the evening, singing and ringing their bells. There are even the mid-ground *Schö-Wüeschte* – a less ugly bunch of *kläuse*. But it's the *Schöne*, bearing extraordinary headdresses carved with symbols of rural life, some as big as a wagon wheel, who steal the show. Many of them carry virtual villages on their heads, decked with miniature farms, houses, cattle, forests and woodchoppers.

Urnäsch has more than its fair share of gasthaus-restaurants, and it is here that Appenzellers like to sit and drink cider, or coffee with schnapps. There is also a local customs museum, **Appenzeller Brauchtumsmuseum** (tel: 071 364 23 22; www.museum-urnaesch.ch; Apr–Oct Mon–Sat 9–11.30am and 1.30–5pm, Sun 1.30–5pm, Nov–Mar Mon–Fri 9–11.30am, Sat–Sun 1.30–5pm), where you can learn more about the local folklore and festivities. Two villages away in **Stein** is a larger, regional folk museum, the **Appenzeller Volkskunde Museum** (tel: 071 368 50 56, www.appenzeller-museum-stein.ch; Tues–Sun 10am–5pm), where you can participate in summer afternoon weaving demonstrations, observe a fine collection of 19-century folk art, or learn about Appenzell cheese production at the *Schaukäserei* cheese exhibition. You can even purchase a home dairy set in its shop and become an amateur cheese-maker.

LAKE WALEN TO LIECHTENSTEIN

Nestled between the mighty Säntis Massif and the landmark seven peaks of the Churfirsten range, is the mountainous **Toggenburg** region. Like the Appenzell to the east, this is a popular area for hiking but also for winter sports, hinging on the resorts of **Wildhaus** ⑭, **Unterwasser** and **Alt St Johann**. Wildhaus is also renowned as the birthplace of the reformer Zwingli. The gingerbread house-like **Geburtshaus Huldrych Zwingli** (tel: 071 999 16 25; Jan–Easter and Pentecost–mid-Oct Tues–Sun 2–4pm; free), with its late-Gothic carvings and wood-beamed ceilings, is one of the oldest wooden houses in Switzerland, dating to 1450, three decades before he was born under its roof.

Walking above Wildhaus.

In the **Rhine Valley**, small wine villages such as **Berneck** and **Balgach** can be found off the main road, then the journey continues southwards along the Rhine to **Werdenberg** with its castle, as well as the oldest wooden housing settlement in Switzerland. To the east is an entirely different country: the **Principality of Liechtenstein**.

This small state has made a name for itself as a domicile with low tax liability for numerous firms, many of which exist only on paper.

The capital, **Vaduz**  is where the reigning prince's family has lived since 1939 in the castle of the same name, which you can walk up to in about 15 minutes via Schlossweg for some lovely views. Down below in the *Städtle* (Small Town) – as the centre is known among locals – is the striking black cube containing the **Liechtenstein Kunstmuseum** (Städtle 32; tel: +423 235 03 00; www.kunstmuseum.li; Tues–Sun 10am–5pm, Thur until 8pm) of fine and contemporary art, which was presented to the state by the present prince's grandfather. It contains several remarkable works of art from the Dutch, Flemish and English schools. Another arts venue for exhibitions and performances is the **Kunstraum Engländerbau** (tel: 423 2 333 111; Tues and Thur 1–8pm, Wed and Fri 1–5pm, Sat–Sun 11am–5pm; free), located on the second floor of the Engländerbau (English Building Art Space) at Städtle 37.

For those interested in philately, the same building houses a stamp museum, the **Postmuseum des Fürstentums** (tel: 423 239 68 46; daily 10am–noon and 1–5pm; free), actually part of the neighbouring National Museum. And for many visitors the **Landes Museum** (www.landesmuseum.li; Tues–Sun 10am–5pm, Wed until 8pm), housed in a former 1438 customs house and princely tavern which Goethe visited, is the favourite, offering an insight into the history and culture of this little mini-state of Europe.

Heading south to **Sargans** , on the southern edge of the principality, there is a defiant-looking **Castle** marking the end of the St Gallen part of the Rhine Valley. Today it houses a youth hostel as well as the **Sargans Museum**.

From Sargans, you can also reach the international spa town of **Bad Ragaz**, and **Pfäfers**, where Paracelsus was the first-ever spa doctor, and where the reformer Zwingli used to go to cure the rheumatism and gout he contracted on military campaigns. Travellers may dare to venture into the wild depths of the **Tamina-schlucht**  (May–Oct daily 10am–6pm). Before the water was piped to the spa, visitors to this famous gorge and health resort used to be lowered in baskets hundreds of metres below into its healing mineral waters, which rise to temperatures up to 37°C (98°F).

The tour continues to **Walensee**  (Lake Walen), via **Walenstadt** to **Weesen**, or to **Quinten**. Here is the gateway to the sunny south; in Quinten one can find kiwi fruit growing, as well as persimmons and figs, and almond, acacia and sweet chestnut trees even flourish in the more sheltered areas.

Vaduz Castle, the official residence of the Prince of Liechtenstein.

PEASANT ART

Peasant art – *Bauernmalerei* – from Appenzell and Toggenburg – occupies a special place in Swiss folk art as a depiction of cherished country life and Alpine farming traditions.

Peasant art or *Bauernmalerei* is characterised by scenes depicting rural life (*bauern* meaning farmers; *malerei* painter). They found their first expression in the 16th century, in rough murals painted on wooden walls, and hand-painted furniture or window panes. Farming tools were being decorated as early as the 18th century, mostly through carving. In the 19th century, it developed into a truly unique Alpine folk art form, unmatched in Europe.

At the beginning of the 19th century, brightly decorated wooden milk-pail bottoms portraying pretty Alpine scenes were all the rage. Meanwhile, long, narrow scenes of Alpine cattle drives, called *Sennenstreifen*, were done for farmers keen to show off their herds. The long boards or strips of paper hung above the door to the cowshed, or in the living room. Another variation is *Senntumsmalerei*, herd painting. Both derive from the word Senn, an Alpine dairy farmer or herdsman. *Wächterbilds* were large-scale portraits of cow herders traditionally painted on window shutters.

All of these art forms were a way of glorifying the tough life of mountain farmers, known as *Bergbauern*, and their indispensible cows. The people here have made a living from cattle breeding and cheese production from time immemorial; economic thinking, as well as daily life and customs, revolved around the animal. While other Swiss regions had more firmly rooted cooperative agricultural traditions, the rolling hills around Appenzell and Toggenburg had extremely high numbers of individual farmsteads – farmers here were their own lord and master, solely responsible for cattle breeding and cheese-making on their holdings.

Peasant art had another popularised offshoot in the small, stylised *Senntums* and *Tafelbilder*, paintings mostly on card or paper. Again themes include cows, herdsmen, farmhands, farm buildings and pastoral landscapes. The cattle drive up the Alp is another favourite. Dozens of men and women made a name for themselves from this art form from the mid-19th century up to World War II. Many examples of their work can be seen in museums all over Switzerland today.

The most respected are the 19th-century masterpieces of the *Senntumsmalerei* (herd painting) genre, in its various forms. The 1854 painting, *Viehweide unter Kamor, Hohem Kasten und Staubern* by Bartholomäus Lämmler (1809–1865) of alpine herders and hunters is one of the most essential works.

A fine example of Appenzell Bauernmalerei from 1854.

BASEL

This ancient city on the Rhine, nestled up against the French and German borders, is best known for its year-round calendar of festivals, crowned by the costumed carnival, Fasnacht.

A historic crossroad city on the Rhine, like its French and German counterparts, Basel's history has been inextricably linked with the great river, of which Victor Hugo once quipped, "The whole history of Europe lies in this river". The fortunes of the Rhine cities have also flowed down that river, and today Basel's cosmopolitan geography and river beauty – coupled with a thriving international arts scene and tomes of history and tradition – are making it a tourist and lifestyle magnet. The friendly and relaxed city is an outward-looking one. Basel is located in a *Rheinknie*, a "knee" or bend in the Rhine, hemmed in to the north and west by the rolling hills and vineyards of Germany's Black Forest and French Alsace. Switzerland's third-largest city may be located in the middle of some of Europe's greatest vineyards, yet the people in this cosy city of 190,000 inhabitants generally prefer to drink beer.

WHERE THREE COUNTRIES MEET

From Basel, along Elsässerstrasse – Alsace Street – it takes about 12 minutes to drive into Saint-Louis in France, and just a few minutes more to arrive in Weil am Rhein in Germany, via Freiburgerstrasse and Basler Strasse. On a fine day, from Kleinbasel, or little

Basel, on the right bank of the city, it is possible to make out the distinctive rugged outlines of the Vosges Mountains to the northwest, which divide Alsace from Lorraine and the rest of France. To the east you can see the first soft ridges of Germany's Black Forest. If Grossbasel, the main city centre on the left bank of the river, were not inconveniently blocking the view, the heights of the Jura Mountains to the southwest would also be visible.

Long ago, the Celts determined certain points in the Jura, the Vosges

Main Attractions

Münster
Pfalz
Museum der Kulturen
Rathaus
Kunstmuseum Basel
Basler Papiermühle
Museum Tinguely
Vitra Design Museum

Maps on pages 266, 276

Basel's Fasnacht carnival.

and the Black Forest and defined an astronomical triangle. Standing near the Münster cathedral in **Basel** ❶ today, you will be right at the centre of it, which may help explain why individuals seeking some kind of theological truth have often felt very much at home in Basel, from 15th-century humanist, Erasmus of Rotterdam, to 20th-century German philosopher Karl Jaspers. From 1521 on, it was the principal centre of humanism and attracted distinguished scholars and teachers from diverse backgrounds. Today, the city's wealth of culture, well-stocked museums, archives and antiquarian bookshops make it a desirable place for a stranger to put down roots.

The local culture here is an unusual and unique mixture. Situated in the Upper Rhine, people here may feel just as much affinity to their fellow Rhinelanders, with whom they have shared strong political and cultural links for centuries, than the rest of Switzerland, which they joined in 1501. Adding to Basel's international atmosphere are the transport links to and from the city, with the tri-national **EuroAirport Basel-Mulhouse-Freiburg** (www.euroairport.com), actually located 6km/ 3.5 miles away in France, plus two major railway stations with links all over Europe: the main international and trans-Swiss **Basel SBB**, and the **Basel Badischer Bahnhof**, a hub for local and regional German trains.

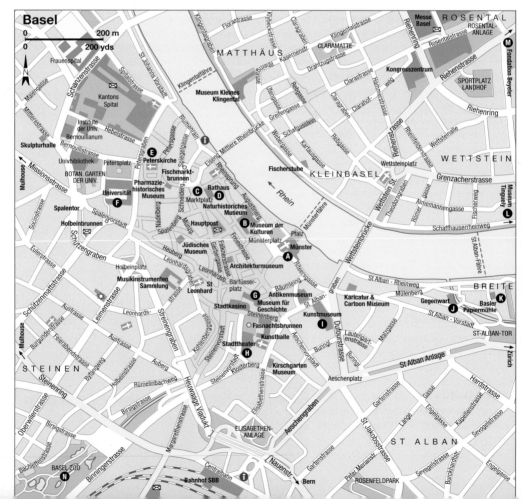

TOURING THE CITY CENTRE

A good launch pad for a tour of the Altstadt of Grossbasel is the **Pfalz**, a lofty viewing terrace alongside the Münster, overlooking the Altstadt and the Rhine. Here you can really get a grip on the lay of the land, in this bracingly transfrontier region, with views through to the Border Triangle – the riverside meeting point of Germany, France and Switzerland. The 100 steps leading up to the Pfalz are just a couple of minutes from the Münster. From up here, Basel is almost indecently exposed to view, though what you see is mainly the area of **Kleinbasel** (Little Basel), the industrial area. Apparently there are inhabitants of **Grossbasel** (Great Basel) who have never been to this section of the city in their entire lives.

You can also see the Rhine forming a long, drawn-out loop, with both ends fading away into the distant horizon. You may well spot a freighter, loaded to the gunwales, pushing its way upriver against the current and squeezing itself underneath one of the low arches of the **Mittlere Brücke**, the main bridge over the Rhine, and the city's first, built in 1225.

A fun way of arriving at the Münsterplatz square and the Pfalz, if ever you are coming from the north bank of the Rhine, is to walk down the riverside Oberer Rheinweg promenade and hop aboard one of the four quaint wooden ferries that that connect Kleinbasel with Grossbasel. For a modest sum, you are transported shakily but safely to the other side of the river – the ferries "Wilde Maa", "Leu", "Vogel Gryff" und "Ueli" make the crossing using only the natural power of the current (year-round roughly 7am–11pm in summer, 11am–5pm in winter).

THE MÜNSTER

If you haven't come by boat, rather from the main railway station (Basel SBB), tram numbers 1, 8 and 10 whizz you in 2–3 minutes to the Bankverein stop, from which you have a 6-minute walk to the red sandstone **Münster** Ⓐ (open Mon–Fri 10am–5pm, Sat 10am–4pm, Sun 11.30am–5pm), the striking cathedral. Its colourful roof tiles and ornately chiseled spindly twin towers date from the 13th century, but most of the Münster was rebuilt in 1356 after a devastating earthquake. Inside, you will find the tomb of the Dutch humanist writer and thinker Erasmus, a leading light of the Renaissance. Other highlights include the St Vincent relief panel, describing the macabre story of his martyrdom, plus an intricately carved pulpit and tombs of lesser-known distinguished *Baslers*.

If you feel like a rest, there is plenty of shade in the Münsterplatz under the 34 evenly spaced chestnut trees. Or you can head straight for the incredible piece of contemporary architectural candy on the other side of the square; one of the most stunning juxtapositions of new and old in all the Rhine major cities. The black shimmering roof of the new-look **Museum der Kulturen** Ⓑ (tel: 061 266 55 00; www.mkb.ch; Tues–Sun

The Old Town of Basel, its Münster bathed in light.

⊙ Fact

Basel's massive exhibition centre is the Messe Basel, on Messeplatz, near the Bad railway station. Trade fairs have been held on the site since the Middle Ages, and during the fair season in spring and autumn it is very hard to get a hotel room in the city.

10am–5pm, first Wed of each month until 10pm) by architects Herzog & de Meuron, which opened in 2011, shields the museum's collection of more than 300,000 ethnological artefacts, from Europe, Africa, America, Oceania and Asia. Like a modern cathedral, its peaked roof of ceramic tiles and new gallery below wrap around the original 1849 museum, nestled in the Münsterhügel (Minster hill).

Around the corner in Augustinergasse, is the **Naturhistoriches Museum** (tel: 061 266 55 00; www.nmbs.ch; Tues–Sun 10am–5pm), covering geology in general, with particular focus on the fossils and minerals of the Alps and Jura regions.

Having heard all about the city's humanists and Nobel prize-winning scientists, about Nietzsche's lectureship at the university and the cultural philosopher Burckhardt, about the painters Holbein and Böcklin, mathematicians Bernoulli and Euler and famous writer Hermann Hesse who penned much of his tenth novel *Steppenwolf* here in 1924, it may be time to adjourn for a beer or a glass of wine.

JOIE DE VIVRE

The *Basler* and *Baslerins* – the inhabitants of Basel, more intimately called the Bebbi – may speak German, but their enthusiasm for food, drink, nightlife and fashionable dress is thoroughly French. Fully refreshed, you might want to take advantage of some of Basel's excellent shops, clubs, bars and fine eateries.

First, head for the **Marktplatz**  (marketplace), where stallholders rub their hands behind heavily laden stands, extolling the merits of their flowers, fruit, vegetables, bread and cheese, where the red of the apples merges into the colour of the splendid **Rathaus** (Town Hall) and swarms of pigeons flutter everywhere. The main wing of this remarkable building is in late-Burgundian Gothic style. The notable clock (1511–12) is the work of a local craftsman; the Basel craftsman's guild built the entire thing, in fact, possibly as an impudent thumb on the nose at the ruling class. They were secure enough to get away with it, too, and even once locked visiting officials inside while staging a party outside on the streets. The wing on the left-hand side and the tower on the right are both 19th-century additions. Venture inside, and you'll find another surprise – more frescoes (a 16th-century feature still seen all around the city).

On the corner of Marktplatz and **Freie Strasse** is the guild house of the wine merchants, the Renaissance-style **Geltenzunfthaus** (1578), and at No. 25 is the guild house of the locksmiths, dating from 1488 but decorated in Baroque style in 1733.

CITY SQUARES

Take a detour up the Totengässlein stairs for a quiet break in **Petersplatz**. This pretty park is marked off on one side by **Peterskirche**, an impressive Gothic church, and on another by the city's university, the **Universität**, home to thousands of young people who give the street scene such vitality each night.

Basel's Rathaus (Town Hall) and Marktplatz.

The area between Marktplatz and **Barfüsserplatz** contains the city's best shops, chic designer boutiques and exclusive department stores. Since most of the narrow streets are closed to cars, this is a pleasant and safe place to walk around. By night, out come the chairs and tables of numerous good (if pricey) restaurants and outdoor bars, all well attended by a youngish set that seems to thrive on dressing up, drinking the light local beer, then dancing the night away at clubs.

On Barfüsserplatz you will find the **Museum für Geschichte** ❻ (history museum; tel: 061 205 86 00; Tues–Sun 10am–5pm) inside the alluring white 14th-century **Barfüsserkirche**, Church of the Barefoot Friars. Part of the trio of museums that make up the Historisches Museum (along with a Museum of Music and Museum of Domestic Culture), the Museum für Geschichte contains Basel Münster treasures, Burgundian war booty, late-Gothic tapestries and the so-called "Lällenkönig" (Babbling King), a crowned head with movable tongue and eyes. Add to that an incredible "Great Cabinet of Curiosities", a compilation of globes, dried plants, crystals, clocks and other antiques and exotica tying in with key personalities from Erasmus of Rotterdam to Jacob Burckhardt.

Just a stone's throw from Barfüsserplatz is one of the city's cultural highlights, the Fine Arts museum (see page 270). On the way there, you pass the whimsical **Fasnachtsbrunnen** (Carnival Fountain), a weird and wonderful mechanical sculpture with continually changing sprays of water, created in 1977 by the renowned sculptor and artist Jean Tinguely (1925–1991), whose career began here in Basel. Today it's equally known as the Tinguely Brunnen. Behind it, the modern **Stadttheater** ❽ (Municipal Theatre), every side of which looks like the back, pushes its way aggressively into view.

ART BASEL

With plenty of art, both old and new, Basel is Swiss art capital, and has carved out a big name for itself on the contemporary art scene with **Art Basel**

Art Basel at the Messe Basel exhibition centre.

☼ Tip

Basel's Jewish district, with its kosher delis and shops, is southwest of the Altstadt (take the bus to Synagoge stop or bus/tram to Basel Zoo Bachletten or Holbeinstrasse stops). The Jewish Museum, Jüdisches Museum der Schweiz, is much closer to the old city at Kornhausgasse 8 (tel: 061 261 95 14; www.juedisches-museum.ch; Mon and Wed 2–5pm, Sun 11am–5pm) and has one of the best collections of Judaica in central Europe.

(www.artbasel.com). Now into its fifth decade (2017 was the 48th edition), the city's international art fair has spread to annual shows in Miami Beach and even Hong Kong. Some 291 of the world's leading galleries gather for the event to show off the works of over 4,000 artists, and to discuss key arts issues in a lively, conversational way.

MUSEUMS AND GALLERIES

Basel offers a choice of three dozen museums, whose range of exhibits caters for every possible taste. This is partly due to the fact that the Basel area established its own special form of patronage, and the people from the wealthy aristocracy, the so-called *Daig* (from the word *Teig*, meaning dough), discreetly supplied the exhibition rooms at regular intervals. Sometimes a particularly wealthy benefactor would commission an entirely new museum.

The leading art light is the **Kunstmuseum Basel** ❶ (St Alban-Graben 16; tel: 061 206 62 62; www.kunstmuseumbasel.ch; Tues–Sun 10am–6pm, Thur until 8pm). Auguste Rodin's *Les Bourgeois de Calais*

welcomes visitors to the oldest art collection in the world. Originally based on the private exhibition rooms belonging to Basilius Amerbach, it includes the most extensive collection of works by Konrad Witz and Hans Holbein the Younger (1497–1543), as well as several paintings by Picasso. Part of its collection was purchased with city funds after the people of Basel took a democratic vote on what to buy for the museum and obtained a loan to do so. Picasso was so touched by their admiration that he donated several more.

The museum also houses an outstanding collection of 19th- and 20th-century art, including work by Gauguin, Van Gogh, Chagall, Klee, Ernst and Kandinsky, as well as paintings by local artist Arnold Bocklein. Dostoyevsky and Lenin are both reputed to have spent hours in front of Holbein's painting, *The Body of Christ*, during their visits to the museum.

In 2016, the Kunstmuseum introduced a new building to complement the main. Connected by an underground passage, the modern slanted

☼ FASNACHT

Basel's three-day Lenten festival is the best chance, albeit rather a strenuous one, for visitors to get a whiff of the real city and its inhabitants.

Beginning on the Monday following Ash Wednesday, at exactly four in the morning, all lights in the city centre are switched off; tens of thousands of people, the *Fasnachtler*, organised into small groups, begin beating drums and playing pipes, their masked faces glowing eerily in the light from their lanterns. Spectators fill the streets to witness the huge but orderly procession, which begins a three-day spectacle of music, dancing and the chanting of satirical songs. The high, piercing sound of the piccolos, blending with the ominous rumble of the big Basel drums, evokes the days when Switzerland was one of Europe's great military powers.

Like all Lenten celebrations in Christian cultures, the roots of the *Fasnacht* are pagan. In its earliest days, the festival was a popular protest, a rebellion against those who did not need to go out into the streets to demonstrate their power and influence; but after the Reformation all such festivals in Basel were banned. *Fasnacht* in its current form has been going for only about 60 years, though many people claim the custom is well over a century old.

grey cube annexe hosts special exhibitions and presentations of art from the collections. (Both are reached in four minutes from the main Bahnhof SBB and the Badischer Bahnhof on Tram no. 2; stop Kunstmuseum.)

In all it has three venues. The **Gegenwart ➊** (tel: 061 206 62 62; Tues–Sun 10am–6pm) at St Alban-Rheinweg 60, a ten-minute walk away, was one of the first entirely contemporary art museums in the world when it opened in 1980 as the Museum für Gegenwartskunst. Its name is a challenge in itself: gegenwart could be read as up to date, contemporary, or, if you take out the w, gegen art – against art. Built with a donation from local philanthropist Maya Sacher, at that time the richest woman in Switzerland, its collection includes works by Swiss artists Giacometti, Klee and Tinguely, and others by Di Chirico, Braque, Dalí, Chagall and Mondrian.

Practically next door, on the river, the **Basler Papiermühle ➍** (Swiss Museum for Paper, Writing and Printing; St Alban-Tal 35–37; tel: 061 225 90 90; Tues–Fri and Sun 11am–7pm, Sat 1–5pm), is a popular attraction. Basel has a long tradition of manufacturing high-grade paper, which is why thinkers like Erasmus turned up here. They knew they could spread their ideas – and the museum does a good job explaining it all. The attached café-restaurant is a popular and inexpensive outdoor lunch spot.

TINGUELY MUSEUM

Continuing east along the riverbank and crossing the Rhine by the Schwarzwaldbrucke, you will come to the **Museum Tinguely ➋** (tel: 061 681 93 20; www.tinguely.ch; Tues–Sun 11am–7pm) at Grenzacherstrasse 210 (Paul Sacher-Anlage 1), with a diverse collection of his quirky kinetic art, melding sculpture with mechanics. Suitable for adults and children, exhibits range from the very strange (such as the 1986 *Mengele Death Dance*) to the very playful. All are testament to Tinguely's fertile mind and his ability to turn the weirdest odds and ends, including bike wheels, old socks and engine cogs, into thought-provoking art. The

Elaborately masked revellers at Fasnacht.

Solitudepark surrounding it is a beautiful riverside park and the perfect place to engage in a little post-art reflection.

The trip out to the astounding and beautiful **Fondation Beyeler** (Baselstrasse 77; tel: 061 645 97 00; www.fondationbeyeler.ch; daily 10am–6pm, Wed until 8pm), some 7km (4.5 miles) away in the northeast residential district of Riehen, is well worth the trip. This private collection encompasses 300 Cubist and Impressionist works from the likes of Klee, Cézanne, Matisse, Picasso, Braque and Bacon. The establishment, which celebrated its 20th year in 2017 with a major Monet exhibition, also stages dazzling, regularly changing temporary exhibitions of contemporary and classical art, while the sculpture-filled gardens are a destination in themselves. (From the Kunstmuseum, tram no. 6 heads here, though you will have a 10-minute walk at the end).

Finally, a few blocks behind the railway station at Binningerstrasse 40, is the lush, renowned **Basel Zoo** (tel: 061 295 35 35; www.zoobasel.ch; daily May–Aug, Sept–Oct 8am–6.30pm, Jan–Feb, Nov–Dec until 5.30pm, Mar–Apr 8am until 6pm), one of the country's best zoos. Besides an impressive array of some of the world's most endangered species, there is a children's area, with pony rides and the usual cuddly animals to stroke.

EXCURSIONS OUTSIDE BASEL

Basel's location at the junction of three nations puts it within striking distance of several tempting destinations. A day trip could take in a number of interesting towns in Switzerland, as well as the delightful surrounding countryside, glorious in spring when the cherry blossom is out, and again in autumn when days are clear, trees are golden and asparagus and grape harvests draw near. Particular towns worth mentioning are **Riehen** (just northeast), **Münchenstein** (just south), and the suburbs of **Bottmingen** and **Binningen** with their country seats and mansions; not forgetting castles such as those at **Pfeffingen**, **Waldenburg** and **Dorneck**; and, finally, delightful little towns and villages such as **Liestal**, **Gelterkinden** or **Pratteln**, all a short journey to the southeast of the city.

You could start by taking a trip back in time at **Augusta Raurica** ❷, the site of some extremely well-preserved Roman ruins just up the Rhine, and its accompanying museum, a 20-minute drive east (Giebenacherstrasse 17; tel: 061 552 22 61; www.augustaraurica.ch; daily 10am–5pm). Here you will find part of a reconstructed Roman town, including an amphitheatre that sometimes hosts concerts, some temples, a Roman brothel dating from the time of the occupation and the Römerhaus, modelled on an urban villa in Pompeii. The museum explains the 2,000-year-old settlement and lays out some exquisite silver items cached by the retreating Romans more than 1,600 years ago.

Rheinfelden ❸, founded by the Zähringen family, can be reached by steamer, a journey taking 2.5 hours, with

Gladiators clash at Augusta Raurica.

boats departing May–Oct from the Mittlere Rheinbrücke in the centre of Basel (or by train, which takes 15 minutes). A relaxed, small-town atmosphere, set against a delightful backdrop, awaits the visitor. The town has its own Rathaus, decorated with ornate frescoes, several churches and museums, and a good range of restaurants. Most day-trippers take a leisurely stroll through the town and then take in the riverside. Rheinfelden is also a spa, claiming some of the saltiest water in Europe with a couple of indoor saltwater baths; the local water is drunk as a medicinal remedy.

In the Jura landscape a 20-minute train ride south of Basel, **Dornach ❹** is home to the Goetheanum (tel: 061 706 42 42; www.goetheanum.org; daily 8am–10pm), world headquarters of Rudolf Steiner's anthroposophical movement. Steiner's "spiritual philosophy" is practiced at the on-site School of Spiritual Science. Designed by him in the 1920s, in an organic, modernist style, the centre also has a splendid park and gardens, a library, café and bookshop open varying hours.

If you have more time, you could make a tour of the wine villages of Alsace in France, just across the border and north; they lie within an hour's driving time. Without a car, you could make the 45-minute train ride to the lovely cobblestoned town of **Colmar**. Alternatively, the Black Forest's country customs, dark gorges and nature-loving ways are easily reachable by car or train, just across the German border. **Freiburg im Breisau**, the pretty bike-loving capital of the southern Black Forest region is a vibrant, left-leaning university town with many gardens and lively bars and eateries. It's just a 40-minute train ride from Basel SBB station by ICE intercity trains. Much closer is the **Vitra Design Museum**, a 15-minutes drive north, in Weil am Rhein, Germany (Charles-Eames-Strasse 2; tel: +49 7621 702 3200; www.design-museum.de; daily 10am–6pm), whose architecture by Frank Gehry is fittingly fabulous for a global design-showcase hub. The museum probes all aspects of design and its relationship with architecture, art and everyday culture.

Rheinfelden.

THE JURA

This mountain range, forming a natural border with France, and comprising the Jura, Vaud and Neuchâtel cantons, offers a rich mix of attractions from Roman remains to vast, unspoilt forests.

According to geologists, the Jura Mountains – a mighty system stretching some 780km (500 miles) long – are among the youngest on the planet. Some 150 million years ago the Jura, an unusually complex mountain range, rose like a reef from the endless sea, much like the neighbouring Alps. Ferns, conifers and ginkgo trees carpeted the slopes of the new land, and the first of the flying reptiles circled above its peaks; then came the first birds, small carnivores and other mammals; the seas teemed with giant dinosaurs, fish, snails, ammonites and innumerable tiny life forms. Fossils, the petrified proof of these creatures' existence, can be seen today in their tens of thousands in the numerous village museum collections of local history.

In the eyes of the average Swiss citizen, the Jura is known as the Confederation's 26th and most recent member (born on 24 September 1978). Much has been written about the labour pains involved; this region in the northwest of Switzerland, which possesses three lakes, has always been – and most likely will continue to be – politically divided. The variations of the landscape are reflected in the diversity of the region's inhabitants.

A DIVERSE PEOPLE

Historians would like to know more about the Raurici, those ancient warriors

The Jura bathed in mist.

and heroes who long ago populated the forests and valleys of the Jura. The Celtic tribe had moved southward through Europe with the Helvetii but in 58 BC had been intercepted by Roman legions at Bibracte. The defeated hordes were sent back north and forced to resettle the regions that they had previously put to the torch. Now the very active Society of Friends of Raurician History from the German-speaking region keeps this Celtic heritage alive.

Others also followed the Raurici, and the Jura's population is surprisingly

Main Attractions
Delémont
St-Ursanne
Porrentruy
Grottes de Réclère
Hermitage of St Verena
Le Chaux-de-Fonds
Neuchâtel
Abbey Church of
    Romainmôtier

Map on page 276

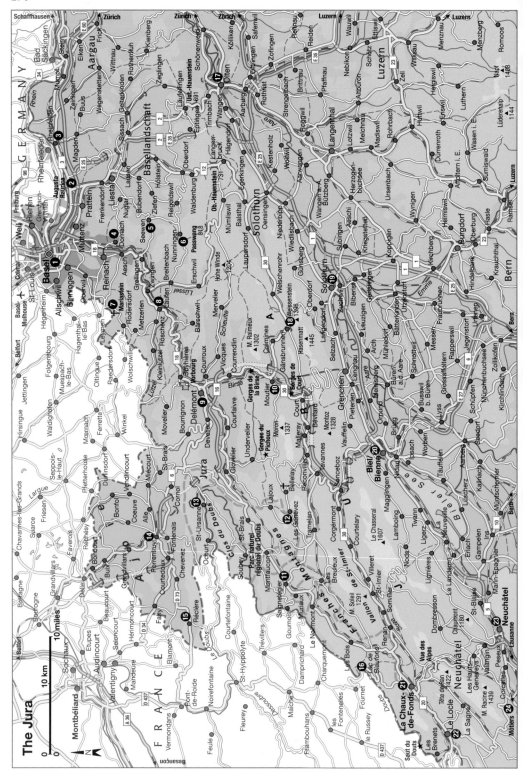

The Jura

varied today: mountain dwellers, with and without bushy beards, who alternate between speaking German and French; artists, many of whom have taken over farms in the region; city dwellers escaping from the stress of everyday life; dropouts; alternative farmers; and many others, all of them in search of a better quality of life.

Switzerland and France both have a share of the Jura mountain range, after all. To the French, as for the Swiss, it is known simply as *Le Jura*; neither has made any effort to distinguish between the two parts by name. Anyone after a more accurate idea should not overlook the fact that these limestone mountains actually extend right across the canton of Schaffhausen and as far as the Franconian Jura in Germany, an area known as "Little Switzerland".

Looking across this range of gentle peaks you can understand why the Jura are often called the "blue mountains". There is no better place to begin a journey here than the River Blauenberg, which separates the rift valley of the Rhein from the Tertiary basin of Laufen. It extends westwards from the gorge at **Angenstein** in the **Birs Valley** to the **Lüssel Valley**, 18km (11 miles) away, where it leaves Switzerland for France.

A counterpart to the Blauenberg is the **Gempen Plateau** to the east; the Birs runs through much of this, too. Several delightful villages can be found on its ridges, including **Seewen** ⑤, 10km (6 miles) east of Zwingen, with its well-known **Museum für Musikautomaten** (tel: 061 915 98 80; Tues–Sun 11am–6pm), holding the largest collection of music boxes and related mechanical musical instruments found anywhere in Europe. More than 300 displays serve as a reminder that the indefatigable Swiss once dominated the music-box business, proving once again they build precision machines like few others.

The plateau forms part of the area beyond the mountains known as **Schwarzbubenland**, south of Basel, in the canton of Solothurn. The largest town here is **Breitenbach**, down in the Lüssel Valley on the **Passwangstrasse**, a magnificent panoramic route running between Laufen and Balsthal, with a view of Schwarzbubenland's loftiest point, **Hohe Winde** (1,204 metres/3,950ft). The ancient capital of the region is **Nunningen** ⑥, 10km (6 miles) southeast of Breitenbach, where the local lords from Solothurn used to rule from **Gilgenberg Castle**, taking advantage of its commanding location in the landscape. Another impressive ruin, **Neu-Thierstein**, lies down in the Lüssel Valley, on a rocky outcrop above the Passwangstrasse: it was once the seat of the rulers of the lower and middle Birse Valley.

The River Lüssel hurries down from the Passwang to join the Birse. Another interesting stream, coming from the Pleigne Plateau, flows towards Laufen and into the broad Laufen basin where it joins the Lüssel. **Lüssel Abbey**, a Cistercian monastery once famous the world over, used to stand on its banks,

Snowshoeing in the Jura Mountains.

in the narrow but highly picturesque Lüssel Valley. Now only a few remains of the monastery walls prove that it stood there at all. Another clue to its existence is the nearby small lake, the **Etang de Lüssel**, which used to serve as the monastery's carp pond.

We can already see the broad plateau of **Mariastein**, the second most important pilgrimage shrine in Switzerland (the most important being Einsiedeln). The Jura rises up, right next to the French frontier, and forms the **Landskronkette**. One of the most curious sites hereabouts is the **Benedictine Monastery of Mariastein** ❼, some 7km (4.5 miles) north of Laufen. The monastery was built in late-Gothic style in 1648, a time when that style of architecture had long since been supplanted by the Renaissance. The facade, however, is neoclassical, and the interior neo-Baroque. The monastery is an instructive place for anyone wanting a crash course in the history of European church building. The main attraction, however, is the Gnadenkapelle, a chapel built into a cave below the church.

The Benedictine Monastery of Mariastein exhibits a mixture of architectural styles.

VITAL PASSES TO THE "FRENCH-SWISS" JURA

Besides the Raurici, the Romans also influenced the area, seeing it as of vital strategic importance. It was they who fortified the crossings from the Belfort Gap into the Alps, vital mountain passes which centuries later the Habsburgs of Austria and the bishops of Basel were equally keen to protect. Castles were built along the length of the passes at great expense: Alt Biederthal, today simply known as "Burg", Blauenstein, Pfeffingen, Frohberg and Angenstein, most of them now in ruins.

In the old days, anyone wanting to go through the mountains followed the course of rivers – the Birse, the Sorne, the Suze, the Alleine and the Doubs. These days the express train from Basel to **Laufen** ❽, the main town in the German-speaking Laufental, takes 18 minutes. On the way it passes the odd-looking **castle** near **Zwingen**. Laufen, whose name comes from the word *Lauffen*, meaning waterfall – has a very neat and tidy appearance. An efficiently run industrialised town, it

is also the starting point for a series of well-marked walking trails into the surrounding countryside.

You might even consider just doing a leg of the long-distance Trans Swiss Trail, which starts in Porrentruy–St-Ursanne in the Jura and ends up in Mendrisio Italy.

It is not just language that marks the difference here: the whole atmosphere has a definite French-Swiss flavour, strongly on show in the town of **Delémont** ❾, the capital of the canton of Jura. Strolling the Grand-Rue, the finest street, you will understand why the bishops of Basel chose to build a château here in around 1716, as their summer residence. The old medieval town remains attractive, with its two ancient city gates, the Porte au Loup and Porte de Porrentruy, a convent dating to 1699 and several interesting churches. A couple of Renaissance-style fountains pretty up the town squares and streets – the Fontaine de la Boule in rue de l'Hôpital, near Place Roland Béguelin, and the Fontaine du Sauvage, in front of the Musée Jurassien, with a statue holding the city's coat of arms.

The people of the Jura have always held public gatherings in front of the **Maison Bennot**, which today houses the excellent **Musée Jurassien d'Art et d'Histoire** (52 rue du 23 Juin; tel: 032 422 80 77; www.mjah.ch; Tues–Fri 2–5pm, Sat–Sun 11am–6pm). It was founded more than a century ago by Abbot and historian Arthur Daucourt, who wanted to "strengthen and revive a love of the region in children's hearts". The museum's displays tell Jura's history through stereotypes and symbols of the Jura, from its flag to Jurassic rocks.

Just outside Delémont, at the entrance to one of the numerous gorges of the River Birse, is **Vorbourg**, a ruined castle sitting on a rocky spur, which also has an important pilgrimage chapel, reached by a walking trail from Delémont.

The Birse curves around the capital, which lies at the mouth of two rivers: the **Scheulte** and the **Sorne**. It was not that long ago that countless watermills, ironworks and sawmills were

Shops in Rue Pierre-Péquignat, Delémont.

ⓘ Tip

The Jura Tourism office in Saignelégier can provide you with information on a variety of walks in the local countryside, from day strolls by the Doubs to legs of the major Via Jura hike and the Trans Swiss Trail (Rue de la Gruère 6; tel: 032 432 4160; www.juratourisme.ch).

still in operation on their banks. From the Vorbourg ruins, there are magnificent views over the Birse gorge, the villages dotted through the Delémont Valley and the town of Delémont itself at its foot. In the distance, it is also possible to make out the jagged series of ravines at Moutier, the **Gorges de la Birse**.

INDUSTRY IN THE SOUTHERN JURA

A short distance south of Delémont, the Birse, until recently, belonged to Bern, for here the river flows on through the **Moutier** region, one of the three districts which stuck with the "old canton" of Bern, rather than breakaway with the Jura when it became, by referendum, Switzerland's 26th and youngest state in 1979. The first change of cantonal boundaries in 163 years was not the last. One of the former districts of the so-called Bernese Jura, Laufen, has since joined the canton of Basel. And in June 2017, Moutier itself narrowly voted to leave Bern and join the Jura pure in a historic referendum.

Saignelégier residents.

Access can be gained to the upper valley here, the **Grand Val**, via the Gorges de la Birse – here you are confronted with magnificent natural scenery. The regional capital, **Moutier ⓾**, could not be more of a contrast. Over the past century this neat and tidy little town has developed into the industrial centre of the Jura (machines, appliances, watches) – a consequence of the tunnel that was built through the Grenchenberg.

The valley basin of Moutier was already an important cultural centre in medieval times. The bygone abbey of **Moutier-Grandval** had its heyday in the second half of the 9th century when noted scholars taught there. The *Great Bible of Moutier-Grandval,* now in the British Museum in London, still testifies to the enormous influence the monastery had as a centre of learning.

From the rue des Gorges in Moutier, the A26 leads southwest to the gorge in **Court**, 8km (5 miles) away. Both ravines are natural traffic hindrances, their military significance known in Roman times. The mountains around the

Gorges de Court, tucked between the ranges of Moron (1,337 metres/4,386ft) and Montoz (1,328 metres/4,357ft), are an ideal place for walkers and mushroom pickers, out of the sombre, heavily industrialised valley.

FRANCHES-MONTAGNES HORSES

The people of the Jura love horses. Since horses particularly like to find footing on ground that is not too hard, the plateau of **Franches-Montagnes**, 1,000 metres (3,300ft) above sea level, is considered ideal horse country.

As if this still needed to be proved, the **Marché-Concours**, Switzerland's largest horse show, has been held in **Saignelégier** ⑪ on the second weekend in August every year since 1897. With its races and equestrian games, it has become a national attraction. The main town in the region, Saignelégier, has a leisure centre, complete with swimming pool, sauna and skating rink. Alternatively, you can take a stroll into the surrounding countryside, where a series of ponds and bogs lie amid suitably unusual vegetation, echoing landscapes much further north – Ireland, Scandinavia and even northern Canada.

The Franches-Montagnes region extends from the Delémont basin all the way to La Chaux-de-Fonds in the canton of Neuchâtel. The air up here is more noticeably bracing, the landscape starker and more barren. Delightful meadows alternate with dark forests of fir trees and with small villages, some of them still very secluded, whose characteristic farmhouses have broad, only very slightly sloping roofs. Particularly fine examples of these can be found in La Bosse, Lajoux, Muriaux, Le Noirmont, Les Prailats and Les Bois.

One peculiarity of the region, however, is its lack of any famous river: the rain instantly seeps away into the soil. On its eastern border, where the former **Abbey of Bellelay** stands (once just as much a centre of learning in the Jura as Moutier), the River Sorne has its source; it flows through the wild and romantic **Gorges du Pichoux**, to the west of Moutier, whose waterfalls were a great favourite with landscape painters of the 18th and 19th centuries. **Bellelay Abbey**, located in the mountains 25km (15 miles) east of Saignelégier, was founded in 1136 and rebuilt in the Baroque style during the 17th and 18th centuries. Also worth a visit is **Les Genevez** ⑫, 4km (2.5 miles) west of Bellelay, where the delightful **Musée Rural Jurassien** (tel: 032 484 00 80; May–Oct Sun 2–5pm or year round on guided group tours) has a collection of farm machinery and implements plus good meals too.

This is also an excellent area for hiking, and a well-developed network of footpaths guides the visitor to places of natural beauty that are still largely intact, despite human intrusion. Efforts have been made recently to increase the popularity of the Franches-Montagnes in winter, too, as a local recreation area for cross-country skiers, dogsleds and the like. Very

The scenic Gorges de Court.

characteristic of the Franches-Montagnes region are its many high moors. The most famous of these is probably the **Etang de la Gruère**, 10km (6 miles) southeast, below Saignelégier. Formerly a millpond, today it is a moor lake of incomparable beauty, and is one particularly good area for picturesque country walks.

DARK BEAUTY

Far away to the west, the **River Doubs** has its source in France, entering Switzerland at Les Brenets in the canton of Neuchâtel, then forming a natural border along a 45km (28 miles) course. The Doubs has cut a deep bed, almost a canyon. Many of the municipalities of the Franches-Montagnes region have land extending down to its lonely banks. The river is of opalesque beauty, flowing darkly onwards and seldom interrupted by weirs. The only important village lying directly along it in this dark valley is **Goumois**, a border crossing 9km (5 miles) west of Saignelégier.

At **Soubey** however, where anglers can be found in their hundreds at weekends, the landscape starts to open up and soon the river changes course, no longer heading for the Rhine but the Saône. Nestled within a curve in the river is **St Ursanne** , a historic town with an ancient stone bridge connecting it with the Clos du Doubs, a tongue of land stretching up to the French border. Just 16km (10 miles) west of Delémont, this is one of the few medieval towns with three intact town gates. It also has the well-preserved Romanesque-Gothic **Collégiale** church, one of the most beautiful buildings in this part of Switzerland, with a Romanesque crypt and Merovingian sarcophagi. The town's well-preserved old quarter and pretty surroundings make it a fine off-the-beaten-track fishing or cycling holiday destination.

At **Ocourt**, 6km (4 miles) to the west, where a distinctive church can be seen standing in the middle of some fields, the Doubs bids *au revoir* to Switzerland.

THE AJOIE

Just as the A16 Transjurane (Trans-Jura) highway, linking the French-Swiss border towns of Delle-Boncourt with Biel/Bienne, 85km (52 miles) away, has revolutionised road travel in this region, train travel has dramatically evolved. Those on the border can reach Paris or Lausanne in roughly the same time by the Belfort-Montbéliard TGV. The local train takes barely 30 minutes to get from Delémont to Porrentruy; half the time it took a decade earlier. En route it stops in Courfaivre, Bassecourt, Glovelier, St Ursanne and Courgenay, passing hilly grazing land, coniferous forest, stretches of almost Alpine-looking grass and broad meadows.

There is also often a hint of Burgundian blue in the sky above **Porrentruy** , a small city of some 7,000 residents, nonetheless the second biggest of Canton Jura and cultural capital of the region. Seen from the castle above, the old town centre is strikingly similar to that of Bern. It took shape with the

Idyllic Etang de la Gruère.

freedom charter granted to town in 1283 by Rudolf von Habsburg, and still retains some of its past flavour. You can sense that most strongly when you stand next to the old city gate, the **Porte de France**, and look up at the magnificent towers and ramparts of the **Château**, perched over the hillside. Home to the Prince-Bishops of Basel from 1524 to 1792, the castle was rebuilt several times after its construction in the 13th century, largely in late-Renaissance style. However, it still retains several of its original buildings, including the so-called "Tour Réfous" (Tower for the Banished) and the sturdy round "Tour de Coq" (Rooster's Tower), which held the archives of the old Bishopric of Basel until 1898. The pavilion of Princess Christine of Saxony came later, in 1697.

Other sights in town include the handsome former hospital **Hôtel-Dieu**, whose museum (Grand Rue 5; tel: 032 466 72 72; Tues–Sun 2–5pm) includes fascinating objects such as a heraldic emblem featuring weird mythical creatures, plus several Baroque-style bourgeois houses with small turrets and courtyards. Five minutes' walk away is the 200-year-old botanical garden, Switzerland's oldest, with an educational trail through 800 plants from the Jura region, medicinal plants, old vegetable and fruit varieties and 600 varieties of cacti. The Jardin Botanique is coupled with another marvel, **Jurrasica** (www.jurrasica.ch; museum Tues–Sun 2–5pm; garden/park May–Sept Mon–Fri 8am–8pm, Sat–Sun 10am–8pm, Oct–Apr Mon–Fri 8am–5pm, Sat–Sun 10am–5pm), a museum whose main pavilion is a small art nouveau treasure, contrasted against the ancient paleontology collections and striking modern architectural elements, sculptures and landscaping in the park.

A good sprinkling of festivals here includes a jazz festival in June and both a rock festival and a folk-music weekend in August. A more local, down-to-earth festival, celebrating St Martin, takes place in November.

The main river in the Ajoie region is the **Allaine**, which splashes its way almost due north towards the Rhône and leaves Switzerland at **Boncourt**.

The ancient stone bridge at St Ursanne.

CHARLES THE BOLD'S LAST STAND

The slopes of the Jura above Concise, on the southwest shores of Lac de Neuchâtel, were the scene of the first battle to take place in the Burgundian wars of 1476.

The Battle of Grandson – named after the nearby castle and town – kicked off the 1476 Burgundian wars. After Bern had declared war on the formidable Charles the Bold, the last Duke of Burgundy, the Confederates defeated his army here, then later at Murten and finally at Nancy, where Charles was killed. These events were captured in

The Battle of Grandson, illustrated chronicle, 1483.

a popular saying: "Charles lost his Gut (possessions) at Grandson, his Mut (courage) at Murten, and his Blut (blood) at Nancy". The main beneficiary of these victories was the cruel and resourceful King Louis XI of France.

Yet the conflicts were vital for Swiss unity too, opening up the way into the west of the country and taking a first step towards bringing Geneva and the Vaud into the Confederation.

"Grandson was the first battle," wrote the military historian Hans Rudolf Kurz, "to feature the successful tactical use of the long pike, which had become an increasingly common weapon for the Confederate army."

Using their long thrusting pole weapons, the Confederates used "pike power" to stave off the Burgundians on horseback, the fleeing soldiers were skewered and the expression "as cruel as a Murten" entered the local language.

The Confederates' sizeable booty from their victory, according to the illustrated 15th-century chronicles by Diebold Schilling, included 400 tents containing valuable tapestries and gold and silver tableware, 400 pieces of artillery, 10,000 horses, wagons by the hundred, 300 powder kegs and 800 crossbows. Coupled with the war purse, all this would have been worth several hundred million of today's Swiss francs.

Yet Charles the Bold's losses at Murten had even more serious consequences for him. Bern's spoils from the war included parts of the territory of the Vaud, until then under the dukes of Savoy's control, such as Aigle, south of Lake Geneva. Bern was also keen to conquer the Franche-Comté region of France, but with fellow Confederates opposed to the idea, they settled for cash reparations instead.

Despite their victory, the Swiss cantons soon fell into deep unrest, winding up with the Diet of Stans treaty in 1481 to avert civil war among members of the Confederacy.

As a result, Fribourg was brought into the fold, and together with Bern jointly ruled over several territories including Murten and Grandson. Thus the glorious history of the lords of Grandson came to an end.

Close by are the mysterious **Grottes de Milandre**. Legend has it that a beautiful maiden emerges here from them from time to time. Alas you probably will not see her as the grottoes are closed to the public. You can, however, visit the **Préhisto-Parc et Grottes** in **Réclère** ❶ (tel: 032 476 61 55; daily Apr–mid-Nov guided tours Mon–Sat 11.30am, 2.30pm; on Sun and in July–Aug additional 4.30pm tour), right on the border about half an hour's drive southwest. To the east of Milandre, are the ponds belonging to the old pottery town of **Bonfol**. This is where to find the best *Dammassine*; a glass of this delicious schnapps will make a fine reward after a hard day's sightseeing.

THE FOOT OF THE JURA

On the **Lac de Biaufond** ❶, created in recent times by artificially damming the Doubs on the border of the cantons of Neuchâtel and the Jura, a boundary stone has stood for more than 1,000 years. Hewn into it is a coat-of-arms depicting the three bishoprics of Lausanne, Basel and Besançon in France.

The territory owned by the prince bishops of Basel once extended as far as the Bielersee. They got their hands on it by a stroke of luck, when King Rudolf III of Burgundy, terrified that the world was going to end on New Year's Day in the year 1000, and keen on securing a place in heaven, gave away large areas of the Jura to the Bishop of Basel.

When people from Solothurn talk about "their" Jura, they usually mean the southern foot of the Jura. For various political, geographical and historical reasons, this region begins at the **Unterer Hauenstein**.

Olten ❶, 50km (30 miles) southeast of Basel and the largest town in the canton of Solothurn, has some interesting features: the old town, with its wooden bridge built originally in the 13th century, and the splendid twin-towered **Sankt Martin Kirche**, dating to 1908. The **Kunstmuseum Olten** (tel: 062 212 86 76; Tues–Fri 2–5pm, Thur 2–7pm, Sat–Sun 10am–5pm, special opening times for groups) has works by local artist Martin Disteli (1802–44). The **Historisches Museum** (closed for

On the Weissenstein.

upgrades until Autumn 2019; Tues–Sat 2–5pm, Sun 10am–5pm) covers local archaeological finds from 40,000 years ago as well as military uniforms, weapons, costumes and ceramics. It also shows the development of the railway, which brought industry to the town and made it an important junction of north-south traffic.

The mountain ridges of the Solothurn Jura go their separate ways at the Unterer Hauenstein, the nearest and most panoramic being the Weissenstein, some 40km (25 miles) southwest of Olten, named for its white chalky cliffs. This ridge is interrupted by the mighty gorge at Oensingen, with **Neu-Bechburg Castle** towering above it. The 1284-metre (4212ft) **Weissenstein** ⑱ peak – the culminating point of the chain – can be reached from Oberdorf by cable car (or by car, except on Sundays and during the winter months). On a clear day, the views extend from Säntis, the highest mountain of northeastern Switzerland's Alpstein range, near Appenzell, through to Mont Blanc. The lofty location is also

very popular for its spa, the **Kurhaus Weissenstein**, built in 1827, now painstakingly restored. Quite a few famous names have spent time here: Napoleon III, Alexandre Dumas, Romain Rolland and Carl Spitteler, awarded the Nobel Prize for his verse composition *Olympic Spring,* in which he made the Weissenstein into a home for gods.

SOLOTHURN – THE FRENCH CONNECTION

The town of **Solothurn** ⑲, which possesses some of the best-preserved Baroque and neoclassical buildings in Switzerland, is unmistakably French in character. Although cut off from the rest of the Catholic federation by the powerful Protestant canton of Bern, it always remained loyal to the Catholic Church and to France; the town even used to maintain an office for recruiting Swiss mercenaries. This formerly rather insignificant place thus grew prosperous, reflected in the town's impressive buildings. Their supreme architectural achievement is the imposing **Museum Altes Zeughaus**

Weekly market at Solothurn.

(Old Arsenal; tel: 032 627 6070; Tues–Sat 1pm–5pm, Sun 10am–5pm), on Zeughausplatz 1, containing arguably the most important collection of weaponry and uniforms in Switzerland.

Another impressive site is the Baroque **Jesuit church**, built in 1680, with its superb Italian-style stucco. The town's backdrop of patricians' houses is dominated by the neoclassical **Cathedral of St Ursus** (daily 9am–noon and 2–6pm, until 5pm in winter) – also known as Solothurn Cathedral, built in 1762 by the Pisoni family of Ascona and still counted as one of Switzerland's greatest Baroque treasures. The interior is even more impressive, with its 11 altars and 11 clocks, while the tower (Easter–Nov 1) provides an excellent vista of the surrounding countryside.

Solothurn is also a good place for museums, notably the superb and free-admission **Kunstmuseum** (Werkhofstrasse 30; tel: 032 624 40 00; Tues–Fri 11am–5pm, Sat–Sun 10am–5pm), containing works by Holbein, Buchser and especially Hodler, to name but a few of the artists.

The surrounding countryside has some hidden attractions. In the wooded Verena Gorge to the north lies the **Hermitage of St Verena**, steeped in legend and set amid almost mystical scenery. You can reach it from Solothurn along a winding forest path by a babbling stream. After a leisurely 20-minute stroll, you arrive at the dainty little hermitage chapel, St Martin's, with its belfry, stone roof and frescoed ceiling, almost engulfed by the Magdalene and Oelberg caves behind. Maintaining a nearly 600-old-tradition, in 2016 the City of Solothurn appointed a divorced ex-policeman from southern Germany to the unusual job of "hermit". His mission is to lead a solitary life as the hermitage caretaker, following in the footsteps of Saint Verena, a third-century hermit.

Travelling west below the Jura ridges between the Weissenstein and Grenchenberg peaks, you will end up within 20 minutes in Solothurn's second largest town, **Grenchen**, which lies on the cantonal border with Bern. This is a rather haphazard collection of houses, dominated by the all-powerful Swiss watch industry.

BIELERSEE WINES AND BERNESE JURA PEAKS

Across the cantonal border is one of Switzerland's more obscure wine regions, the **Bielersee**, spreading out from the northern shores of the lake towards the foothills of the Bernese Jura. Winemakers here produce whites from Chasselas grapes, one of the two dominant varieties along with Pinot Noir. Pinot Gris and Chardonnays are also popular, as well as the occasional sparkling vin mousseux, or schaumwein, made with Pinot Noir. One of the Jura's highest points, the tiers of forest, limestone ridges and Alpine meadows of the Chasseral Regional Nature Park offer amazing views of the Alps, and a hiking and biking paradise. Below,

Autumn in the Bielersee.

on its southern flank, is the Plateau de Diesse – Tessenberg at the heart of the vineyards; seated at around 800 metres (2625ft), like a big sun terrace, helping the grapes here to ripen slowly. A cute little funicular baptised the "vinifuni" (officially the Ligerz-Tessenberg-Bahn), travels up through the vineyards from Ligerz on the lakeshore, to Prêles on the Tessenberg. You can also get there by foot through the Twannbach Gorge. There are many hiking and biking trails all over these mountains and slopes, from Mont Sujet to Prés-d'Orvin and Twannberg to Magglingen.

A lovely vineyard path with views of the Bernese Alps also links lakeside Twann and Ligerz, 2.6km (1.6 miles) apart. Twann is a 7-minute train ride from Biel, or 20 minutes from Neuchâtel; it also has a pier with boat connections. Opposite, sticking out into the lake, is St Peter's Insel – a skinny peninsula and haven for birds and plants where the philosopher Jean-Jacques Rousseau said he spent "the six happiest weeks of [his] life" in 1765.

Old Town square and Venner Fountain, Biel.

Bielersee is the northernmost of the three Jura lakes, and along with the Lac de Morat and Lac de Neuchâtel had its water levels deliberately lowered in the 19th century. The reason for this was twofold: to reclaim land, and to act as a preventive measure against malaria and other epidemics, which struck in 1868. At the northwest end of the lake lies the only bilingual town in Switzerland, **Biel** ⓴ in German, or **Bienne** in French. Its older quarter is definitely worth a visit, with several well-preserved 16th-century houses and fountains.

The windy **Taubenloch Gorge**, a narrow defile that leads to the pass of Pierre Pertuis, was considered inaccessible until almost the end of the 19th century. The path, hewn from rock in 1890, is still as popular with naturelovers as it was from the outset. From Biel, a road leads to **St-Imier**, about 25km (15 miles) to the west, the self-proclaimed watch capital of the country, whose busy citizens claim an innate ability to make watches.

This valley, dominated by **Mont-Soleil**, used to contain a Benedictine monastery given to the Bishop of Basel as a present in 999. The Romanesque **Collegiate church** is all that remains of it, but is well worth visiting. In springtime you will find wild daffodils, Alpine violets and gentians growing here in their thousands.

Venture from here into an area inextricably linked with watchmaking. Heading southwest for about 20 minutes through the Parc naturel régional du Doubs (see page 282), will bring you to **La Chaux-de-Fonds** ㉑, then Le Locle, both on the edge of the forest. The pair are part of a 2009-listed Unesco site recognised for its unique and ingenious "watchmaking town-planning": a result of industry and urban planners working together so tenaciously to make these remote Jura towns into a global watch-industry hub. They did so over several decades in the early 1900s after fires hit the area. A century on, the "mono-industrial" set up has not only been well preserved, but is still alive. 1,000 metres (3,300ft) above sea level, La Chaux-de-Fonds – the metropolis of the Neuchâtel Jura – is a relatively modern town; designed on a drawing board, right angles predominate here. It is also famed for being the birthplace of the great architect Le Corbusier, and poet Blaise Cendrars.

The region's main clock-making museum, **La Musée Internationale d'Horlogerie** (tel: 032 967 68 61; Tues–Sun 10am–5pm), is found here at 29 rue des Musées. Its treasures and quirky displays include a watch made of wood, gilded Baroque royal timepieces, music-playing automatons, marine chronometers and robots. In the park in front of the museum is an extraordinary sculpture, a giant luminous steel carillon which sets in motion every quarter of an hour, capping off the museum's blend of modernity and antiquity in a sensational way.

Le Locle ㉒, on the French border, is only 7km (4 miles) away. A relatively large town, it's here that the watchmaking industry is said to have truly got ticking. Most of the first watchmakers were farmers who needed to earn a bit of extra money in the cold winters; farming in such a mountainous area was not a very viable pastime. Le Locle has its own museum of watches and other mechanical creations, the **Musée d'Horlogerie du Locle**, located within the **Château des Monts** on the Route des Monts (tel: 032 933 89 80; www.mhl-monts.ch; Tues–Sun, May–Oct 10am–5pm, Nov–Apr 2–5pm). Its other attraction is a 3km (2-mile) long lake resembling a fjord, **Lac des Brenets**, beyond the cliffs known as the **Col des Roches**. The River Doubs, which enters Swiss territory here, was dammed up by a prehistoric landslide. The biggest attraction here is the waterfall, the **Saut du Doubs**, which plunges nearly 30 metres (98ft) into a rocky gorge.

THE NEUCHÂTEL JURA

The Haut Jura Neuchâtelois extends all the way up to **Les Verrières**, 35km (20

◎ Eat

Fondue, the Swiss national dish, is taken very seriously in the Jura: the distinctive mixture of melted cheese, white wine and kirsch was invented by the people of Neuchâtel – though Fribourg and the Vaud also claim it as their own.

La Musée Internationale d'Horlogerie.

miles) southwest of Le Locle. **La Bré-vine**, about halfway between Le Locle and Les Verrières, is also known as the Siberia of Switzerland because temperatures there can drop sometimes even as low as −40°C (−40°F).

Nearby is the quiet **Lac des Taillères**. There are several ways to approach the Neuchâtel Jura; one of them is from Neuchâtel itself, heading north on highway 20 via the **Vue des Alpes Pass** to La Chaux-de-Fonds. The pass was not given its name in vain: the view is magnificent, and extends for miles.

Neuchâtel ㉓, at the bottom end of the lake of the same name, and lying wholly on Swiss territory, is a very old town at heart. It was founded in the 11th century by the counts of Neuenburg, who turned the **castle** above the town into a mighty fortress. The **Collegiate church**, which Count Ulrich II built next to it in 1147, makes it clear how important this town – which has now developed into a very lively commercial centre – used to be in former days. More proof of this can be found in the town's fine museums. One of the best of these is the **Museum of Art and History** (Esplanade Léopold-Robert 1; tel: 032 717 79 25; Tues–Sun 11am–6pm), which has a large collection of old clocks and watches and other antiques.

TACKLING THE TRAVERS VALLEY

The Jura should really be tackled in hiking boots. Those who are up to it should gain access to the heights of the Jura from Lac de Neuchâtel by crossing the **Val-de-Travers**, a lateral valley that made quite a name for itself in the 19th century: on the slopes of the **Creux du Van**, the most impressive limestone cirque in Europe, 1,200 metres (4,000ft) wide and 2,000 metres (6,500ft) long, there grows a plant known as wormwood, from which absinthe is derived. In the 19th century the valley developed into quite a lucrative producer of the liquor. It was once referred to as "La Fée Verte" (the green fairy) for its hallucinatory properties, stemming from the addictive thujone, a component of the

The impressive, natural Creux du Van.

local plant. Inevitably, the authorities eventually stepped in to stop its manufacture. In 2009, the former towns and villages of Môtiers, Couvet, Travers, Noiraigue, Boveresse, Fleurier, Buttes, St-Sulpice and the Bayards melted into one identity under the new city of Val-de-Travers, formerly just a geographic location.

Its cultural centre and oldest hamlet is **Môtiers** ㉔, 25km (15 miles) west of Neuchâtel. There are several fine patrician houses to be found along Grande Rue, where you will find museums dedicated to regional history and crafts, to absinthe, to vintage cars and to Australian Aboriginal art. Among them too is the **Musée Jean-Jacques Rousseau** (tel: 032 860 11 94; open on demand), recalling the famous philosopher and writer who lived and worked here from 1762 to 1765.

From here, you might want to head to one of the absinthe distilleries or the Maison Mauler, which was founded in 1829. Not only does it produce an excellent award-winning sparkling drop, but it does so within a classified heritage monument, the former Benedictine monastery of Le Prieuré St-Pierre (tucked into a courtyard off the main street; tel: 032 862 03 03).

THE VAUD JURA

One of the oldest and most important buildings in all Switzerland can be found on the border between the Neuchâtel and Vaud Jura: the former 10th–11th-century **Abbey Church** of Romainmôtier (Chemin Derrière-l'Eglise; daily 7am–6pm), whose 8th-century pulpit and 14th-century frescos have been lovingly restored to an immaculately authentic condition. Romainmôtier, 16km (10 miles) southwest of Yverdon-les-Bains, was formerly the centre of the music-box and musical automata industries, and the concerts held at the abbey on Sunday afternoons through summer help keep the traditional alive today.

The rest of the southernmost tip of the Jura (see page 141) includes the Vaud region to the south and east of Lac de Neuchâtel, as well as the adjacent canton of Fribourg.

Luzern's Kapellbrücke was reconstructed following fire damage in 1993.

THE LUZERN LOWLANDS

This central region of rounded hillsides and valleys is dominated by the elegant historic city of Luzern, one of Switzerland's first major tourist resorts.

The Luzern lowlands, which are made up of several beautiful valleys, extend from Luzern itself in a northwesterly direction towards the canton of Aargau. These valleys have been given their distinctive topography by the ice masses and moraines of the Reuss Glacier. Three great lakes – the Baldeggersee, the Hallwilersee and the Sempachersee – are the legacy of the last period of Ice-Age glaciation more than 10,000 years ago.

In the northern area closest to Aargau, these valleys, interspersed by ranges of gentle hills, are used predominantly for arable farming. To the south where there is more rain, cattle farming dominates. There is a lot to explore in the lowland regions closest to Luzern, including the ancient and picturesque towns of Beromünster, Sempach and Willisau. Along its southern rim, the topography changes again as it rises towards the pre-Alpine and Alpine regions of Aarau.

TOURIST CENTRE

The city of **Luzern ❶** is one of Switzerland's premier tourist destinations, though of far less commercial and financial importance than Basel or Zürich. It is the largest town in Urschweitz and the cultural capital of central Switzerland, but has always been treated as a somewhat separate entity by the rest of the inhabitants of the Lake Luzern area.

Roughly 200 years ago, poets discovered the beauty of the mountains here, and the verses they penned in celebration provided the first publicity material for promoting tourism in central Switzerland. Because of its geographical proximity to the Alps, the town of Luzern developed into a convenient base for mountaineering expeditions. Lying 439 metres (1,440ft) above sea level, just 10km (6 miles) away to the southwest is Mt Pilatus, overlooking

Main Attractions
Kappellbrücke
Sammlung Rosengart
Richard Wagner Museum
Zug
Sempach
Bremgarten
Schloss Lenzburg

Maps on pages
294, 298

Riverside dining, Luzern.

the city and some 73 Alpine peaks from an altitude of 2,132 metres (6,994ft).

Early tourism altered the town's appearance quite considerably. Until the 19th century Luzern managed to retain its medieval city walls. Though sections were razed, 870 metres (2,850ft) of the 1400-built **Musegg-mauer** still stand and from Easter to September you can walk along the top of the ramparts, which afford a wonderful panorama of the city and its lake. Climb up to them either via the staircase in the outer edge of the wall that you will find just up from the Nöl-liturm, the most southwesterly of the wall's nine towers, or via the Schirmer-turm, one of the central fortifications.

The city's first big hotel was built in 1845. Others soon followed, mostly on the northern shore of the lake, facing both the sun and the Alps. Then the quay was built, so that locals and tourists could boost their wellbeing by walking along the banks of the Vier-waldstättersee, literally "lake of the four forest cantons", as Lake Luzern is officially known. (Between the cantons of Luzern, Unterwalden, Schwyz and Uri, its shores total 162km (100 miles) in length.

THE HEART OF SWITZERLAND

Historically, Luzern perhaps fancied itself as the Swiss capital. In the old Swiss Confederation, which it joined in 1332, up until the Burgundian Wars (1474–77), Luzern adopted a kind of "senior" role, and the emissaries of the individual towns often used to meet here. In the 16th century this role was gradually taken over by Zürich, but by then Luzern was the undisputed centre of the Catholic towns. From 1798 to 1799, for a few months only, it became Switzerland's official capital.

When the federal state was formed in 1848, Luzern was not even considered as a potential capital. Not until 1917–18 did the city become the headquarters of the Confederate authorities. Many people consider Luzern to be the secret capital: if Bern is the head of Switzerland, and Zürich the hand, then Luzern can certainly pride itself on being the heart.

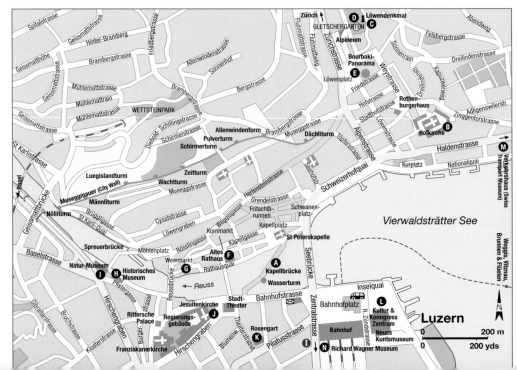

As far as culture is concerned, this is arguably the case. Start a tour by crossing with the throngs what was once the oldest roofed wooden bridge in Europe, the **Kapellbrücke** Ⓐ (Chapel Bridge), painstakingly reconstructed after a fire in 1993. The bridge has two particularly interesting features: first, the fascinating cycle of pictures in its roof truss, second, the famous octagonal water tower, the **Wasserturm**, halfway along. This bastion of the 13th-century fortifications was once used as the town treasury. Luzern claims it as the most photographed icon of Switzerland.

Downstream is the **Spreuerbrücke**, a near contemporary of the original Kapellbrücke, which has survived better than its bigger sister. It is well worth crossing for its series of paintings illustrating the dance of death, executed between 1626 and 1635 by Kaspar Meglinger.

CITY ATTRACTIONS

Even on a short walk through this pedestrian-friendly town you can cover a number of interesting sights. Only a few steps from the Nationalquai on the northern lakeshore is the **Hofkirche** Ⓑ (Collegiate church), formerly part of a Benedictine monastery and later a secular canonical foundation. The arcaded churchyard, which is reminiscent of an Italian cemetery, commands a good view of the lake. Take a short detour to see the **Löwendenkmal** Ⓒ (Lion Monument), an immensely moving sculpture of a dying lion, hewn directly into the rockface over a pond; Mark Twain described it as the saddest piece of rock in the world. Full of aching pathos, the monument commemorates the 786 Swiss officers who died defending Louis XVI and Marie-Antoinette in the attack on the Tuileries Palace in 1792 during the French Revolution.

Alongside the Löwendenkmal, at Denkmalstrasse 4, is the **Gletschergarten** Ⓓ (Glacier Garden), with its intriguing glacial potholes, eroded during the Ice Age by the sheer force of melting water, seeping through fissures and reaching speeds of up to 200kph (124mph) by the time it whirled to the bottom of the glacier.

The eclectic **museum** (tel: 041 410 43 40; www.gletschergarten.ch; daily Apr–Oct 9am–6pm, Nov–Mar 10am–5pm) here includes a remarkably disorientating mirror maze made for the Paris Exhibition of 1896.

Heading south towards the old town, you arrive at the Löwenplatz with its **Bourbaki Panorama** Ⓔ (monument and museum; tel: 041 412 30 30; www.bourbakipanorama.ch; daily 9am–6pm), housing the enormous circular painting by Edouard Castres depicting the retreat of the dejected French Army of General Bourbaki into Switzerland in 1871 during the Franco-Prussian War.

From here, you might want to spend some time strolling the Altstadt, window shopping in the old town's chic boutiques, relaxing on a café terrace, or enjoying the architecture of its many squares. On **Hirschenplatz**, several houses sport richly painted facades.

> **Ⓘ Tip**
>
> On 5 December, the town of Küssnacht, in Zug canton, holds a bizarre, candle-lit festival in which men and women parade the streets wearing bishops' mitres.

The poignant Löwendenkmal.

Sunrise over Luzern with the Rigi behind.

A minute's walk away towards the river Reuss is the **Kornmarkt**, once a medieval marketplace, where you will find the **Altes Rathaus** ❶ (Town Hall), built between 1602 and 1606 by Anton Isenmann. Its facade was strongly influenced by the Florentine early-Renaissance style, while the hipped saddleback roof reflects local traditions. From here, Kornmarktgasse leads into another ancient market square, the colourful **Weinmarkt** ❶, whose fountain is a replica of the original, now preserved in the city's Historical Museum.

TOP MUSEUMS

Continuing west, cross the river on Spreuerbrücke to get to the **Historisches Museum** ❶ (tel: 041 228 54 24; www.historischesmuseum.lu.ch; Tues–Sat 10am–5pm), on Pfistergasse 24, which counts among its stylishly presented exhibits the suit of chainmail that Habsburg Duke Leopold III was wearing at his death in the 1386 Battle of Sempach (see page 43). Nearby, on the riverside Kasernenplatz is the **Natur-Museum** ❶ (tel: 041 228 54 11; www.

naturmuseum.ch; Tues–Sun 10am–5pm), a natural history museum with plenty of hands-on exhibits.

Walking along the Reuss in the direction of the lake, you pass the **Jesuitenkirche** ❶, on Bahnhofstrasse, Switzerland's oldest large Baroque church, built in 1666. It contains the first examples of stucco by the Wessobrunn School of artists. The nearby Franciscan church is also worth visiting.

Heading east, you will soon come to a hidden art gem at Pilatusstrasse 10, the **Sammlung Rosengart** ❶ (Rosegarden Collection; tel: 041 410 35 33; www.rosengart.ch/en; daily Apr–Oct 10am–6pm, Nov–Mar 11am–1pm and 2–4pm), an incredible private collection featuring more than 300 works by Picasso, Paul Klee and another 23 Impressionist, Modernist and Abstract artists from Chagall and Kandinsky to Modigliani and Miró.

CULTURAL ATTRACTIONS

Luzern is also one of the best places to tune into Swiss culture, such as the overpowering din of the Guggenmusik bands during the Fasnacht carnival (see

page 270), or the far more harmonious sounds of the Summer Festival, a month-long event from around mid-August to mid-September with some 100 concerts. Pulling in international classical music talent – soloists, conductors and composers – the festival takes an annual theme, often grounded in not just musical realities but political ones: in 2017, it was all about identity, migration and globalisation.

Most of the programme unfurls in the **Kultur und Kongresszentrum** ❶ (KKL Luzern), looming over the lakeshore in front of the railway station. Opened in 1998, it has some of the best acoustics of any international concert hall.

The fine arts **Kunstmuseum** (tel: 041 226 78 00; www.kunstmuseumluzern. ch; Tues–Sun 11am–6pm, Wed until 8pm) is housed inside the same stunning Jean Nouvel building on the Europaplatz; for architecture fans, it is no doubt just as interesting as the collection of contemporary art and 19th-century Swiss landscapes found inside.

Opposite, on the northern side of the lake, is the **Verkehrshaus** ❿ (Swiss Transport Museum; tel: 041 370 44 44; www.verkehrshaus.ch; daily summer 10am–6pm, winter until 5pm), in another arresting building, on Lidostrasse 5. It contains highly interactive, fun exhibits on virtually every conceivable method of mechanical transport, including space modules and cable cars, as well as probes into technology (at the i-factory) and a chance to walk your way all over Switzerland at the Swissarena, a 1:20,000 scale aerial photograph of the nation. An annexe houses some 300 works by one of Switzerland's greatest contemporary artists, Hans Erni (1909–2015), some of them displayed in a sculpture garden. He was a restless explorer of contemporary culture, technical and ecological issues; one series of murals, *Panta Rhei*, portrays great philosophers and scientists who have influenced the development of Western thought. Alongside that is a painting corner for creative littlies.

The vast complex also includes Switzerland's largest cinema (great for rainy days; tel: 041 375 75 75), a Chocolate Adventure and a Planetarium.

The Richard Wagner Museum.

Back on the other side of the lake, in the tranquil edge-of-town villa of Tribschen, is the **Richard Wagner Museum**  (Richard Wagner Weg 27; tel: 041 360 23 70; www.richard-wagner-museum.ch/en/wagner; Tues–Sun, Apr–Nov 10am–5pm, June–Sept 10am–6pm). In this house, between 1866 and 1872, the great composer wrote his "Siegfried-Idyll" in honour of his second wife, Cosima. Many other prominent figures gathered here including Franz Liszt, Friedrich Nietzsche, Gottfried Semper and King Ludwig II of Bavaria, who were among Wagner's closest friends. The museum houses a collection of musical instruments and the composer's personal effects.

MOUNT PILATUS

Luzern's resident titan, Mount Pilatus, eclipses all of this dazzling lakeside culture and history somewhat. Sitting at its door, just 4km (2.5m) to the southwest as the crow flies, cable cars and cogwheel trains will take you to its peak. The cable car leaves from Kriens, seven minutes by car, three minutes by non-stop train (on the Engelberg line), from Luzern. The cogwheel train travels between Alpnachstad and Pilatus Kulm, on the world's steepest rack railway. Alpnachstad is a 20-minute drive and pretty much the same by train (Line S5). Luzern Tourism's "golden tour" day trips are highly recommended, including a boat trip, the train, aerial cable car and gondola ropeway around Mount Pilatus and back to Kriens (Tourist Information; Zentralstrasse 5; tel: 041 227 17 17; www.luzern.com; May–Oct).

THE REUSS AND AARE BASINS

From Luzern, the Reuss flows in a northerly direction towards the Rhine. To the northeast lies the canton of Zug, one of Switzerland's smallest regions, also bearing traces of the Reuss glacier across its landscape. On the old road from **Küssnacht** to Immensee, which used to connect Lake Luzern and the Zugersee, lies the **Hohle Gasse** (sunken lane) and the **William Tell Chapel**. It was here, in 1307, at the foot of the massif known as the **Rigi**, that Gessler,

the Habsburg bailiff, who had forced Tell to shoot the apple from the head of his son, was killed (see page 39).

For many, the Rigi is unmissable, whether that means climbing it or scaling it by train to see over a dozen lakes from its summit, possibly at sunrise, as Mark Twain did. A 15-minute drive from Küssnacht will reach either Vitznau or Arth-Goldau, both of which have stations for the cogwheel train for the Rigi Kulm, the highest (1,797 metres/5,895ft) peak. The Rigi Bahnen, as its called, is just one way of getting there; there are also cable cars connecting various points (www.rigi.ch), and if you want to stay overnight, there are many hotels, guesthouses and chalets too.

Travelling 30km (19 miles) to the northeast of Luzern, you come to **Zug ❷**, on the shores of its lake, the Zugersee. This is one of the smallest cantonal capitals in Switzerland, but it nevertheless plays a bustling economic role in the region.

Founded in the 13th century, Zug has a wealth of interesting sights. The castle, which was once the residence of the Habsburg governors, today houses a city and cantonal cultural history museum, **Museum Burg Zug** (Kirchenstrasse 11; tel: 41 728 29 70; www.burgzug.ch; Tue–Sat 2–5pm, Sun 10am–5pm). Its various rooms each present a different theme, with interactive stations allowing you to design your own wallpaper, play a game with an old deck of cards or look at a model of Zug to see it expand from a sleepy fishing village to industrial hub.

Just in front of the museum is the late-Gothic **St Oswald Kirche**, with its fine choir stalls and striking 52-metre (170ft) high Zytturm clock tower, sporting blue and white painted tiles in cantonal colours. If you want to climb it, call or drop by Zug Tourismus (Bahnhofplatz; tel: 041 723 68 00) and ask for instructions on attaining the key.

Also of interest are the imposing mansions on the lakefront and richly decorated 16th-century Brandenberghaus,

at St Oswalds-Gasse 17, which houses the **Afrika-Museum** (tel: 041 711 04 17; Mon–Fri 8.30–11.30am and 2pm), run by the St Petrus Claver Sodalität sisterhood of nuns. This is a small but interesting collection of stuffed animals and 19th and 20th-century artefacts from Africa, including a bizarre and rare nail-fetish idol from the Democratic Republic of Congo.

LUZERN CANTON

The fact that Luzern and the canton of Luzern are mainly Catholic is something that can be experienced first hand in **Beromünster ❸**, a neatly kept historical town, just to the west of Baldegger See, which grew up around a monastery founded in 981 by Bero von Lenzburg. Each Ascension Day the impressive "Ascension Ride" takes place: over 100 riders, including the lay canons from the foundation, take part in this church procession on horseback, entering the town in the afternoon. This old ceremony is associated with blessing the fields and checking the boundary markers. Beromünster's needle-spired

⊘ Eat

A local speciality of Zug is the Zuger Kirschtorte, a rich cherry cake, with a notoriously high alcohol content.

Atmospheric Zug.

St Michael's Minster is worth checking out for its wedding-cake rococo interior, composed of dolphin-blue stucco, the paisley-style heraldic shields of past provosts and canons emblazoned on the whitewashed walls of the portico.

Sempach ④, northeast of Luzern, was the site of a momentous event in Swiss history; the Battle of Sempach (see page 43) is described in every school textbook. It occurred on 9 July 1386, when a small Swiss force managed to defeat Duke Leopold III of Austria. The battle site is 4km (2.5 miles) northeast of town, where you will find a simple chapel with a remarkable fresco of the battle. A commemorative parade in military dress is held here on the first Saturday of July every year. A more contemporary struggle took place to salvage the once heavily polluted **Sempachersee** (Sempach Lake). Thanks to artificial oxygenation, and much stricter water protection laws, the project was a success – good news for the lakeside **Vogelwarte Sempach** bird-watching area, one of Switzerland's most important bird sanctuaries.

Little ones will love the engaging exhibits at Schloss Lenzburg.

WILLISAU AND AARGAU CANTON

Willisau ❺, a fortified town on the northeastern boundary of the Napf region, is centred on one broad, flag-lined medieval street. It has established itself as the venue for a jazz festival (running from 31 August to 3 September every year) offering an eclectic mix of music, even jazz improvisations from members of the local yodelling club. Here at Willisau we are already in the Napf region, which also contains the world-famous cheese production Emmental area (see page 124).

Most of the region downriver of the Reuss from Luzern belongs to the German-speaking canton of Aargau, the least mountainous region of Switzerland. It is here that the Habsburg family had its origins. There are numerous castles and manor houses dotted along the route here, reminders of the days of chivalry and the life of the landed gentry, or *Junkertum*, in the rococo period. Aargau is now largely reformed, but memories of the Habsburgs also evoke the old Catholicism that still survives in the former Benedictine abbey in **Muri ❻**, a town that lies halfway between Aarau and Zug. Founded in 1027, and one of the great centres of religious art in Switzerland, the monastery was remodelled in Baroque style by Caspar Mosbrugger in 1695. The Loreto Chapel in the north walk of the former cloister has served as a family vault of the Habsburgs.

Some 9km (6 miles) due north of Muri is the delightful little town of **Bremgarten ❼**, which has many medieval and Baroque buildings and a covered wooden bridge across the Reuss. The town received its charter from Rudolf of Habsburg in 1256, and has retained an air of Catholic supremacy for which it was once renowned.

HISTORIC SITES AND SPA WATERS

The three major rivers of the region – the Aare flowing northeast from Aarau, the Reuss in the middle streaming north from Luzern and the Limmat heading northwest from Zürich – converge before running north to the mighty Rhine. Many historical seats of power lie in the wedge of land between the Aare and Limmat, culminating in the north at the so-called Wasserschloss, near Turgi, at the confluence of the three rivers. The landscape, with its distinctive fields, forests and meadows nestling among rows of hills, is romantically reproduced in pastoral paintings on many of the castle walls.

Two of the better-known castles are at **Lenzburg** ❽ and **Wildegg** ❾. Both have museums, and go to great lengths to give visitors a flavour of their rich history and keep breathing life into the historic sites. **Schloss Lenzburg** (tel: 062 888 48 40; www.schloss-lenzburg.ch; Apr–Oct Tues–Sun 10am–5pm) is strongly geared towards children, and sure to delight them. Exhibits include a realistic, fire-breathing dragon to scare off visitors (part of a dragon research station), a display on knighthood and nobility and a children's museum.

Afterwards you can relax in the gardens or at the castle café, or embark on the Castle Fox Trail treasure hunt. On top of that, the castle stages a programme of public tours, displays of old crafts and a medieval market.

Perched on a hilltop and reached via an avenue of beautiful walnut trees, evocative **Schloss Wildegg** (tel: 062 887 12 30; Tues–Sun 10am–5pm) is an offshoot of the Swiss National Museum. The castle's decorated chambers and halls have been wonderfully restored, and decked with period furniture and exhibits of armour. Outside you can enjoy the landscaped Baroque-style gardens, which include cultivated plots of rare herbs, fruit and vegetables presented in a flamboyant way: tomatoes in a star formation and blue potatoes growing alongside flowers. Parts of the castle date back to the 13th century.

A few kilometres to the southwest of Brugg, **Schloss Habsburg** ❿ (Apr–Oct Tues–Sat 10am–10.30pm, Sun 10am–9pm, Nov–Mar Wed–Sat 11am–10pm, Sun 11am–9pm) is the obvious place for understanding the Habsburg history of

Enjoying a sunset dip at Sempachersee.

this region, and of Europe. On the Habsburg Royal Tour you will learn of the rise and fall of the famous dynasty, in the family fiefdom itself. The restaurant is also worth a visit (tel: 056 441 16 73; hours as above) for its rich Swiss cuisine and the pleasant, bucolic view.

Known to the Romans as Vindonissa, the town of **Windisch**  stands on the Aare close to its confluence with the Reuss, just to the southeast of Brugg. Here there is a Roman amphitheatre that once had room for 10,000 people; today all that remains is a low, circular wall. But many of the excavations ended up in **Brugg** at the **Vindonissa Museum** (tel: 056 441 21 84; Tues–Sun 10am–noon and 2–5pm), in an art nouveau building realised by the architect Albert Froelich in 1912, who was active in both Berlin and Brugg. Its entrance evokes a Roman gate; alongside is a sculpture of the legendary Capitoline wolf who suckled Romulus and Remus, while the walls are engraved with heads of Roman emperors.

Outside the city walls lies the elegant former 14th-century abbey, **Kloster Königsfelden**, with its magnificent stained glass, dating from the 1320s. It was the murder of Albert I of Habsburg in 1308 that led his wife and daughter to see to its construction, as a way of assuring his salvation.

A little further southeast, **Baden**, too, can pride itself on its Roman past: appearing in the writings of Tacitus as Aquae Helvetica. Situated on the left bank of the Limmat above an abrupt bend, this ancient spa town is now an industrial centre. In the 19th century, when spas were the height of fashion in Europe, the town boomed on its Roman bath heritage. The prospect of naked female flesh drew Casanova here in 1760, but nowadays visitors are drawn more for taking the curative treatments in the sulphurous waters than for love.

Those not in need of healing should take a stroll through the marvellously intact old town, the ruins of Stein Castle towering impressively above. The **Landvogtei-schloss**, the bailiff's castle, which dates from 1414 to 1712, houses a historical museum (tel: 056 222 75 74; Tues–Wed and Fri 1–5pm,

Snow-capped Baden.

Thur noon–7pm, Sat–Sun 10am–5pm). The town's other major attraction is the **Langmatt Foundation** (tel: 056 2002 8670; www.langmatt.ch; Tues–Fri 2–5pm, Sat & Sun 11am–5pm), at Römerstrasse 30, which has a marvellous collection of Impressionist and Fauvist art.

AARAU AND ZOFINGEN

Standing on the River Aare to the southwest of Baden is **Aarau** ⑬, a town with an attractive medieval nucleus of tightknit lanes and solidly constructed buildings. In 1798, Aarau became the first capital of the new federal Helvetic Republic, but this honour lasted a mere six months and it had to content itself with being recognised as Aargau's cantonal capital in 1803. Even that status has not gone uncontested: even today it sometimes struggles to be recognised as the centre of this heterogeneous patchwork canton, which consists of almost a dozen small towns and several rural regions that were formerly of equal importance. Aarau's role as a seat of the cantonal government, however, has definitely contributed greatly to the outward appearance of the town.

Its most impressive landmark is one of the old city clock towers: the **Oberturm** (mostly 16th century, but parts date from 1270), which has an intriguing Cubist-inspired *Dance of Death* mural on the south side, painted by local artist Felix Hoffmann in 1966.

The last Aargau town before we return to the Luzern lowlands is **Zofingen** ⑭, which lies to the southwest of Aarau on the road that leads between Olten and Luzern, via Sempachersee (Lake Sempach). This is a small industrial centre with a remarkably well-preserved historical core, dating back to the high Middle Ages. It was in Habsburg hands from 1251 and its ramparts were besieged by the Bernese in 1415. With its imposing-looking Baroque buildings, it also provides a fine example of the numerous towns that were founded here in the high and late Middle Ages and which determined the entire pattern of settlement in Switzerland. Two mosaic floors from a large **Roman Villa** very close to the town are another reminder of earlier inhabitants of this area.

> **Ⓣ Tip**
>
> Near to Aarau, in the town of Schönenwerd, are the headquarters of world-famous Bally shoes, with a Museum of Footwear in the former owner's villa.

Aarau's Old Town.

Rütli, the birthplace of modern Switzerland.

CENTRAL SWITZERLAND

The historic cantons of Uri and Schwyz in the southern Lake Luzern region are home respectively to the Rütli meadow, fabled site of the declaration of the Swiss Confederation in 1291, and the Swiss Army Knife.

Historically speaking, a sensible starting point for a journey through Central Switzerland would be a small meadow known as the **Rütli**, on the western shore of the **Urnersee** (Lake Uri), part of Lake Luzern. Here on 1 August 1291, as the legend goes, a historic pact was made by the cantons of Uri, Schwyz and Unterwalden to seal the Swiss Confederation (see page 41). Whether an oath really occurred here is uncertain, but the Federal Charter, signed in the same year between the three forest cantons, is fact. 1 August 1291, the day freedom from the Habsburgs began, thus marks the Swiss National Holiday. The mythical oath of Rütli (the *Rütlischwur*), meanwhile, was dramatised in Friedrich Schiller's 1804 play *Wilhelm Tell*, about the Swiss national hero of independence.

CRADLE OF THE CONFEDERATION

In the 11th to the 13th centuries, as cities including Bern, Luzern and Fribourg developed, skilled craftsmen settled in the once remote valleys of Uri, Schwyz and Unterwalden. (Today, Unterwalden is made up of the two cantons of Obwalden and Nidwalden.) These "little cantons", as 19th-century travellers later called them, gained strategic importance with the opening

Altdorf is the capital of Uri canton.

of the St Gotthard Pass, and the development of a new trade route.

In the final years of the 13th century, they must have comprised an astonishingly lively body politic, as the seeds sown by the formation of the Confederation began to take hold with shifting cantonal alliances.

Nature, aided by the Vierwaldstättersee – the lake of the four forest cantons, as Lake Luzern was originally known – had ensured the regions of Inner Switzerland, *Urschweiz*, were not forced to maintain harmonious and

○ Main Attractions
Rütli
Bürgenstock
Treib-Seelisberg funicular
Bürglen
Schwyz
Einsiedeln Abbey

Map on page 306

lasting relations with one another. It was thus obvious that Schwyz would start trying to extend its influence, first against Arth, Zug and Küssnacht, then against Einsiedeln and out into the Linth Plain. Until the 19th century, Uri could only be reached from the north by crossing the lake, and was thus only able to extend its influence eastward in the direction of the Urseren Valley, a short way into Glarus, and in the direction of the southern Alpine valleys. Finally, in 1865, work was completed on the Axenstrasse – a narrow road built along the steep eastern shore of the Urnersee from Brunnen, at last linking Uri with the north.

The old forest-canton of **Unterwalden**, stuck in the valleys with the lake and mountains on all sides, never had any real chance to expand. Instead the Unterwaldner just argued among themselves, resulting in the creation of the cantons of Obwalden and Nidwalden, which are separated by a high moor and dark forest.

As the centuries progressed, the powerful leaders of Schwyz, the cosmopolitan cattle drivers of Uri and the rather introverted Obwaldner and Nidwaldner – all situated in close proximity to each other in this compact area – developed ways of life, economic patterns and political cultures that were distinctively different from one another. Despite losing its religious grip and political importance, the centre-right Christian Democratic People's Party (Christlichdemokratische Volkspartei der Schweiz, CVP), one of the "big four" national political parties, founded in 1912, still dominates in the predominantly rural Catholic cantons of Central Switzerland.

Whether this splendid isolation will last is questionable. What with the corridor for goods traffic, the future trans-Alpine rail link coming here and the increasing attraction of the area for holiday and second homes, the place may not be able to remain a charming backwater forever.

ENTERING FROM THE SOUTH

To avoid using Luzern as a starting point and begin a visit to Central

Switzerland at one of its outermost points, it is best to enter **Obwalden** canton from the south via the **Brünig Pass ❶**. Today there is a road as well as the **Brünig Railway** with its carriages offering panoramic views across the pass. In the Middle Ages a barrier blocked the way here, denying access to the lords of the Bernese Oberland who were eager to expand their territory. The steep terrain falling off towards **Lungern** provided the canton with extra protection against conquerors and invaders.

Travelling north along highway 4, after **Giswil** the landscape gets a lot broader and gentler and also provides enough room for the **Sarner See**, a small and typical resort lake, ringed by gentle hills with the higher Alps towering beyond. Even further north, the towns of **Sachseln ❷**, nearby **Flüeli** and the **Ranft**, form the centres of an important pilgrimage. Niklaus von Flüe, Switzerland's only saint, was born in Flüeli in 1417; after an active life in local politics he spent 20 years fasting and praying in the remoteness of the Ranft. His remains, visited by about 100,000 pilgrims each year, have been kept in Sachseln's church since 1934. No wonder, then, that the area is full of guesthouses and hotels. Indeed, Switzerland's first motel was built in Sachseln.

It is true that **Sarnen ❸**, the capital of the canton of Obwalden a few kilometres north, has no saints to speak of, but it does have a modern and architecturally remarkable **monastery** and the Baroque **Church of St Peter and St Paul**. The town's hill, the **Landenberg**, provided an attractive setting for the *Landsgemeinde* (vote), which from 1646 until 1998 was held outdoors annually on the last Sunday in April. The **Rathaus** (Town Hall) contains the so-called *Weisses Buch* (White Book), which includes the earliest account of the history of the Confederation, written during the 1470s.

Of all the local-history museums in Central Switzerland, the one in Sarnen, the **Historisches Museum Obwalden** (Brünigstrasse 127; tel: 041 660 65 22; mid-Apr–Nov Mon–Sat 2–5pm) is the best endowed and provides a comprehensive overview of the culture and history of the region. Exhibits include a number of prehistoric items, Roman material from the settlement of Alpnach, weaponry from the Middle Ages, various examples of religious art and pictures and sculptures by local artists from the 17th century until the present day.

Leave Sarnen and head to **Alpnachstad ❹**, 7.4km (4.5 miles) north, on the southwestern tip of the Alpnachersee, a small branch of Lake Luzern. Here you can board the world's steepest rack railway, the Pilatus Bahnen, which takes 30 minutes to travel up the rock face to the summit of **Mount Pilatus**. At 2,120 metres (6,959ft), the Pilatus Kulm, as it's known, offers unparalleled views of the Alps, out across the entire lowlands.

Tip
If you are a fan of church architecture, have a look inside Sarnen's church, which is beautifully decorated, especially the chapel ceiling.

The Pilatus Bahnen scales the rock face of Mount Pilatus.

⊙ Tip

Be sure to take a ride in one of the cable cars at Engelberg, which have cabins that rotate, providing riders with a 360-degree view of the surrounding valley.

THE NIDWALDEN

Anyone wanting to head to **Nidwalden** canton, which unfurls from the southern shore of the Lake Luzern towards the Uri Alps, can do so via the attractive route northeast through Kerns and the dark Kernwald forest and across the practically flat Ice-Age valley to the capital **Stans ⑤**. The village, which has a small aircraft industry (of Pilatus air force craft), has been painstakingly restored and cleaned up over the years. Two sites reflect the wealth and power of the Nidwalden patricians of the past. The first, located in the old town, is the Renaissance-Baroque manor and garden, **Höfli/Rosenburg**, with its 1566 coffered ceilings and Biedermeier furnishings, once a museum. It now houses a cultural centre and an inn, the Wirtschaft zur Rosenburg (Alter Postplatz 3; tel: 041 610 24 61; Wed–Thur 9am–11pm, Fri–Sat 9am–midnight, Sun 9am–10pm). The second, just outside the centre, the **Nidwaldner Museum** (Wed 2–8pm, Thur–Sat 2–5pm, Sun 11am–5pm) is located in another charming house,

the Winkelriedhaus and juxtaposes regional history against contemporary art. The early-Baroque church, old Romanesque tower and Gothic ossuary dominate the village square, which also contains a monument to Arnold von Winkelried who, legend has it, helped a Confederate army out of trouble near Sempach in 1386 by throwing himself on to a flurry of enemy lances.

Although it is not strictly within Nidwalden, but is in fact part of Obwalden, **Engelberg ⑥**, 25km (15 miles) south, is simpler to reach on an excursion from Stans. With its excellent walking country, hills and lakes, it is a popular winter and summer resort. Its **Benedictine abbey** was founded in the 12th century and remodelled in the Baroque style between 1730 and 1737. The abbey contains an important library and also doubles as a boarding school.

Because of its location, Engelberg is an active winter resort area. Skiing and especially snowboarding are popular – there are several schools teaching both skills – but the slopes

Mountains loom over the attractive village of Engelberg.

are not as carved up by trails as they could be and the town has not yet been given over completely to tourism. As a result, a visit here makes a pleasant outing, attracting a surprisingly youthful crowd. The **Laub Wall** of the Titlis is a death-defying run, however, for experts only – do not go up there without plenty of experience and insurance.

For a more gentle summertime activity visitors can take the sequence of cable cars and lifts from Engelberg to the summit of the **Titlis**, which at 3,239 metres (10,627ft) is the highest peak in this part of Switzerland. Besides astounding views, you will also have the opportunity to walk atop a glacier (along a carefully marked road) and enjoy drinks from a bar built in an ice cave. The ride to the mountaintop and glacier can be costly but is worth it for the view across the valley to numerous, jewel-like lakes and other towering peaks including Mount Pilatus (2,121 metres/6,959ft) near Alpnachstad. Smaller summits such as **Brunni** (1,402 metres/4,600ft) to the east and **Fürenalp** can also be reached by cable car, which operate from the Engelberg area.

HIGH ABOVE THE LAKE

Another interesting excursion from Stans, this time heading north via Stansstad, leads to the top of the **Bürgenstock** ➐ mountain (1,128 metres/3,701ft), with its cluster of late 19th-century hotels and incomparable views over Lake Luzern. A small path leads along a rock face to the **Hammetschwand lift**, a rocket-like elevator that whisks you 152 metres (500ft) up to the summit at hair-raising speed, in under a minute (May–October). It's hard to believe that this technological marvel – the highest outdoor lift in Europe – has been functioning since the early 1900s. Visitors to the old Grand Hotel here have included Charlie Chaplin and Sofia Loren, while Audrey Hepburn was married in the Bürgenstock Chapel. In 2017, the stunning Bürgenstock Resort opened (tel: 041 612 90 10, www.buergenstock.ch), incorporating the old but redesigned Palace Hotel, and adding a couple more, including the Waldhotel

Expect superlative panoramas from the top of the Hammetschwand lift.

⊙ Tip

Guided expeditions are led into the Hölloch ("Hell's Hole") Caves in Muotathal, 30 minutes' drive from Schwyz. The cave system is one of the longest in Europe, with huge chasms and potholes (contact Trekking Team AG for details; tel: 041830 28 45; www.trekking.ch).

by Italian architect Matteo Thun, and a tavern and pension in an 1879 chalet. Add to that a massive wellness centre and Alpine spa set in the forests. A reborn version of the old funicular railway connecting the mountain with Luzern and other hiking trailheads and panoramas is to be added to the hotel.

If you bypass Bürgenstock, you might travel east instead to Lake Luzern, which looks almost Mediterranean on a sunny day. In **Beckenried**, 10 minutes from Stans, you can take a boat along the lake's southern shores to **Treib**, then a funicular up to the **Seelisberg** plateau, some 800 metres (2,624ft) above Lake Luzern and the Rütli meadow. Here you can hike along the Swiss Path, constructed as part of Switzerland's 700th birthday celebrations in 2001. It leads south for 15km (9 miles), past the little castle of **Beroldingen**, down to **Bauen** and along a passageway cut out of the rock to **Seedorf** ❽, where you can rejoin the motorway. The total trail length is 35km (22 miles), and parts are wheelchair accessible.

The Baroque church, the tower of the lords of Seedorf, the small 16thcentury castle and the nearby convent form a delightful ensemble, called the Benedictine Kloster, built in 1197 and renovated in 1695. They also make it instantly clear that this place must once have been a very important shipment point for goods coming across Urner See. From here they would have been transported throughout the canton via the St Gotthard Pass towards the south.

East of Seedorf is **Altdorf** ❾, the capital of the canton of Uri, which lies on another old route, leading from **Flüelen** via Altdorf east into the **Schächental**, and also heads in the direction of the St Gotthard Pass. A reminder of the city's former importance and busy traffic is the **Fremdenspital**, a hospital that offered refuge to pilgrims, and sick and impoverished travellers. The patrician houses, and the **Capuchin monastery,** high up on the mountainside where the Counter Reformation in Switzerland took root, hint at the wealth generated by the brisk trade across the St Gotthard Pass.

Altdorf and nearby **Bürglen** are particularly connected with the legendary origin of the Confederation. It was in Altdorf that William Tell defied the hated bailiff, Gessler, and as a result was forced to shoot an apple off his son Walter's head (see page 39). Tell's house supposedly stood on the site of the tiny 1582 **Tellskapelle** (Tell's Chapel) in Bürglen, near the parish church on Kirchplatz and richly decorated with frescoes after a renovation in 1949. Opposite is the **Tell-Museum** (tel: 041 870 41 55; www.tellmuseum.ch; July–Aug 9.30am–5.30pm, May–June and Sept–Oct 10–11.30am and 1.30–5pm) on Postplatz. Its important collection of objects, documents and other archive material relating to "Switzerland's hero of freedom" extends outside to other sites around Lake Luzern. In Altdorf, for instance, there is a much-photographed bronze statue by Richard

Beckenried.

Kissling, and **Tell Theatre** built in 1925, where Schiller's *Wilhelm Tell* is regularly performed. On the old route to the St Gotthard Pass, south of Altdorf, are the ruins of a **castle** that once belonged to the Lords of Attinghausen.

A key part of the Tell-Museum's signposted "open-air exhibition" is the lakeside **Tellsplatte Sisikon**, marking the place where Tell apparently leapt off the sheriff's barge in a heavy storm. The chapel here, oft confused with that in Bürglen, was built in 1879 on the site of a 14th-century church and features four great frescos by 19th-century Basel painter Ernst Stückelberg, depicting the Rütli oath and apple-shooting scene.

TRAFFIC PAST AND PRESENT

Over a period of roughly 600 years, travellers and goods would leave Flüelen and Altdorf and head south along a route now marked by Autoroute No. 2, in the direction of the St Gotthard Pass and Italy, past the Von Silenen Residence Tower in **Silenen**, past the castle of Zwing Uri near **Erstfeld**, to the 18th-century church in **Wassen**. In the early days the journey was done mostly on foot or, at best, on horseback. Later, after a road had been constructed, people travelled by coach and wagon. From 1882 onwards traffic used the rail tunnel and, since 1980, the St Gotthard road tunnel.

The valley, narrow and dignified, and for centuries dominated only by the thundering sound of the River Reuss, is now filled with the sound of heavy traffic 24 hours a day; even worse, the clear mountain air is being polluted by exhaust fumes. While it is still possible to ascend the wild Schöllenen ravine on foot along the old mountain trail and hike all the way to the St Gotthard Pass, complete silence and really fine hiking can only be found high up in the lateral valleys: in the **Urseren**, and in the **Göschener**, **Maderaner**, **Meien** and **Schächen** valleys.

In the 1940s there was a plan to flood the whole of the Urseren Valley in a massive hydroelectricity scheme. It was only when the locals ejected the gentlemen from the lowland electricity board out of their valley that the entire plan, which seems crazy now, was eventually dropped. Today the valley is one of the few skiing areas in Switzerland that can guarantee snow every winter.

In the Schächen Valley stories are still told about General Suvorov and his Cossack troops, who fought Napoleon and the French on Swiss soil; although he brought war, devastation and hunger to the country, the general's forced marches across the St Gotthard, Kinzig and Pragel passes earned him the respect and admiration of the local inhabitants.

ELEGANT EDIFICES

The canton of Schwyz had its own experience of Suvorov: the general, forced to retreat from the French, moved east via **Muotathal** ❿ in the direction of Glarus and incurred heavy losses. It is assumed that the **icon** that hangs in the

> ⊘ **Fact**
>
> The castle at Attinghausen was where Freiherr von Attinghausen, who featured in Schiller's William Tell play, died in 1321.

William Tell statues, like this one in Altdorf, are found throughout Switzerland.

parish church (1792) in Muotathal was left behind during this retreat. Nothing is known of the origins of the 8th-century **Merovingian reliquary** that forms part of the church treasure, though the hamlet of Muotathal, as well as nearby **Illgau** and **Morschach**, was populated as early as the 10th century: something quite astonishing for such a remote area, lying deep in a forested gorge of the River Muota.

Northwest of Muotathal is the capital of the canton, **Schwyz** ⓫. Despite some uncontrolled construction in the past, the historic town centre retains traces of its old character, notably the broad square and richly decorated Baroque **Church of St Martin**. A dozen or so townhouses with imposing facades and extensive gardens once graced the square. Today only a handful of traditional 17th- to 18th-century patrician houses remain, interspersed with modern structures.

Particularly noticeable is the Baroque-influenced **Ital Reding-Haus** (tel: 041 811 45 05; www.irh.ch; Apr–Oct Tues–Fri 2–5pm, Sat–Sun

The 13th-century Bethlehem Haus, Schwyz.

10am–4pm), a museum within a magnificent 13th-century farmstead (or *Hofstatt*), set against an Alpine backdrop. Guided visits take in the 17th-century mansion and medieval Bethlehem Haus, the oldest wooden house in Switzerland, dating to 1287, decked with 16th-century murals and other treasures. The edge-of-town complex also contains the district library, Kantonsbibliothek.

The grand **Bundesbrief Museum** (Bahnhofstrasse 20; tel: 041 819 20 64; www.bundesbrief.ch; Tues–Sun 10am–5pm; free) in the town centre is most famed for containing the original Federal Charter of 1291, the **Bundesbrief**. The Museum of the Swiss Charters of Confederation – as it's known in English – was the Federal Charter Archive until 1992, but has gradually transformed into a modern history museum. As well as exploring the history and myths of the charter, and its place in Swiss national identity, it also holds other documents from Swiss and cantonal history, plus a collection of pennants, flags and banners.

Also of interest in Schwyz is the **Rathaus** (Town Hall), opposite the Church of St Martin. It is not open to the public but its splendid facade is decorated with a series of frescoes illustrating different events in Swiss history.

Other places of historical significance to the northwest of Schwyz include the ruins of the **Gesslerburg** in Küssnacht (seat of the Habsburg governor Gessler, killed by William Tell), the ruins on the island of **Schwanau** on the Lauerzer See and the **Hohle Gasse** ("sunken lane", where Tell killed Gessler), near **Immensee**. Visitors may also see the last remaining pieces of *Letzine* (barrages) at Arth, Morgarten, Rothenturm and Brunnen. The ruins and remnants are all testimonies to the series of battles fought against the local nobility and the House of Habsburg at the beginning of the 14th century.

The municipality of **Gersau**, 12km (7 miles) west of Schwyz, has the warm *Föhn* wind, as well as its sheltered position by the lake, to thank for the fact that it can support both chestnut trees and palm trees; both grow in profusion. A further attraction is the well-constructed road that runs from **Brunnen** to **Küssnacht**, some 28km (17 miles) to the northwest, along the shore of the Vierwaldstättersee, via Gersau, Vitznau and Weggis. The scenic route is full of bends and, along some stretches, almost like the corniche at Monte Carlo. From Gersau it is about 20km (12 miles) to the **Astrid Chapel**, between Merlischachen and Küssnacht, overlooking the Vierwaldstättersee. Inside the chapel is the grave of Queen Astrid of Belgium, who died in a car accident in the town in the 1930s, and who is venerated almost as much as a saint.

Nearby **Merlischachen**, about 9km (5 miles) south of Küssnacht, is a small village, containing a few grand farmhouses, which is worth the slight detour to make a pleasant break in your journey. The Swiss Chalet Hotel, brightened by geraniums and small red lanterns, is a thoroughly romantic place to stay, and in the Schloss Hotel – popular with honeymooners – you can sleep in a 1963 pearl-white Jaguar MK 10.

MONASTIC COMMUNITY

The high valley of Sihl, some 26km (16 miles) north of Schwyz on Highway 8, is renowned for its countryside of moors and meadows. In summer the **Sihlsee** – the country's biggest artificial reservoir – is a haven for water sports, fishing, lakeside camping and swimming. At the heart of the valley is the town of **Einsiedeln ⑫**, a historic place of pilgrimage, second only to Compostela in Spain, due to its Benedictine Abbey, **Kloster Einsiedeln** (Tourism office tel: 055 418 44 88; church daily 6am–8.30pm, until 9 in summer; guided tours of the church and abbey available). Its history dates back to the 10th century when Eberhard, the provost of Strasbourg's cathedral, founded a monastic

Lake Luzern and Pilatus.

community here. Duke Hermann of Swabia donated to the monastery a portion of land to farm, igniting years of conflict in the holy place. Under Habsburg control, it was locked in a long and bitter dispute with the town folk of Schwyz over rights to the cattle-grazing land. In 1314, a band of locals attacked the abbey, took the sleeping monks prisoner, drank the abbey's wine and desecrated the religious relics.

The abbey, whose prince abbots minted their own coins, lost much of its secular power in 1798 as a result of the revolution.

During the 17th and 18th centuries, pilgrimage to the Black Madonna statue in the marbled **Gnadenkapelle** (Our Lady Chapel) reached a height. The shrine is dedicated to the monk, Meinrad of Einsiedeln, martyred here in 861, and attracts nearly a million visitors a year from all over the world.

The deterioration of the Romanesque-Gothic abbey over the years led to its reconstruction, including the building of the splendid Baroque church, consecrated in 1735. Widely regarded as one of the finest examples of Baroque architecture in Switzerland, this is where today's monk community meet daily for church services. It lies at the heart of the abbey, whose wings shoot off in varying directions around it.

After visiting the abbey, you might want to drop into Einsiedeln's ram and gingerbread museum – the **Schafbock und Lebkuchenmuseum** (Kronenstrasse 1; tel 055 412 23 30; www.goldapfel.ch; Jan 1-Easter Sat, 1.30-4.30pm, rest of year until 6; free) occupies several rooms of the *Goldapfel* (the golden apple), a heritage-protected 1896 house. The museum alone will make you hungry, with its displays of early 20th-century baking utensils for making soft gingery *Lebkuchen*, often dipped in dark chocolate. Thankfully the family-run museum also has what it calls a "nostalgia shop", where you can buy traditional biscuits and chocolates, so you don't have to relegate them to simple memory.

The lavish interior of the Kloster Einsiedeln.

Alpine sheep herding in Belalp, Valais.

SWITZERLAND

TRAVEL TIPS

TRANSPORT

GETTING THERE

By air

There are five international airports in Switzerland: Zürich and Geneva are the main points of entry, followed by Basel, Bern and Lugano. Swiss is the national airline, with flights to some 100 European and worldwide destinations. Numerous airlines, including budget operators such as Easyjet and Ryan Air, have flights from the UK to Geneva, Zürich and Basel, but increasingly also operate flights from Switzerland directly to other locations too, without going via their home bases. Airlines operating flights to Switzerland from the US include American Airlines, British Airways, Air France, Continental, Lufthansa and Delta.

The airports in Zürich and Geneva have their own railway stations, which are part of the national fast-train network. In both these cities there are regular trains running between the airport and the main city railway station. The EuroAirport Basel-Mulhouse-Freiburg is actually situated in France, but only a 5-minute drive to Basel. The journey by bus to Basel takes about 20 minutes on Line 50: EuroAirport – Bahnhof SBB (Basel railway station).

There are many domestic flights between the Zürich, Basel and Geneva international airports. Regular and charter airlines as well as local air-taxi services fly in and out of the Bern-Belp, Lugano-Agno, Gstaad-Saanen, Sion and Samedan-St Moritz airfields.

The SBB national rail offers a flight-luggage service, standard and express, for those arriving/leaving Geneva and Zurich airports. Instead of lugging baggage around the airport, rail passengers can have it unloaded from the plane and

forwarded directly to its destination point, which includes all Swiss railway stations. The same goes for the return journey – you can check in your luggage at any railway station, up to 24 hours in advance with the standard service, and have it sent directly through to your hometown airport from the town where you've been staying.

Travellers can also check in to flights at main railway stations (including Basel, Bern, Geneva, Lausanne, Lugano, Luzern, Neuchâtel, St Gallen and Zürich) and obtain a boarding pass up to 24 hours prior to departure. All the information about this and the flight-luggage services is available online and at every railway station in Switzerland.

The national carrier is **Swiss** (www.swiss.com). Its offices abroad include:
Canada: tel: 1-877 359 7947
UK: tel: 0345 601 0956 (reservations 24 hours a day)
US: tel: 1-877 359 7947

By train

By combined Eurostar London–Paris, then TGV-Lyria services connecting France with Switzerland, you can travel from the UK to Switzerland in as little as 5.5 hours.

Comfortable intercity trains connect Switzerland with all large cities in the surrounding countries. These trains have comfortable first- and second-class compartments and leave every hour. For further information contact the **Swiss Tourist Information Centre** in your country or ring the free number of the **Switzerland Travel Centre (STC)** on 00800 100 200 30 (www.myswitzerland.com). The number in the UK is (0)20 7420 4934. All timetables on the national train network are available online at www.sbb.ch to download and print.

From the Swiss Tourist Information Centre you can also obtain the latest train timetables as well as the following travel tickets:

Discount **Gruppenfahrkarten** (group tickets), for groups of 10 or more.

Swiss Travel Pass: a personal network ticket issued for four, eight, 15 or 22 days or one month, or for three–six or eight days out of 15 days or a month (referred to as a **Flexipass**), which enables its bearer unlimited mileage on SBB and many private railways, postbuses and boats (and in 30 cities and towns on buses and trams too). **Rail Europe** is also a very good place to purchase the Swiss Travel Pass and offer very competitive deals: www.raileurope.com/rail-tickets-passes/swiss-pass.

The **Swiss Card** is good for a round-trip ticket from one of the Swiss borders or airports to a holiday resort area located in Switzerland. The Swiss Card is valid for a month – also gives a 50 percent reduction on most other journeys you make (check mountain railways, some might not be included).

The **Swiss Transfer Ticket** is a free return ticket from the border or airport to your holiday resort. It is valid for one month. Note that you have to buy it outside Switzerland, ideally at the tourist office in your own country.

A **Regional Card** is a ticket (offered in some regions), which is valid for 15 days of which you can travel five days for free in a limited region. Ask tourist information in your country.

The **Swiss Half Fare Card** offers a 50 percent reduction on normal tariffs for trains, boats and postbuses throughout Switzerland.

Direct information from the rail company SBB: tel: 0900 300 300; www.sbb.ch.

By car

When Switzerland joined the EU's Schengen zone in December 2008, systematic passport controls at road border points was done away with, but customs rules are still in effect. The most important Swiss border crossing points, such as that between Basel and France, are manned 24/7. Many small border crossing points are manned at specific times, or not at all.

If you come into Switzerland by car, trailer, caravan, camping car or motorbike and plan to use the national motorways, you require a Swiss motorway fee sticker (or vignette) to stick on the vehicle's front windscreen (Swiss rental cars have a vignette, so you don't need to purchase one). The vignette is valid for a calendar year, regardless of when you buy it, and can be purchased at post offices, petrol stations and garages in Switzerland, Swiss Touring Club outlets (TCS; www.tcs.ch), as well as most overseas automobile associations. The price is CHF40. The Swiss Federal Customs Office provides all the information in English about vignettes and other customs requirements: www.ezv.admin.ch.

Yellow Swiss Postal Service bus.

GETTING AROUND

Public transport

Switzerland maintains an extensive transport network (the second most dense in the world). Nearly every area can be reached comfortably by train, postbus or boat. Many mountains can be reached by rail. **Tickets** for trains, postbus and boats can be obtained at railway stations or at the tourist office. You can also buy tickets directly, though more expensively, on every postbus and Intercity train.

All the necessary **public transport information** is available online at the various websites listed below. Alternatively, information on the train, postbus and boat connections is available at all railway stations – they will print out the date and time of the connection you need (often complete with departure platform number).

Where there are no rail services, hop on one of the yellow buses owned by the **Swiss Postal Service**. These vehicles don't just serve the most remote areas (for example, Juf, the highest village in Europe that is inhabited year-round, located at

☉ Taxis

Taking a taxi in Switzerland is relatively expensive; rates vary from place to place. There are fixed prices charged for extra services (luggage, etc.), which are posted in the taxi itself. The tip is included in the fare.

2,126 metres/6975ft), but cover a lot of the rural areas too.

Regularly scheduled **boats** cruise all the big lakes. There are also **steamships** to put you in a nostalgic mood on Lake Geneva/Lac Léman, Lake Zürich/Zürichsee, Lake Brienz/Brienzer See and Lake Luzern/Vierwaldstätter See. It's also possible to take a trip along the Rhine, Rhône, Aare and Doubs rivers.

In cities, towns and larger villages, **trams** and **buses** operate. Some larger destinations such as Zürich have a local train network (S-Bahn) that includes connections to the airport. Buying tickets at machines is widespread practice, and given you can choose your language, it's a good way to go.

The Swiss love public transport timetables. You can get them for literally every train, tram or bus. But make sure you arrive in good time, since the country's public transport is extremely punctual.

Swiss Railway (SBB/CFF/FFS): Hochschulstr. 6, 3000 Bern (office opening hours: Mon–Fri 7.30am–noon, 1–5.30pm); for all rail enquiries, tel: 0900 300 300; www.sbb.ch.

Post Bus: www.postbus.ch. Their website is also in English and provides useful information on all kinds of offers by post, including online shopping.

By train

It's easy to get about by train in Switzerland and many Swiss prefer this method of travel themselves. Ask at railway stations or at the tourist office for special offers and excursions regularly available for travellers.

Thanks to regular departures and exceptional punctuality, you won't have to wait very long for a train in Switzerland. Intercity, rapid and regional trains have direct connections to all cities and most holiday-resort regions. Trains leave every hour, and sometimes every half-hour between the major cities such as Zürich–Bern,

⊙ Mountain railways

There are numerous spectacular **rack (or cogwheel) railways** and **funiculars** in Switzerland, plus hundreds of **cable cars** and **chairlifts** to carry you up some of the highest peaks. Add to that **underground trains such as** the Metro Alpin in Saas Fee, the world's highest altitude railway, where you can travel inside the mountain to an elevation of almost 4,000 metres (13,000ft). Timetables are available in railway stations and at local tourist information centres.

Zürich–Luzern, Bern–Lausanne, Geneva–St Gallen and many others. You can obtain free timetables for either the Intercity or regional trains, or a print-out of times, changes, etc. from all railway ticket desks.

If you don't wish to carry your luggage on an excursion, there's an express luggage service where you can send your bags (for 12 francs per item plus a flat rate of 30 francs for express shipping; maximum 25kg per item) to the destination in advance for later pick-up. The drop-off, pick-up service is available at more than 30 railway stations.

Similarly there is an "express door-to-door luggage" option between departure hotels to destination hotels provided at more than 30 locations. International luggage delivery and advance luggage check-in prior to flying are also available. Information is available at railway stations or by visiting: www.sbb.ch, or **the Swiss Rail Service**, tel: 0900 300 300.

There is a **lost property** office at every railway station. They are well organised and can trace lost luggage nationwide. If you know the specific train on which you lost an item, staff will phone through immediately to see if it can be found, and will send it back to you at the earliest opportunity.

There are trains with dining cars and minibars in operation each day (normally on all intercity and inter-regional trains). If you plan to travel in a large party or during meal times, you'd be wise to reserve a table in advance.

By car

If you plan to enter Switzerland by car, you are required to be in possession of a passport, a motor vehicle registration and a valid national driving licence.

Wearing a seat belt is mandatory and children under the age of 12 must sit in the back seat. Motorcyclists are required by law to wear helmets. Driving while the alcohol level in your bloodstream exceeds 0.8 mg per millilitre is illegal.

On all country roads the maximum speed is 100kph (60mph); on motorways 120kph (75mph); within city limits 50kph (30mph).

Parking places

Motor vehicles are increasingly banned from city centres, with the number of pedestrian zones increasing. It's wise to leave your car somewhere on the city outskirts or in a car park.

If you want to leave your car in the city centre, there are some short-stay parking areas (from half an hour to a few hours) with parking meters. These only accept small change, so it is useful to carry 1-franc coins with you.

Road information

For information on road conditions in Switzerland, the best English-speaking source is **ViaMichelin**, as it is for all road and itinerary information trans-Europe: www.viamichelin.com/web/Traffic.

Breakdowns

Foreign car drivers can dial 140 (the same telephone number applies throughout Switzerland) for help in the case of a breakdown. One of

⊙ Petrol stations

At many petrol stations along the motorways as well as in cities you can purchase fuel around the clock with credit cards and sometimes with cash (10, 20 and 50 SFr notes). Prices, as everywhere, vary depending on the fuel market and location, often with higher prices in more remote mountainous regions. One of Switzerland's biggest retailers, Coop, has a network of some 90 roadside Coop Pronto shops, and dozens of them include filling stations. The pit-stop café-shops are usually open seven days a week from 6am–11pm. The petrol is self-serve 24-7.

the five action centres of the Swiss Touring Club (TCS) will answer your call and put you in touch with the closest repair shop or mobile help. If you are in possession of a letter of safe conduct, issued by your own automobile association, breakdown aid will be delivered free of charge by the TCS Road Patrol. There are emergency telephones positioned on the highways at 1.6km (1-mile) intervals. You'll also find TCS and ACS (Swiss Automobile Club) emergency telephones along remote stretches on pass roads.

In the case of an accident resulting in injury, it is mandatory to inform the police. If there are no injuries but damage is done to a vehicle, it is still advisable (but not obligatory) to call the police. Throughout Switzerland dialling 117 will connect you with the police.

Special regulations

Private vehicles with studded tyres are permitted on country roads only between 1 November and 31 March. Such vehicles are forbidden to drive on motorways and major thoroughfares (clearly designated as Autobahn or Autostrasse).

There are special regulations that apply specifically to trailers, caravans and boats. Further information is available from automobile associations or from the Swiss customs officials posted at the borders.

Tunnels and passes

Road tunnels

The Great St Bernard Tunnel (5.8km/3.5 miles) connects Valais to the Aosta Valley (in Italy). The price of the toll is contingent upon the type of vehicle you are driving and starts at SFr 27. If the return trip is made within 30 days cars are awarded a 30 percent discount, and buses 20 percent. It is also possible to purchase a booklet containing several toll tickets.

The Munt la Schera Tunnel (3.5km/2.25 miles) between Zernez and Livigno (in Italy) is open 8am–8pm. One-way tickets for private cars are SFr 9, plus SFr 2 for each occupant.

It is necessary to obtain a motorway vignette for passage through the St Gotthard Tunnel (connecting inner Switzerland to Ticino, 16.8km/10.5 miles) and for the highway leading to the San Bernardino Tunnel (between Graubünden and Ticino,

6.6km/4 miles). You will not have to pay additional fees inside the tunnel.

Car hire

Hiring a car in Switzerland is expensive. There are car rental agencies in all cities of any size, so you'll have no trouble renting a vehicle. The minimum driving age is between 20–25 depending on the rental company. In the larger railway stations tourists travelling by rail can take advantage of the car rental service operated by the Swiss Federal Railways. If coming from elsewhere in Europe, a cheaper alternative might be to hire a car in advance from your home country.

Car hire firms

The main international car hire firms are represented throughout Switzerland. The telephone numbers are listed below:
Avis tel: 0848 811 818
Budget tel: 0844 844 700
Europcar tel: 0848 808 099
Hertz tel: 0848 822 020

Cars on trains

Cars are transported through Alpine railway tunnels according to a timetable. Additional trains are employed during Christmas and Easter holidays.
Albula tunnel, Thusis-Samedan, up to 10 daily departures; www.rhb.ch
Furka tunnel, Oberwald-Realp, at least 16 daily departures; tel: 027 927 77 77; www.mgbahn.ch
Lötschberg tunnel, Kandersteg-Goppenstein, at least 33 daily departures; tel: 0900 55 33 33; www.bls.ch
Vereina tunnel, Klosters Selfranga-Sengalins, daily departures every 30 minutes; tel: 081 288 37 38; www.rhb.ch
Oberalp tunnel, Andermatt-Sedrun, four–five daily departures; tel: 027 927 77 77; www.fo-bahn.ch

For Albula and Oberalp it is essential to call the embarkation railway stations in advance and make a reservation for your car:

The Vereina car transporter.

Albula: tel: 081 288 37 38
Oberalp: Andermatt tel: 041 888 77 51; Sedrun tel: 081 949 11 37
Furka: Realp tel: 041 887 14 46; Oberwald tel: 027 973 11 41
Lötschberg: Kandersteg tel: 033 675 18 88; Goppenstein tel: 027 939 11 69. At all other embarkation stations it is not possible to reserve in advance.

Further information on schedules and prices (including those applicable to buses, trailers, motorcyclists, etc.) can be obtained at Swiss Tourist Information centres or railway stations.

In order to spare car drivers a time-consuming journey to their holiday destination, European railways offer **Transport Trains for Cars**, with sleepers and/or couchettes.
Vereina: information tel: 081 288 37 38

Mountain passes

Information on relevant mountain passes can be found in each chapter. Check for openings and real-time traffic news before heading off on **ViaMichelin**. The other extremely useful source of information on the passes is **The SwitzerlandMobility Foundation**: www.wanderland.ch/en/services. Also visit www.alpen-paesse.ch/en.

Here is a list of the principle mountain passes and their general opening season:
Albula
(2,312 metres/7,586ft)
(Graubünden) Tiefencastel–La Punt, May–Oct.
Bernina
(2,328 metres/7,638ft)
Pontresina–Poschiavo, all year (in winter mostly closed at night).
Brünig

(1,008 metres/3,307ft)
Meiringen–Sachseln, all year.
Flüela
(2,383 metres/7,819ft)
(Graubünden) Davos–Susch, April–Nov (in winter use Vereina Tunnel).
Forclaz
(1,526 metres/5,007ft)
Martigny–Le Châtelard, all year.
Furka
(2,431 metres/7,976ft)
(Valais) Gletsch–Andermatt, June–Oct.
Great St Bernard/San Bernardino
(2,469 metres/8,100ft)
(Graubünden) Martigny–Aosta, June–Oct (tunnel passage open all year).
Grimsel
(2,165 metres/7,103ft)
(Bernese Oberland) Meiringen–Gletsch, May–Oct.
Klausen
(1,948 metres/6,391ft)
(Central Switzerland) Altdorf–Linthal, May–Oct.
Lukmanier
(1,914 metres/6,280ft)
Disentis–Biasca, May–Nov.
Nufenen
(2,478 metres/8,130ft)
Ulrichen–Airolo, June–Oct.
Oberalp
(2,044 metres/6,706ft)
(Graubünden) Andermatt–Disentis, May–Nov.
San Bernardino
(2,065 metres/6,775ft)
Thusis–Bellinzona, June–Oct (tunnel passage open all year).
St Gotthard/Passo San Gottardo
(2,108 metres/6,916ft)
(Central Switzerland) Andermatt–Airolo, June–Nov (tunnel passage open all year).

Simplon
(2,006 metres/6,582ft)
Brig–Domodossola, all year.
Susten
(2,224 metres/7,297ft)
(Bernese Oberland) Innertkirchen–
Wassen, June–Oct.

Tours by train

Glacier Express

St Moritz–Zermatt (7hrs 30 mins), or
Davos–Zermatt or vice versa (7hrs).
This route provides the traveller with
291km (182 miles) of varied scenery
through the enchanting landscape
of the Alps. On the slowest express
train in the world, complete with a
"panorama wagon", you'll make
your way through 91 tunnels, over
291 bridges, across the 2,033-metre
(6,777ft) Oberalp Pass and through
the longest metre-gauge railway
tunnel in existence.

The steepest parts of the stretch
are accomplished by virtue of rack
railways. You can partake of a midday meal in the tastefully decorated
dining car.

Bernina Express

Chur–Tirano or vice versa (4hrs 35
mins).
The highest crossing of the Alps by
train is made on the *Bernina Express*;
with a 7 percent gradient it is the
steepest non-rack railway in the
world. During the 145km (90-mile)
ride the train first ascends to the
Albula Line at 585 metres (2,860ft)
above sea level (Chur), before reaching Pontresina at 1,774 metres
(5,913ft). From here the express
heads over the Bernina Pass (2,253
metres/7,510ft) to descend twisting and turning all the way to Tirano
(429 metres/1,430ft). In just a short
while passengers can experience the
complete range of vegetation zones
from the Piz Bernina Glacier (4,049
metres/13,497ft) to the palm trees of

The Golden Pass Panoramic train.

Tirano in Italy. When the weather is
good, some trains offer open "panorama wagons" – an unforgettable
experience. You can travel further
on to Lugano by a connecting bus in
Tirano.

Palm Express

St Moritz–Lugano (4hrs), in summer
and autumn.
The *Palm Express*, a connection
between postbus and railway, travels from the snow and glaciers of
the Alps to the palm-fringed regions
of southern Switzerland and back
again. This express connects the
Engadine and Upper Valais with
Ticino, St Moritz and Zermatt with
Ascona (where passengers remain
overnight), before continuing on to
Locarno and Lugano.

Additional information can be
found on the postbus website at
www.postauto.ch/en/excursion-tips/
palm-express, through Swiss tourism
offices, or online at www.swisstravel-
system.com.

Golden Pass Route

Luzern–Interlaken–Zweisimmen–
Montreux or vice versa (5hrs 6 mins).
This is one of the classic Swiss train
journeys. It leads through charming scenery from the banks of Lake
Luzern to the Swiss Riviera. You
travel on the narrow-gauge SSB
Brünigbahn to Interlaken and continue on from there with the BLS to
Zweisimmen. At Zweisimmen you'll
change back to the narrower gauge
MOB tracks all the way to Montreux
– an especially pleasurable experience in the panorama wagons with
their enormous picture windows.

Lötschberg-Centovalli
ExpressTrain

Locarno–Domodossola (1hr 30 mins).
This narrow-gauge track makes its
way through romantic Centovalli
and connects the two great European railway lines over the Simplon
and Gotthard passes. The journey takes you 52km (33 miles)
over bridges, idyllic gorges and
up inclines, some of which have
a gradient of six percent, as well
as through stretches of Italy.
The round-trip journey Zürich–
Gotthard–Centovalli–Simplon–
Lötschberg–Brig–Zürich is an
extra-special treat, which can be
accomplished in a single day.

Wilhelm Tell Express

The *Wilhelm Tell Express* (6hrs) runs
daily from May to mid-October.
This route, connecting Central
Switzerland with Ticino, includes

⊘ Swiss station experience

Railway stations in Switzerland
are often an attraction in their own
right, with excellent facilities. You
can dine out at a good restaurant
on the station concourse, or shop
in supermarkets (open in the
evenings), or use the 24-hour
vending machines, which dispense
bread, milk and even salami.
There are luggage lockers at all

stations except tiny country halts,
which come in three sizes. You can
use them for several consecutive
days without problem.

Platforms are marked out in
sectors and the PA will announce
which sector your carriage will be
arriving at, to save you running up
and down the length of the train.
All in all, a civilised experience.

passage in a steamboat. You can sit back and enjoy the sights from the huge saloon or panorama wagons.

During the ferry ride a delicious midday meal is served in the "Salon Belle Epoque".

This is a packed and varied day excursion from Luzern to Locarno/Lugano and back again.

Heidi Express

Landquart–Davos–Berninapass–Tirano or vice versa (4hrs 40 mins). Like the *Bernina Express*, the 145km (90-mile) route traverses the Bernina Pass but first leads from Landquart up the lovely Prättigau Valley past Klosters and Davos. After Davos the landscape becomes more rugged, with raging mountain torrents. From the train you can see a wide range of Alpine flowers and in the Bernina area you will encounter shining glaciers.

After a stopover in Tirano (Italy) the route takes you through the Valtellina Valley back to Lugano (only in summer).

As you will cross the Swiss border during this journey you will need your passport or identity card.

Voralpen Express

Romanshorn–St Gall–Rapperswil–Arth-Goldau–Luzern or vice versa (2hrs 39 mins).
This Pre-Alp Express takes you through the Alpine foothills of Switzerland and along various lake sides. It is worth stopping off en route to make a small excursion to any one of the following: Cloister of St-Gall, Säntis Mountain, Appenzellerland (where the cheese comes from), the Children's Zoo in Rapperswil, Cloister of Einsiedeln, the Wildlife Park in Goldau, Rigi Mountain or the Transport Museum in Luzern.

Allalin Express

Bern or Interlaken–Lötschberg–Brig–Saas Fee or vice versa (2hrs 50 mins).
The journey first takes you from the canton of Bern through one of the highest tunnels in Europe (Lötschberg) into the canton of Valais. From the train you can see the foothills of the Rhone Valley wine region, and also the snow-capped mountains rising all around. In Brig the bus waits to take you on an exciting journey uphill to Saas Fee, one of the country's famous ski resorts. If you haven't had enough sightseeing yet there is an option to take the Alpine Express from Saas Fee to the world's largest glacier grotto at 3,500 metres (11,480ft) above sea level.

Note: these scenic routes are also possible on ordinary trains where you pay no extras. Of course, you can just do one part of a route and then return if you wish. Or you can pay for an excursion as part of a package holiday. In general, it is hard to find a long train journey that is not pleasant in Switzerland, since the country is so small and the variety of the countryside so expansive – you'll always have interesting scenery to look at en route.

Road tours

By postbus

Swiss postbuses offer a comfortable and safe way of travelling through the Alps. Tours are offered throughout Switzerland. Examples include a triple-pass journey (over the Grimsel, Furka and Susten passes, starting from either Meiringen in the Bernese Oberland or from Andermatt in the canton of Uri), and a quadruple-pass trip (over the Grimsel, Nufenen, Gotthard and Susten passes, commencing in Meiringen) in Central Switzerland.

During lengthy journeys with the postbus (for example from St Moritz to Lugano), a generous break is allowed to give travellers plenty of time for a bite to eat. You can get more information at the **Swiss Tourist Office** or at any of the regional offices. Visit www.postbus.ch.

By bicycle

If you are in possession of a valid ticket, you can have your bicycle transported by train or boat. It is also possible to get your bike aboard a postbus, but space is quite limited and you must be sure to make arrangements in advance.

It's no trouble bringing your own bike into Switzerland.

Cycle routes: There are over 6,000km (3,730 miles) of marked bicycle paths in country areas. There are more than a dozen long-distance cycle routes throughout Switzerland, as well as hundreds of regional paths, mostly well away from traffic. You can obtain a map showing the long-distance routes from tourist offices. **Switzerland-Mobility** also has a bike-dedicated information site, with all routes, interactive maps, safety information and lodging suggestions along the way (and all provided in English at www.veloland.ch). The Veloland site also serves as a cycling-holiday booking platform, most of them offered by Zürich-based bike tour operator **Eurotrek** (www.eurotrek.ch). Another serious cycling tourism set up (and a Switzerland Tourism member), is **Bike Switzerland** (www.bikeswitzerland.com), whose highly visual website will give you a very good virtual tour of the trips they do in the Jura and the Alps.

◷ Bicycle hire

Nearly every railway station in Switzerland that lies within or near the extensive network of bike routes has top-condition, modern bicycles for hire. The national railway SBB, linking up with regional rail services such as Rhaetian Railways, are increasingly getting in on the rail-bike hire scene. Hire bikes in advance either online or by phoning a specific station, then collect your bike from the station and start your cycle tour. You can find their bikes for hire at 200 locations throughout Switzerland, including at more than 80 railway stations. You can return bicycles and e-bikes hired at a railway station to the same station, and usually also to any other station with bike-hire facilities. Prices for a day are approximately CHF30–35, with road and mountain bikes, tandems and children's bikes also available. The Swiss Rail's RailAway tickets, bought online or at the ticket counter, include various combined offers (train and bike hire): www.sbb.ch.

Ensure, especially during the summer, that you make bookings in advance. If you are in possession of a Swiss Travel Pass you get a discount.

In some cities, such as Zürich and Bern, you can get free bike hire when you leave your ID card and a small cash deposit with the hire company.

A - Z

A

Accommodation

Choosing a hotel

There are around 5,000 hotels in Switzerland, amounting to more than 270,000 beds. This includes hotels, motels, pensions, mountain sanatoria and luxury spa and wellness resorts. There are an additional 26,000 chalet and holiday apartments and 600 youth hostel beds. The Swiss Hotels Association, **Hotellerie Suisse** (www.hotelleriesuisse.ch), classifies hotels from one to five stars, or without stars as a "Swiss Lodge", or a "Garni" (bed and breakfast). The best hotels in each star category are designated "Superior".

For more information, call or visit the website of **Switzerland Tourism**, the national tourism promotional board (Tödistrasse 7 Zürich; tel: +41 44 288 11 11 or toll-free number 00800 100 200 29; www.myswitzerland.com), or one of its offices **abroad** (see page 331).

All hotel and holiday bookings can be made via its website, linking with the booking platform of the **Switzerland Travel Centre** (STC; www.switzerlandtravelcentre.ch), a joint venture between Switzerland Tourism, the Swiss Hotel Association and Swiss Railways SBB.

Hotel listings

Information and prices can be found on MySwitzerland.com, which lists about 2,000 hotels according to city and region, or holiday type, as well as at **Swiss Hotels** (www.swisshotels.com, tel +41 848 848 408), a brand of the STC.

Camping

For outdoor lovers, there are some 55,000 camp sites, of which about a fifth are open in winter. You can obtain a listing of regional camp sites along with a map of Swiss camp sites from the tourist office, and there is plenty of information available online at **MySwitzerland**.

Outside the boundaries of official camp sites, caravans and trailers may only be parked with the permission of the property owner, the relevant local authority or from the police. Spending one night at a public car park is tolerated in many cantons. If you decide to do this, it's a good idea to inform the closest police station or the local authorities beforehand.

The Swiss Touring Club (TCS; tel: 022 417 20 20; www.tcs.ch) runs a network of sites, which it sells through its online booking platform (only in German, French and Italian). It also publishes a camping guidebook, and can provide maps and other information.

SwissCamps (http://swisscamps.ch) on the other hand, the website of the **Swiss Camping Association** (Verband Schweizerischer Campings), has a full listing and search engine in English, with an interactive map.

Youth hostels

Of the 52 youth hostels run by the **Swiss Youth Hostel Association**, 42 carry the Swiss Lodge certification from hotelleriesuisse, of which it has been a member since 2013. That says a lot about their quality. From country castles to city villas, most offer double and four-bedded rooms. Dormitories are rare. Open to anybody, regardless of age. You don't need a membership card, but if you are planning to stay for long periods it is worth buying one (online or at any of the hostels; 22 francs up to 18 years and for seniors, 33 francs for adults). They are valid in 4,500 other youth hostels around the world, and bring some discounts and other deals. All the hostels are bookable via the association website, www.youthhotel.ch, or by telephone: 01 360 14 14.

Swiss Backpackers runs about 40 hostels, often centrally located in towns and cities with competing prices. No membership is required (tel: 062 892 26 75; www.backpacker.ch).

In more peaceful nature locations, you can find some 100 hotels that belong to the Bern-based **Naturfreunde Schweiz.** Run by individuals, they are often located in picturesque historic buildings as well as forests or by lakes (tel: 031 306 67 67; www.naturfreunde.ch).

The Swiss Alpine Club

There are over 150 club huts in the Alps, which are intended not as holiday lodgings but starting points (base camps) for mountain-climbing expeditions or high-Alpine ski tours. Plenty of information on them is available on the website of the Bern-based **Swiss Alpine Club** (Schweizer Alpen-Club), which has a hut search engine and booking platform as well as maps and other information (Monbijoustrasse 61, Bern 23; tel: 031 370 18 18; www.sac-cas.ch).

Holiday apartments

Other than through the dependable holiday rentals portal of My Switzerland and the Swiss Travel Centre (http://chalet.myswitzerland.com/holiday-rentals), one of the main agencies for apartments and holiday homes, with approximately 3,500 on its books, is **Interhome** (tel: 043 810 91 26; www.interhome.com). Of course it competes today with **Airbnb** and all the other online rental and holiday booking sites.

For travellers on tighter budgets, or for those who prefer simple lodgings, there are plenty of smaller hotels and inns. All of these plus

B&Bs, furnished apartments, country inns, farm camping and mountain inns are listed on the Swiss Tourism website and available in brochure form from its local offices.

You can stay in private rooms (ask at the tourist office) and even sleep on straw at some farms: the brochure **Schlaf im Stroh** is issued by the tourist office.

Agritourism

Sleep in Straw is an initiative of **Agritourism Switzerland**, which is another relatively inexpensive and highly enjoyable way of coming up close with the countryside. Agrotourismus Schweiz has 320 properties under its wing, including farm accommodation – not just straw but rooms, holiday homes and dormitory beds – as well as enjoying fresh farm produce. Its website has plenty of online information and a booking platform: www.agrotourismus.ch.

Admission charges

Charges to get into museums and other places of interest are no higher than anywhere else in Europe, with most museums charging around 8–10 francs. There are discounts for under 16s and children (under 12) often go free. Ask at tourist offices about the **Swiss Museum Pass** (www.museumspass.ch), which covers about 500 museums around the country. The public transport **Swiss Pass** also entitles you to free admission to all museums in the Swiss Museum Passport scheme. An International Student Identity Card (ISIC) entitles the holder to all sorts of discounts on admission prices.

B

Budgeting for your trip

There's no doubt about it, Switzerland can be an expensive place to take a holiday, with costs about 10 percent higher than many other European countries and 20 percent higher than Australia and the US. Even on the most budget of budget trips you'll still need to bank on a bare minimum of 80 francs a day for hostel accommodation, transport, three basic meals and some modest nightlife; 100 francs

would be more reasonable and 200 francs would allow you to do more and stay in simple hotels.

Hotel costs are likely to be your biggest expenditure; expect to pay more than the average in big cities and popular ski resorts. You can save money by staying in hostels (around 35 francs a night) or cheap hotels (around 80 francs a night), which are basic but clean and comfortable.

Eating out can be expensive, but there are plenty of self-service and fast-food restaurants in most towns and cities where you can eat for less. A good tip is to go to the main railway station, which will usually have bars and cafés selling healthy sandwiches, kebabs, roast chicken and hot quiche. Department stores such as Migros and Coop have restaurants where you can get a nourishing meal for around 12 francs.

Business hours

As a general rule Switzerland-wide, shops open daily from 8/9am–6.30pm Monday to Friday, and until 5/6pm on Saturday, though in smaller towns and villages, even in some cities, they generally close between midday and 2pm. In the German-speaking cities in particular, many department stores and other larger shops have late-night trading one night a week, generally Thursday or Friday, until 8pm. Grocery shops often stay open later on weekdays, beyond 7/8pm but are closed on Sundays, except at railway stations, airports and other transport hubs, and in resort areas.

Over recent years shopping hours have been liberalised in many areas, though there are big disparities from region to region, and particularly between French- and German-speaking cities. Shops in German-speaking cities tend to stay open later. This is the case, for example, in Zürich, where shops are allowed to open Mon–Sat 6am–11pm. Though only a few exercise that right, many shops are open at least until 8pm. On Sundays, only shops in railway and petrol stations are allowed to open. In Geneva, on the other hand, many service shops close for lunch between noon and 2pm.

Offices countrywide tend to observe the 8am–noon and 2–5pm hours, while banks open Mon–Fri 8.30am–4.30pm. Money can still be changed at the Change/Cambio

bureau at airports and railway stations, open daily from 6am–9/11pm, as well as at convenient currency-exchange machines at the main airports.

Post office hours vary dramatically too. In smaller towns and cities, hours are generally 8.30am–noon and 1.30–6pm Mon–Fri, and Saturday until noon. In the major cities, however, they are open from 8am–8pm, and in some cases, the regular counter is open Mon–Sat from 6.30am–10.30pm. The postal system in Switzerland is as efficient as its transport; on the postal website, www.post.ch, you can check any details for any office across the country in English.

Government and other official offices open Mon–Fri 8am–noon and 2–5/6pm.

In general, museums open Tues–Sun 10am–5pm. Many larger museums have also started opening during the evenings, generally on Thursday, while smaller and regional museums are often only open half days (mostly an afternoon) or at weekends. In any case, to avoid disappointment, it's a good idea to check exact opening hours prior to setting off, either by phone or online.

Business travellers

It's not surprising in a country renowned for its financial expertise and service sector that business travellers are well catered for. Even the trains are geared up for work, with Wi-Fi access and "quiet carriages" where you won't be disturbed. In major cities there is an ever-increasing choice (and competition) of quality mid-range hotels where 150–200 francs a night will get you a good room Wi-Fi and breakfast included in the price.

Because most Swiss speak good English, business travellers find meetings and negotiations easy. Many Swiss dress smartly but informally for the office, although for very important meetings a jacket and tie – a smart suit for women – is a good idea. On its website, Switzerland Tourism has an extensive section on meetings, with a meeting planner, venue finder and links to incentive itineraries, the best business hotels and themes for business meeting, (www.myswitzerland.com/en/meetings.html).

C

Children

There are many different possibilities for enjoyable family holidays in Switzerland. Ask at the Swiss Tourist Office for more information.

All family-friendly accommodation, as well as activities, holiday ideas, adventure parks and animal farms are listed on the Swiss Tourism website under Interests/Family Trips: www.myswitzerland.com/en/interests/family-trips.html.

Special playgrounds for kids are often provided, as well as special attractions at reasonable prices. Travelling with children is easy in Switzerland; the Swiss railway makes special arrangements for families, such as the family card, where children up to 16 years travel free when travelling with their parents. Information is available from all railway stations.

Climate

Located in the centre of Europe, the Swiss climate is influenced by maritime and continental air masses. Summers are mostly warm at lower altitudes, although they can be quite wet with frequent thunderstorms. Winters are generally cold with plenty of cloud, snow and fog.

The high mountains mean great differences can occur within just a short distance – one valley can be sunny and dry while the next is shrouded in mist. The Ticino area bordering the Italian lakes is markedly warmer and sunnier than the rest of the country throughout the year.

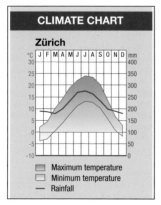

⊘ Holidays with kids

The non-profit social tourism association, **Reka**, has a network of holiday villages and holidays geared to families in Switzerland (www.reka.ch; tel +41 31 329 66 99). Ask for the brochure "Familienferien" at tourist offices.

Don't forget to bring along a warm fleece, raincoat, waterproof boots and an umbrella, even in the height of summer, and likewise, sunglasses and sunscreen even in the depths of winter.

Weather reports

When in Switzerland, for an up-to-date weather report dial 162, or visit: www.meteo.ch. Weather reports are also intermittently broadcast on Swiss radio and television. Since the Alps function as a climatic divide, weather broadcasts distinguish between the north side of the Alps, southern Switzerland and the Engadine.

Crime and safety

In comparison with other countries, Switzerland is very safe and there is little crime. Nevertheless, it is better not to walk at night-time in some parts of the bigger cities. Ask for advice at your hotel or in a tourist office. Pickpocketing can happen in crowded places, such as on public transport and in supermarkets, so be attentive. The police emergency number everywhere is 117.

Customs

Tourists are allowed to take the following goods into Switzerland duty- and tax-free:
250 units/g cigarettes/cigars/other tobacco products
5 litres of alcohol up to 18% vol. and 1 litre of alcohol over 18% vol.

If in doubt, please inquire in advance at a **Swiss Customs Office** or at: www.ezv.admin.ch.

D

Disabled travellers

Contact **Mobility International Schweiz**, at Froburgstrasse 4, 4600 Olten; tel: 062 206 88 35; www.mis-ch.ch. They provide a list of easy-access accommodation and a hiking brochure for those with mobility difficulties.

Nautilus Reisen, Froburgstrasse 4, 4601 Olten; tel: 062 206 88 30; www.nautilus.ch organises its own tours and arranges holiday bookings for the disabled.

Cato, Limmatstrasse 275, 8005 Zürich; tel: 01 440 41 00; www.cato-reisen.ch specialises in activity holidays and guided group tours for the disabled with or without able-bodied companions.

You can get information on special services on public transport for travellers with disabilities at most railway stations. In the UK, **Holiday Care** provide practical advice, support and information for disabled travellers and their families; visit www.holidaycare.org.uk or tel: 0845 124 9971 for information.

A list of ski schools with professional assistance for the disabled is available at **Schweizerischer Zentralverein für das Blindenwesen**, Schützengasse 4, 9000 St Gallen; tel: 071 223 36 36; www.szb.ch.

E

Electricity

The voltage in Switzerland, as in most of Europe, is 230V/50 Hz. Switzerland uses 2-pin (type C) and 3-pin (Type J) plugs and most power sockets are designed so that either of these can be used (the 3rd is an optional grounder). The standard European continental plug with two round pins, applied for many electrical travel products, may be used without a problem. Adapters are available in most hotels for other voltages (or bring your own).

Embassies and consulates

Australia Consulate-General: Chemin des Fins 2, 1211 Geneva/Grand-Saconnex, tel: 022 799 91 00; www.geneva.mission.gov.au
Canada: Kirchenfeldstrasse 88, 3005 Bern 6, tel: 031 357 32 00
UK: British Embassy Bern, Thunstrasse 50, 3000 Bern 15, tel: 031 359 77 00
US: Sulgeneckstrasse 19, CH-3007 Bern, tel: 031 357 70 11

Swiss embassies

Australia: 7 Melbourne Avenue,

Forrest/Canberra ACT 2603, tel: 02-6162 8400; www.eda.admin.ch/australia

Canada: 5 Avenue Marlborough, Ottawa, Ontario K1N 8E6, tel: 613-235 1837; www.eda.admin.ch/canada

New Zealand: Level 12, Maritime Tower, 10 Customhouse Quay, Wellington 6011, tel: 64 4 472 15 93

UK: 16–18 Montagu Place, London W1H 2BQ, tel: 020-7616 6000; www.swissembassy.org.uk

US: 2900 Cathedral Avenue N.W., Washington, DC 20008-3499, tel: 202-745 7900
Consulate, 633 3rd Avenue, 30th floor, New York NY 10017, tel: 212-599 5700; www.swissemb.org

Entry requirements

Visas and passports

Travellers from most European countries, the US, Canada, South America, Australia and New Zealand must be in possession of a valid passport but do not need a visa for a stay (for business or pleasure) of up to three months.

Etiquette

The reputation the Swiss have for being ultra-conservative is somewhat misleading. Their apparent reserve is usually superficial and borne more out of a deep respect for order and polite behaviour than any sense of superiority. One of the small joys of Switzerland is that people – most of them anyway – turn off their mobile phones when they go to a restaurant; or if they do leave it turned on, they'll step outside to make or take a call. Talking loudly on your mobile in a quiet café or on the bus will not endear you to people, so follow the Swiss example and use your phone with consideration.

The Swiss are usually punctual and will also expect you to be so. A handshake is fine for a first meeting, but if you know people well it's traditional throughout Switzerland to exchange three kisses on alternating cheeks. If you're having dinner, don't start slurping your wine before anyone else; the host will usually propose a toast and you shouldn't drink until he or she has done so. For the toast, hold the wine glass by the base and clink glasses with everyone. Before you eat, wish everyone guten appetit, or in French areas, *bon appetit*, though in Swiss German, as

spoken outside the big cities, you are more likely to hear en *Guete*.

Dress codes are more relaxed than you might expect. If you're invited for dinner, smart-casual clothes are fine, with neat jeans and open-necked shirts or blouses.

F

Festivals and events

Music and film festivals

January–April
Solothurn Film Festival (Jan); Fribourg Film Festival (Mar)

May
Bern International Jazz Festival; Schaffhausen Jazz Festival; Nyon International Documentary Film Festival; Rose d'Or International Television Festival, Luzern.

June
Gurten Open-air Rock and Folk Festival in Bern; Zürich Caliente, the biggest Latin festival in Switzerland; Solothurn Literature Days; Zürich Festspiele, an arts festival (June–July); Wilhelm Tell Festspiele in Interlaken (June–Sept); Ascona New Orleans Music Festival (June–July).

July
Saas Fee Alpine International Music Festival; Festival Jazz in Lugano; Montreux Jazz Festival; Klassik-Musikwochen in Braunwald (GL); Arosa International Jazz Festival; Fribourg International Jazz Festival; Verbier Music Festival (end July–beginning Aug); Yehudi Menuhin Festival in Gstaad (July–Aug); Classical concert weeks in the Engadine (July–Aug); Luzern International Blues Festival; Davos International Music Festival – young artists in concert (July–Aug); Open-air theatre performances in Ballenberg's Freilichtmuseum, near Brienz (July–Aug); Leukerbad Clown Festival; Nyon (VA); Paléo International Open-air Rock Festival; Thuner Schlosskonzerte, classical music festival in Thun; Tibor Varga, classical music festival with violin competition in Sion (VS; July–Sept).

August
Neuchâtel Busker's Festival; Luzern International Music Festival;

International Festival for music and lyric poetry in Montreux (Aug–Sept); Interlaken Music Festival (Aug–Sept); Music weeks in Locarno/ Ascona (Aug–Oct); Locarno International Film Festival; Willisau (Luzern), a jazz festival (end Aug–beginning Sept); Fribourg International Folklore Festival.

September–November
Cinemusic in Thun – an international festival of music and film; International Festival of Alpenfilms in Les Diablerets; International Jazz Festival in Zürich (Nov).

Traditional festivals and events

There are numerous festival traditions throughout the year. For more information and tickets visit **Switzerland Tourism**, www.myswitzerland.com or **Swiss Ticket Corner**, tel: 0848-800 800; www.ticketcorner.ch. Another good website is: www.events.ch.

January
Vogel Gryff in Basel (January 13, 20 or 27th); Kläusenacht in Urnäsch near Appenzell (New Year's Eve); Lauberhorn Ski World Cup downhill ski racing in Wengen (mid); Inferno giant slalom ski race in Mürren (late); international hot-air ballooning week in Chateau d'Oex (late).

February
Horse racing on St Moritz's frozen lake (early); Cresta Run toboggan competition in St Moritz (mid); Fasnacht carnival in Basel and Luzern and many other towns and villages (mid); in the Lötschen Valley there are the terrifying masks of "Dirty Thursday" and the "Good Lord's Grenadier" (mid-February–early March).

March/April
Chalanda Marz in Graubünden, with its ringing chimes (1st); Fridolinsfeuer in Glarus and the Good Friday Procession in Mendrisio (6th); Sechseläuten in Zürich (spring festival; first Monday after 21 March).

May
May Day celebrations in many places (1st); Landsgemeinde in Glarus, public voting on local issues (early); Valaisian champion's meeting of Cow Fighting in Aproz (mid).

June
Celebration in many villages of taking cattle up to the Alps (early);

Tour de Suisse cycle race (mid); Celebration of the Battle of Murten/Morat with flower parade (22nd).

July
Swiss Open tennis championship, Gstaad (early); Aarau Youth Festival (first Friday in July); Medieval Festival in St Ursanne, Jura (mid).

August
Swiss National Day, with fireworks, parades etc. everywhere (1st); Zürich Street Parade: giant techno dance party (early); Fêtes de Genève in Geneva (early); Marché-Concours horse festival in Saignelégier, Jura (early); Chur Festival (late); Lausanne international Rollerskating Championships (late); Fribourg International Folklore Festival, with yodelling and typical Alpine sports events (late).

September
Bern Festival (early); Zürich Knabenschiessen, with funfair (mid); La Bénichon in Fribourg, a traditional thanksgiving festival (mid); Aarau Backfischet, children's parade with Chinese lanterns (second Friday in Sept); International Horse Race in Luzern (mid). There are grape-growing festivals in Fribourg, Neuchâtel, Lugano, Lutry, Morges and other villages throughout the month.

October
Celebrations in many villages of bringing cattle down from the Alps (early); Basel Autumn Fair, food fair (late).

November
St Martin's Market in Vevey and Porrentruy, a food festival (early); Zibele-Märit onion fair in Bern (4th Monday).

December
Claus Hunt in Küssnacht on Rigi and in Arth (6th); Escalade in Geneva (around 11th); Lichterschwimmen in Zürich, illuminated boats on the Limmat River (mid/late).

H

Health and medical care

Medical treatment
The quality of medical treatment in Switzerland is very high. In case of emergency, go to the nearest doctor or to the Emergency Station in the nearest hospital. Unlike in most other countries, the emergency numbers for police etc. are different: dial 144 for an ambulance, 117 for the police and 118 for the fire department.

Cities and larger villages have emergency doctors, dentists and out-of-hour clinics. Their contact numbers can be obtained by dialling 111 or 144; you can also get contact details of 24-hour pharmacies. Alternatively, find pharmacy details online by tapping your location into **SOS Pharmacie** at www.sos-pharmacie.ch.

I

Internet
You will be able to be online with fast efficient internet in Switzerland, even if you don't have roaming. Many airports, cafés, restaurants and hotels, offer free internet; while Swiss rail offer free Wi-Fi at an increasing number of stations.

The pocket Wi-Fi service **Travelers Wi-Fi Mobile Hotspot**, offers unlimited 4G access throughout Switzerland – sharing your access with up to 10 devices from CHF6 a day. Order online and have it delivered to the hotel of your choice or pick it up at Zurich airport. www.travelerswifi.com

Outside of that, operators such as **Swisscom** have major networks with some 1,700 hotspots, charged by the hour, day or month. You can also buy prepaid SIM cards for unlimited surfing for up to five devices.

Note that the 2017 free-rate roaming agreements between EU countries and EEA countries do not apply to Switzerland.

LGBTQ travel
Attitudes among the Swiss towards the LGBTQ community are progressive. All cities have gay hubs where there are gay bars and entertainment venues. The age of consent for gay sex is 16, the same as for heterosexuals. A law recognising same-sex unions came into effect in 2007. In January 2007, two men from Ticino, aged 89 and 60, became the first couple in Switzerland to join in a same-sex union. Switzerland's de-facto gay capital is Zürich, where around 4,000 people join a massive Pride parade every June. There's a similar annual event in Geneva.

Lost property
Major railway stations and airports have lost-property offices or small police stations where you can report something missing or try to claim something that you've lost. Police and security guards at stations and airports are zealously efficient and often take bags and suitcases to lost-property offices if the owner isn't nearby, so don't wander off and leave your bag unattended. If it is taken away you'll have to prove that it's yours before you get it back.

M

Maps
There's no shortage of any kind of map for Switzerland, from road maps that can be bought at petrol stations to maps of cycle routes and high-quality 1:60,000 scale maps of every inch of the country, useful for hikers and climbers. Bookshops and adventure-travel retailers in cities and many towns stock a great selection.

Many post offices in Switzerland also stock a range of maps. **The Swiss Travel Center** is a great online resource for purchasing maps published by both Hallwag, and Kummerly and Frey (tel: 031 850 3131; www.swisstravelcenter.ch). The former publish city maps, hiking, biking and wintersports maps, the latter regional maps, hiking and cycling maps and leisure guides.

Basic city and town maps, often of a high quality, can be picked up free at a local tourist office, and increasingly interactive maps are available online to allow you to virtually visit in detail ahead of an actual visit, to map out your stay.

Media

Newspapers
The Swiss newspaper *Blick* can be found everywhere, from the largest city to the smallest village, as well as in most restaurants and bars. The leading daily newspapers, in terms of journalism quality, include the German-speaking *Neue Zürcher Zeitung*, held in high esteem abroad, Zürich-published *Tages-Anzeiger*,

and French-speaking Le Temps, followed by regional newspapers, such as La Tribune de Genève, Basler Zeitung and Berner Zeitung. The Corriere del Ticino is the Italian-speaking region's favoured local newspaper, though many prefer Milan's leading daily, the Corriere della Sera, as an international news source. The greatest readership however, goes to the online German-language news site, 20 minuten: www.20min.ch.

In the cities and bigger holiday resorts you will find the usual selection of foreign newspapers and magazines.

Television and radio

Television and radio in Switzerland are of a fairly high standard both technically and with regard to content, in particular the news. Swiss television has stations in German, French and Italian. There are also local television stations in some of the larger cities.

In all of the bigger cities and the major hotels and holiday resorts you can receive foreign television stations such as BBC World, CNN and others.

As well as the official Swiss radio stations there are many local stations, from which you may be able to glean information concerning your holiday destination. **Radio Switzerland International** has sections in many foreign languages, including English (www.swissinfo.org/eng).

Money matters

There is no limit regarding the amount of foreign currency, as well as other means of payment, travellers are permitted to take with them upon either entering or leaving Switzerland. The unit of currency

⊘ Public holidays

New Year's Day 1 January
Good Friday, Easter Monday March/April
Ascension Day May/June
Whit Monday/Pentecost May/June
Federal Thanksgiving Day 3rd Sunday in September
National Day 1 August
Christmas Day 25 December
Boxing Day 26 December

in Switzerland is the Swiss franc (Schweizer Franken, SFr), which is issued in five, 10 and 20 centimes, half a franc (50 centimes) and one, two and five franc coins. Notes are issued in 10, 20, 50, 100, 200 and 1,000 francs.

Traveller's cheques, foreign currency and other means of payment can be changed into Swiss money at banks, bureaux de change (marked as Change or Cambio, located in city and town centres as well as at railway stations and airports), travel agencies and hotels. Most Swiss banks also accept Eurocheques. Travellers can often settle their bills in larger hotels, shops, department stores and restaurants with foreign money. Ask for the rate of exchange; in most cases it will be slightly worse than the current rate.

P

Postal services

The Swiss Post Office (www.swisspost.ch) is a paragon of efficiency. Within Switzerland, 98 percent of first-class letters ("A-Post") posted before 6pm arrive the next morning. The charge for a standard letter is one franc and for a large letter 2.20 francs. For overseas mail there are three services: the urgent courier service, which is the fastest and most expensive, priority and standard. A priority letter to another European country costs from the standard 1.40 francs (for a 20g letter), or 1.50 francs for priority, and up to 40 francs for a "Maxi Letter" weighing up to 2kg. To a country outside Europe you'll pay 1.70 francs for a standard letter, 2 francs priority. For sending parcels you can buy useful "flatpack" boxes in various sizes, which you assemble yourself. All these prices are easily found online so you can estimate the cost before you head to the post office. Many have ATMs for cash withdrawals as well as shops where you can buy envelopes, computer accessories and maps. Poste restante services are available throughout Switzerland for a charge – CHF20 francs for two weeks – purchased at the counter or by phone (only CHF8 online). You'll need to ask senders to address the letter to the branch of the post office where you intend to collect, and show your passport.

R

Religious services

Religious services are held in either French or German, although there are a small number of Anglican churches that have a weekly service in English. The website of the **Intercontinental Church Society** (www.ics-uk.org) lists churches which minister in English, including churches in Wengen, Kandersteg and Thun. In Bern, the Anglican church, St Ursula's in Jubiläumsplatz, has Sunday services at 8.30am and 10am.

S

Shopping

What to buy and where

There is an enormous choice of mementos, national and local specialities to take home. Interesting purchases from different regions include rock crystals from Alpine areas, painted ceramics, wooden utensils and vessels, glassware (Glasi Hergiswil near Luzern is famous and open for visits; www.glasi.ch), and music boxes from Sainte-Croix in the Jura, or from Alscher in Interlaken or Reuge, Geneva. Not forgetting dolls in folkloric costumes, carved wood from the Brienz area, and copious lace and embroidery, silk scarves, shawls and ties. Fabric Frontline in Zürich is a cult label in the latter case, and also has designer silk fabric by the metre, while more traditional scarves and Alpine designs are found in mountainous areas. Other truly Swiss Alpine keepsakes include bells and leather accessories from the Appenzell area, Swiss Army knives (Victorinox is the main brand, Wenger has turned more to travel gear and watches). And as for the iconic Swiss gifts available almost everywhere, you can't miss the chocolate, cheese, wine and schnapps, and of course jewellery and watches – 90 percent of production was once concentrated in the Jura's Watch Valley – the so-called "Land of Precision", along the Watchmaking Route pivoting on Porrentruy.

If you're searching for something typical of good quality – fashion accessories, tableware and toys, bells, books, ceramic jugs and music boxes, flags and fondue sets – take a look in one of the **Schweizer Heimatwerk** (Swiss Handicraft) shops (www.heimatwerk.ch). They're located in Zürich, at Zürich airport, in Basel and Luzern and Geneva airport, and are staffed by competent sales assistants who can tell you anything you'd like to know. For jewellery and watches visit the famous **Bucherer** in Zürich, established in 1888.

In smaller towns it's best to buy directly from the source, at small art and craft ateliers or established local artisan companies.

Chocolates

These can be found in any food store. Look out for real Swiss chocolate, brands such as Lindt and Sprüngli, Nestlé and Frey. Home-made chocolates such as pralines are sold in bakeries and confectioners in most villages. In Zürich you will find the best ones at **Sprüngli** and in the lovely old-fashioned **Café Schober**.

Cheese and sausages

Swiss cheese is for sale in every grocer's shop, but if you have the opportunity, buy regional cheese directly from village dairies or on mountain farms – they are authentic and taste especially fine. Famous cheeses include: Appenzeller, Emmentaler (Bern region), Gruyère and Vacherin Fribourgeois (Fribourg area), Sbrinz (originally from Brienz), Schabziger (Glarus area), Tilsiter (eastern Switzerland), Raclette (Valais), Tête de Moine (Jura) and Formaggelli (Ticino).

There are various kinds of sausages that originate from different regions. Try to purchase them from a good butcher. Varieties include: Klöpfer (Basel area), St Gallen Schüblige, Bratwürste (pork, beef or a mixture; the Appenzell area), Waadtländer (Vaud), Longeoles (pork; Geneva), Coppa (salami; Ticino), Salsiz (salami; Bündner) Bindefleisch (dried, sliced meat).

Wines

In western Switzerland, Valais, Ticino, Grisons and other wine regions, look out for wine farms. A lot of them sell directly to the customer, or in wine shops and in larger food stores. Wine brands include white Chasselas, Epesses, St Saphorin (from the Lavaux, Geneva/Vaud area), red Dôle (Valais area), red Merlot (Ticino), Maienfelder Blauburgunder and Veltliner (Grisons area).

Desserts

Try – or take home – the famous *kirschtorte* (cherry schnapps tart) in Zug or the Engadine, *nusstorte* (nut tart) in Graubünden, *Rüeblitorte* (carrot tart) from the Aargau, filled *Meringuen* from Meiringen (BE), *Délices* (a sort of bagel) from Geneva or filled *Amaretti* (Tessin).

Shops normally open daily 8/8.30am–6.30pm, on Saturday until 4pm. In smaller towns many close between noon–2pm. Some confectioners in the holiday resorts and larger towns are open on Sundays.

Student travellers

An International Student Identity Card (ISIC) entitles the holder to all sorts of discounts on admission prices, air and international train tickets, hostel accommodation, bars, clubs, shopping and ski lifts. You can get your card, along with all sorts of other information about student and youth travel, from the **International Student Travel Confederation** (www. istc.org). If you are not a full-time student, but aged under 26, or you are a full-time teacher or professor, the International Youth Travel Card (IYTC) or International Teacher Identity Card (ITIC) offer similar benefits and are also available from the ISTC.

T

Telephones

Telecommunications in Switzerland are very good. The Swiss dialling code from abroad is +41. To make a call from Switzerland first dial 00 then for the UK, 44; 1 for the US and Canada; and 61 for Australia. Be careful when using hotel telephones for anything but local calls: the charges are generally steep.

Cards for calling from public telephones can be bought at post offices, railway stations, petrol stations and kiosks. Among them is the so-called **Taxcard**, also available at Swisscom Shops for CHF 5, CHF 10 and CHF 20. (Some phones accept coins but they are a dying breed). There are many **pre-paid international phone cards** offering even better value, which are also available at kiosks, minimarkets, post offices and some railway stations. These use a toll-free number then a pin code for making your call.

Mobile phone reception is often poor in mountainous regions. While driving, phones must be used on hands-free.

Some helpful telephone numbers are listed below:
Directory assistance: 111
Police emergency: 117
Tourist information and snow reports: 120
Roadside assistance: 140
Weather forecast: 162 (German, French and Italian only)
Up to the minute road conditions: 163
Seasonal Avalanche Bulletin and Pollen Bulletin: 187

Tipping

Hotels, restaurants and bars are legally obliged to include a 15 percent service charge in their bills, which means tipping is not necessary. It is, however, appreciated, so if you're satisfied with the service you could round up the bill as locals often do. Waiters, porters and taxi drivers expect a franc or two.

Toilets

Public toilets are usually very clean and well maintained, whether they're in railway stations or pubs. The Mr Clean franchise of public toilets operates at many railway stations and airports, where you'll pay either one or two francs. Supermarkets and department stores also have good toilets. In some restaurants toilets are for customers only and there's a security code to get in – the code for the day is often printed on your receipt, so don't throw it away.

Tourist information

The **Swiss National Tourist Office** provides information, addresses and links for all tourist-related subjects. It also sells tickets, tours, package tours and makes hotel bookings. Their global offices are not open to the public. Contact is by the toll-free phone numbers or by email. They will then send details by e-mail or post brochures to you. You can book your entire holiday online through their travel and hotel platforms, starting at www.myswitzerland.com (email: info@myswitzerland.com; free call tel: 00800 100 200 29).

The **Switzerland Travel Centre** is the country's so-called destination management company, in short a national travel agency; they sell any Swiss holiday. It is jointly owned and operated by Switzerland Tourism, the national rail, SBB and the Swiss hotel association, Hotellerie Suisse. The STC has offices at home as well as in the UK and Germany, the latter two of which are open to the public.

Offices abroad

Australia: Switzerland Tourism
Tel: 0011 800 100 200 30
Email: info.aus@myswitzerland.com
Canada:
Switzerland Tourism
Tel: 1-800-794-7795
Email: info.caen@myswitzerland.com
UK:
Switzerland Tourism
Tel: 00800 100 200 29 (free-phone)
Email: info.uk@myswitzerland.com
Switzerland Travel Centre (Covent Garden, open to the public)
1st Floor, 30 Bedford Street, London WC2E 9ED
United Kingdom
www.switzerlandtravelcentre.co.uk
Tel: 020 7420 4934
Email: sales@stc.co.uk

⊙ Matterhorn guides

If you are planning to climb the Matterhorn, Switzerland's most famous peak guides can be contracted through Zermatt's **Alpine Centre** (Bahnhofstrasse 58; Postfach 403, CH-3920 Zermatt; tel: 027 966 24 60; email: alpincenter@zermatt. ch; www.zermatt.ch/alpincenter). The standard cost for the four to five hour ascent is around 1215 francs per person, which includes transport and half-board accommodation at the Hörnli mountain hut, but not equipment hire or insurance (there is a cancellation fee in the event of bad weather).

Alternatively, visitors who would simply like to stay overnight up the mountain – and avoid a strenuous hike – can experience a night in the Hörnlihütte Base Camp Matterhorn (tel: 027-967 22 64) or reserve a room at the adjacent Belvédère guesthouse (tel: 028-67 22 64), both of which are at an altitude of 3,260 metres (10,696ft). Reservations for both can also be made online: www.hoernlihuette.ch.

US:
Switzerland Tourism
Tel: 1-800-794-7795
Email: info.usa@switzerland.com

Local tourist offices

The main city and regional offices are listed below:
Basel city & region: Bahnhof SBB, Centralstrasse 10, 4051 Basel; tel: 061 268 68 68; email: info@basel.com; www.basel.com; also Stadt-Casino am Barfüsserplatz, Steinenberg 14, tel: 061 268 68 68
Bern: Bern Tourismus, Bahnhofplatz 10a, 3011 Bern; tel: 031 328 12 2; email: info@bern.com; www.berne.com
Bernese Oberland: BE! Tourismus AG, Thunstrasse 8, 3005 Bern; tel: 031 300 33 00; email: info@madeinbern. com; www.madeinbern.com
Bernese Oberland Interlaken region: Interlaken Tourismus, Marktgasse 1; tel: 033 826 53 00; email: mail@interlakentourism.ch; www.interlakentourism.ch
Bernese Jura: Office du Tourisme du Jura Bernois, Avenue de la Gare 9, 2740 Moutier; tel: 032 494 53 43; email info@jurabernois.ch; www.jurabernois.ch
Eastern Switzerland/Lichtenstein: St Gallen-Bodensee Tourismus, Bankgasse 9, 9001 St. Gallen; tel: 071 227 37 37; email: info@st.gallen-bodensee.ch; www.st.gallen-bodensee.ch
Fribourg city & region: Fribourg Tourisme, Place Jean-Tinguely 1, CP1120, 1701 Fribourg; tel: 026 350 11 11; www.fribourgtourisme.ch
Geneva: Genève Tourisme, Rue du Mont-Blanc 18, 1201 Geneva; tel: 022 909 70 70; www.geneve.com
Graubünden: Graubünden Ferien, Alexanderstrasse 24, 7001, Chur; tel: 081 254 24 24; email: contact@graubuenden.ch; www.graubuenden.ch
Luzern: Luzern Tourism, Zentralstrasse 5 6002 Luzern; tel: 041 227 17 17; www.luzern.com
Jura: Jura Tourisme, Rue de la Gruère 6, 2350 Saignelégier; tel: 032 432 41 60; www.juratourisme.ch
Vaud & Lake Geneva Region: Office du Tourisme du Canton de Vaud, Avenue d'Ouchy 60, CP1125, 1001 Lausanne; tel: 021 613 26 26; www.region-du-leman.ch
Neuchâtel: Neuchâtel Tourism, Hôtel des Postes, CH-2001 Neuchâtel; tel: 032 889 68 90; www.neuchateltourisme.ch
Ticino: Ticino Turismo, Via Canonico Ghiringhelli 7,Casella Postale 1441, 6501 Bellinzona; tel: 091 825 70 56; www.ticino.ch

Valais: Wallis Promotion Rue Pré-Fleuri 6, 1951 Sion, tel: 027 327 35 70; email: info@valais.ch; www.valais.ch
Zürich: Tourist Information, Zürich main station (Hauptbahnhof/HB), 8023 Zürich, tel: 044 215 40 00; email: info@zuerich.com; www.zuerich.com

Tour operators

The main **Swiss Tourism** website, www.myswitzerland.com, will lead you through all the various activities, experiences and events available from its database of more than 10,000, giving contact details for both regional and city tourism companies as well as specialised tour companies within those interests. There is also a list of major international tour companies working with them at www.myswitzerland.com/en-in/touroperators.html.

Farm holidays

Holidays on the farm are a popular pastime. Swiss Tourism has some 300 places listed and bookable on its website (http://farm.myswitzerland.com/on-the-farm).

Such down-to-earth holidays offer the best opportunity to get to know the country and its inhabitants; they are especially suitable for families with children. In some places it is possible for a child (aged six to 14) to stay unaccompanied with the farmer's family, allowing them to participate actively in farming life.

Another useful resource is the agriturismo association, **Agritourismus Schweiz**, which has an English website and booking platform for more than 280 properties across Switzerland: www.agrotourismus.ch/en.

Cultural holidays
Martin Randall Travel
10 Barley Mow Passage, London W4 4PH; tel: 020 8742 3355; www.martinrandall.com
One-week holidays covering art, architecture and music, including three- to six-day trips to the International Jazz Festival in Montreux (July) or five days at the Luzern Festival (August).

Holidays by train
Swiss Railway train holidays are sold as packages on its website, including train tickets, hotels and special offers for the region you wish to stay in.

For example, the eight day/seven night Grand Tour of Switzerland (from CHF 1375) takes in Zürich–Interlaken–Montreux–Zermatt–St. Moritz–Lugano–Luzern. Other shorter trips and "Panorama Trips" are all available on the website along with various rail passes, including the Swiss Rail Pass. See www.sbb.ch. The organisation of these holidays is usually seamless, building in baggage and bike services if required.

Many of the same trips are offered by **Rail Europe**, who are incredibly reliable and competitive in their pricing. Visit www.raileurope.com/europe-travel-guide/switzerland.

Health resorts, mineral springs and spas

The Swiss wellness industry is alive and well. Of some 80 health hotels, resorts and spas spread across the country, there are several distinctive wellness destinations including Scuol in the Engadin, with its mineral springs and curative waters, the thermal springs of Baden and Leukerbad in the Valais – the Alps largest wellness resort. MySwitzerland.com provides detailed information on all the spas and their various characteristics and attractions, as well as contact details. Many of the spas offer various pools, Roman and Turkish baths, saunas and solariums. A handful are classified as medical spas, and specialise in different remedial treatments as well as having beauty therapies in a separate spa. Notable ones in this category are the Medical Health Center at the Grand Resort in Bad Ragaz, the pioneering Clinique La Prairie medical

retreat on Lake Geneva's shores at Clarens-Montreux and Curhaus, with its 18 treatment rooms in the new Sir Norman Foster-designed wing of Zürich's Dolder Grand.

W

Websites

The best place to start surfing is at the **Swiss National Tourist Office** (www.myswitzerland.com), whose vast well-organised and easily navigated site provides all the information you need about the country, as well as hotel bookings, transport details, snow reports and walking guides. For train travel you can book online at www.sbb.ch, while you can book tickets with the national carrier Swiss at www.swiss.com. For Swiss Travel Passes, book via **Rail Europe** (www.raileurope.com), which offers many discounts and deals and often ends up significantly cheaper than through the Swiss National Railway. The latter network should nonetheless be used for all other single journeys within the country. As well as running like clockwork, it too offers good promotions.

For hostels www.youthostel.ch has everything you'll need including online booking, while there's excellent hotel information and reservations at www.swisshotels.com. Swissinfo (www.swissinfo.com) is an excellent all-round site about all things Swiss, with news, weather, and sections dedicated to music, travel and culture.

Weights and measures

The metric system is used. Food such as cheese, meat and portions of salad are priced per 100g not per kg.

What to bring

The golden rule when packing for Switzerland is to pack for all four seasons, whichever season you're travelling in. Summers can be hot so you'll primarily need lightweight clothing, but at altitude it can still be cold, windy and misty, so make sure you've got some warm gear, especially if you're planning on hiking. In winter you'll need to be well prepared for extreme cold, which means good-quality outdoor clothing, thermals, gloves and hats. Remember several layers of thin clothing keep you warmer than one or two layers of cumbersome thick clothing.

Good-quality sunglasses and sunscreen are an absolute must at any time. The sun in the Alps can be sizzling and you'll burn very quickly if you don't take care. Your itinerary will dictate the specifics of what you pack – no need for expensive hiking boots if you're only wandering around the shops in Interlaken and Zürich.

If you're planning a more adventurous trip, you'll need to take or rent gear such as tents and skis. A raincoat or rain jacket is useful at any time of year and for rainy city days it's worth packing an umbrella. There are fountains all over the place where you can fill up a water bottle with potable Alpine water, so pack or buy a decent water bottle and carry it with you in a small day pack.

What to wear

It's unlikely you'll need to take anything formal, unless you're planning a night at the opera. The Swiss dress well and always look neat, but they are rarely showy. For dinner you'll be fine in smart trousers or jeans with a simple shirt, or a blouse for women. Wear a tie if you want, but many men don't bother unless it is a very formal occasion. For après-ski people wear comfortable trousers, warm boots and a ski jacket. Visitors to ritzy resorts like Gstaad and St Moritz take things a bit further, but there's no need for an expensive fur coat or ermine boots, especially in today's casual-glam environment.

Outdoor swimming pool, LeCrans Hotel and Spa in Crans-Montana.

LANGUAGE

WHAT TO SPEAK WHERE

About 64 percent of Swiss people speak Schwiizerdütsch or Schwiizertüütsch (occasionally also called Schwyzerdütsch), a variation of German; but don't be afraid to try standard German on them, as they grow up with High-German at school and it is the official written language. The three other official languages are French, used by about 19 percent of the population in the western part of Switzerland; Italian, used by roughly seven percent of the Swiss in the southern part of Switzerland, especially in the Ticino; and Romansh, spoken by 0.6 percent of people in some regions of the canton Graubünden. All Romansh-speaking and a lot of Italian-speakers also understand and speak German. But in the French-speaking part of Switzerland you would be more successful speaking English than German.

Swiss people are in general friendly and patient, and will take the time to listen to foreigners who do not speak their language fluently.

Since a lot of English vocabulary is related to German, travellers will often recognise many helpful cognates: words such as *Hotel*, *Kaffee*, *Milch*, *Markt* and *Bett* hardly need to be translated. You should be aware, however, of some misleading "false friends".

☉ The alphabet

Learning the pronunciation of the German alphabet is a good idea. In particular, learn how to spell out your name.
a = ah, **b** = bay, **c** = tsay, **d** = day, **e** = ay, **f** = ef, **g** = gay, **h** = hah, **i** = ee, **j** = yot, **k** = kah, **l** = el, **m** = em, **n** = en, **o** = oh, **p** = pay, **q** = coo, **r** = ehr, **s** = ess, **t** = tay, **u** = oo, **v** = fou, **w** = vay, **x** = eex, **y** = eepseelon, **z** = tset.

There is one rather puzzling characteristic of the Swiss: even when speaking German proper, they borrow many words from the French, such as *billet*, *lavabo*, *porte-monnaie* and *merci*; this is especially the case if they are speaking about eating.

BASIC RULES

Even if you speak no German at all, it is worth trying to master a few simple phrases. The fact that you have made an effort is likely to get you a better response. Increasing numbers of German-speaking people practise their English on visitors, especially waiters in cafés and restaurants and the younger generation. Pronunciation is the key; they really will not understand if you get it very wrong. Remember to emphasise each syllable.

Whether to use *"Sie"* or *"Du"* is a vexed question; increasingly the familiar form of "Du" is used by many people. However, it is better to be too formal, and use "Sie" if in doubt. You address people with "Sie" or, if you know their names, you address them *Herr* (Mr) or *Frau* (Mrs), and attach the relevant surname. To say Herr or Frau without surnames sounds rather ridiculous in German. If you say "Du", then you attach (if you know the name) just the first name. When entering a shop always say, "guten Tag", and "danke, auf Wiedersehen", when leaving.

WORDS & PHRASES

Greetings

hello *Guten Tag* or, more familiar, *Hallo*
OK *In Ordnung*
goodbye *Auf Wiedersehen*

good evening *Guten Abend*
good night *Gute Nacht*

Introductions

What is your name? *Wie heissen Sie?*
My name is... *Ich heisse...*
Do you speak English? *Sprechen Sie englisch?*
I am English/American *Ich bin Engländer(in)/Amerikaner(in)*

Useful words/phrases

How much is it? *Wieviel kostet das?*
I don't understand *Ich verstehe nicht*
Please speak more slowly *Sprechen Sie bitte langsamer*
Can you help me? *Können Sie mir helfen?*
I'm looking for... *Ich suche...*
Where is...? *Wo ist...?*
I'm sorry *Entschuldigung*
I don't know *Ich weiss es nicht*
No problem *Kein Problem*
Have a good day! *Einen schönen Tag!*
That is it *Das ist es*
Here it is *Hier ist es*
There it is *Dort ist es*
Let's go *Lass uns gehen*
See you tomorrow *Bis morgen*
See you soon *Bis bald*
Show me the word in the book *Zeigen Sie mir das Wort im Buch*
At what time? *Um wieviel Uhr?*
When? *Wann?*
What time is it? *Wieviel Uhr ist es?*
yes *ja*
no *nein*
please *bitte*
thank you (very much) *danke (vielmal)*
you're welcome *bitte* or *gern geschehen*
excuse me *Entschuldigung*
here *hier*
there *dort*
today *heute*
yesterday *gestern*
tomorrow *morgen*
now *jetzt*
later *später*

⊙ False friends

False friends are words that look like English words but mean something different, for example:
Der Car **coach**
Es geht can sometimes mean walk, but is usually used to mean working (the TV, the car etc.) or going well.

right away *sofort*
this morning *heute morgen*
this afternoon *heute nachmittag*
this evening *heute abend*

On arrival

I want to get off at... *Ich möchte in ... aussteigen*
Does this bus go to...? *Fährt dieser Bus nach...?*
What street is this? *In welcher Strasse sind wir?*
Which line do I take for...? *Welche Linie muss ich nehmen nach...?*
How far is ...? *Wie weit ist ...?*
Validate your ticket *Entwerten Sie Ihr Billet*
Airport *der Flughafen*
train station *der Bahnhof*
bus station *der Busbahnhof*
bus *der Bus*
bus stop *die Bushaltestelle*
platform *das Perron*
ticket *das Billet*
return ticket *das Retourbillet*
hitchhiking *Autostop*
toilets *die Toiletten*

At the hotel

This is the hotel address *Das ist die Adresse des Hotels*
I'd like a room *Ich möchte ein Zimmer*
single/double... *Einzelzimmer/ Doppelzimmer*
...with shower *...mit Dusche*
...with bath *...mit Bad*
...with a view *...mit Aussicht*
Does that include breakfast? *Ist das Frühstück inbegriffen?*
May I see the room? *Darf ich das Zimmer anschauen?*
washbasin *das Lavabo*
bed *das Bett*
key *der Schlüssel*
elevator *der Lift, der Aufzug*
air conditioning *die Klimaanlage*

Sightseeing

town *die Stadt*
Old Town *die Altstadt*

abbey *die Abtei, das Kloster*
cathedral *die Kathedrale, das Münster*
church *die Kirche*
mansion *das Herrschaftshaus*
hospital *das Spital*
town hall *das Rathaus*
nave *das Kirchenschiff*
stained glass *das Glasfenster*
staircase *das Treppenhaus*
tower *der Turm*
walk *der Rundgang*
country house/castle *das Schloss*
Gothic *gothisch*
Roman *römisch*
Romanesque *romanisch*
museum *das Museum*
art gallery *die Kunstgalerie*
exhibition *die Ausstellung*
tourist information office *das Verkehrsbüro*
free *gratis*
open *offen*
closed *geschlossen*
every day *täglich*
all year *das ganze Jahr über*
all day *den ganzen Tag*
swimming pool *das Schwimmbad*
to book *reservieren*

Shopping

Where is the nearest bank (post office)? *Wo ist die nächste Bank (Post)?*
I'd like to buy something *Ich möchte (etwas) kaufen*
How much is it? *Wieviel kostet das?*
Do you take credit cards? *Nehmen Sie Kreditkarten?*
I'm just looking *Ich schaue nur ein bisschen*
Have you got...? *Haben Sie...?*
I'll take it *Ich nehme es*
I'll take this one/that one *Ich nehme das hier/das dort*
Anything else? *Noch etwas?*
size *die Grösse*
cheap *billig*
expensive *teuer*
enough *genug*
too much *zu viel*
a piece... *ein Stück...*
each *das Stück (eg, bananas, 4 Fr. das Stück)*
emergency exit *Notausgang*
bill *die Rechnung*
chemist *die Apotheke*
bakery *die Bäckerei*
butcher *die Metzgerei*
book shop *die Buchhandlung*
library *die Bibliothek*
department store *das Warenhaus*
grocer's *das Lebensmittelgeschäft*
tobacconist *der Tabakladen, der Kiosk*
market *der Markt*

supermarket *der Supermarkt*
junk shop *das Brockenhaus*

Dining out

breakfast *das Frühstück*
lunch *das Mittagessen*
dinner *das Abendessen*
meal *die Mahlzeit*
first course *die Vorspeise*
main course *die Hauptspeise*
made to order *auf Bestellung*
drink included *Getränk inbegriffen*
wine list *die Weinkarte*
the bill *die Rechnung*
fork *die Gabel*
knife *das Messer*
spoon *der Löffel*
plate *der Teller*
glass *das Glas*
napkin *die Serviette*
ashtray *der Aschenbecher*

Menu

Frühstück und Snacks/ Breakfast and snacks

Brötchen *rolls*
Brot *bread*
Butter *butter*
Ei *egg*
... weiche Eier *boiled eggs*
... Eier mit Speck *bacon and eggs*
... Eier mit Schinken *ham and eggs*
... Spiegeleier *fried eggs*
... Rührei *scrambled eggs*
Honig *honey*
Joghurt *yogurt*
Konfiture *jam*
Crêpe *pancake*
Pfeffer *pepper*
Salz *salt*
Zucker *sugar*

Hauptgerichte/Main courses

Fleisch *Meat*
Blutwurst *black pudding*
Braten *roast*
Bündnerfleisch *dried meat*
Ente *duck*
Entrecôte *beef rib steak*
Fasan *pheasant*
Froschschenkel *frog's legs*
Gans *goose*
Gnagi, Schweinsfuss *pig's trotters*
Huhn/Poulet *chicken*
Kalb *veal*
Kalbsleber *calf's liver*
Kaninchen/Hase *rabbit*
Lamm *lamb*
Leber *liver*
Leberwurst *liver sausage*
Nieren *kidneys*
Schinken *ham*
Schwein *pork*

Salami *salami*
Schnecken *snails*
Spiessli *kebab*
Steak *steak*
Voressen *stew of veal, lamb or chicken with creamy egg sauce*
Wildschwein *wild boar*
Wurst *sausage*
Zunge *tongue*
wenig gebraten, bleu *rare*
mittel gebraten, à point *medium*
gut gebraten, bien cuit *well done*
grilliert *grilled*
gefüllt *stuffed*

Fisch/Fish

Aal *eel*
Auster *oyster*
Egli *small regional fish*
Felchen *regional white fish*
Forelle *trout*
Hecht *pike*
Hummer *lobster*
Kabeljau, Dorsch *cod*
Krevetten *shrimp*
Lachs *salmon*
Langustine *large prawn*
Muscheln, Moule *mussel*
Meerfrüchte *seafood*
Sardellen *anchovies*
Schalentiere *shellfish*
Thunfisch/Thon *tuna*
Tintenfisch *squid*

Gemüse/Vegetables

Artischocke *artichoke*
Blumenkohl *cauliflower*
Bohne *bean (green or dried)*
Chips *potato crisps*
Cornichon *gherkin*
Erbsen *peas*
Grüner Salat *green salad*
Haselnuss *hazelnut*
Kartoffel *potato*
Kefen *snow peas*
Knoblauch *garlic*
Kohl *cabbage*
Lauch *leek*
Linsen *lentils*
Mais *corn*
Nuss *nut, walnut*
Pastinake *parsnip*
Petersilie *parsley*
Pilze *mushrooms*
Pommes frites *French fries*
Radieschen *radish*
Reis *rice*
Salatgurke *cucumber*
Sellerie *celery*
Spargel *asparagus*
Spinat *spinach*
Steinpilz *boletus mushroom*
Trüffel *truffle*
weisse Rübe *turnip*
Zucchini *zucchini/courgette*

Zwiebel *onion*
roh *raw*
gedämpft *steamed*
gekocht *boiled*

Obst/Fruit

Ananas *pineapple*
Apfel *apple*
Birne *pear*
Erdbeere *strawberry*
Feige *fig*
Grapefruit *grapefruit*
Himbeere *raspberry*
Kirsche *cherry*
Limone *lime*
Mango *mango*
Mirabelle *yellow plum*
Pfirsich *peach*
Pflaume *plum*
Rotebeere *redcurrant*
Traube *grape*
Zitrone *lemon*
Zwetschge *prune*

Desserts/Dessert

Glacé *ice cream*
Käse *cheese*
Kuchen *cake*
Schlagrahm *whipped cream*
Torte *tart*
Vermicelles *Chestnut purée with whipped cream*

Table talk

I am a vegetarian *Ich bin Vegetarier*
What do you recommend? *Was empfehlen Sie?*
Do you have local specialities? *Haben Sie lokale Spezialitäten?*
I'd like to order *Ich möchte bestellen*
That is not what I ordered *Das ist nicht, was ich bestellt habe*
Is service included? *Ist der Service inbegriffen?*
May I have more wine? *Ich möchte noch Wein, bitte.*
Enjoy your meal *Guten Appetit!*

In the café

drinks *Getränke*
alcoholic drinks *Alkoholische Getränke/Drinks*
coffee *Kaffee*
... with milk or cream *... mit Milch oder Kaffeerahm*
... decaffeinated *koffeinfrei*
... black espresso *Espresso*
... American filtered coffee *filtre*
tea *Tee*
... black tea *Schwarztee*
... herbal infusion *Kräutertee*
... peppermint *Pfefferminze*
... rosehip *Hagebutte*

... camomile *Kamille*
... vervain *Eisenkraut*
hot chocolate *heisse Schokolade*
milk *Milch*
mineral water *Mineralwasser*
fizzy *mit Kohlensäure*
non-fizzy *ohne Kohlensäure*
fruit-flavoured carbonated water *Mineralwasser mit Aroma*
freshly squeezed orange juice *frisch gepresster Orangensaft*
full (eg, full-cream milk) *voll*
fresh or cold *kalt*
beer *Bier*
... bottled *in der Flasche*
... on tap *offen*
wheat beer *weissbier (white, cloudy beer)*
pre-dinner drink *Aperitif*
with ice *mit Eis*
neat *trocken*
red *rot*
white *weiss*
rosé *rosé*
dry *herb*
sweet *süss*
sparkling wine *Schaumwein*
house wine *Hauswein*
local wine *Landwein*
Where is this wine from? *Woher kommt dieser Wein?*
carafe/jug *Karaffe/Krug*
... of water/wine *... Wasser/Wein*
half litre *einen halben Liter*
mixed *panaché (beer with lemon mineral water) or gespritzt (white wine with water)*
after-dinner drink *Digestif*
cherry brandy *Kirsch*
pear brandy *Williams*
plum brandy *Pflümli*
cheers! *Gesundheit! or Zum Wohl!*
I have a hangover *Ich habe einen Kater*

In Switzerland table wine, and sometimes also mineral water, is served in measures of 100cl (one decilitre). Usually you order *2 Dezi, 3 Dezi, einen halben Liter* or *einen Liter*. If it is a very good wine, you have to order a whole bottle, which can vary in size.

Emergencies

Help! *Hilfe!*
Stop! *Halt!*
Call a doctor *Rufen Sie einen Arzt*
Call an ambulance *Rufen Sie eine Ambulanz*
Call the police *Rufen Sie die Polizei*
Call the fire brigade *Rufen Sie die Feuerwehr*
Where is the nearest telephone? *Wo ist das nächste Telefon?*
Where is the nearest hospital? *Wo ist das nächste Spital?*

I am sick *Ich bin krank*
I have lost my passport/purse *Ich habe meinen Pass/mein Portemonnaie verloren*

On the road

Where is the spare wheel? *Wo ist das Reserverad?*
Where is the nearest garage? *Wo ist die nächste Garage?*
Our car has broken down *Unser Auto hat eine Panne*
I want to have my car repaired *Ich möchte mein Auto reparieren lassen*
It's not your right of way *Sie haben kein vorfahrt*
I think I must have put diesel in the car by mistake *Ich glaube, ich habe irrtümlicherweise mit Diesel getankt*
the road to... *die Strasse nach...*
left *links*
right *rechts*
straight on *geradeaus*
far *weit entfernt, weit weg*
near *nahe*
opposite *gegenüber*
beside *neben*
car park *der Parkplatz*
over there *dort drüben*
at the end *am Ende*
on foot *zu Fuss*
by car *mit dem Auto*
town map *der Stadtplan*
road map *die Strassenkarte*
street *die Strasse*
square *der Platz*
give way *den Vortritt lassen*
dead end *die Sackgasse*
no parking *Parkieren verboten*
motorway *die Autobahn*
toll *die Gebühr*
speed limit *die Tempolimite*
petrol *das Benzin*
unleaded *bleifrei*
diesel *der Diesel*

water/oil *das Wasser/das Oel*
puncture *die Reifenpanne*
bulb *die Batterie*
wipers *die Scheibenwischer*

On the telephone

How do I make an outside call? *Wie telefoniere ich nach auswärts?*
I want to make an international/local call *Ich möchte eine internationale/lokale Verbindung*
What is the dialling code? *Wie lautet die Vorkennzahl?*
I'd like an alarm call for eight tomorrow morning *Ich möchte morgen früh um acht Uhr geweckt werden*
Who's calling? *Wer ist am Apparat?*
Hold on, please *Warten Sie bitte*
The line is busy *Die Leitung ist besetzt*
I must have dialled the wrong number *Ich bin falsch verbunden*

Numbers

0 *null*
1 *eins*
2 *zwei*
3 *drei*
4 *vier*
5 *fünf*
6 *sechs*
7 *sieben*
8 *acht*
9 *neun*
10 *zehn*
11 *elf*
12 *zwölf*
13 *dreizehn*
14 *vierzehn*
15 *fünfzehn*
16 *sechzehn*
17 *siebzehn*
18 *achtzehn*
19 *neunzehn*
20 *zwanzig*

21 *einundzwanzig*
30 *dreissig*
40 *vierzig*
50 *fünfzig*
60 *sechzig*
70 *siebzig*
80 *achtzig*
90 *neunzig*
100 *hundert*
1,000 *tausend*
1,000,000 *eine million*

Days and months

Days of the week

Monday *Montag*
Tuesday *Dienstag*
Wednesday *Mittwoch*
Thursday *Donnerstag*
Friday *Freitag*
Saturday *Samstag*
Sunday *Sonntag*

Months

January *Januar*
February *Februar*
March *März*
April *April*
May *Mai*
June *Juni*
July *juli*
August *August*
September *September*
October *Oktober*
November *November*
December *Dezember*

Saying the date

20 October 2017 *der zwanzigsteOktoberzweitausendundsiebzehn.*

Seasons

spring *der Frühling*
summer *der Sommer*
autumn *der Herbst*
winter *der Winter*

BOOK SHOPS AND WEBSITES

A large selection of books in English can be found in the **Orell Füssli** book shop in Zürich (Bahnhofstr. 70; tel: 01 211 04 44; www.books.ch), self-proclaimed "Number One Address for English Books in Switzerland", with a large selection of UK and US titles, along with a dedicated children's department. You can also browse and order titles online. In Geneva, **Payot Librairie** (Rue de la Confédération 7; tel: 022 316 19 00; www.payot.ch) on the Rive Gauche counts many English and international titles among its 10,000 books. Bern meanwhile has **Stauffacher** (Neuengasse 25-37; tel: 031 313 63 63), with a great selection.

Also have a look at **Bergli Books** which publishes Swiss and intercultural titles such as a *Cartoon Survival Guide to Switzerland* (www.bergli.ch).

BACKGROUND

Why Switzerland? by Steinberg Jonathan. A thorough examination of Switzerland through its history, politics, language and religion.
Swiss Watching: Inside the Land of Milk and Money by Bewes Diccon. In this Financial Times Book of the Year, Diccon intelligently dispels the myths and clichés to reveal the real Switzerland.
A Concise History of Switzerland by Clive H. Church and Randolph C. Head. An engaging journey through Switzerland's past.
La Place de la Concorde Suisse by John McPhee. A shrewd insight into the Swiss Army's role in Swiss society.
Ticking along with the Swiss, Ticking along too, Ticking along free by Dianne Dicks. Collections of personal stories from English-speaking writers, teachers, translators, etc., living in Switzerland.
Cupid's Wild Arrows: inter-cultural romance and its consequences by Dianne Dicks. Personal experiences of 55 authors of many nationalities.
Perpetual Tourist by Paul Bilton. The Englishman who lives in Switzerland started to write his diary in short notes to remind him what to write to his family in England.
Culture Shock! by Shirley En-Wong. A guide to customs and etiquette.
Inside Outlandish by Susan Tuttle. Snapshots in prose about the never-ending questions: What am I doing

here? Can I call this place home?
Laughing Along with the Swiss by Paul Bilton, who describes the funny side about Switzerland and the Swiss.
A Taste of Switzerland by Sue Style and John Miller. Descriptions of Swiss food, folklore, history and 50 recipes and tips on restaurants and hotels.
The Surprising Wines of Switzerland by John C. Sloan. A look at Swiss wine, describing the wine tradition, products and places, with lots of practical tips.

FICTION

Hôtel Du Lac by Anita Brookner. Booker Prize-winning novel about a writer staying on the shores of Lake Geneva.
Prisoner of Chillon by Lord Byron. Famous poem telling the story of monk François Bonivard during his imprisonment at the Château de Chillon.
The Manticore by Robertson Davies. The aftermath of a mysterious death is interpreted through a series of conversations between the victim's son and a Jungian psychoanalyst.
Man in the Holocene by Max Frisch. A beautiful novel about mortality and man's insignificance.
Peter Camenzind by Hermann Hesse. Protagonist Peter Camenzind travels in search of new experiences. A tale of lost idealism and redemption.
Not To Disturb by Muriel Spark. The household staff at a mansion near Geneva wait for a preordained crime of passion, eager to tell their stories to the press.
Heidi by Johanna Spyri. The quintessential Swiss children's book, about a young girl growing up in the Alps.
The Magic Mountain by Thomas Mann. Mann's greatest work on a group of patients and their discussions about love, death and war, in a sanatorium in Davos during World War I.

The Pollen Room by Jenny Zoë. The writer describes a marriage break-up through the eyes of a child.
Steppenwolf by Hermann Hesse. Hesse's best-known novel is about profound social deconstruction.
Masquerade and other stories by Robert Walser. Poems and short stories about the writer's life in Zürich, Berlin, Biel and Bern.

OTHER INSIGHT GUIDES

Other Insight Guides to this region include: *Western Europe, Germany, France, Italy* and *Italian Lakes*.

⏱ Send Us Your Thoughts

We do our best to ensure the information in our books is as accurate and up-to-date as possible. The books are updated on a regular basis using local contacts, who painstakingly add, amend and correct as required. However, some details (such as telephone numbers and opening times) are liable to change, and we are ultimately reliant on our readers to put us in the picture.

We welcome your feedback, especially your experience of using the book "on the road". Maybe we recommended a hotel that you liked (or another that you didn't), or you came across a great bar or new attraction we missed.

We will acknowledge all contributions, and we'll offer an Insight Guide to the best letters received.

Please write to us at:
Insight Guides
PO Box 7910
London SE1 1WE
Or email us at:
hello@insightguides.com

CREDITS

PHOTO CREDITS

COVER CREDITS

INSIGHT GUIDE CREDITS

Distribution
UK, Ireland and Europe
Apa Publications (UK) Ltd;
sales@insightguides.com
United States and Canada
Ingram Publisher Services;
ips@ingramcontent.com
Australia and New Zealand
Woodslane; info@woodslane.com.au
Southeast Asia
Apa Publications (SN) Pte;
singaporeoffice@insightguides.com
Worldwide
Apa Publications (UK) Ltd;
sales@insightguides.com
Special Sales, Content Licensing and CoPublishing
Insight Guides can be purchased in bulk quantities at discounted prices. We can create special editions, personalised jackets and corporate imprints tailored to your needs.
sales@insightguides.com
www.insightguides.biz

Printed in China by CTPS

All Rights Reserved
© 2018 Apa Digital (CH) AG and
Apa Publications (UK) Ltd

First Edition 1993
Fifth Edition 2018

Every effort has been made to provide accurate information in this publication, but changes are inevitable. The publisher cannot be responsible for any resulting loss, inconvenience or injury. We would appreciate it if readers would call our attention to any errors or outdated information. We also welcome your suggestions; please contact us at:
hello@insightguides.com

www.insightguides.com

Editor: Helen Fanthorpe
Author: Tamara Thiessen
Head of Production: Rebeka Davies
Update Production: Apa Digital
Picture Editor: Tom Smyth
Cartography: original cartography Mike Adams, updated by Carte

CONTRIBUTORS

This edition of *Insight Guide: Switzerland* was thoroughly updated by **Tamara Thiessen**, a Paris-based, Australian-born, Swiss-loving travel writer, photographer and editor (www.tamarathiessen.com). She built on the contributions made by the team of writers in previous editions, including **David Dalton**, **Marianne Flueler-Grauwiler**, **Rowlinson Carter** and **Klaus Speich**.
This book was edited by **Helen Fanthorpe** and the index compiled by **Penny Phenix**.

ABOUT INSIGHT GUIDES

Insight Guides have more than 45 years' experience of publishing high-quality, visual travel guides. We produce 400 full-colour titles, in both print and digital form, covering more than 200 destinations across the globe, in a variety of formats to meet your different needs.
Insight Guides are written by local authors, whose expertise is evident in the extensive historical and cultural background features. Each destination is carefully researched by regional experts to ensure our guides provide the very latest information. All the reviews in **Insight Guides** are independent; we strive to maintain an impartial view. Our reviews are carefully selected to guide you to the best places to eat, go out and shop, so you can be confident that when we say a place is special, we really mean it.

Legend

City maps

	Freeway/Highway/Motorway
	Divided Highway
	Main Roads
	Minor Roads
	Pedestrian Roads
	Steps
	Footpath
	Railway
	Funicular Railway
	Cable Car
	Tunnel
	City Wall
	Important Building
	Built Up Area
	Other Land
	Transport Hub
	Park
	Pedestrian Area
	Bus Station
	Tourist Information
	Main Post Office
	Cathedral/Church
	Mosque
	Synagogue
	Statue/Monument
	Beach
	Airport

Regional maps

	Freeway/Highway/Motorway (with junction)
	Freeway/Highway/Motorway (under construction)
	Divided Highway
	Main Road
	Secondary Road
	Minor Road
	Track
	Footpath
	International Boundary
	State/Province Boundary
	National Park/Reserve
	Marine Park
	Ferry Route
	Marshland/Swamp
	Glacier / Salt Lake
	Airport/Airfield
	Ancient Site
	Border Control
	Cable Car
	Castle/Castle Ruins
	Cave
	Chateau/Stately Home
	Church/Church Ruins
	Crater
	Lighthouse
	Mountain Peak
	Place of Interest
	Viewpoint

INDEX

MAIN REFERENCES ARE IN BOLD TYPE